PIONEERS PEDDLERS & TSADIKIM

THE STORY OF JEWS IN COLORADO

IDA LIBERT UCHILL

UNIVERSITY PRESS OF COLORADO

Copyright © 2000 by the University Press of Colorado
International Standard Book Number 0-87081-593-8

First edition, Sage Books ©1957
Second edition, ©1979

Published by the University Press of Colorado
5589 Arapahoe Avenue, Suite 206C
Boulder, Colorado 80303

All rights reserved.
Printed in the United States of America.

The University Press of Colorado is a cooperative publishing enterprise supported, in part, by Adams State College, Colorado State University, Fort Lewis College, Mesa State College, Metropolitan State College of Denver, University of Colorado, University of Northern Colorado, University of Southern Colorado, and Western State College of Colorado.

The paper used in this publication meets the minimum requirements of the American National Standard for Information Sciences—Permanence of Paper for Printed Library Materials. ANSI Z39.48-1984

Library of Congress Cataloging-in-Publication Data

Uchill, Ida Libert.
    Pioneers, peddlers, and tsadikim : the story of Jews in Colorado / Ida Libert Uchill.—3rd ed.
      p. cm.
    Includes bibliographical references (p.) and index
    ISBN 0-87081-593-8
    1. Jews—Colorado—History. 2. Colorado—Ethnic relations. I. Title.
F785.J5 U3 2000
978.8'004924—dc21

                                                                00-047981

Cover design by Laura Furney

CONTENTS

Dedication	4
Preface to the Third Edition	5
Abbreviations	8
Pike's Peak Adventure	9
"The Big Excitement"	11
"Go West, Young Man"	26
The Territorial Years	32
Otto Mears—"Moses of the Roustabouts"	50
Furthering the Cause of Monotheism	69
Gaining the "Needful"	90
"Papa Had a Cold"	114
Benevolence, Brotherly Love and Harmony	128
"The Hebrew in Politics"	144
"Extra"	152
The Forms of Hatred	156
The Yiddish-Speaking Jews	165
Acceptance and Rejection	188
West Denver, "Brooklyn," and West Colfax	194
Minyanim and Congregations	204
The *Shtetl* in Denver, Colorado	223
"The Tents"	241
Papa Spivak	249
Tsdokoh Expanded	259
The Muller Scandal and the United Community	265
The Jewish Press	277
Zionism	280
The Jews Outside Denver	283
The Sublime Ones	297
Jews in the Armed Services	307
Chronology	309
Acknowledgments	325
Bibliography	327
Index	334

In loving memory of my father
PAUL LIBERT
1892–1951
And to my mother
FANNIE PEPPER LIBERT
who begged me to dedicate this book not to her
but to the "unknown righteous" men and women—the Tsadikim—
who quietly helped build a Jewish community.
And this Third Edition to my daughter
VICKI UCHILL

Preface to the Third Edition

God cannot alter history. Historians can.
—Samuel Butler

More than forty years ago the first edition of this book appeared. During those years the most frequent question posed to me regarded the word in the title, *tsadikim*. *Tsadik*, the singular, is not an easy word to define. It is derived from the noun *tsedek* (frequently transliterated *zedek*), meaning "justice" and "righteousness." (The feminine is *tsadayket*.) A tsadik embodies all the virtues Judaism propounds, but a tsadik is not a "saint" because Judaism frowns on asceticism. From the root comes *tsdokah*—loosely, "charity." Tsdokah differs from charity because the recipient has a moral right to what he or she receives, and has the obligation, no matter how poor, to give tsdokah in turn. If the word "pioneers" (usually those who came before 1861) stands for history, and "peddlers" stands for "economics," then "tsadikim" stands for the religious life and the resulting institutions.

Next most frequently I am asked why and how I wrote this book. One incentive, in 1949, was to answer the mother from Wisconsin who was surprised that my children were allowed to go to preschool with hers. I needed to know more about my community. I found only two articles on the subject. That fall, leaving my children with my mother, I started my research.

I proceeded slowly and carefully until 1954, when Rabbi C.E.H. Kauvar and philanthropist Adolph Kiesler hired Dr. Allen Breck to write a history of the Jews in Colorado. Although Dr. Breck and I have a cordial relationship, I knew that I had to finish my manuscript before my target date, the Denver Centennial in 1959, because the Jewish community was not likely to support two histories, even if both of us found publishers. Moreover, my book would not have the support of the communal leaders, although the Allied Jewish Council voted not to support either book. I achieved the distinction of writing the first book on the subject, but I gave up the time I would have spent exploring local Jewish folklore. Fortunately, having the master publisher, Alan Swallow, accept my manuscript helped assuage my disappointment.

Another disappointment is the distortion, albeit well-meaning, of my research on Frances Wisebart Jacobs. She was *not* a founder of the National Jewish Hospital, and the bust of her in the lobby is not of the tiny woman with the large eyes, generous mouth, and prominent nose.

Because she was a loved and admired national figure, the Jewish Hospital believed that her name on the building would attract financial support. A similar decision was made years later to name a community hospital for General Maurice Rose. (Because "General" was removed, few remember the furor when his widow strenuously objected to his name on a Jewish institution and had him buried under a cross.)

When I first mentioned her name fifty years ago, only one person, Pearl Wolfson, knew who she was, and one person remembered as a child seeing her and believing she had "something to do with sorting clothes for the poor."

She was not honored by the United Way of which she was one of four founders. Despite my pleas, it was Milt Morris who succeeded in getting that national organization to recognize her, and Elaine Clearfield who convinced the city of Denver to name a park for her. Unknown in 1949, today she is the best-known Jewish woman in Colorado history, and the subject of highly imaginative storytellers as well as one of the myths I inadvertently created.

Some of the errata that were not the result of this book include:

> Altman, Colorado, is listed in Bernard Postal's *Jewish Tourist Guide* as being named for a Jew. His family wrote me in 1955 that he was not a Jew. Postal acknowledged the correction, but it was too late to prevent the repetition.
>
> Joe Washer of the Cotopaxi colony did not die young as reported. He divorced his wife, who was a cousin, remarried, and helped found the JCRS.
>
> The Star of David on the Tivoli tower, on other buildings, and on beer bottles, has nothing to do with Judaism. It is an accepted beer symbol.

West Ridge, a housing project in West Colfax, is not "Wheatridge" with "a preponderance of Jewish families." Only one Jewish family lived there. The wrong benefactor is credited.

As for my errors, where possible I corrected them in the accompanying chronology. Those for which there was no date follow:

> On page 168, the road described from Central City to Idaho Springs is the "Oh-My-God" road in Virginia Canyon. Caroline Bancroft said the women took the lower, safer road.
> On page 174, the Harts came from Falmouth, England.
> Possessives in place names are now incorrect. "Sloan Lake" and "St. Anthony Hospital" are the correct renditions.

Rules do exist for transliterating Hebrew, but with proper names I followed the organization's spelling, changing it when the organization changed it. As for dates, when lacking precise information I listed a date when a person or institution was first mentioned in print.

Since the first edition, I have new sources to thank. First is the talented Christopher Leppek of the indispensable *Intermountain Jewish News*. The staff's generosity is rare. I also thank historian William Kramer for directing me to the work of historian Hynda Rudd. My late friend Lil Goodstein's son, historian Dr. Phil Goodstein, continuously challenged my facts, forcing me to re-examine them. I am most pleased to have the support of the two experts, synonymous with Colorado history, Dr. Stephen J. Leonard and "Dr. Colorado," Thomas J. Noel.

Did I collect any folklore? Just what floats around in my memory. I learned from Protestants that Catholics built orphanages and Jews built tuberculosis sanitariums. I learned some tasteless songs.

To the tune of "The Bear Went Over the Mountain":

> We are the jolly consumptives,
> We are the jolly consumptives,
> We are the jolly consumptives,
> Hock, tschu, ping.

To the tune of the Toreador song we warned a victim of tuberculosis:

> To-re-ador, don't spit on the floor.
> Use the cuspidor.
> That's what it's for.

Some Yiddish words in the text need defining. The word *catooteh* is a euphemism for tuberculosis, and *catootnik* for the victim of the disease. It is derived from the Hebrew "quarrel." A *gnossinik* is not the same as the Greek *gnostic*. It was applied to anyone who might be an agnostic, a socialist, or a free-thinker.

I am surprised how many people never heard that the obscene words "KKK" stood for were "Koons, Kikes, and Katholics."

It is too late to capture the folklore of the early years, but it is not too late to start compiling the events of the last forty years. *Pirke Avot* (*Sayings of the Fathers*) admonishes, "You are not obligated to finish the work, but neither are you free to desist from it."

Abbreviations

AJY	*American Jewis Yearbook*
Art. Inc.	Articles of Incorporation
BMH	Beth Ha Medrosh Hagodol
BB	B'nai B'rith
DJN	*Denver Jewis News*
DPL	Denver Public Library
WmSF	William S. Friedman
IJN	*Intermountain Jewish News*
ICA	Inventory of Church Archives
JCRS	Jewish Consupmptives Relief Society
JO	*Jewish Outlook*
RA	*Reform Advocate*
RMN	*Rocky Mountain News*

Pike's Peak Adventure

The story of the Jews in Colorado would be no different from the story of the Jews in any other place in America, nor would it differ greatly from that of their non-Jewish neighbors, were it not for the unexcelled climate of the region. A natural stage was provided in the arid country for the Jews upon which they were to enact their ancient drama of *tsdokoh* (righteousness), the traditional concept of charity that couples love of fellow man with responsibility for fellow man.

Eliminating, or alleviating, human misery in any form is a fundamental in *tsdokoh*. The most prevalent form of misery that faced the nineteenth-century Jews in Colorado was tuberculosis, the mysterious and dread disease, which became so widespread after the Industrial Revolution that it became known as the "White Plague." In Colorado, even before the disease was understood or given its proper name, the Jews began their battle on behalf of suffering man as early as 1878.

Aside from the victory over the disease, in which the Jews in Colorado played an important part, there is the abounding narrative of adventure in the wilderness, of the establishment of Judaism and the forms it took in the Rocky Mountain region, and the stories of colorful individuals who rose to leadership in their communities as Americans and as Jews.

Before the beginning of this account there were Jews in the region, but history is as silent concerning the coming of the first Jew as it is about the coming of the first man into the West. Although the civilized world had long speculated on the origin of the Indians as red-skinned descendants of the Lost Ten Tribes, the oft-refuted belief does not draw the curtain apart for Jewish entrance into Colorado. Even a less popular theory that *Marranos* (secret Jews) may have accompanied the Spanish *conquistadores,* although it opens a vast area for research, does not have a part in Jewish history in Colorado. Neither would a study of the personnel of the parties accompanying the French and American explorers, nor those of the trappers and traders, be part of the history of the Jewish communities of the state.

An accurate and authentic beginning could be made in 1851, when the first established store in Costilla (a town today on the Colorado-New Mexico border) was opened by Moritz Beilschowsky (who appears to have been a Jew) and his partner, William Koenig.[1] Not even this event nor the fact that another known Jew was in the boundaries of Colorado in 1853, are of significance to this story. It is, however, important to note that this Jew was Solomon N. Carvalho, who accompanied General John C. Fremont on his last and most dangerous expedition in the far west. Fremont, the "Pathfinder," had launched a group of thirty-three men into the wilderness in the rigorous winter, to learn first-hand the most difficult conditions under which a rail-line to the Pacific might have to operate. As the official daguerreotypist, and thus the first photographer of the Rockies, Carvalho wrote an account of the adventures of the expedition, *Incidents of Travel and Adventure in the Far West,* which has earned an important place among the early descriptions of the uncivilized region.

For the beginning of the adventure of the Jews in Colorado, an event that took place in May, 1858, is chosen: the finding of the first "color" of gold in the Platte River. The effect of this event was felt when the news of it reached the East. By that time, it was too late in the year to undertake the 600-mile journey across the Great Plains. Not until the following spring would the mighty army of gold-seekers be ready to pour into the barren American desert, bound for Pikes Peak.

In this group came the first Jews who were to make Colorado their home and build a Jewish community.

FOOTNOTES

[1]Frank Hall, *History of Colorado,* III, p. 329; *Colorado State Business Directory,* Denver, lists M. Beilschowsky in Conejos from 1879 to 1884; *RMN,* July 6, 1880; p. 8, col. 2; "Moritz Bielschowsky, solid democrat of Conejos is doing the capital." There were more than a dozen Jews in the San Luis Valley [see Ch. "Jews outside Denver"] before Colorado became a state. Since intermarriage was the rule among them, and Judaism died with them, these Jews are not here considered pertinent to the story of the Jews in Colorado.

"The Big Excitement"

1

In the spring of 1859, after the snows had melted sufficiently and green shoots of grass were underfoot, 100,000 men, women, and children left the banks of the Missouri River. With guides, or by guidebook, they began their brave march west. Outfitted according to their means, the wealthier came by stage or horseback, families came in covered, ox-drawn wagons, and the poor walked, pushing their possessions before them in carts, or carrying them on their backs.

Emblazoned on the covered wagons was the brave slogan, "Pike's Peak or Bust." They pushed their way against hunger, thirst, exhaustion, and frequently against hostile Indians. About half of them could not fulfill the bold challenge. Those who lived turned back, earning the derisive name of the "go-backs." Admitting their defeat, they had crossed out "Pike's Peak or Bust," and substituted, "Busted, by God."

The half who were brave enough, or better equipped, finally caught their first glimpse of what appeared to be stationary, low-lying clouds on the horizon—the unbelievable spine of the continent—the Rocky Mountains. There lay their vague destination, Pike's Peak.

After Zebulon M. Pike had sighted America's famed mountain, the entire region had become known as Pike's Peak. But the peak, some seventy miles to the south of the goal of the Fifty-niners, was not where the gold of 1858 had been found. Instead, journey's end was at the two little towns on the banks of Cherry Creek, where it trickles into the sluggish, shallow Platte River. On the west side of the creek was the town owned by the Auraria Town Company, and on the east bank was the town owned by the Denver Town Company. To the north of the Platte was still another, the Highland Town Company property.

When the spot was reached, the travelers, who had journeyed for weeks, sometimes at the rate of two miles an hour, were bitterly disappointed. There was no gold. All they found were two treeless, dusty, little villages, with no comforts and no future. After cursing those who had inspired the great "hoax," another half of the adventurers who had reached the settlements left the region.

For the 25,000 who remained, the trip was soon justified. Gold had already been discovered. The secret held since January, 1859, came out that summer, along with that of another discovery made in May. The gold had been found in the mountains, not along the Platte River. Immediately, the mountains were covered by prospectors. Although there was little time for contemplation, the optimistic pioneers along the Platte now noticed the intense electric blue of the skies, the clear, invigorating air, and the majestic mountains so deceivingly close. This suddenly looked like a good place to stay.

During the first year of the "big excitement" (as the goldseekers termed the year of discovery of gold in the region) one dozen known Jews came into the area. It was neither persecution nor hunger that brought these "German" Jews west. They were already economically secure in the United States, although the nation was still suffering from the Panic of 1857. Instead, they sought the freedom of movement, the joy of expansion, and the excitement of the frontier at the foot of the continental barrier.

These Jewish pioneers had much in common. Most of them were young men, under thirty. All but three were unmarried. Although none of them was native American, they had come to the United States as children or youths, and knew the language of the country well. The majority had come to the country before the large wave of immigration from Central Europe after 1848. It has been claimed that the Jews brought the Masonic degrees to the United States and that "The annals of Freemasonry ... disclose the earliest Jewish settlers in various localities."[1] In the group of pioneers almost all were Freemasons, who were completely at ease in the large group of Masons in the West. They were comfortable, too, in the large group of Germans who had left the East.

Over and over again the names of these dozen pioneers appear in the infancy of civilizing the region. Their stories are the stories of the West, of Colorado, and of Denver, Central City, South Park,

California Gulch, and the myriad mining camps, some of which in the decades to come died and became "ghost towns."

2

Zadek (a righteous man) is the middle name of the members of the Salomon brothers who played a leading part in the Pikes Peak region. They were Frederick Zadek Salomon, Hyman Zadek Salomon, and Adolph Zadek Salomon. Hyman Z. was the earliest known Jewish arrival in the small village. He came in February,[2] before the great wave of Argonauts that followed in the spring. Apparently he did not remain to welcome his older brother, Fred Z., in June, but seems to have returned to Las Vegas, New Mexico, where he and his brother began to lay plans for the establishment of the merchandising firm they would eventually build. In the fall of the year he was back.

Hyman Z. gave the date of his birth and birthplace as September, 1832, Prussia. In the same record Fred Z. gave April 10, 1830, Poland, as his date of birth and birthplace. Both were born in Posen, which in the game of international boundaries lost two-thirds of its Jews. These Central European Jews from German-speaking Prussia were called the "German" Jews.[3]

On Fred Z.'s arrival in the United States, he entered business in New York. From there he went to the South, where he contracted yellow fever. Hyman Z. was in Cincinnati and summoned Fred. Both then went to Dubuque, and from there in 1858, to Las Vegas, New Mexico.[4] There Fred Z. joined the J. B. Doyle firm. Although Hyman Z. was not so closely identified with that firm, he, too, worked for Doyle.

Early in 1859, Fred left for St. Louis by stagecoach to bring back the first stock of goods for the Pikes Peak region. At Independence, Missouri, Fred loaded an ox-drawn wagon train with goods bound for the region to which the stampede was now under way. He halted his train at the lower crossing of historic Bent's Fort on the Santa Fe trail. Leaving the train behind, he came on horseback, or by mule, to the little villages on Cherry Creek to ascertain if the area was safe enough to bring his goods into it.

Finding things comparatively safe in the frontier towns, he sent back word to have the train follow him. It was ten days later that the "astonished and delighted" pioneers witnessed the sight of the provision-laden, ox-drawn train come down Cherry Creek. Fourteen years after the entrance of Fred Z. into Denver, the *Rocky*

Mountain News, January 1, 1873, in reminiscing, recorded the spectacular arrival of the city's first leading merchant:

> June 22, 1859, there arrived in Auraria a dapper little businessman, mounted on the deck of a mule. He registered himself at Smoke's Union Hotel as Fred Z. Salomon. . . . Fred made a friendly call at Uncle Dick Wootton's [the "inn" of the celebrated frontiersman], wiped his lips, picketted his mule down on the bottoms . . . and began "flaxing around." In a few hours a mammoth wooden storehouse was planned and it soon began to assume shape near the corner of Ferry and Fifth streets. But lumber was distant, carpenters few, and wages half an ounce per day in gold dust. About ten days later a noise of cracking whips and "gee, whoa, haws," coming down the valley of Cherry Creek announced the arrival of an old-fashioned train of huge white-topped wagons, each drawn by 5 or 6 yoke of oxen, and loaded with $30,000 worth of goods, marked J. B. Doyle & Co. Fred's other name at the time was "Co." The new store was not ready and the train "coralled" in front of Uncle Dick's (there was where all weary pilgrims brought up in those days). The result of a parlay was the moving out of the old man's bottles and glasses; the pioneer saloon was suppressed and dry groceries took the place of wet ones. Fred took command of the first general mercantile house established in Colorado.

The *News* office was in the attic overhead. It was already an old settler, dating its first issue, April, 1859. From its press came the bulletin: "New Goods Just Received. Only 50 days from the Missouri River. J. B. Doyle & Co."

It is possible that the rival towns made a bid at that time that he locate in one of them, for the records of the Auraria Town Company on July 31 show that, "On motion Fred Z. Salomon is donated two donation shares on condition that he locate a store in Auraria."

Hyman moved from Las Vegas to Auraria, and both brothers, working for J. B. Doyle, opened the store. Until the supplies were put into the large new store, they were scattered in half a dozen log cabins, and "no small excitement prevailed" when the hungry miners learned how extensive and valuable a lot of merchandise it was.

Toward fall a second train arrived for the Doyle firm. With it came O. J. Goldrick, the Irish scholar and father of the Denver Public School system. The "professor" arrived in full dress: "Broadcloth, plug hat, and lavender kid gloves," all frayed and fingerless, but faultlessly adjusted. He drove in, cracking a bullwhacker's whip with a flourish, and hurling epithets at the oxen in Latin. The elegant Goldrick had joined Salomon's train at the Missouri river. When the teamsters struck, Goldrick took command of the lead team, and as a bullwhacker trudged patiently beside the teams all through the summer. At the old Santa Fe crossing the train had divided. When Fred Z. had brought half of the train into Pikes Peak in July, the other half had gone with Goldrick to Fort Barclay in New Mexico, where the Doyle firm had an extensive establishment. Three months later Goldrick brought the balance of the train to the Cherry Creek branch of the Doyle firm.

During the year of the "big excitement," Hyman Z. acquired a partner, J. H. Ming. Together they started a train of six wagons freighted with provisions for the newest diggings at the foot of the Continental Divide in South Park. Said the *News*:

> These wagons are regular prairie freighters, and each carries about two tons. . . . The idea that the Rocky Mountains can only be penetrated in a few places is fast being dissipated. They are accessible almost at every point, not only with animals, but with heavily laden wagons.[5]

In a few weeks, Ming and Salomon were ordering additional supplies. The mines "were exceedingly rich and the miners were making money." The claims were much richer than had been suspected. Each had yielded more than $1000 in the short time since discovery. "Every man with a good supply of the needful on hand," the enthusiastic *News* reported.[6] Hyman Z. remained in South Park in the Tarryall diggings. The miners "holed up" that winter as much to protect their claims as to avoid the untried winter.

Tarryall was reputedly a rough camp, with miners jumping each other's claims, earning for it the nickname of "Grab-all." A new camp not far away is believed to have chosen pointedly for itself the name of Fairplay. That November Hyman Z. called together a meeting of the citizens at his and Ming's store (also referred to as Ming, Doyle & Co.) to form a debating society. Under a code of by-laws and regulations it was named the "Tarryall Lyceum," with Hyman Z. as secretary.[7] Nobody commented on the incongruity of a lyceum in "Grab-all."

In early spring, 1860, Hyman Z. returned to the settlements. The snow of beautiful South Park was eighteen inches deep at level, and on the eastern side of the Divide for a distance of twenty-five miles it was three or four feet deep. Leaving the Divide, he had met about fifty men going in. "The first party had pack animals and about 40 men were shovelling a road through."[8]

While Hyman Z. was in the mountains, Fred Z., with still another partner, named Tascher, began the manufacture of lager beer at their brewery in Auraria, "the first ever brewed in the Territory of Jefferson. . . . As soon as the lager is a little aged our citizens will have an opportunity of indulging in a drink not deadly in its effect, and which we hope will materially decrease the present consumption of strychnine whiskey and Taos lightning."[9] The first of December the beer was in abundant supply at J. B. Doyle & Co. The newspaper upstairs, which had been in constant and heady debt to the firm below for "certain black bottles, labeled, Old Cognac"[10] had something more for which to be grateful.

In the spring of 1860, Fred Z. left for St. Joseph, Missouri, where he purchased his stock for the winter of 1860-61. On his return he reported that his trip on the Central, Overland, California and Pike's Peak Coach had taken him less than six days. Business, he said, was very dull in St. Louis and on the River. Nearly all the trade there was being done with the Pikes Peak country, and an immense quantity of merchandise was on its way.

While awaiting the arrival of his train, "Messrs. Salomon & Co." were completing construction of their lager beer cellar, eighty feet by twenty feet, nine feet high to the base of the arch, with a stone wall two feet thick and floor and ceiling of gypsum cement. After he sold this business it became one of the leading breweries in the region.

When the goods Fred Z. had purchased in the East arrived, it proved to be the most immense stock any of the pioneers had ever seen. The thirty-five wagon train with three-hundred head of cattle thundered into town with so much merchandise it had to be divided between several stores. Branch stores were opened in Canon City, Mountain City, and Golden Gate, where the miners could obtain their supplies "at hand." There were one hundred tons of groceries, hardware, and other staple goods. Said the *News*, "Their immense three-story block fairly groans under the immense stock."

The building certainly did groan, as the *News* had said on November 15. The next day the building crashed with a blast heard throughout the settlements. The center foundation wall had settled more than two feet, carrying the heavy pillars running through the lower room, with a resultant cave-in of the first and second floor. No one was injured by the heavy shower of merchandise.

The pioneers came to the rescue and the next day Fred Z.'s card appeared in the newspaper, thanking everyone for helping him remove his goods from his "late" store. The loss was $5,000, and repairs estimated at $2,500. The roof and all three floors had to be replaced. A new three-story brick building replaced the one which had collapsed, supporting the claim that Fred Z. built the first brick building in Denver.

Fred Z.'s name was in the newspaper almost every day. At the brewery his company was selling fresh baking yeast daily. When twenty stolen horses on the way to New Mexico were found, it was "F. Z. S., Esq." who took descriptions of the animals in an effort to locate the owners. He worked on the committee for the Church Festival sponsored by the Episcopalians, in their effort to build a church. He was elected, unanimously, treasurer of the newly-organized Denver Chamber of Commerce in October, 1860. At that early period he began his efforts to bring transportation into the region with his request that the Chamber ask the citizens of Denver to raise $1000 to complete the St. Joseph, Maryville and Denver rail and wagon road into Denver.

Not so much is recorded in the *News* about Hyman Z. in 1860. The younger brother had been sent to Canon City to operate the Doyle branch store there. However, he sent the *News* a small bottle of coal oil taken from a spring about five miles from the town, which he believed to be the same as found in Pennsylvania. Measures, he said, will be taken to sink wells for oil gathering on a large scale.

As the region grew, so the position of the Salomons grew. It was augmented with the coming of a younger brother, Adolph Z., before the first decade was over. Before continuing with the saga of the Salomons, the coming of the other Jews and events of the early years should be examined.

3

Between the coming of Hyman and Fred Z., a few other Jews had entered the region. The towns they found were far bigger than those Hyman had seen in February. Auraria had one hundred and fifty houses, two hotels, one baker, one printing office, two saloons, one blacksmith, one carpenter and cabinet maker, one tin shop, one tailor, and two meat markets. Denver City, separated from Auraria by Cherry Creek, which was described as one hundred feet wide and three to twelve inches deep, had one hundred and fifty houses, five stores, two hotels, one printing office and two saloons.[11] Auraria boasted the pioneer newspaper, the *Rocky Mountain News*.

Most of the buildings were of hewed logs, some of earth, and were covered with "Mexican roof," as the earth roofs were called, or with the tarpaulin covers that had been removed from the prairie schooners. The most recent roofs had pine shingles. The few trees found by the pioneers east of the Rockies were the cottonwoods along the Platte River, and the *News* pleaded to "Save the Trees." Baths were taken in Cherry Creek or the Platte. All of the dust of the plains in the villages, which was ankle deep mud when it rained, was a part of Kansas Territory.

The second oldest member of the little Jewish group to be greeted by this sight arrived in May. Julius Mitchell at the age of forty-seven was old enough to be the father of many of the Jewish Fifty-niners. Like the Salomons he was born in Posen. A well-educated man, who had learned English in Europe, he came to the United States in 1835[12] where he immediately became a citizen in New York. There he engaged in the mercantile business and acted as a sales agent for a large fur company. He married in 1844, and although doing well, went west to Leavenworth, Kansas, where he remained until the Pikes Peak excitement, when he left his family behind, and set out west alone. In Denver he opened a large grocery and outfitting business. Before the year was over he was joined by his eleven-year-old son, David. As the patriarch of the little Jewish group on the banks of Cherry Creek, he officiated at the first Jewish High Holiday services during the fall of the very first year, 1859.[13]

Later writers described him as a man of decided liberal belief, who conceded to others the same right of expression whether their views were more orthodox or less. Mitchell was the first of a large group who came from, or through, Leavenworth, where a Jewish community existed, and which was one of the principal outfitting points of the Pikes Peak region.

During the same month Leopold Mayer also left Leavenworth, where he had been engaged in the grocery business. It took him sixty or seventy days to make the trip. Walking along beside an ox-team, he covered the entire 600 miles by foot. Several writers claim that he was accompanied by Abraham Goldsmith and Simon L. Wels on this trip.[14] Although the first city directory lists A. Goldsmith as a member of the Mayer firm, coming from Leavenworth, and residing, as did Mayer, in Denver City, neither Mayer's son, Adolph, nor the descendants of the Goldsmith family believe that they came west together.

Mayer was born in Alsace-Lorraine, and came to the United States at the age of nine. In Lafayette, Indiana, he sold matches and there began his lifetime of adventures. He followed the building of the railroads, particularly the building of the Union Pacific, and was present at Promontory Point when the East and West were joined in the first transcontinental road. Of all of the Fifty-niners only the sons of this Jewish pioneer remain in Denver in the mid-twentieth century. The story of Mayer's life is to be found in Denver, San Luis, and Saguache.

Although only Abraham Goldsmith [also Goldschmidt] is listed in the first city directory, there were two brothers, Abraham and Henry, married to two sisters, who made the trip west. The two young couples came from Munich. For four or five months they were on the sailboat bringing them to the United States. The voyage was a hazardous one, with their ship blown to the shores of Nova Scotia. In the United States they tried farm lands in Illinois and Missouri. In Denver City they filed homestead claims, and in October, 1859, Abraham held a grant of Denver lots.[15] On the death of Henry's wife, the first Jewish organization in the Rocky Mountain region was formed.[16]

4

In June, one of the leading Jews of the city arrived. Abraham Jacobs, who was born in Frensdorf, Germany, in 1834, came to the United States at the age of nine. After clerking in Louisville, Cincinnati, and Lexington, he came to Omaha in the summer of 1857 and ventured into business for himself. Next, in Denver, as was typical of Jewish activity during the period, he formed a partnership with a non-Jew, Albert Buddee.

Their store, across the street from the Doyle Company and *News* office, was described as a "finely finished frame building 22 feet by 70. Two stories high. The front in supurb style."[17]

On October 1st, A. D. 1859, A. L. 5859, more than 40 Masons assembled in the hall of Auraria Lodge to witness and participate in the first regular communication of Masons in the territory now known as Colorado. This hall was on the second floor of a two-story frame building on Ferry Street belonging to Br. Abraham Jacobs.[18]

In the same history in which the above appeared, were recorded the names of those present, which included:

> Br. F. Z. Salomon, Montezuma Lodge, No. 109, Santa Fe. . . .
> Br. A. Goldschmidt, Weston Lodge, No. 53, Missouri. . . .
> Br. A. Jacobs, Capitol Lodge, No. 3, Nebraska Territory. . . .

At a subsequent meeting Simon L. Wels of Templar Lodge, No. 203, New York City, was a guest. Fred Z. was elected treasurer of the Auraria Lodge U. D. (Under Dispensation) and was later a signer of the petition to create out of it Denver Lodge No. 5 (other lodges in the mining camps having picked up the intervening numbers).

Another of Jacob's contributions to Masonry is recorded with:

> A notable incident in connection with the location of the Lodge room is that Bro. A. Jacobs, who fitted up for us the first permanent Lodge room in his building on Ferry St. about 30 years ago, vacated in 1889 the home he and his family had occupied for 15 years, and watched it torn down to make place for the new temple we are now about to occupy.[19]

This lodge in 1889 became the leading lodge in the state, and the repository of the state's Masonic records.

One of the enterprises with which Jacobs was identified was called "The Fashion." The *News* commented with frequency on the establishment, "over which Jacobs presides with accustomed suavity of manner. It is the most elegant place you can drop in to refresh the inner man and read the latest papers."[20] The newspaper did not refer to the establishment as a saloon. Either it was not, or the fact that the Masonic Hall was in Jacobs' building constrained the editor. Yet, Masonry in the region did not frown on alcholic beverage, then regarded a necessity in the masculine frontier towns. It was well that the *News* did not mention it, for the woman Jacobs married soon after was active in the Women's Christian Temperance Union.

Jacobs and Buddee engaged in the real estate business, sold Pikes Peak Grindstone, obtained ten miles west of the city, and had on exhibition a specimen of marble from a quarry forty miles north of the city. The *News* speculated, "Who knows but the

Pike's Peak marble quarry may yet be called for completion of the national capitol?"[21] Anything was possible in the treasure chest of the Rockies, and the pioneers were like children in a toy store, displaying curios as well as ore specimens in their store windows. Every natural phenomenon was investigated.

With still another partner, Jacobs opened the Jefferson House in September with an inauguration dinner, honoring the brief-lived Territory of Jefferson. Only a handful of citizens appeared for the festivities. A bridal ball he staged in January, 1860, was one of the earliest of such elaborate entertainments.

In December, 1859, at a "Citizen's Meeting," Jacobs was elected a member of the city council from Auraria. The city council served both towns. Although Jacobs lived in Auraria where he had been granted one donation share in the town company,[22] and a strong rivalry existed between the two towns and its merchants, he was a prime mover in uniting them. The name of Auraria stuck fast on the pioneer's tongues. In April, 1860, a moonlight ratification meeting was held on what was to become the Larimer Street bridge and the two towns were united, with Abraham Jacobs acting as secretary of the meeting. Auraria became Denver City, West Division.

Jacobs' name was found on memorials to Congress, petitions for civic betterment, and performing such duties as opening the polls. But when he was suggested as a candidate for mayor he turned down the proposal.

Both Jacobs and Fred Z. were founders of the Auraria and Denver Chess Club and Literary Society, which met in Jacobs' building. Fred Z. was elected vice-president and Jacobs treasurer. The "Law and Order" movement centered about this building and its occupant, the Masonic Lodge. When Fred Z. was nominated for the legislative council on the Law and Order ticket, the signers were prominently identified with the lodge.

In November, 1859, the area ceased to be "Pike's Peak." A constitution was adopted for the new territory of Jefferson, carved out of the territories of Nebraska, Kansas, New Mexico and Utah. This territory lasted until February 28, 1861, when it became the Territory of Colorado by Congressional law.

The last day of 1860 Buddee and Jacobs announced the dissolution of their partnership. Buddee had been engaging in mining and planned to continue his search for gold. Jacobs continued with the established business, until 1861, when he moved his store to Central City.

5

Very little is recorded about the other Jewish Fifty-niners. The name of Simon Wels almost always appears with that of Abraham Goldsmith in the Denver Lodge which succeeded Auraria U. D. In 1872 he was a charter member of the B'nai B'rith lodge. The following year the lodge called a special meeting to grant him a traveling card when he was leaving for a visit to Europe.[23] In 1874 he requested, and was granted, a withdrawal card from the lodge.

Joel Gottlieb [also Gottleib] who arrived in 1859 and remained in the West for the rest of his life was, unlike his contemporaries, a East European Jew. His birthplace was Plonska, Russian Poland. At fifty-three he was the oldest of the Jewish pioneers, but never seems to have assumed the leadership that his age warranted. Joel had a younger brother, Joseph. Since both were referred to as "J. Gottlieb," and at least one historian credited Joseph as being one of the pioneers of the Jewish community, it is likely that both brothers were in the Pikes Peak region in 1859.

In the first city directory of 1859, Joel Gottlieb is listed under "merchants," and as being formerly of St. Louis. The same name also appears in Chicago in 1837. He owned a great deal of property in Denver at the time of his death, according to his will, which also lists property purchased in Virginia City, Montana, in 1864. He is listed in a Utah directory in 1867. Both he and Joseph seem to have spent a great deal of time in Utah, and it was the Euphrates Lodge of the B'nai B'rith of that state that conferred one of the order's degrees in Utah upon Joseph in 1876, to the chagrin of the Denver lodge, which did not quite know whether he deserved the degrees and membership.

Joel petitioned the Denver lodge in 1873 and was accepted. A few months later he resigned and requested the return of the fees he had paid for the second and third degrees of the order. The following year he died. From his will can be noted that even before Colorado became a state, the Jews were already grouped together on the basis of origin. His will was witnessed by Jews of similar East European birth, and the executor, a Russian Jew, married Joel's widow. Joel left everything to Flora, his wife, with the exception of three bequests to nephews. To Joseph he left nothing. The younger brother's reputation was not of the best. Although he was championed by some, he was not completely acceptable to the conservative Jewish community. Joseph's first wife, Ellen, died in 1879 at the age of 30, leaving him with four children. Two years later "Justice Whittemore tied the knot for Joseph Gottleib and Ella Grabosky in a strictly private ceremony." The following year his oldest son died, and in 1890 his second son died. At the time of his death in 1898 he left three children, born to his second wife. A month after his death another son died.

Joseph seems to have been principally engaged as a pawnbroker. After the Temple Emanuel was erected, he held the note on the building as late as 1876. His first application to membership was rejected in 1875, but accepted in 1878.

Grumpert Goldburg, listed in the city directory of 1859 as being in the auction and commission business in Auraria, did not remain long in Colorado. In August, he was at the diggings in Gregory Gulch, engaged in mining. From Colorado he went on to a mining camp in Montana, then named "Last Chance Gulch." He married Helena Morris in Denver in 1863, and returned with his bride to the camp which was renamed Helena.[24]

Among the few family men was Simon Nathan, who brought his wife and baby with him. Nathan was born in Kempen, Poland, in 1826 and came to the United States in 1852, later than most of his pioneer co-religionists. He settled in New Orleans, where he remained for four years. From there he went to Leavenworth, where he married Anna Zucker in 1857. During the following year, their first child, Edward, was born. As soon as the baby was old enough, the three joined a covered-wagon procession bound for Pikes Peak. The Nathans settled in California Gulch (Leadville) which was enjoying its first "excitement." One of the early births recorded in the region, and the first or second among the Jews, was that of Louis Nathan, born in Hamilton, October 7. 1860.

Late in the fall another Jew arrived from Leavenworth, Louis Rothchild, who opened a clothing store and completed the group of known Jews.

It is probable that there were other Jews in the region, but either they did not remain long enough to be noted, or they chose to separate themselves from their fellow-Jews. One such Jew was the French- and German-speaking Joseph Block, who came from France. He married a beautiful Catholic girl and brought up his children according to her religion. The family lived in Crested Butte for most of Block's life. In early Denver, where Block was a butcher, he took no part in the activities of the small Jewish group, yet he gave employment to at least one Jew.[25] He never denied being a Jew and was on friendly terms with the Jews. The *b'rith milah* (traditional ceremony of circumcision) of a son appears in Dr. John Elsner's record book, with the notation "5 years old for Joseph Block, Nov. 27, 1869, Isaac ben Joseph, chloroform." He also buried a child in the Jewish cemetery.[26]

FOOTNOTES

[1] Paul Masserman and Max Baker, *The Jews Come to America;* Peter Wiernik, *History of the Jews in America,* p. 111.

[2] Hall, *History of Colorado,* II, p. 551. H. Z. Salomon gave the date of his arrival as February 15, 1859.

[3] The fine line of distinction between the Central European Jews and East European Jews, was not the boundaries of divided Poland, but the simple test of language. "German" Jews did not speak Yiddish, East European Jews did. This book follows the common (and incorrect but convenient) usage.

[4] Denver *Republican,* Nov. 3, 1888. Obituary.

[5] *RMN,* Oct. 27, 1859.

[6] *RMN,* Nov. 17, 1859.

[7] *RMN,* Dec. 8, 1859.

[8] *RMN,* Feb. 23, 1860.

[9] *RMN,* Oct. 27, 1859.

[10] *RMN,* Aug. 13, 1859.

[11] *RMN,* May 21, 1859.

[12] *RA,* Oct. 31, 1908, p. 10, col. 3.

[13] *Ibid.* Almost all sources agree, except *Republican,* Jan. 1, 1911, p. 6: "First meeting of Jews . . . on a summer evening of 1860."

[14] *RA,* p. 10, col. 1.

[15] Henrietta Bromwell, "Fifty-Niners Directory," p. 110.

[16] *RA, op. cit.,* p. 48, col. 3. The name of Henry was supplied by his daughter-in-law, Mrs. Sam Goldsmith.

[17] *RMN,* Nov. 3, 1859.

[18] Denver Lodge No. 5, "Fiftieth Anniversary."

[19] Proceedings of the M. W. Grand Lodge of A. F. & A. M. of Colorado, p. 45.

[20] *RMN,* Sept. 30, 1859.

[21] *RMN,* Jan. 25, 1860.

[22] "Town Record" of Auraria Town Company, Oct. 15, 1859.

[23] BB minutes, Apr. 2, 1873.

[24] Joel Gottlieb may have been related by marriage to Grumpert Goldburg His wife, Flora, was the daughter of Mrs. Esther Morris, and sister of David Morris of Helena, where Goldburg lived. Both Gottlieb and Goldburg are

mentioned in Leon Watters' book, *The Pioneer Jews of Utah*. Watters does not indicate that the city of Helena was named after Mrs. Goldburg.
[25]Louis Anfenger received his first job from Block as a bill collector.
[26]Mrs. Augusta Hauck Block. Joseph Block's daughter-in-law, agrees that a son was buried in the Temple Emanuel cemetery, because it was the best one in the area. She is certain that no *b'rith* was ever performed for his sons.

"Go West, Young Man"

1

The eyes of the entire nation were upon the Pikes Peak region. Horace Greeley crossed the Great Plains in 1859 to see for himself. He reported carefully the opportunities of the West, without overlooking the hardships to be endured in gaining them. Yet, so far as his readers were concerned, his report had said only, "Go West, Young Man, and Grow with the Country."

Business was good in the pioneer settlements. Before the end of 1859 the *News* published a list of receipts of gold dust since the opening of many of the pioneer establishments, which included:

J. B. Doyle, receipts $2,528, shipments $2,268.

L. Mayer & Co., receipts $824, shipments $456.[1]

A newly created minting firm in Denver announced that its gold was nearly as perfect as regular mint issues. The Homestead bill had the support of the young Republican party, and brick and tile were being furnished from the east side of the Platte River for builders in the fire-conscious arid city.

Thus was the attraction of the West enhanced. After the winter of 1859-60, more than double the number of Jews who had come the previous year arrived in the settlements. Some of them remained, but as the weather warmed, most of them moved on into the mountain camps or nearby supply points.

The term "Fifty-niner" applies to all the pioneers who came into the region before it officially became Colorado Territory on February 28, 1861. The Jewish Fifty-niners of 1860 and early 1861 differed little from their predecessors. With a few exceptions they were again the merchants, the young single men, and, with two exceptions, the "German" Jews. An early East European Jew, Alexander Rittmaster, who came from Suwalki, Poland, is said to have arrived during this early period. The other exception

26

was Wolfe Londoner, who was to become Denver's mayor before the century was over. Wolfe was born in New York City. His older brother, Julius, who came west the same year, was born in Prussia.

Again, most of them were Masons who took an active part in the established lodges and helped create new ones in the mountain camps. Many of them were connected with outfitting houses in Leavenworth, and were either moving the firm into the new territory, or opening branch stores. Some of them were related. Others knew each other previously.

Newspaper items revealed the entrance of most of them into the territory:

In April, "H. Poznansky, Esquire, of the well-known house of Poznansky and Cohen,"[2] opened a clothing and dry goods store, superintended by "J. Sands of the popular house of A. Sands and and Brothers in Leavenworth."[3] The store was named the New York Clothing Store. The name of Poznansky, or Poznanski, appeared for many years in Denver, Central City, Buena Vista, and Leadville. Almost each time it appeared it was prefaced by different initials. "Felix Poznanski" and "Phillip Poznanski" are mentioned on the rare occasions that full names were used. Just how many Poznanskis there were is not known, nor even if they belonged to the same family.

New advertisements in the *News* in the beginning of 1860 included that of "S. Schayer, hats, caps, gloves and furs. Also makes to order and cleans. Ferry St."[4] There was an H. Schayer,[5] as well, and is likely the Herman Schayer who signed the charter of the B'nai B'rith lodge in 1872.

Salomon Schulein of New York purchased the Arcade building at the corner of Larimer and F Streets and divided the building into two stores, one for his clothing store and the other half as a dry goods store.[6]

One of the most frequently encountered names in pioneer western merchandising history is that of Abraham Hanauer. His firm "Hanauer, Dodd & Bro." came into Colorado through their stellar salesman, Wolfe Londoner. Hanauer was in Denver in October, 1860, subscribing to the rules and regulations of the Denver Chamber of Commerce.

Known Jews in the Territory of Jefferson included the names of the following men, each of whose names appears again later in the history of Colorado: Leopold B. Weil; the Deitsch brothers,

Isadore, Jonas and Moritz (who may have arrived in 1859); Solomon Nathan (whose identity is easily confused with that of Simon Nathan, since the *News* referred to both as "Mr. S. Nathan," and to compound the confusion, each had children named Louis and Edward); Samuel Arkush; Adam Kuhn and his partner, B. Hellman; Solomon Holzman; I. H. Kastor, and his brothers-in-law Henry and Joseph Kline and Louis Trapp.

These names were found together in various partnerships from time to time. Thus, the Sands and Holzmans were partners, Kastor was part of the firm S. Schulein, Kastor & Co. and later was in partnership with Henry Kline and Bernard Berry. In Central City, A. Sonneberg and the Deitschs were in business together. From these partnerships came marriages, some of them arranged by fathers and brothers for their lonely partners in the West.

From Abraham Lincoln on down, Biblical names were in vogue. Coupling the Old Testament names with the abundant German surnames in the region, a name offered little clue to the religion of its bearer, perhaps a welcome anonymity to the handful of Jews. Some of the names, not identified with Jewish groups in later years, yet very likely Jewish, were those of the partners Loeb and Kleinstein, and William Rosenfeld.

Many of the pioneers of 1860 were "boomers." Some of them who took an active part in the early days in the territory of Jefferson were only temporary residents, who made their permanent homes later in other Rocky Mountain states. From the group, Hanauer settled in Utah, and Grumpert Goldburg in Utah and Montana. The Kuhn brothers, Adam and Abraham, were later in Montana and Utah, and I. H. Kastor in Wyoming. Isadore Strassburger, Louis Hershfield, and Arthur Mortiz were said to have pioneered in Pikes Peak before following the boom that created Virginia City, Montana.[7]

2

In the saga of Colorado wit and humor, Wolfe Londoner was the darling of the newspapermen and writers of his day. The pioneers found his humor hilarious. His accounts of early days in Colorado were prolific and were widely quoted, as well as carefully preserved. As a practical joker, his boisterous pranks with, and on, his intimate friend, the children's poet Eugene Field, kept the community howling with pain or delight. Field himself was a Denver newspaperman who wielded his pen, not with the poetic gentleness that earned him fame, but with piercing newspaper thrusts at all who came within its range.

The account of Wolfe Londoner's coming into the region is given here not so much because he was a representative Jew (he left Judaism early), but because it was the most complete of any of the Jewish Fifty-niner stories, and is basically like those given by many another young immigrant from the "states," Jew or non-Jew.

The first Londoners, Julius and Wolfe, to arrive in the West, came from a wealthy merchant family in Prussia, also cited as Poland, where the original family name had been Wolfe. But from their frequent travels back and forth to London, their neighbors began to ask, "How are the Londoners?" Thus, according to one legend, the new surname was born.

While the facts may well be embroidered, the historian W. B. Vickers gives the story of the arrival of both brothers as it was undoubtedly told by Wolfe:

Although they had all the advantages of wealth, both brothers were restless and adventurous. Julius, who was seven years older, worked in his father's store until he was eighteen and then left for California, where he clerked for a time in a San Francisco store. He made three journeys to California before 1856, trying business in Los Angeles and in the Mormon community of San Bernardino. As a member of the Vigilante Committee in San Francisco he was present during its reorganization in 1856, and during its subsequent reign during which many of the desperadoes were hung and the city cleared. He then returned east to Dubuque, where he took charge of his father's store. The following year he went to St. Louis and remained there until he came west to Pikes Peak in 1860.

Wolfe left home at the age of thirteen, boarded a California-bound steamship, and made his way to the Pacific Coast. There he found employment in a hotel at $125 a month, with his board thrown in. Next, the youngster went to work for a "celebrated" auctioneer and was soon making $200 a month. He saved enough money to open a grocery of his own and remained in California about four years. But his parents became anxious and he returned to New York.

Wolfe was in charge of a family branch store in Iowa. The business prospered until the Panic of 1857. With what was left, his father moved the business to St. Louis, and Wolfe was placed in charge of the family in Iowa to await receipt of funds from St. Louis to take the family down the Mississippi. He was soon sent the sum of twenty dollars. But Wolfe

> being heartily tired of his life of enforced inactivity in Dubuque, without waiting for further remittances, determined to attempt the removal to St. Louis at once. . . . Going to the levee, he accosted the most genial-looking captain then on the river and asked him what he would charge to take himself, his family and their goods to St. Louis. The fare was $15 a passenger, but as his family must be small—he was then under 20—the good-natured captain . . . offered to take them for $25. This was more than young Londoner had, and he proposed to pay $15, and the balance as soon as he could earn it in St. Louis.
>
> To this the captain finally consented, and a ticket was accordingly issued to "Wolfe Londoner and family." Hurrying home, he loaded their household effects on two drays and sent the family, consisting of seven persons, on board the boat, with directions to secure berths and hold them while he remained with the goods. It was not until the boat had put out from the wharf and was several miles down the river that he ventured to approach the clerk, who by this time, was quite anxious to see the holder of the tickets of the family that had appropriated so many of the staterooms.
>
> At the clerk's office he met the captain, who charged him with deceiving him. "No," said young Londoner, "upon my word, every one of that party is a member of my family." Looking at him in astonishment, the captain asked him to explain. "Well, captain, I will tell you, although I seldom speak of it, and hope you will not, in the future. I married a widow."

In St. Louis he met Hanauer, an old friend of the family, who employed him in his firm, then engaged in freighting across the plains and in merchandising in Colorado and New Mexico. Early in the spring of 1860, Wolfe left St. Louis. He joined the firm's wagon train at Atchison. On the first day out the party made a distance of five miles. On the second day, as he was comfortably seated in one of the wagons, he was discovered by the "Mexican wagon master, or *major domo,* who disregarding his protestations that he was sent out by the owners of the train, ordered him to vacate his seat at once."[8] Of this trip he says:

> I walked most of the way and had a terrible experience with a pair of hob-nail boots, regular miner's brogans, with

spikes sticking out in a formidable manner . . . the nails tortured me, so I walked barefoot 100 miles. We met some Indians and I traded my shoes for several pairs of moccasins. . . . There were no flies here when I reached Denver—no, that is no joke; flies came with the increase in population. . . .[9]

Julius, who came out the same month, traveled more comfortably by stagecoach.

Almost on arrival, Wolfe was sent to Canon City as a representative of the firm, where he built a solid business housed in a solid store—the first stone building in the town. From Canon City he was sent to California Gulch where he operated another branch store. While there he was appointed county clerk and recorder of Lake County, and held, as well, the offices of county treasurer and county commissioner in the booming ore-rich mountain country. He remained there until 1865, when he turned the business over to his youngest brother, Joseph.

The careers of both brothers are part of the early history of Colorado. The rest of Wolfe's story is more appropriately told with that of the political activity of the early settlers. As for Julius, his name appears in the founding of many of the Jewish organizations of Denver.

FOOTNOTES

[1]*RMN*, Sept. 17, 1859.
[2]*RMN*, Apr. 30, 1860.
[3]*RMN*, May 16, 1861.
[4]*RMN*, Oct. 22, 1860.
[5]Hall, *History of Colorado*, III, p. 551.
[6]*RMN*, Oct. 19, 1860.
[7]Bernard Postal and Lionel Koppman, *A Jewish Tourist's Guide to the United States*, taken from thesis by Rabbi Benjamin Kelson, "The Jews of Montana."
[8]W. B. Vickers, *History of the City of Denver*, p. 497-8.
[9]Alice Polk Hill, *Tales of the Pioneers*, p. 121.

The Territorial Years

1

On February 28, 1861, while Fred Z. Salomon was in Washington attending the inauguration of Abraham Lincoln, the territory of Colorado was established. However, the pioneers' joy in having their own government was soon tempered by the attack on Fort Sumter and the outbreak of the Civil War. The new territory was on the side of the Union, although within the pioneer group there were men from the South who expressed strong feelings for the Confederacy. Within the local governments and the Masonic groups there was unity, whatever their members' national sentiments.

By the end of September, Colorado volunteers formed the First Regiment, which later won the Battle of La Glorieta, ending the Confederate threat in the West. The government had not provided any money for military equipment for the patriotic fighting men, so the territory's first governor, William Gilpin, issued drafts on the national treasury in payment to the merchants who were supplying the regiment. When the drafts were presented in Washington, the government refused to honor them and the money the pioneer merchants had tied up in the paper reached about $400,000.

Several merchants ran advertisements similar to that of D. Sands: "Important notice. On all our goods bought of us for which payment is made in coin, we will make a discount of 10 per cent."[1]

Another problem, possibly created by the war, was encountered by S. Schulein, who advertised in the *News* that he had read that many marriageable women were on their way west. The women did not materialize (travel was dangerous enough without the added peril of getting through a country at war) and Schulein found himself with fifty "fine wedding suits."[2] By October he was ready to dispose of part or all of his entire stock of goods "at lowest wholesale cash price for government drafts, allowing 100 cents for each dollar."[3]

The Doyle company rented their newly repaired store to the government for a warehouse "at the magnificent sum of $400 per month."[4] Fred Z., in charge of the warehouse, advertised "an invoice of sabres, belts and sashes, with which officers can now provide themselves." The merchandise was purchased in St. Louis and came by express, risking seizure by the Rebels; this compelled a higher price in Denver, "but not too high considering."[5]

The war brought other troubles. While Messrs. Hellman and Kuhn with three or four friends sat around the stove in their store one evening, they were robbed of more than $1,200 worth of clothing by twenty-five persons whom they believed to be soldiers. The robbery was something of a mystery. The merchants had been "deceived" by a man acting "as being impressed by officers" to take supplies, and who said that the quartermaster would take care of payment the next morning. The *News* was of the opinion that the managers of the store were not very well versed in army regulations and frontier doings.[6]

With the victory of the Battle of La Glorieta, and the government making good the claims on the dishonored drafts, the territory was able to recruit two more regiments to participate in the war, and also to fight the Indians with whom trouble was increasing.

Fred Z. left in May of 1862 for Fort Union and Santa Fe. He reported that it was being said that Kit Carson had been appointed colonel of the First New Mexico Regiment. A Hanauer, Hyman Z., and Fred Z. made several trips to visit the Colorado boys, carrying letters and messages to them from home. Before leaving on one trip Fred Z. gave a group of friends a big champagne supper at Charpiot's Restaurant and the newspaper reported a "most magnificent time."[7]

That fall "Doyle, Salomon & Co." were given a contract for transporting the First Regiment to Fort Scott. A few hours after receiving the contract the firm had ready, and under way, twenty wagons.[8] The patriotic pioneers subscribed to a testimonial fund to equip the Colorado First Regiment with a band.[9] Abraham

Jacobs brought the *News* a six-pounder ball from the Battle of Valverde and a grapeshot from Pigeon's Ranch.[10]

The Civil war and the Indian uprisings were not the only serious troubles faced by the pioneers. On the morning of April 19, 1863, at two-thirty, fire swept through Denver, burning out the business section of the town, and leaving an estimated damage of $250,000. Poznanski and Cohen, who had recently built fireproof buildings, were completely wiped out. They could well envy— for a time—the merchants who had moved their establishments into the mountains.

Rebuilding began immediately, but the effort was partly wasted, for a year later, May 20, 1864, the innocent trickle called Cherry Creek, which some of the pioneers had followed into Denver, became a wall of violent fury. Rains and melting snow had swollen the creek, which burst into the newly rebuilt settlement and completely engulfed West Denver and the bottomlands around the point where the Creek meets the Platte. Water, mud and debris destroyed everything the pioneers had labored to build with so much difficulty. The city hall, a small frame building in the creek bed, disappeared, and with it the iron safe in which were kept all the records and documents since the Cherry Creek settlements were born.

Twenty lives were lost. The damage was estimated at a million dollars. After the flood there were many changes. J. E. Zalinger, a freighter, had just hauled his last load of freight into town, when it was carried off by the flood. Zalinger gave up freighting, and he and his wife, Brunetta, moved to what became University Park, where they built a house and began raising crops.[11]

The flood had an important effect on the rebuilding of Denver. A movement eastward to higher ground began, and the principal expansion of Denver from there on was eastward.

Early in the 60's more than half of the Jews in the state were in the mountains, with most of them in or around Central City. Not only gold was now being sought. The first paying silver mine had been located, and silver was on its way to enriching the new region.

Although the Civil War and Indian troubles had hindered the growth of the territory, the ore of the mountains, pouring into the stream of business, was increasing the wealth of the territory slowly but steadily. In 1866 the items that indicated a more luxurious way of life appeared in the *News*: gold watches, 185;

34

carriages, 116; piano fortes, 26. In Denver, incomes over $3000 included those of Isadore Deitsch at $7,702; his brother Jonas, the same amount, and that of Phil Trounstine, a new partner and brother-in-law of Abraham Jacobs at $4,393.[12]

2

The importance of the Salomons, particularly that of Fred Z., mounted with their ever-increasing activity on behalf of the territory. Fred Z. had taken the lead, not only among the Jews but in the larger community as well, as a successful businessman and as one of the most civic-minded men in the region.

According to his nephew (also Fred Z. Salomon of St. Louis) the pioneer had been a Forty-niner participating in the California Gold Rush. But Fred Z. in appearance and demeanor was far different from the traditionally rough-and-tumble gold prospectors of the day. According to his nephew,

> He was a little under average height, was almost a dude in the type of his apparel, dressed immaculately, always carried a cane, and in the majority of cases wore a high hat. He ran the most lavish living establishment possible for a bachelor to adopt, and was a great entertainer.[13]

His social life did not suffer from the lack of a wife. On the contrary, Alice Polk Hill, in her *Tales of the Pioneers*, repeated a story told her by Mrs. William Byers, the wife of the editor of the *Rocky Mountain News*:

> Fred Salomon's dinners "took the shine off of everything." He was considered the most punctiliously polite man in the settlement, a reputation fairly won and well preserved. . . . His was a bachelor's home, with a bona fide ground floor, and furnished with pine tables and three-legged stools. On one occasion he gave a dinner to his lady friends, and it was a meal that would have delighted the most fastidious epicure.
>
> After the repast, the ladies, thinking it time to take their leave, requested Mr. Salomon to bring their wraps. Instead of protesting against the brevity of their stay, he instantly complied with their request, saying, "Certainly, ladies, certainly I will, with the greatest of pleasure." When the force of his speech dawned upon him, he hastened to apologize, at the same time nervously searching for his handkerchief to mop his perspiring brow. It was a long time before he heard the last of his after dinner politeness.

As a leading figure in the organization of the Colorado Pioneers Association, those few records of pioneer days in existence today are in some measure due to his foresight. The first meeting of the Fifty-niners was called to order by Fred Z. in 1866. The group decided to admit to membership only those pioneers who were in the region before it became Colorado Territory. The organization adopted a uniform of "black felt hat, red flannel shirt (with white collar and black cravat), black pants, black belt, and a silver badge with '59' inscribed on it, to be worn on the right breast." The membership fee was $1.00, and included the registration of the pioneers in a book which provided space for the name of the pioneer, the date of his entrance into the territory, and his date of birth and birthplace.[14] In 1879 he and B. F. Zalinger were among twenty-eight incorporators of the State Historical Society.[15]

His early social activities were interwoven with his civic ideas. From the Auraria and Denver Chess Club and Literary Society and the early Chamber of Commerce eventually grew the Denver Public Library. On his death he left $2000 for the purchase of books by the Chamber. This bequest was said to be the first of its kind in the city.[16]

He took part not only in the founding of his Masonic lodge but also in the activities of other pioneer lodges. In 1862 he was appointed Grand Pursuiviant of the Grand Lodge of Colorado. In later years he was an incorporator and officer of the non-Jewish Lotus club, to which many of the social leaders of the late 80's belonged.[17]

Masquerades were very popular from the earliest days until after the turn of the century. On many lists, particularly those of the Turnverein, his name appears as attending in dignified costume. Fred Z. did not come in gunny sacking but as a red coat officer or one of a quartet of hunters. Among his intimates were all the prominent men of the territory. He seems to have been especially close to Byers, the editor of the *News*, who had frequently thanked him in the newspaper for his gifts, sometimes "enough to set up a Yankee peddler in business for himself."[18]

He traveled widely: to the Doyle establishments in the Southwest; to the army forts during the Civil War; to the East Coast, particularly Washington; and periodically abroad. These travels were not merely for his pleasure, but also to help the territory. The *News* tried to gather specimens to take to the Paris Exposition in 1867 in order to publicize the region. Upon his retirement in 1885, he took his nieces, the daughters of H. Z., with him to Europe, and was planning to extend his travels to Palestine, when he decided to return to Colorado.[19]

His business enterprise was not confined to the Doyle Company or his early brewery. From the first he worked on the constant problem of the region—water. On November 30, 1859, the Capitol Hydraulic Water Company was organized with a capital stock of $500,000. The company brought water from the Platte River six miles above Auraria by ditch across the plains into the settlements. Fred was on the board of directors through the years when the company became the Platte Water Company, which he began to serve as president in 1868. In 1874 he made a proposal to furnish the city with water, or that the city buy out the company. The *News* favored the city buying the company for the offered price of $50,000, "which is cheap."[20]

One city alderman did not agree that the price was cheap and said that the Jews had made a corner on the city just as they had done 1800 years earlier. Abraham Jacobs wrote a stinging letter to the alderman. Under the heading: "A Jew's Reply to Alderman Case," Jacobs wrote that he had come to the city in 1859 to better his pecuniary condition, and was willing to leave it to the citizenry if he had not been highminded, upright, and honorable. He pointed out that he was once an alderman and refused to run for mayor although urged. The Ditch, he said "is worth all asked for it, and I would not sell it for that price if it had been mine. . . . What are the alderman's religious views, and what sins did his ancestors commit that he has become a wanderer?" Jacobs added that the alderman had been appointed through one of the most corrupt bargains ever made, and got more than thirty pieces of silver. "If this alderman had been subsidized by the Platte Water Company, the price would not have entered into consideration."[21] The Platte Ditch controversy set off much comment. Another letter appeared in the *News* signed "Mendelsohn," pointing out that religious belief had nothing to do with the matter.[22]

Fred Z. and his brother prospered in the Doyle Company. First it became Doyle, Salomon & Co., then Doyle, Salomon & Bro. For a time after death of J. B. Doyle in 1864 (while serving in the territorial legislature) it was known as Hanauer, Salomon & Co. It finally became Salomon & Co. and so remained when the company moved from the Elephant Corral, where it was located after the flood of 1864. The firm moved eastward with growing Denver until January 1, 1873, when the *News* reported: "With the closing of the year, there passed from the list of mercantile firms, the earliest and oldest of the list—the wholesale house of Salomon Bros." The wholesale business was given up, and the company continued with retailing and small jobbing. The *News* estimated that the firm had averaged half a million dollars a year during the fourteen years of its existence.

Fred Z. was a loyal and energetic Republican. Among the many offices he held was his appointment as treasurer of the Territory of Colorado. When the merchants of Denver and Central City sought to establish a uniform rate for gold dust, Fred Z. took an active part and was also the instigator of the first mining exchange in the 70's. He helped organize the Merchants Protective Association, which kept an alphabetical file of all persons with bad credit. Fred Z. was elected president of the association, and Julius Londoner served on the board of directors.

From 1875 to 1879 he served as president of the Denver Board of Trade. The Union Pacific had by-passed Denver in favor of Cheyenne. After many unsuccessful attempts by the Board to bring a railroad into Denver, Fred Z. helped negotiate a contract for the building of a railroad. The pioneers expended half a million dollars in grading, tieing, and bridging, to bring the railroad into the city. The work began in May, 1868, and the Denver Pacific was fully completed and formally accepted in 1870. On St. John's Day all the Masonic bodies in the city turned out to celebrate and lay the cornerstone of the proposed Union depot.[23]

There were many other activities and honors. In 1866 he was chosen a director of the First National Bank. In 1872 he signed the articles of incorporation for the organization of a sugar beet company. The incorporators believed that they could raise beets with a higher saccharine content than those raised in Germany. At the time the idea was premature. Years later growing and refining sugar beets became one of Colorado's principal industries. He also took part in the discussion toward forming an agricultural society in 1861; was present, as a member of the committee, at the welcoming of Ulysses S. Grant; led a successful fund-raising for the victims of the Chicago fire, raising $10,000 in two days, and offered his help to the victims of the fire that all but demolished Central City in 1874. Not the least of his accomplishments was the founding of the town of Greenland in Douglas County in September, 1875.[24]

In his Jewish activities, he was a charter member of the B'nai B'rith Lodge in Denver, and its second president. However, he withdrew from the lodge in 1874.[25] He took part in the first religious services in 1859, but did not join Congregation Emanuel for sometime after it had been founded.

Fred Z.'s contemporaries were honored by the naming of cities, counties, and natural points of interest. Even a few Jews were honored in a lesser degree. But for this pioneer, not even a street is named. Although he was mourned by the city, his named ceased to appear almost immediately after his death in 1888 at the age of fifty-eight.

Hyman Z. took part in almost all of the activities in which Fred Z. was the leader. He and his wife and two daughters lived on Curtis Street, next door to the Tabor Grand Opera House, which was built in 1881 and for which H. Z. had sold Tabor two of the lots for $16,000.[26] His house was new in the days when Indians leaned on his picket fence asking for handouts, when trains were halted not too many miles distant from the town for passengers to shoot bison from the windows, and when a walk from their home to any point west or south was through open prairie.

Like his brother, he was a charter member of the B'nai B'rith lodge in Denver, but instead of withdrawing as Fred Z. had, he merely dropped out of the order.[27]

According to their nephew, both Fred Z. and Hyman Z. probably had more friends and associated with more non-Jews than with Jews. This was not true of their younger brother, Adolph Z., whose efforts in Denver were almost completely for the Jews.

The younger brother settled in Colorado in quite a different way from those of his pioneer brothers. It was the idealism of Horace Greeley that determined where and how Adolph Z. would make his contributions to the people of Colorado. Greeley's love affair with the West, which had already been declared, blossomed into a Utopian dream a decade later. The visionary editor and his agricultural editor, Nathan C. Meeker, launched an effort to establish a model colony in the West. With the New York *Tribune's* columns calling for idealistic "temperance men, ambitious to establish a good society" on a location chosen by Meeker in northeastern Colorado, a flood of subscriptions swamped the

Tribune office, totalling $100,000. The first Union Colony was born.[28]

With Meeker as president and Greeley as treasurer, the colony organizers outlined their proposals and attracted a diverse group of idealists, including P. T. Barnum, Greeley's friend and already a famous showman. "Mr. Meeker's idea at the time he made his first proposal for a colony was to have one church edifice. However, there was no religious test as a condition for membership." It was also "worthy of note that scarcely any Germans were among the original colonists . . . and are still scarce because of their love for lager beer," David Boyd, a Greeley historian, commented. He also noted the lack of Catholics, particularly Irish Catholics, because of the prohibition of liquor, and found it hard to understand why there were so few Negroes in the colony, since the colonists were not only Republicans, but also Abolitionists.[29]

In Colorado, Meeker named the townsite Greeley, and in 1870, in accordance with the life-long preachings of the newspaperman, the charter was written forbidding liquor from its boundaries forever.

Adolph Z. had made several trips to Colorado where he operated a store for an English ditch digging company in Evans, the Union Pacific terminus near Greeley. He became interested in the ideals of the colony, and brought his store into the town, leasing the Hotel de Comfort. The business could well have been a forebear of the twentieth-century department store, except that Salomon sold items undreamed of in the more modern one. Coffins and farm machinery, as well as clothing and hardware, filled the store, which soon embraced a full block, with a tin-roofing department across the street. For fifty miles around, farmers came to his store, the only one in the area.

Adolph became a trustee of Greeley and a devoted protector of the colony's interests. One of these was the handling of the large potato crop raised there. He sold his store and built one of the first potato warehouses in the vicinity. "In the meantime," his daughter, Amy Salomon Lifton, writes, "he thought the farmers near Greeley were being cheated in the prices they received for their potatoes (then Greeley potatoes were as famous as Idaho potatoes in later years). So he formed the first potato pool," giving thousands of dollars in profits to the Weld County farmers. The family has a picture of him labeled "the Potato King."

Inadvertently he became a farmer. Lending money rather liberally, and extending credit too generously, he was forced into the operation of many farms and stock ranches. "This was not a particularly voluntary procedure on his part, but became necessary to protect his interests. He was not particularly successful in picking to whom he made loans," his son, Fred Z., writes.

Another of his achievements, as yet undocumented, was his successful introduction of alfalfa in the west. In the 60's he had brought with him some seed, called *lucern* in Germany, which he sold to Colorado farmers. "It was so sensationally successful, sometimes turning in four crops a year, that soon the government took notice of it, and asked him to return to Germany, charter a ship, and bring back a whole shipload, which was distributed by the Department of Agriculture."[30]

His daughter also mentions, "Another thing which didn't turn out so well: He was the first person ever to bring the zipper to this country. It was invented in Germany, but do you know, he could not think of a thing to do with it, and let the whole thing go."

Hyman Z. had married Cecilia Joel, the first woman of the Salomon family, who had come out in a covered wagon from Crawfordsville, Indiana. In 1871, Adolph Z. married her niece, Matilda, who as a seventeen-year-old girl came out to visit her aunt. Mrs. Salomon's wedding dress, given to the State Historical Society in Denver, is still displayed on appropriate occasions in the mid-twentieth century.

After Nathan C. Meeker was massacred at the White River Agency, historian Boyd points out, not only his family but also his memory was destined to suffer cruel neglect at the hands of the great majority of the people of Greeley. At the first public meeting called for the purpose of expressing the sentiments of the people concerning the Meeker massacre, the question of a monument was raised. A. Z. Salomon offered the resolutions, suggesting that the name of Main Street in Greeley be changed to Meeker Avenue, and that a portrait in oil be placed in the town hall. For a time nothing was done. Then a monument and subscription was proposed. A. Z. Salomon pledged $50, as did P. T. Barnum, and others. Boyd comments: "Not one of the Town Board, who ordered the place to go into mourning, and the flag to hang at half-mast for five days, gave a cent, save A. Z. Salomon. Some may call him a Jew, and in the sense that he a descendant of the race that founded the Christian religion, he is. But he was the most public spirited merchant Greeley ever had."[31]

The A. Z. Salomon family left Greeley in 1885 and moved to Buffalo, where Mrs. Salomon's family lived, but A. Z. did not care to settle there. The pull of the West was too strong. He returned to Colorado the following year and opened a store on Sixteenth Street. In 1893 the Panic put him, as well as almost everyone else on Denver's main business street, out of business. The family moved to one of its many ranches, where they remained for a few years.

In Denver, A. Z. volunteered much of his time to the Jewish Relief Society, serving as its corresponding secretary for several years. His wife held the office of president of the Hebrew Ladies' Benevolent Society. Amy, their daughter, who was called "one of the most ardently altruistic young ladies of the city,"[32] engaged in similar activity. She worked in Judge Ben Lindsey's famed juvenile court, and in that connection was made chairman of the Council of Jewish Women's committee to start a settlement house for the East European Jews. "I battled with those wild Indians single-handed until we got a few more interested," she says.

A. Z., like his brothers, joined the B'nai B'rith lodge in Denver, but unlike them remained a member until his death in 1910.

3

"I did not leave New York on account of ill-health," was the opening statement with which Colorado's first Jewish physician addressed a staff meeting of the National Jewish Hospital almost a half-century later. Whatever the doctor's intent in opening with this remark, it was understood by every one present.[33] He had said what many another immigrant in the West had said, but not all of them had told the truth, because there was a stigma attached to being a "consumptive." He also said, in effect, that in 1866 Colorado was already a mecca for the victims of tuberculosis.

John Elsner's life was an adventure story filled with contrasts. According to his biographers, his father, Leopold Elsner, was a famous physician who had led 2,000 students under Louis Kossuth during the Hungarian revolution. Leopold Elsner, like Kossuth and Carl Schurz, left for the United States. His son, John, who was born in Vienna, May 8, 1844, received his early education in New York and then returned to Europe where he continued his education in Prague.

The majority of the male members of the Elsner family had been physicians for 400 years. John Elsner continued the tradition by completing his education in Bellevue Hospital Medical College in New York and taking a special course in ophthalmology and otology, receiving a degree from the New York Ophthalmic Hospital. During the Civil War, although still a student, he served as U. S. Sanitary Commissioner, and in 1863 was appointed U. S. Surgeon of the United States receiving ship *Ohio* at Charleston.[34]

Why a worldly young man of twenty-two with a cultured background should leave the civilized city of New York for the frontier has been answered by the story of the other pioneers. In Elsner's case, a group of wealthy men in the East had organized a mining company in Central City, called the Onondaga. The young doctor, who had just finished his education, left immediately for Colorado Territory. He went as far as Waterloo, Iowa, by rail. There he met a train of twenty-seven covered wagons, Colorado-bound.

It was a slow trip, hampered by the heavy mining machinery in the wagons. Also impeding the movement of the party, was its fear of Indians. Having encountered the red men along the way, the group had to corral the wagons and station picket guards every night. The trip took nearly forty days, with the doctor on horseback, or walking, although he owned half-interest in one of the wagons.

The Denver Elsner found in 1866 was even more the "wild west" than the settlements of 1859 and 1860 had been. He described the scene on one of the principal streets of the business district: The sidewalk on the right side of the street was covered with tables, over which the most noted gamblers known supervised games of chance. The center of the street was crowded with bullwhackers and ox trains. When the bullwhackers were paid off for their three or four months on the plains, they headed for the tables where they lost every cent they had, and within a few minutes their revolvers and watches as well.

Into this scene, Elsner appeared with silk hat and umbrella.

> After 24 hours I found a placard on my door with skull and cross-bones at the top, and underneath printed: "Dispose of your hat and umbrella, as it is a violation of the vigilantes." It was not necessary for me to do this, as the following day I missed my umbrella. The hat was cut into two parts. From than on I wore a felt hat.

As one of the five physicians in Denver when he arrived June 6, 1866, he had ample opportunity to practice all of his medical knowledge in the territory. "When I first came to Colorado someone was shot almost every night. . . . It gave an opportunity for many gunshot wounds to be treated." In 1868 the doctor performed what he believed to be the first operation for stones in the bladder. The anaesthetic was administered by Dr. D. O. Heimberger, another Jewish pioneer physician. The operation was successful, and Elsner performed a similar one three months later on Lucien Maxwell, the owner of the fabulous Maxwell Grant, with the government furnishing an ambulance and a squad of soldiers for escort to the southern part of Colorado and back.

During the settlers' troubles with the Indians, an army major offered $1,000 to anyone who would ride through Indian country to remove a bullet from a wounded man. Elsner accepted the offer, saved the man's life, and returned unharmed.

In 1870 Elsner was appointed county physician. There was still no hospital in Denver. "I collected the patients, who were lying in hen houses and barns, and were treated heretofore for so much a visit; established a small hospital with 29 beds on Ninth Street on the West Side." He served as county physician for six years; attending not only all the patients in the hospital, which was in time enlarged, but also the insane, the prisoners of the jail, and all the "outdoor" patients of the county. This hospital was the beginning of the county hospital.

Elsner told how he called together all the medical men of Denver in his home, where he served a banquet and organized the first medical society in the territory—out of which came the Denver Medical Society as well as the state medical society. At this meeting the group elected Elsner as a delegate to the American Medical Association convention in San Francisco. There he was appointed chairman of a committee on "The Diseases Peculiar to Colorado," was elected an honorary member of the state society of California.[35]

The meeting which took place April 4, 1871, in Elsner's home also marked the beginnings of the Gross Medical College, the first such institution in the region, where Elsner held the chair of theory and practice for fifteen years. An attempt at a literary school for higher education was also made in Denver with Elsner appointed professor of physiology and hygiene. The classes were so small that the school was soon turned into a "bath establishment."[36]

In his spare time he studied geology, paleontology, mineralogy, and crystallography. His collection of fossils and crystallized minerals was purchased for the state of Colorado in 1895 by the commissioner of mines. This collection, for which the state took more than a decade to pay, formed the basis of the mineral collections of the state, later housed in the state historical museum.[37] Aside from a long list of medical affiliations, Elsner belonged to at least a dozen varied national and international societies. He also served as First Assistant Surgeon with the First Battalion of Colorado.[38]

In his Jewish activities, Elsner was a charter member of the B'nai B'rith, and an early president of the organization (1874). As an early member of the Reform congregation, he delivered an address at the dedication of Temple Emanuel. Almost simultaneously he was a member of the first Orthodox quorum. In the mansion the first meeting to organize the Denver Hebrew School was held. There, too, visiting Zionists debated with the Temple's anti-Zionists. In addition to his activity in the Temple, he was president of the Colorado branch of the Jewish Theological Seminary, from which came the rabbi of the traditional synagogue.

His most valuable contribution to Jewish history in the region is the meticulous record[39] he kept of all the circumcisions he performed as *mohel* (one who circumcizes according to Jewish law) of the frontier. From the first entry in May, 1867, until 1905, he recorded the date, age, Hebrew name of the child, and the name of the father. Where there was something unusual, such as the circumcizing of a young man, there were notations such as, "chloroform administered," or where a child had to be re-operated, a note naming the prior *mohel*. The entries also contained the name of the city, and in Colorado, until 1876, the letters "C.T."— Colorado Territory.

Not all of the children were eight days old, the minimum age for the ceremony, and usually the maximum. Travel to the mining camps was not always easy. Thus, when Elsner came into a camp, he took care of all the boys born since his previous visit. Even with this record it is difficult to ascertain how many Jewish boys in the territory were ritually circumcized. The operation could also have been performed by Dr. Heimberger or Rabbi Elkin of the Temple, or the family could have taken the child east where a family ceremony could be conducted.

From the slender book, containing 169 entries, it can be learned that the ceremony was conducted for some children whose descendants are not Jews and that Dr. Elsner cared for Jewish children as far south as Santa Fe, north as Cheyenne, and east as North Platte, Nebraska. This was part of a practice said to extend from the Missouri River to Salt Lake City. That any of the Orthodox Jews used his services after 1880 is unlikely, since a *schochet* (one who slaughters animals for food according to the ritual) was in Denver at least that early. A *shochet* is invariably a *mohel* as well.

In 1867 the doctor married Lena Zalinger, a daughter of the pioneer freighter, Joseph E. Zalinger, and his ex-wife, Brunetta.[40] Lena Elsner was a gentle and lovable woman, well known for her great generosity. Unfortunately, she was almost as well-known for her kleptomania. Her "shopping" excursions kept the embarrassed doctor in difficulty, trying to pay the mounting bills that resulted. When he could, he would return the merchandise to the stores, whom he had informed to bill him for anything she took. The Elsners had one daughter, Rosalind, or Rose, as she was better known, who was reputed to have been a beautiful girl. They also adopted a son, Edward, who had been left with them by actors playing in the city.

Most of all the Elsners enjoyed their role as patrons of the arts, particularly of the theater. According to the newspapers and those who visited in their home, among their intimate friends the Elsners numbered Mrs. Scott-Siddons, Frederick Ward, Joseffy, Emma Abbott, Herman the Great, Edwin Booth, Adelina Patti, and David Warfield. Jenny Lind was said to have been a friend of the doctor's before he came to Denver. When Oscar Wilde came to the "wild west," the Elsners entertained at dinner, "with the dinner board covered with flame-colored satin, with beige guipure incrustations and yellow roses as a centerpiece." The Elsners' royal blue dinner set was on the table, consisting of Haviland and Dresden. The newspaper many years later reported that Wilde had written, "that he had never sat down to such a banquet as he had 'at the foot of the Rockies.' "[41]

The entire community was impressed by the activities of the Elsners and their home, which was originally owned by Wolfe Londoner. Even before the city auditorium was built across the street, the Elsner home was a landmark in the city. No one ever forgot a visit to the house:

> They entertained more lavishly than any Jewish family in town. My parents often went to these elegant parties, where

the food was served on plates belonging to Napoleon. . . . The house was so full of modern paintings, old Sèvres, curios, and antiques that it was almost impossible to move around.[42]

Dr. John Elsner was universal in his interests. He was equally universal in his choice of friends. The man at whose office millionaire Nathaniel P. Hill was launched as a candidate for the United States Senate,[43] was a doctor to Negroes and Chinese and a "medicine man" to the Indians.

It was only natural that a family so well-known, and so different from the rest of the community, should become public domain. Legends grew up about the family, to which were added all the unusual things they did: Mrs. Elsner's wearing gloves and a Paisley shawl when neither was particularly stylish, and her hiding of the things she had picked up so that the doctor could not return them. One young girl, sent with a message to the mansion, never forgot the eating arrangement of the family:

> The doctor was eating in a tiny room, so full of teakwood furniture, you couldn't turn around. Mrs. Elsner was eating in the huge dining room at the end of a very long table, and since she was a small woman, the effect was *very odd*. I asked where Rose was and received the reply that she was eating in her room.

With the death of Dr. Elsner in 1922 the community looked with interest and curiosity toward what would happen to the remaining members of the family. Six years after the doctor's death, the newspapers reported that the "famous Elsner home was to give up the ghost."[44] The house was torn down, and only a small building, which had been the doctor's office, remained. Mrs. Elsner died in 1929. Edward, who had left Denver for the New York stage, spent very little time in his home town. The site of the mansion became a parking lot. Rose, who was still a nice looking woman, became a penny-pinching recluse. The newsboys in the neighborhood announced that she pulled up every board in the building that remained, looking for treasure, or, as is more likely, for valuables she believed her mother had hidden.

Screaming at her help and customers, the daughter of the cultured physician became an unkempt "character" on the streets of Denver. Despite this, the parking lot across from the city auditorium made money, the first real money in many years. It took all of Rose's strength to make a living and pay off the debts she had inherited.

Rose died in 1943 at the age of seventy-three. As soon as her death was known, those treasures she left, and the money she had made on the parking lot, were claimed by a ne'er-do-well, who said he had been her husband. Lacking proof, he claimed that he was her common-law husband. Everything she left became his. Decked out in new finery, the man, who had turned up only after her death, had Rose buried without even a marker in the Emanuel Cemetery, of which her father had been a trustee in its earliest years. Most of the possessions Rose had left he sold in Denver, burning every scrap he found of the family papers, and bought a half interest in the Woodbury mansion overlooking the city on the north side of the Platte. Ironically, he had little opportunity to enjoy his "ill-gotten" new wealth. One sordid story after another was climaxed by his death of cancer with the money dissipated in schemes of his own.

Colorado's most popular tale of the pioneers is the story of millionaire H. A. W. Tabor and the beautiful Baby Doe, for whom he left his first wife. As a United States Senator he staged a magnificent wedding for his once-divorced bride in Washington. Subsequently Tabor lost all his money, but Baby Doe remained steadfast to him and later to the Matchless, the mine he believed would make them wealthy again. She became a recluse and died in poverty, heartbroken at the activities of a daughter who had been most unorthodox in her behavior.

Baby Doe, wearing a miner's shirt and cap, appeared at the Elsner home, where a newspaper reporter had come to interview Mrs. Elsner. Mrs. Elsner, who remembered better days for both families, was greatly disturbed.[45] Her husband dead, her daughter always displeased with her, and her adopted son in New York, completed an almost comparable situation. In retrospect, the obvious question occurs: was her distress for her friend, or for her own broken family?

FOOTNOTES

[1] *RMN*, Nov. 8, 1861.
[2] *RMN*, June 11, 1861.
[3] *RMN*, Oct. 9, 1861.
[4] *RMN*, Oct. 1, 1861.
[5] *RMN*, Oct. 14, 1861.
[6] *RMN*, Jan. 29, 1862.
[7] *RMN*, Aug. 21, 1862.
[8] *RMN*, Oct. 23, 1862.
[9] *RMN*, Dec. 4, 1862.
[10] *RMN*, June 11, 1862.

[11] *DJN*, July 20, 1921, p. 4.
[12] *RMN*, June 26, 1866, p. 4.
[13] Correspondence, Fred Z. Salomon, St. Louis, nephew of Fred Z. and son of Adolph Z.
[14] *RMN*, June 23, 1866, p. 1. This record is very likely the one from which the information in Hall, III, 551 ff., is copied. Hall cites its authority as the records of the Colorado Pioneer's Association.
[15] Art. Inc., July 11, 1879.
[16] Rena Reese, "History of the Denver Public Library"; *RA*, *op. cit.*, p. 9.
[17] Art. Inc., Feb. 7, 1887; *Denver City Directories*, 1888-1895.
[18] *RMN*, Dec. 1, 1859.
[19] *Republican*, Nov. 3, 1888, p. 4.
[20] *RMN*, July 1, 1874.
[21] *RMN*, May 23, 1874. In 1882 Jacobs helped sell the ditch to the city.
[22] *RMN*, May, 25, 1874.
[24] *Colorado Magazine*, XVIII, p. 68.
[25] BB Ledger, I, withdrawal card granted June 4, 1874.
[26] *Colo. Mag.*, *op. cit.*, p. 41.
[27] BB ledger, I, suspended, Sept. 11, 1875.
[28] William Harlan Hale, *Horace Greeley*, p. 309.
[29] David Boyd, *A History: Greeley and the Union Colony of Colorado*, p. 225.
[30] There are no official records kept by the Department of Agriculture recording the introduction of alfalfa into the United States. George Washington is known to have used an alfalfa seed, but not with the success achieved in the West. Alvin T. Steinel, *History of Agriculture in Colorado*, p. 411: "No crop has developed so many claimants for the honor of [its] introduction. . . ."
[31] Boyd, *op. cit.*, p. 363.
[32] *RA*, *op. cit.*, p. 12.
[33] John Elsner, M.D., "Reminiscences," Denver *Medical Times*, XXVIII, No. 1.
[34] Joseph Emerson Smith, "Jewish Builders of Colorado," *IJN*, Sept. 15, 1939.
[35] Colorado State Medical Society, *A Jubilee Volume*.
[36] *Medical Times*, *op. cit.*
[37] State Bureau of Mines, *Biennial Report*, 1909-1910.
[38] Major John H. Nankivell, *History of the Military Organizations of Colorado, 1860-1935*.
[39] John Elsner's *B'rith Mohel* records. Many names and dates for this work were verified through this record book.
[40] Marriage Certificates, Denver, Index No. 17, p. 94.
[41] *RMN*, magazine section, Jan. 29, 1928, p. 7.
[42] Correspondence, Amy Salomon Leifton.
[43] *RMN*, magazine section, *op. cit.*
[44] *Ibid.*
[45] *Ibid.*

Otto Mears — "Moses of the Roustabouts"

1

The soldiers who volunteered to fight the Confederacy were soon pressed into protecting the settlers, as the angry Indians increased their attacks on the widening stream of white men moving westward. In 1865, Hyman Z. Salomon, returning from Alkali Station on the route used by the pioneers, reported that he had talked to General H. H. Heath, who was organizing an expeditionary force against the Plains Indians.[1]

For the next three years, as the railroad began to push into Indian land, the uprisings mounted, until no white man was safe crossing the plains. Traveler after traveler, like Fred Z. Salomon, reported attacks on their stagecoaches.[2] The terror had to be ended. In 1868, with the important Battle of Beecher Island, the danger of crossing the plains, at least, was terminated.

This was the battle of the fifty scouts, in a sand bar in the middle of the Arickaree River, against 500 Indians, led by the notorious chief Roman Nose. One of the "hand-picked" scouts was a twenty-year old Jewish clerk, Sigmund Shlesinger, who was described as "in all respects unfit for the service; a Jew, small, with narrow shoulders, sunken in chest, quiet manner and piping voice, but little knowledge of firearms and horsemanship; he was indeed unpromising as a son of Mars."[3]

Yet when the battle was over, his colonel wrote, "There was no sphere of gallantry or usefulness in which he was not conspicious." Shlesinger, who was born in Hungary, was working in Leavenworth with the soldiers guarding the construction of the Union Pacific Railroad, which was infuriating the Indians, when the call for volunteers was made. "Slinger," as he was called, was immortalized in two books,[4] and was the subject of a long poetic tribute, the closing lines of which were:

> When the foe charged on the breastworks
> With the madness of despair
> And the bravest of souls were tested,
> The little Jew was there.[5]

Shlesinger's exploits in Colorado ended with the battle and he returned east. Another Jew, small in stature, who came into the territory during the same period, remained and became in many ways synonymous with the early history of the territory and state. Otto Mears was as "unpromising" in appearance as Shlesinger. Of him David Lavender says in *The Big Divide*: "He looked colorless: undersized, scraggly-bearded, dark of complexion. But life had honed him down, both physically and mentally, until he was as sharp and as resilient as the stub end of a piece of bailing wire."[6]

In the only existing account[7] of his life, as told by himself in 1926, Mears said: "I was born May 3, 1840,[8] in Kurland, Russia. My father died when I was a year old. He was born in England. My mother was born in Russia, or Kurland, as it was called, and died when she was forty years old."

When his mother died her brother took him into his family. Mears' twelve cousins did not get along with him. The orphan was then sent to one relative after another—to England, New York, and, finally, San Francisco. He arrived there in 1851, only to find that the last of his father's four brothers had left for Australia. Since no one suggested he follow to that continent, he remained in San Francisco. Selling newspapers, tinsmithing, and working for a storekeeper became the youngster's means of livelihood. He later related, "I had to get up early in the morning and take a team and go ten miles and load a car with merchandise, but first I had to milk the cows. In lifting the large bundles . . . I hurt my back."

The slight youngster with the bad back tramped from gold field to gold field until he was twenty. He took out his naturalization papers, casting his first vote for Abraham Lincoln, and when the Civil War broke out he joined the First Regiment of California Volunteers, Company H, as a private in the infantry. In New Mexico he fought the Confederates at Valverde and Pigeon's Ranch. In his total of three years with the army, he served part of the time under Kit Carson in the Navajo War, in which the famed frontiersman brought about a peaceful surrender of the Navajo.

Discharged from the army, he went to Santa Fe, where the German Jewish traders had been among the first Americans in the area. While working for one Jewish firm and in partnership in another, he made valuable connections for his own merchandising ventures. With another young Jew, Isaac Gotthelf, he came into Colorado. Mears and Gotthelf, who were at first associated in business in Santa Fe, Taos, and Costilla, were partners in many ventures thereafter. In the old town of Conejos, Mears opened his first Colorado store.

At the time, the government, for its army post in nearby Fort Garland, was paying the high price of twenty dollars for a hundred pounds of flour, and lumber was worth eighty dollars for a thousand feet at the mill. Since there was neither a saw mill nor a grist mill in the entire county, which was then the entire southwest corner of the territory, Mears seized the opportunity to build the first such mills in the region. Since iron materials were very scarce, Mears had everything at his mills, except the saw, constructed of wood. The wooden wheel was tied with rawhide, and the stones for the grist mill were of lava found in the vicinity.[9]

When the grist mill was completed, there was not enough wheat being raised there to keep it running; so the resourceful Mears homesteaded a farm in the upper part of the valley to grow wheat for the mill. To save time and effort, he brought the first mower, reaper, and thresher into the San Luis Valley in 1867. The Spanish-speaking natives refused to use it, as they claimed the machine was stealing the wheat. By the time the grain was grown, the price of flour had dropped so low that it did not pay to sell it to the government. Mears had to hunt another market and found a new and more ravenous one had mushroomed to the north. A new "excitement" had broken out above the Arkansas Valley at Granite and California Gulch.

The little "pathfinder" met his first challenge. From Saguache to the Arkansas Valley there was no wagon road, and only a trail crossed Poncha Pass. Mears was anxious to get over the pass with his wheat to a mill being built in the Arkansas Valley. With an ax and shovel he broke through. Governor Gilpin became highly interested in the road and suggested to Mears that he construct it on such a grade that it could be utilized for a railway, which the governor said would certainly be built over that pass. After he sold the wheat, Mears went directly to Denver where he paid $5.00

for his first toll-road charter. Mears had found and built his first path, the wagon road to the San Luis Valley from the Arkansas River.[10]

In Saguache, the county just carved out of Conejos, where Mears had his farm, he built a house-store combination.[11] Governor Cummings (whose Thanksgiving proclamation the Jews bitterly protested in 1865) appointed Mears as the first treasurer of the county. Taxes were paid to Mears in furs or buckskins in lieu of money, of which the people in the sparsely settled county had very little. These he brought to Denver and sold, turning over the proceeds to the territorial treasurer.

Life in Saguache was not dull. "In 1867 a rumor spread that the Utes from the White River Agency to the north were going to attack," Mears recounted.[12] He built a barricade around his house and stationed the men of the area there. The women indoors were put to making bullets out of chunks of lead chopped and melted over the fire and poured into molds. Word was sent to Fort Garland, ninety miles away, and the group prepared itself to stave off the Indians until help arrived.

It took two days for two companies of infantry to arrive. Saguache Creek was swollen and flooded over when the soldiers reached it, albeit just ankle deep. In the black night the soldiers marched forward towards it in lines abreast, each with a heavy gun and cartridge belt with sixty rounds of ammunition. When they came to the edge of the creek they could not see it, not only because it was dark but also because they were wading in the shallow water which had spilled over the banks.

The whole first line of men slipped over the edge. Pulled down by their guns and belts, they promptly submerged. But they uttered not a sound, for fear of alerting the Indians who were certainly lurking about. The second line marched right into the river. With second company piled on top of the first, the creek was filled with two companies of floundering, speechless infantrymen.

The well-soaked soldiers, clambering out of the water, were greeted by an unguarded stockade around the well-lighted house they had been sent to protect. Ouray, the Ute chief, and some of his braves had already brought Mears the news that the White River Indians had been persuaded to go back.

Mears observed, "The soldiers would have been useless anyway, with their guns and ammunition soaked."

2

The hand of destiny lay heavy on the slight shoulder of Otto Mears. Even in the grizzliest story in the annals of the Rockies, he played the part of a detective.

A party of five prospectors disappeared in the western mountains in the blizzard of 1873. Their guide, Alfred Packer, a petty convict, appeared alone, unusually sleek and well-nourished after his ordeal, in the store of Mears and Gotthelf in Saguache. There he purchased a horse from Mears for which he offered to pay in bank notes. Mears, suspecting them to be counterfeit, as Packer's reputation for passing bad notes was well-known, asked him for another. Packer then produced a different pocketbook from the first and gave Mears another bill in place of the note Mears had rejected. In doing so, he displayed a red printed draft, such as were used by the Wells-Fargo Express.

Mears said nothing to Packer but promptly reported the matter to General Charles Adams of the Ute agency, who was in the vicinity. Adams, who had no jurisdiction in Saguache, asked Mears to induce Packer to go with him and Mears to the agency where he had authority. At the agency began the long questionings that finally led to Packer's confession, not only of robbing his five companions but also of killing and eating them as well.[13]

Mears' apprehension of Packer and Packer's sentence to life imprisonment were not the end of the "cannibal" case. Years later, when Mears was an important public figure, the beautiful and fearless reporter Polly Pry discovered the man-eater in prison and decided that Packer should be pardoned. The governor, Charles S. Thomas, refused to do so. Polly then launched a series of articles designed to free Packer.

One of her articles in the Denver *Post*, January 3, 1900, read:

> Governor Thomas has refused to pardon Packer because he has a client and a friend. . . . He calls himself the governor-maker of Colorado. . . . I herewith present him to you. His name is Otto Mears. You all know him. He is a trader who always has a new scheme and who never gets the worst of a bargain.

Polly asserted that Mears came in from Washington to see that Governor Thomas did not parole or release Packer, and incidentally added that the governor wanted Mears' picture in the capitol building.

With all of Polly's stories in the paper and her exhaustive articles on other murderers and rapists who had been pardoned, Packer was paroled. It is said that the man-eater turned vegetarian for the rest of his life.

3

Much had happened to Mears in the years since he had carved his first road over Poncha Pass. His two best-recorded contributions were his road-building and his negotiations with the Indians to clear the way for the miner and farmer. To accomplish the latter he had begun very early.

After he had brought his first road over Poncha Pass, he met and married a German girl in Granite in 1870. Mary Kampfshulte, who had come to Colorado with her brother for his health, became Mrs. Otto Mears. She stayed quietly in the background, although she shared in at least one adventure in her husband's career. The following incident recounted by Mears must have occurred while Mears was negotiating with the Indians to accomplish what became known as the Brunot Treaty:

> I made a trip to the Uncompaghre Agency, where the city of Montrose now stands. Ouray was head chief then and I wanted to see him. The distance was 150 miles, and I went in a buggy with my wife and baby. When we were nearly to the place, we found that the river was badly flooded and we could not ford it. We had to get across for we could not stay where we were. Finally, I thought of a plan. I had two empty oat sacks, for, of course, we had to carry all our provisions and fodder for the horses with us. I filled these sacks with rocks and tied one on each end of the back axle, and I drove my rig full speed.
> The horses swam, dragging the buggy after them. The buggy could not upset, because the two loaded sacks held it down, just as two anchors would. The water rose to our waists as we sat in the buggy. My wife held the baby up in her arms. I tried to guide the ponies. When we reached the other side I heard the firing of guns and an Indian ran past me. Ouray came out and called to me to come into the house as quickly as I could. He lived in a "doby" house and after we went in he barred the doors and windows. He said that the Indian we had seen had been sent out by the Northern Utes to try to induce his Indians to rebel and join with them in an insurrection against Ouray as chief.
> When Ouray heard this he ordered the Indian shot. He told us there would be trouble during the night. We did not sleep much, but kept on the lookout as Ouray felt that the Northern Utes would come down on him. We were not par-

ticularly comfortable in between these two fires, the Northern Utes on the one hand and Ouray with his Indians on the other.

The next morning all being quiet, I hitched up and drove on to the government agency ten miles away. On the road we passed the dead body of the Indian we had seen shot the night before. We stayed at the agency ten days, and when we came back, the body still lay as we had seen it. It was badly decayed and covered with buzzards, who were eating the flesh, but not one of Ouray's Indians could be induced to bury it.[14]

The small boy who had left Russia before he was ten strangely never lost his heavy Yiddish accent. This did not deter him from learning the difficult language of the Utes. As one of the few white men who spoke to the Indians in their tongue, he won the devotion of Ouray, who knew English, but refused to speak it to those who refused to speak his language.[15] To Mears, who treated the Indians as equals, they listened with respect. With the increased pressure of the white man on them, they turned more and more to Mears.

After the Battle of Beecher Island in northeastern Colorado, the Western Utes had made a promise to move into the region west of the Continental Divide. But silver discoveries in the San Juans were pushing them out of the land that had been promised them. The government tried to buy the Indians' lands, but the Utes refused to sell. The Indian commissioner, Felix Brunot, turned to Mears, whose friendship with Ouray was well-known. Mears proposed that Ouray be offered a $1000 salary for ten years. To Ouray he suggested that he was getting old, and, being chief, he should have an income so that he could live without hunting and selling buckskins. In addition the trader proposed that the government agree to pay the Indians the interest on half a million dollars. Ouray accepted and signed the treaty by which the government received the territory that includes the counties of Hinsdale, San Juan, Ouray, San Miguel, Dolores, Montezuma, and La Plata— most of the counties Mears helped carve out of Conejos county. A priceless new land was opened to the miner's pick and the farmer's plow.

Mears, Ouray, and eight lesser Indian chiefs were invited to meet the Great Father, President Grant, and for a trip through the eastern states, which Mears had never seen.

The Brunot Treaty was not a success. The $25,000 annuity allotted the Indians was squandered as fast as it was received. The agency was moved and a new agency established on the White River, with Nathan C. Meeker, the New York *Tribune's* founder of the Union Colony at Greeley, as the Indian agent.

Meeker, rigidly dedicated to the agrarian ideals of Greeley, insisted on imposing the white man's ways. The Indians, who regarded farming as woman's work, deliberately set about to make Meeker's life, and that of the settlers there, as miserable as possible. One incident led to another in a chain of two-sided resistance climaxed by the dreadful tragedy, the Meeker massacre. The state was horrified. The Indians had to go. Mears and others, under escort arranged by Chief Ouray of the Uncompahgre Utes, were taken to the White River Ute Agency and succeeded in rescuing the women still held captive.

That fall eleven Indians were ordered to come to Washington with Mears to have a talk with the "Great Father." Another trip followed, with the perpetrators brought to Washington by Mears. Meeting with the President and Carl Schurz, a new treaty was formulated and new commissioners appointed. Of the five, Mears was the youngest of the group. He knew the Utes better than the others did and was willing and able to saddle a horse and ride miles over wild terrain.

The commissioners brought the treaty to the Indians, who refused to sign it because of the clause that the new reservation would be at the junction of the Grand and Colorado Rivers, or in territory adjacent to it. The Indians wanted to know exactly where, and the commissioners could not tell them until they had a majority of signatures on the treaty.

The resultant deadlock was a task Otto Mears was best fitted of the group to break. Despite the death of Chief Ouray at this important time, when he was the Indian on whom the government had most depended for signatures, Mears was successful in getting the treaty signed.[16]

Mears and the other Colorado commissioner, Judge Thomas A. McMorris, realized that the plan to build a reservation at the junction of the two rivers in Colorado would only lead to more trouble. Mears stated that "for the benefit of Colorado it would be better to keep the Indians out of the state." The land in the Uncompahgre was valuable and the whites would soon want it. Since the treaty had said that the Indians should be located at the junction of the two Colorado rivers or "in territory adjacent thereto," the Colorado commissioners decided that Utah was adjacent territory.

When the Indians found that it was not the site of the junction that had been selected, they refused to move. Again it looked as though there might be incidents, but the general-in-command, who had charge of moving them, was not one to hesitate. About two o'clock in the morning he sent for the commissioners to sign the order to move the Indians.

With their signatures on the order, the general had the Indians surrounded and gave them two-hour notice to move. The Indians tried to argue, but the adamant general repeated that they had two hours. In two hours they were ready.

As the Indians began their exodus, Commissioner Mears rushed through Salt Lake to the selected site and managed to have the necessary provisions and buildings ready for the new agent before the Utes arrived. Some of the Indians tried to kill Mears, claiming that it was through Mears that they were removed.

There seems to be a trace of self-justification in a letter he is said to have written to an old friend shortly before his death in 1931:

> Had the Utes been agricultural they would still occupy Western Colorado. Ouray, my friend, saw this, and on his Uncompahgre farm raised extensive crops to show his people their security and salvation. But they would have none of it, and like the useless tribes since the dawn of time, they had to move on.[17]

Less than a month later the city of Grand Junction was founded in the heart of rich agricultural country.

4

During these same years Otto Mears was busily engaged in certain ventures for which he has received little recognition. As a newspaper publisher he was so far outshadowed by his reputation as the "Indian Commissioner" and the "Pathfinder" that little attention is paid to his efforts in journalism.

In 1872, Mears had started a newspaper in Saguache, the *Saguache Chronicle,* to advertise the San Luis Valley. The resultant population growth there has been attributed to his editorials boosting the soil, climate, and wealth of the region. When the first silver "excitement" broke in the San Juan mountain, Mears, with others, built a string of wagon roads from Saguache to Lake

City. In Lake City which Mears and his partners incorporated with Isaac Gotthelf as a trustee of the town company, he began publication of a newspaper, the *Silver World*, June 17, 1875, to advertise the silver and lead of the new mining camp. Since there were as yet no houses in Lake City, Mears printed the first issue in a tent. The entire edition was carried by its editor, Harry Wood, over the range to Del Norte on snowshoes. Historians agree that the publication of this paper started the Lake City boom.

After the removal of the Indians from the Uncompahgre, Mears became an incorporator of Montrose and was connected with the first newspaper published there. He is said to have been an owner of the first newspapers published in Ouray, Salida, and Bonanza, as well.

Mears had begun his political career in Saguache as county treasurer, using his store and merchandise for political purpose when expedient. His critics claim that he influenced elections by giving prospective voters hams, bacon, and flour. According to Anne Ellis in her *Life of an Ordinary Woman*, this pleased the women more than the men, who preferred whisky. But Mears, who was not a drinking man, had had one unpleasant experience with the angry wives of Saguache. After a drunken brawl, one of the participants was killed. While all the men were out burying the body, their wives marched into the Mears store, smashed the barrels of whisky, and poured the liquor into the road in front of his store. Mears stood by silently watching the destruction, biding his time. When he sent out his bills, the husbands found the $400 to $500 worth of whisky they had never tasted apportioned on their bills.

His activity as Indian commissioner had taken him to Washington, where he negotiated for at least two contracts to deliver the U. S. mail. One contract, for which he and a partner bid $2,179 per year to carry the mail ninety-five miles from Fairplay to Oro City (Leadville) over the precipitous Park Range, was never executed.[18] The contracts which he did fulfill called not only for ingenuity but sometimes for sheer physical effort as well. Using an old burro trail, Mears devised a plan of delivering the mail by dog train with sleds, with cabins spaced at thirty mile intervals along the route to change the dogs during the winter deliveries.[19] On one occasion his hired carriers refused to attempt the flooded, muddy road of spring. If he failed to make that delivery, he would be subject to a fine so heavy he would be ruined. He strapped the mail sack to his back and waded through the ice and snow, which was sometimes waist deep. It took him almost a week to cover the seventy-five miles, but he beat the government deadline.

By 1876, the year of Colorado's admission to statehood, Mears was one of the best-known and most politically influential men in the state, holding the balance of power in the Republican party through the counties he had helped create. The two houses, in joint sessions, chose Mears as a presidential elector, and the electors at their meeting chose Mears as the messenger to Washington. This was the crucial election, in which Colorado, the youngest state of the union, held the decisive vote. Mears carried the vote to Washington which elected Rutherford B. Hayes president of the United States.

5

"The grade is four parts vertical and one part perpendicular,"[20] the Ouray *Solid Muldoon,* Colorado's colorful and candid newspaper, declared. The newspaper was describing one of Mears' most famous toll roads, but the description could apply to almost all of his toll roads and railway trackage in the jagged San Juans.

His narrow-guage roads have been recognized by Lucius Beebe and other writers of the stories of America's most exciting railways. The Hollywood motion picture industry has portrayed the thrilling beauty of the region and used Mears' roads to add to the excitement. Only by traveling his roads can one appreciate the unusual terrain his roads conquered and embraced. How much more the achievement of having carved them from the unyielding masses of granite!

Mear's first nine wagon roads, built from 1867 to 1886, totaled a mere 302 miles but had cost $325,000 to build. Towns only a few miles apart, but separated by such gorges, peaks, and cliffs that it was easier to go several hundred miles around them than to cross over to them, were linked together. None of the existing railroads was interested in competing for road building in a region where there was scarcely an acre of tillable land. Mears had it to himself, and he built roads to, and between, almost every camp and large mine, relishing the fact that his feats were considered impossible.

His original nine wagon roads were:

From the South Fork of the Arkansas across Poncha Pass,

which opened communication between the Arkansas and San Luis valleys; seven miles, built in 1867.

From Saguache to Lake City, creating a more direct route than existed from the San Luis Valley to the San Juan mining region; ninety-six miles, built in 1874.

From Barnum station on the Lake City road to Lake City, to Cimarron, and thence to the Uncompahgre Indian Agency, twenty miles below Ouray; eighty miles, built in 1877.

From Mears Station on Poncha Pass over Marshall Pass to Gunnison; fifty miles, built in 1879.

From Dallas Divide to Telluride; twenty-seven miles, built in 1880.

From Sargent's, six miles below Telluride, to Ames; six miles, built in 1881.

From Ouray up the Uncompahgre to Poughkeepsie Gulch; seven miles, built in 1883.

From Red Mountain to Silverton; seventeen miles, built in 1885.

From Silverton to Animas Forks; twelve miles, built in 1888.

Mears was not satisfied with his toll roads for long, and soon moved into railroading, converting his toll roads when possible and building new ones where necessary. The narrow-gauge tracks (three feet wide), climbed grades of as high as seven per cent. The appreciative miners and settlers marveled at his ingenuity. Particularly impressive, was the Ophir Loop, with its one-hundred-foot trestle, over which the train hurtled down with frightening speed.

From the roads linking Ouray, Ironton, Red Mountain, and Silverton; and Rico, Ophir, and Telluride, he threw out spurs to the major mines in the area, making it profitable for the miners to bring out the ore that had been previously packed out by mule team. With ore selling for as low as $80 a ton, the miners were yet able to make a profit, and Mears, who derived his revenue from the monopoly of the traffic, had more money to invest in more railroad building.[21]

His narrow-gauge from Silverton to Red Mountain and Ironton cost $725,000 for seventeen miles. The breathtaking "Rainbow Route," which was so named because it made a bow in its path over the crest of a mountain, was awing in the grandeur of the scenery and famed for the ingenious switchbacks that made a grade estimated from five percent (212 feet ascent to the mile), to six and even seven per cent. An earlier toll road over the same route had had an ascent of twenty-one per cent.[22]

At the site of his toll station at Bear Creek Falls, on the road which later became the Million Dollar Highway, the people of the San Juans blasted a hole in the stone of the mountain, to place a tablet honoring the "Pathfinder."

Not only had Mears helped increase the wealth of the region, but he had also linked the lonely camps together. For his years of efforts he was known throughout the state as "the Uncrowned King of the San Juan," and it is small wonder that many an oldtimer used the epithet, "By God and by Otto," until his dying day. Yet not even the Million-Dollar highway is named for its creator. Outside of Mears Junction, on his first road over Poncha pass, and a mountain near Dallas Divide, no part of the region is named for him.

The Panic of 1893 interrupted Mears' labors in Colorado. Mears lost almost all of his roads, and his Rio Grande Southern Railroad passed into the hands of a receiver. Called east, he began the building of a line from Washington, D. C., through Maryland to Chesapeake Beach. Mears told the newspaper reporters in Denver later that he had beat the schedule, which had started too slowly to please him. To hasten the work, he hired two bands to play alongside the Negro construction crew. The Negroes sang and swung their axes to the musical beat. When one band tired, the other played. According to Joseph Emerson Smith, Mears grinned and pronounced his feat "A nice Jewish trick."

Mears showed his originiality in other ways. He had issued passes on his railroad to his friends. Mere slips of cardboard did not please him, and he began to design passes which became coveted gifts for more than what they represented. He started with buckskin, and soon designed 500 passes of solid silver, silver watch fobs, lockets, and silver-and-gold filagree oblongs. Josie Moore Crum, who wrote the "The Otto Mears Passes," regards them as unique, saying, "In all railroad history no others like them have ever been issued."[23]

6

When Mears, who had rarely sought political office, became the chairman of the Board of Capitol Managers, an honorary appointment he accepted after many years of service to the state, he had a typical Mears suggestion for the state's most important building, then under construction: "Cover the capitol building dome with gold!" In the heart of Denver, the dome fifty years later gleams with its second coat of gold leaf.

Inside the glittering dome are sixteen stained glass windows separating the interior from the sky above. Each window is a portrait of an outstanding pioneer of the state. When they were to be chosen, the board of capitol managers asked the curator of the state historical society to prepare a list of prominent pioneers. During the decisions, a petition was submitted by residents of the San Juans asking that Mears be so honored, but Mears declined. He regarded it as being in poor taste to accept in view of his position as chairman of the board. By the unanimous vote of the Colorado legislature, the board was directed to place a full figure portrait of him in stained glass outside the Senate chamber. Mears was the only living person so honored.[24]

Mears was accused of bribery on several occasions and his honesty questioned by the press. Yet his contemporary, Dave Day, the sharp-tongued editor of the *Solid Muldoon* of Ouray, who once had as many as forty-two libel suits against him, talked of Mears far differently from the way in which he discussed other public figures. Few issues of the newspaper did not mention the "Hebrew pathfinder." It was Day who had dubbed him the "Moses of the Roustabouts."

Said the *Muldoon,* in 1890: "Otto is one man in San Juan who is always returning good for evil. He has done more for the San Juan than any other ten men in the country, and at the same time been the recipient of more curses than even the *Muldoon.*"[25] When another publication praised Mears, the *Muldoon* pointed out, "We are pleased to note that he is now being affectionately handled by the press. As for the *Muldoon,* it has been Otto's main and only organ for years. . . . Blessed Otto."[26]

When the Wolfe Londoner election was under fire for fraudulent balloting,[27] the *Muldoon* was disgusted and took to task "such pure (?) statesmen as Senator Edward O. Wolcott, Otto Mears, and others," who had been part of the election campaign, and happily reported that year, "We take pleasure in announcing that the 'Pathfinder' is out of politics for the year ending July 1, 1891. Sensible Otto."[28]

Mears was not out of politics. In 1903 the newspapers reported, "Hon. Otto Mears, speaker of the Third House Gives Banquet." The banquet, which cost $10 a plate or $3 per plate and $7 per set of glasses, put Mears in the position of peacemaker in the Republican party.[29] Actually the party was a Republican caucus.

When Mears was given a $1,000 span of matched trotters by a

friend, the *Muldoon* wryly commented that he "could well afford to have thrown in a landeau and set of gold mounted harness."[30] Mears seems to have engaged in mining from time to time. Not only did the *Muldoon* list claims he had filed, but in his pension records in the National Archives dating from his participation in the Civil War, he gave his occupation as "miner and railroader."

An insight to his character can be given by the men who worked with him and for him. Shortly before his death Arthur Ridgway, who had been Mears' chief engineer, told of Mears' kind and honest treatment of him and his crew. He said Mears had been admired for his skill and willingness to work alongside his men. No matter what his position was among the great men of the state, he never was afraid to soil his hands, dismantling and assembling the complex machinery of his trains as expertly as any of his crew. Sometimes they forgot how small in stature he was. To them and to the citizens of the San Juan he was a king.

And he was obeyed like a king. David Lavender gives a stirring account of an event that took place in Mears' seventieth year when a flood closed the trackage of the Denver and Rio Grande in Animas Canyon just before the onset of winter, and just before the area had a chance to lay in winter supplies. Mears, with two hundred and fifty men, began to clear the tracks immediately but was stopped because he lacked coal to keep the work trains running.

> Mears toured the town, appealing to mills, to stores, to homeowners. "Give us your coal!" The people shivered. Emptying the bins at the mines meant stopping production; at home, the threat of freezing. And suppose the tracks weren't rebuilt in time? Suppose their last bits of fuel were burned to no avail? Suppose. . . .

Men, women, and children, from the entire town of Silverton, brought Mears their precious coal. The tracks were cleared in time for the winter supplies to reach what would soon be a snowbound village in the lofty San Juans.

7

While he lived it never occurred to anyone who knew him that Otto Mears could be other than a Jew. After his death, however, cautious writers picked up the fact that his father was born in England and began to refer to Mears as the son of an English father and Jewish mother. As recently as 1952, a short biography stated that he was "Born in Russia, his father an Englishman," and that the services of the Episcopal Church were held at his burial. All of the facts were true, but the careful writer did not mention that Mears was a Jew.

When Mears died in June, 1931, his body was cremated, and a month later, his ashes were scattered over the mountains around Silverton. The late Bishop Fred Ingley of the Colorado diocese, who was in the area at the time, was asked to officiate at the services. A careful check of the records of the diocese in Denver by Mrs. Ingley disclosed that Mears had never joined the Church in Colorado.

Unlike his friend Wolfe Londoner, who had left Judaism, Mears while in Colorado joined the Temple[31] and the B'nai B'rith and served as a trustee of the Jewish Hospital during the years when it was known as the Frances Jacobs Hospital.

During the same year in which a daughter was born in Saguache, and received and baptised in the Unitarian Church there,[32] Otto Mears presented his petition for membership in the Denver B'nai B'rith Lodge.[33] Because he lived out of the city, the "secretary was instructed to ask for a dispensation to confer three degrees at one time upon Mr. Otto Mears."[34] On November 13, 1880, "Mr. Otto Mears appeared and received the degree of our order." Although he did not live in Denver until late in the century, his name appears in the minutes in 1882 and 1888. At one election of officers he was appointed a teller.[35] When the question of the alleged anti-Semitism of a candidate for public office was brought before the lodge, Mears was appointed on a committee to investigate the man.[36] On another occasion when the question of aiding a member whose need was in doubt, Mears voted to aid the man.[37]

More can be learned from the ledgers and cash receipt books of the organization. From the time he joined until the last available cash receipt book (1921), Mears paid more than any other member. Part of the sum which he paid as late as 1921 was his participation in the Covenant Endowment Fund of the organization, but he also paid regularly to the building fund of the lodge, to a war fund, and to other funds when he was living in Pasadena, at least five years after he left Denver.[38]

The *American Israelite* reported on May 25, 1893, that "Hon. Otto Mears, the president of the Rio Grande Southern Railroad, has been elected a trustee of the Jewish Hospital."[39] Since that was the year Mears was building a rail-line in Washington, D. C., and the Denver Jews were campaigning all over the country for funds, it is not hard to guess what his assignment was.

In addition to his partnerships with several Jews, he was an intimate friend of the rabbi of the Temple, William S. Friedman; and with Dr. Elsner, to whom he gave one of his silver passes. He is known to have given similar passes to his partner Isaac Gotthelf and to Gotthelf's partner Leopold Mayer as well.[40] Fred Z. Salomon of St. Louis says, "He was an intimate friend of my uncle Fred. I saw them together at many occasions, but never saw his wife with him at any of them."[41] During the Russian pogroms of 1905, Mears gave $100 to help the Jews of Russia, one of the largest contributions made in the entire Rocky Mountain region.[42] He made no attempt to cut himself off from his people. Back in Lake City, when he was publishing the *Silver World,* an issue of October 12, 1878, reported that Rosh Hashanah services were held in Charles Weinberg's home—the first time such services were ever held in the San Juans.

One of the people who knew him best, was Joseph Emerson Smith, the veteran Denver reporter who saw the railroad builder daily. If the press frequently gave Mears trouble, the reporters regarded him with respect. Before he released any news he would give the reporters a chance to investigate and verify the facts. He would then telephone the news into the newspapers. Soon young Smith felt he could confide in the important man. At the time young Smith's ambition was to become an Episcopalian clergyman. A wealthy man offered to finance him while he took the orders. Smith came to Mears for advice. Gently, Mears told him that when he had come to America he had wanted to become a rabbi and would have had he "had an encouraging hand" to help him. "Don't let a little pride stand in your way," he told Smith earnestly. It is hard to imagine the frontiersman as a rabbi.

There is no reason to believe that Mears' parents were not both Jews. A Jewish girl in Kurland was not apt to marry a Christian in the 1830's, and had she, it was unlikely that she would have remained there with her family. The Jewish communities of Kurland, while not so pious as some of the other east European Jewish communities, were no less strict on intermarriage.

It is equally unlikely that a Jewish boy would be sent to his non-Jewish relatives, no matter how poverty-stricken the family. Moreover, the uncle he missed in San Francisco may well have been the same Mears who, in 1854, subscribed to the rebuilding of the Melbourne Hebrew Congregation.[43]

Few Jews in the state rose to the height of Otto Mears. Although he is well-remembered in the San Juans, the later Jewish community never heard of him. Even the B'nai B'rith took no notice of his death in the minutes of 1931. Among the Jews, only the *Intermountain Jewish News* commented on the death of the man who was once the best-known Jew in the state, and whose name was once a by-word.[44]

An oft-repeated story has it that at one time the governor of Colorado, on boarding a streetcar in Denver, found that he had forgotten his fare. Said the conductor, who put him off, "I wouldn't let you ride this car without paying, even if you were Otto Mears himself."

FOOTNOTES

[1] *RMN*, Dec. 26, 1865, p. 1, col. 3.
[2] *RMN*, May 28, 1867, p. 4, col. 2.
[3] Postal and Koppman, *Jewish Tourist's Guide to U. S.*, p. 70.
[4] General James B. Fry, *Army Sacrifices;* Cyrus Townsend Brady, *Indian Fights and Fighters.*
[5] Col. George A. Forsyth, "Frontier Fights and Thrilling Days of Army Life," *Harper's New Monthly Magazine*, June, 1895.
[6] David Lavender, *The Big Divide*, p. 93.
[7] Otto Mears dictated his biography to the secretary of Arthur Ridgway, in 1926. The original manuscript appears to be lost. In this chapter the quotations are taken from Lavender, *op. cit.*
[8] Mears gave the date of his birth as 1840. In his pension application, he gave his date of birth as 1841. Correspondence from files of General Services Administration, Washington, D. C.
[9] Sidney Jocknick, *Early Days on the Western Slope.*
[10] *Ibid.*
[11] Lavender, *op. cit.*, p. 95.
[12] T. F. Dawson Scrapbook. Volume 62, "Early Days in San Juan Country." Source not noted.
[13] Hall, *op. cit.*, III, p. 245.
[14] Hill, *op. cit.*, p. 412.
[15] Lavender, *op. cit.*, p. 98.
[16] Just how he accomplished this is told in many histories, but Lavender doubts the story. Correspondence.
[17] *Denver Catholic Register*, Feb. 27, 1941, p. 9. Joseph Emerson Smith quotes a letter from Mears to an old friend written shortly before Mears' death. The language does not sound at all like Mears', cf. "Otto Mears" in *Pioneers of the San Juan*, I, pp. 16-21.
[18] Mail Contract No. 17039, General Services Administration, Washington, D. C.

[19] Lavender, *op. cit.*, p. 143.
[20] Quoted by Muriel Sibell Wolle, *Stampede to Timberline*, p. 434.
[21] *Ibid.*, p. 415.
[22] *Ibid.*, p. 449.
[23] Crum, *op. cit.*
[24] Levette J. Davidson, "Colorado's Hall of Fame," *Colorado Magazine*, XXVII, No. 1, p. 25.
[25] *Solid Muldoon*, Feb. 28, 1890.
[26] *Ibid.*, May 2, 1890.
[27] See Londoner.
[28] *Solid Muldoon*, Oct. 11, 1890.
[29] *Denver Republican*, Mar. 7, 1903.
[30] *Solid Muldoon*, July 25, 1890.
[31] Temple Emanuel Membership Roster, January 27, 1899.
[32] Born Nov. 25, 1879, baptized, June 2, 1880, from Mears papers, State Historical Society, Denver.
[33] BB minutes, I, Jan. 26, 1879.
[34] *Ibid.*, Feb. 9, 1879.
[35] *Ibid.*, Dec. 23, 1880, III, p. 98-99.
[36] *Ibid.*, II, p. 180, Oct. 8, 1882.
[37] *Ibid.*, Mar. 10, 1889.
[38] The records of the Endowment Fund and his petition may still be in existence.
[39] WmSF Scrapbook.
[40] Crum, *op. cit.*
[41] *RMN*, Jan. 2, 1883, p. 8, Col. 4. Mrs. Mears and Mrs. Wolfe Londoner attend Standard Club party.
[42] *JO*, Dec. 1, 1905.
[43] Rabbi L. M. Goldman, *The History of the Jews of Victoria in the 19th Century*, refers to a Mr. Mears as a contributor in the building of the Melbourne Hebrew Congregation at the time it was being rebuilt in the 1850's. This fact was brought to the writer's attention by Mr. Jack Carson of Melbourne, Australia.
[44] *IJN*, June 26, 1931, p. 1.

Furthering the Cause of Monotheism

1

Considering the intimacy of the publisher of the *Rocky Mountain News*, William N. Byers, with the pioneer Jews, it is strange that the newspaper rarely referred to the Jews in the region as such.[1] While Jewish activities in the East were given considerable space, until 1865 the *News* did not mention those of the little Jewish group on Cherry Creek. Jewish life is supposed to have begun during the first year of settlement. The High Holiday of Rosh Hashanah fell on September 29, 1859.

At these services, all accounts agree, Julius Mitchell took charge, but the accounts vary as to the participants, agreeing only on Fred Z. Salomon, Abraham Jacobs, Leopold Mayer, and Mitchell. The services were said to have been held in a store building on Sixteenth and Larimer Streets.

The day following Christmas, the Denver City and Town company directors, who were wooing the settlers to establish on the east side of Cherry Creek, adopted a resolution: "On motion of R. E. Whitesitt, that the trustees of the Hebrew Synagogue be donated ten lots, providing they build a house of worship in Denver City within eight months from this date. Said house to cost not less than $700." The motion was carried,[2] but no synagogue was built in eight months, nor in eight years.

In Judaism, not only the days of religious observance but also the rituals of personal observance must be observed at specific times. Of all rituals, death insists on more immediacy than most, because burial must take place before sundown, or on the following day. It can only be postponed by the Sabbath, but the human remains must be buried by the following day.

The little band of Jewish pioneers was called together during

1860 to perform the last rites for the wife of Henry Goldsmith, who died in giving birth to the first Jewish girl baby born in Denver, Clara Goldsmith. No records of the funeral, nor of where Mrs. Goldsmith was buried, exist, but according to a later account a society was formed then and there for the burial of the Jewish dead.[3] Although there is said to have been a cemetery used by the Odd Fellows and Masons on Fifteenth Street on high ground just across the Platte River,[4] the Jewish group seems to have used for their first burial the ground on the eastern plains, later known as the Capitol Hill Cemetery. Leopold Mayer and Abraham Jacobs defrayed the expense of a fence around the cemetery.[5]

That the same cemetery was again used within a few years may be gathered from an obituary in 1862, when the body of a young man, Morris Abrams of St. Louis, who died in Central City, was buried from the A. Goldsmith residence in Denver.[6] Apparently the Goldsmiths were actively interested in the plot while they remained in Denver.

The group formed for burial is said to have been known as the Hebrew Burial and Prayer Society, and also as the Hebrew Cemetery Association. All accounts agree that the following men took part in the first Jewish organization: Abraham Goldsmith, brother-in-law of the deceased, Abraham Jacobs, Julius Mitchell, and Isadore and Jonas Deitsch. Other lists, which vary as to one or more members, include Leopold Mayer, Joseph Gottlieb, Phillip Poznanski, Abe and David Steadhouse, Fred Z. and Hyman Z. Salomon, and A. Sonneberg, a partner of the Deitsches, and at whose place in Central City the young man, Abrams, had died.

Although the group had not been organized specifically for religious services, it met at least three times a year: Passover, Rosh Hashanah, and Yom Kippur. Services were held in a building on the corner of Fifteenth and Larimer Streets, in the Tappan Block at the corner of Fifteenth and Market Streets, and in the pioneer Denver Theatre.

Mitchell conducted services, at least until the arrival in May, 1861, of David Kline. Kline was born in Bohemia, and came to the United States at the age of nineteen. He landed in New Orleans and remained there a year, then moved to St. Louis. There he joined the Bohemian congregation, where services were held in a loft. From there he went on to Leavenworth, where he assisted in the formation of a Jewish charity society. After a thirty-day trip by prairie schooner, he arrived in Denver and went into the dry-goods business. Until Denver had a rabbi, Kline and Mitchell served as the community's religious leaders, officiating at weddings and arranging the holiday services. While the records show only the marriage certificates signed by various judges, Mitchell and Kline performed most of the ceremonies. Early marriages included that of Rosa Lobinstein to Henry Kline, but not all the marriages were mentioned in the newspapers. The weddings of Grumpert Goldburg to Helena Morris in Denver in 1863,[7] and of Samuel Arkush and Flora Goldbaum that same year do not appear there or in the city records.[8] Many of the pioneers returned to the East to marry and then brought their brides back with them.

Another Jewish religious leader arrived in Denver in 1865. Charles M. Schayer, born in Kempen, Prussia, in 1827, arrived in New York in 1861 and entered into the cigar trade. Four years later he came to Denver and opened a wholesale cigar business. Schayer, who had an excellent Hebrew and German education, was able to lead the religious life of the settlers. In Denver, and later in Leadville, he served as a rabbi until ordained rabbis could take over.

Until 1865, Jewish life is barely discernible in the territory. The newspapers neither commented on the Jewish holidays nor on the burial and prayer society. On the other hand, when a Moses Adler, who was in Denver in the early 60's, was sent to prison,[9] the newspaper did not identify him as a Jew as was customary when a Jew committed a crime. The question presents itself: Was it because the small group of Jews preferred that the larger community not be aware of their presence while their number was so few, or was it that their reverence for democracy insisted that they identify themselves only as American citizens? It does not seem possible that Byers, who recounted the activities of the Salomon brothers and Abraham Jacobs so minutely, did not know that they were Jewish. They sat together in Masonic lodges and built the first cultural organizations in the city. It is almost certain that Jacobs taught Byers his first Masonic lesson, when they were still in Nebraska.[10]

After the long period of silence, the *Rocky Mountain News*, by contrast, seemed suddenly filled with news of Jewish activity.

With the High Holidays in the fall of 1865, the *News* commented wonderingly, "Today is some sort of a holiday for the Jewish persuasion, unknown to us gentiles. Business houses kept by that class in town are closed from 'rosy morn' till dewey eve."[11] Better informed, the next day the newspaper explained that "Yesterday was the Jewish year 5626, a gal-a-day with them. This will account for closing of business houses of this class yesterday. We hope our readers will understand no disrespect meant to our Israelite friends in the local columns of last eve."[12] At the end of the month, Yom Kippur was explained as well as the holidays "Tsukes," and "Simchas Tore."[13]

If the editor had been puzzled by the Jewish holidays, his further surprise can be imagined when he received the following letter which he published that November: Headlined "An Inquiry," the article addressed to the editor, read:

> Allow us, through the columns of your paper to address a few words of inquiry to His Excellency, Gov. A. Cummings. Are we of the Jewish persuasion included in the Proclamation for Thanksgiving, "requiring all good people of Colorado to assemble in their respective places of worship and render unto God devout Thanksgiving for the riches of his grace, manifested through His Son, Jesus Christ?" If so, we have never in the United States of America seen a proclamation excluding Jews from participating.
> Jews do not worship God through Christ, and by the above proclamation we are excluded. Respectfully yours, H. Z. Salomon, Jo. Deitsch. Denver, Nov. 18, 1865.

In the same issue on the second page a letter signed by an "Israelite," takes the same stand, pointing out that President Johnson gave the proclamation correctly, but that the governor went further without constitutional precedent and "excludes and debars by sectarian proclamation. . . . In all honor and regard for the ancient and ever-enduring religion we love and profess, we can thank the God of both Christian and Jew."

A few days later the *News* answered on page one: "To the public. We deprecate bad feeling. The Jewish residents are our very best and most enterprising citizens." The newspaper did not think that the governor meant to interfere. "We won't take sides as we are a non-sectarian journal." The paper hoped that the breach and cause would be removed.[14]

By December, the Jews seemed to be determined not to leave the issue alone. Again, on the first page, the newspaper said that it had no idea of being intolerant. "This is a Christian nation, and similar expressions are found throughout it." The Jews should have better judgment than to quarrel, especially with the odds ten to one against them, said the *News*, and insisted the proclamation was intended in a general sense. "It is no such interference as laws in nearly all states requiring observance of the Sabbath day." The *News* went on to praise Governor Cummings' good character.[15] A year later, and on a different issue, the same governor so lavishly praised was as thoroughly denounced.[16]

This Thanksgiving proclamation protest may have been spontaneous, but it was not original. The Jews of the eastern United States had made similar protests even earlier. The Jews of Denver, out on the frontier, were never cut off from the world. While distances were great, the population in between was small, and Cincinnati, America's early home of German Jewry, was almost next door. Correspondence, periodicals, and travel kept the Colorado Jews well informed of the Jewish events in America.

As far as the communities of the territory were concerned, the Jews had identified themselves. Thereafter Jewish activities were reported in the *News*. For the holidays of 1866, the newspaper announced: "Religious services will be held by the Israelites of Denver, corner Larimer and H Streets, commencing Tuesday evening at 6:30, until Wednesday, 6 p.m."[17] While the members of the group varied in their observances, apparently only one day of Rosh Hashanah was observed. The day of Atonement, services for which were held in the old Denver Theatre,[18] was mentioned and the following week, "Tskes and Simchas Torah" were again described. It was that Yom Kippur that twins were born to Joseph Kline. His son Samuel J. writes, incidentally, that his uncle Henry officiated at these services and was "probably the only Jew in Denver competent to do so." This is strange because most histories give David Kline that credit. S. J. Kline does not even mention him. That the Kline family was more religious than the other pioneers cannot be determined; however, on one occasion the father, Joseph, rode horseback eighty-five miles so that he could spend the "fall holiday at home."[19]

A feeling of permanence was felt in Denver. Within a few years the pioneers created the first permanent Jewish organizations. In the second decade of the region's history there came out of the pioneer burial society the Hebrew Benevolent Society and the official Hebrew Cemetery Association in 1871, the B'nai B'rith and Hebrew Ladies' Benevolent Society in 1872, and the Congregation Emanuel in 1873. The idea for the B'nai B'rith was said to have been first suggested in the insurance office of Louis Anfenger, and for the Congregation Emanuel at the *b'rith* of his son, Milton.

The congregation and the lodge shared the same rooms for worship and meetings, with the lodge paying the hall rent and the congregation the fuel and light bills. How the congregation worshipped may be surmised from the minutes and comments made in later years. That the group was influenced by the Reform movement in Cincinnati was obvious; yet the services in the beginning were Orthodox, by comparison with what they became later. The men prayed in Hebrew and kept their heads covered during services. It is even said some of the women sat apart from the men during the services. Certainly the right to worship as they pleased was not denied the members of the congregation which called itself Reform.

In 1874 the constitution was drawn up, and by October a resolution to erect a building was passed. The daughters of M. Rothschild, in London, sent a $60 contribution. In December lots were purchased in East Denver at Nineteenth and Curtis Streets for $1800 for the purpose of erecting the first Jewish house of worship in the territory.[20] The Hebrew Ladies' Benevolent Society raised funds for furnishing the temple by staging a fair.

The building was completed and occupied in 1875. The *News* devoted a half column to the dedication, which took place on the High Holidays that year. The newspaper described the building as thirty by sixty feet, of brick and costing $3000, excluding the furnishings of $1000 more. The ark was not complete but already had the Torah in it.

Said the *News*: "At 6:30, the building was well-filled, the gentlemen sitting with their hats on. To the music of a choir and organ, the procession, with the congregation's two oldest members (one of whom was Julius Mitchell), each carrying a torah, began." Dr. Elsner opened the program, and, "The Hon. Herman Silver gave a very pertinent and forceful address, and then followed the regular new year services, which lasted a long time." Services were held the following day, and a discourse was delivered by Dr. Elsner. "The New Year has thus dawned upon this progressive and liberal or Reformed congregation of the Israelite community." The *News* gave as the reason for the building and the congregation, "the hope of the Jews for furthering the cause of monotheism of the last 3,500 years."[21]

The liberality of the congregation was revealed in later minutes when instructions were given to Abraham Jacobs, "to procure, at the risk of the congregation, 50 sets of *minhag America* prayerbooks for the use and sale for the benefit of the congregation."[22] The *minhag America* (America custom) was the Reform prayerbook, which as a liberal interpretation of Judaism was a radical departure from the old traditional form. In the United States, especially around Cincinnati, where its founder, Isaac Mayer Wise, guided the movement, it rapidly became synonymous with the German Jew. Many of Colorado's early Jews had lived in Cincinnati and the surrounding region and were already influenced by the movement.

Most of the pioneers had to follow a religion easier for them to keep on the frontier where it was all but impossible to observe the Sabbath. It was even more difficult to keep the dietary laws. The few attempts made were quickly abandoned. Obviously, since these early Jews had not come from fear or hunger, they were well aware that the ritual would be one of the first things they would have to give up in the West. During this period it would take more than adventure to lure an observing, traditional Jew into the West.

What amount of risk Jacobs took in purchasing the prayerbooks has not been recorded. The movement away from Orthodox Judaism was now well under way. During the following year, 1876, the "hat controversy" began. From the minutes of the Temple, it appears that whether or not the head was covered during services was one of the last vestiges of traditional Judaism to be debated within the Temple. After much argument no resolution was passed, each worshipper doing as he saw fit. A later peruser of the minutes wrote in the margin, "That's the question. Whether 'tis nobler to act a civilized people, or to keep sacred the foolish customs of an infant religion."[23]

Another interesting problem posed itself to the congregation during the same period. Joseph Block and his family were assigned a pew during the High Holidays. The only Joseph Block in the territory at the time was the pioneer butcher, who had married a Catholic girl. After the notation on the reservation of the pew, the minutes continue, "that no one else not of our persuasion be admitted to service."[24]

In 1877, Isaac Mayer Wise was invited to "lecture at the synagogue."[25] That year the congregation joined the Union of American Hebrew Congregations.[26] Thereafter, there was little misunderstanding as to where the congregation stood in the observance of the ritual. A permanent Orthodox *minyan* (religious quorum of ten), said to have been organized the same year, may have been the result of the Temple's new affiliation.

The bulk of the Jewish pioneers of '59 and '60, and the latercomers joined the Temple. B'nai B'rith and the Temple Emanuel, the only two organizations to survive from the 70's under the same name, were for many years the center of Jewish life, not only for Denver but also for many of the Jews of the mining camps and country towns. The German Jew, unlike his East European brother, maintained these two original organizations from their inception to the present. If he was dissatisfied he resigned in writing, or, from the B'nai B'rith, either by requesting a withdrawal card or by not paying his dues. It may have occurred to him to set up a rival house of worship, or to launch a rival service organization, but such aspirations at a time when the state's entire Jewish population in 1877 was said to be 422[27] were not promising.

2

Within the Temple, as it grew, life was not always peaceful, with two recognizable problems constantly before the congregation for many years—financial and ministerial. Of the former, even when times were good in the little city and the promise of great wealth lay ahead, the congregation was too small to raise the money it needed to pay for the kind of a rabbi it wanted.

The problem of finding a suitable minister is not peculiar to the Jews. In fact, it is strange that in a religion where the conducting of religious services is not dependent upon a minister so much emphasis was placed on the personality of the rabbi. Was it the need of the congregation for a minister, or was it the wish of the Reform Jews to be like the rest of the church-going community, that created so much traffic in the selection of a rabbi? The minutes offer a clue when they record that the requirements of a prospective rabbi include his ability to lecture in English and German.[28]

The fact that the congregation was not homogeneous in religious practice contributed to the inability to find a suitable rabbi. It was the only organized congregation in Denver from 1873 to 1877, but the minutes of 1875 refer to an "existing congregation," from which the Temple was planning to buy its *Sefer Torah* for $50.[29] Although this congregation was very likely the remnant of the old burial and prayer society, the fact that it existed and had not yet affiliated with the new congregation presented the problem of pleasing this group, in the hope that its members would join.

With Rev. A. H. Fleischer—a language teacher at Wolfe Hall, and listed in the 1873 city directory as the rabbi of Congregation Emanuel—a procession of rabbis began which lasted for sixteen years. Each rabbi presented a problem to the congregation. After serving the Temple for less than two years, one rabbi wrote to a local Christian minister that he had renounced Judaism, and would never serve in a Jewish temple again. Another was paid off and promptly sent back to his home. Still another could no longer serve because of ill health. A later rabbi left Judaism, after he had "retired," but lived out his life in Denver, a strange, cultured, and very poor man of Sephardic background.

Of the last, the *Republican* gave part of his life story, headlined, "A Famous Jewish Rabbi Dies an Agnostic at 83." The obituary told of his birth in Amsterdam in 1818, where his family lived after fleeing the Inquisition. Coming to the New World in 1854, he had held pulpits throughout the United States and as far south as Curaçoa in the West Indies. In Denver he served the Temple Emanuel in 1885 until old age forced his retirement. Thereafter, he eked out a bare living in Denver as a teacher of languages. During these years he abandoned all religious belief and began to proclaim his belief in "the God of Science," publishing a pamphlet entitled, "The Fallacies of Religion, Its Delusions, and Evils." Nevertheless, when his end came, he asked to be buried as a Jew, with a Jewish burial. While he lived he had alienated many friends, but at his death the newspaper reported that the most Orthodox in the city would follow his body.[30]

If ever a congregation had a problem rabbi, the Temple had one in the early 80's. One young woman from the Jewish community's cultured families wrote of him: "He was no fool, but he had no manners. He proposed marriage to my seventeen-year-old sister in the Denver Horse Car, and she nearly exploded with laughter." He became so offensive that many of the most important members of the congregation resigned. Not the least of his grievous sins was his ridicule of the Orthodox Jewish religion from the pulpit. With the resignation of the Salomons and others, the board looked accusingly at the rabbi, who said he would take a cut in salary to offset the loss and would double his efforts to serve the cause of Judaism.

Having made the offer, he was not prepared to make the sacrifice, and had many interesting comments to make on the matter. Arguments flew back and forth between the rabbi and the board, with interested parties accused of carrying tales. In an exquisite handwriting, a copy of a letter sent to the rabbi was spread in the minutes of the Temple, and in Hebrew, with an English translation, was written, "Thou shalt not go as a calumniation between thy people." It is likely that the rabbi was too radical for his congregation. During the period when he served, the Temple was still not so far removed from Orthodox Judaism as it was to become in the 90's. The minutes still referred to the building as the "synagogue."

3

When the congregation was sixteen years old, it found the rabbi who served it for almost fifty years, and was its titular head, until he died in 1944. Rabbi William Sterne Friedman, even after his death, still lived as the symbol of Reform Judaism in Denver. Rabbi Friedman at twenty-one was an American product. Born in Chicago, reared in the Cleveland Orphan Asylum, and educated at Hebrew Union College, he was prepared for a ministry to the first generation of American Jews. On March 15, 1889, the *Jewish Voice* confidently reported: "Mr. Friedman left last morning for Denver, where he will preach next Saturday, and where, in all probability, he will be elected to become their rabbi after he will have graduated next June."[31]

Rabbi Friedman had much in his favor: he was an eloquent orator, who could move his audiences, Jewish and non-Jewish, to tears. He was a man of great dignity and fine bearing, and of such strong conviction that he refused to compromise on any issue. His friendships were with the intellectual, civic, and religious leaders of the community from the first. In a short sketch written on the life of Monsignor William O'Ryan, in the *Glory that was Gold*, the writer comments on

> ... Father O'Ryan's devoted friendship with Rabbi Friedman. They met within two weeks after Dr. Friedman's arrival in 1889. Since then no week has passed when both were in the city without some exchange of interest between these two stirring and exalted characters. For over forty years Denver has been fortunate in their citizenship.[32]

His sermons and speeches were quoted in the newspapers regularly. Editorials heaped praise on his head, and the congregation proudly acted as host to the many Christians who attended services in order to hear Rabbi Friedman. With such influence, he was soon leading the congregation into avenues of thoughts from which most of it would never return. His beliefs were those of the Reform branch of Judaism at the nadir from traditional Judaism. He had been a student in Cincinnati when the Pittsburg Platform of 1885 was formulated, and under its principles he was a part of the extreme left in Judaism. He renounced much of the Oral Tradition: the ritual, customs, ceremonies, the beliefs in the coming of the Messiah, the return to Zion, and the attitudes of the traditional to all of these. On one occasion he called the Bible a "fetish," stirring up a small tempest.[33]

One of his first acts was the introduction of the confirmation of the young people on Sunday, "which illustrates the progress made from the bounds of ancient tradition," according to the *Republican*, May 26, 1890. At an early debate the question of whether it was advisable to change the Jewish Sabbath from Saturday to Sunday was debated, with the audience deciding that "the present order of things, was best."[34] On this score Rabbi Friedman was adamant. He wanted the Sabbath day kept holy, but the fact that the question was even debated shocked the non-members.

The East European Jews of Denver, Orthodox or otherwise, were soon angry with him on any number of counts. As the idea of Zionism became stronger in the Jewish community after the turn of the century, and the pogroms increased following the Kishinev massacre, he became more and more imperative in his stand against a Jewish national state. Only at the death of Theodor Herzl did he relent his attack on the Zionist leader, to comment, "If nothing else Herzl's movement brought back indifferent alienated Jews,"[35] and to deliver a eulogy at a memorial meeting.[36]

Nevertheless the Orthodox East European Jews were forced to admire him and more than that, to be grateful to him on many occasions. He served as a vital link between them and the Christian community and zealously defended their rights as American citizens. When a Jew turned Christian missionary appeared in West Colfax—the heart of the Orthodox section—in *tallis* and *tefillin* (prayer shawl and phylacteries) he shocked the Jews with an apostatic address. Had it come from a Christian there would have been resentment, but from a Jew, using the sacred reminders, it was infuriating. At least one group of husky young men felt it to be so. They followed the *meshummed* (apostate) into town, and in the first convenient dark alley administered a beating. The shocked community is said to have voiced its indignation freely. Rabbi Friedman came to the defence of the Orthodox Russian Jews and pointed out that this was a family matter.[37] When a local newspaper misquoted a leader of the humane society as deploring the methods of Jewish slaughter, Friedman came to the defence of the ritual method at the same time pointing out that it was not followed by his Americanized congregation.[38]

Immediately on his arrival he became identified with almost every form of charity existing in Denver and a prime mover in many new ones formed thereafter. He brought to the attention of his congregation the need for a kindergarten for the Jewish children west of the creek, where most of the recent East European immigrants lived. When the Jews were asked to appoint a member of the Jewish community on the board of the state's Associated Charities in 1891, the Temple suggested its rabbi, who served for many years as president of the state Board of Charities and Corrections, supervising all state and county institutions, including the penitentiary, the insane asylum, and the homes for orphans and the blind.

When Rabbi Friedman came, the Associated Charities had already been organized and the Charity Organization Society of Denver incorporated in 1887. Rabbi Emanuel Schreiber was listed as one of the earliest participants, although Rabbi J. Mendes de Solla was the rabbi of the Temple at the time. Actually the only Jewish member of the five founders of the forerunner of the Community Chest was Frances Wisebart Jacobs. Rabbi Friedman became so active in the organization, that he was honored as one of its founders for fifty years, even though he had not come to Denver until 1889.

Honors were heaped on the head of the Temple rabbi. In 1906, the University of Colorado conferred the degree LL.D. on him, while he was holding a chair as professor of Hebrew at the school. Among the many organizations he served was the Denver Library Commission and the Hospital Saturday and Sunday Association, the latter an organization to help the "delicate-minded poor whose pride forbade care in the county hospital."[39]

His most important accomplishment was the high respect he

Frances Wisebart Jacobs, 1890. *Denver Republican.*

Temple Emanuel on Curtis Street. Numa L. James Collection.

Otto Mears's Million Dollar Highway. Courtesy of Colorado State Highway Department.

Otto Mears's silver pass made for John Elsner. Courtesy, Morris Abbott.

Temple Aaron, Trinidad. Courtesy, *Intermountain Jewish News*.

Henry Plonsky. *Reform Advocate*, 1908.

Dr. Charles D. Spivak. Ruth Oppenheim collection.

Mogen David. Photo by author.

The Shwayders standing on a Samson suitcase. Courtesy, *Intermountain Jewish News*.

created for the Jews and Judaism. Speaking and writing everywhere and for every publication, he dramatically presented the case of the Jews, so that the good feelings of Denver toward the Jews may be traced to him in ample measure. When angry, his dramatic powers came into full play. In 1905 he accused the Church of fostering hatred of Jews with: "There isn't a Jewish child who lives in a block of Christian Denver, who is not taunted by Christian children and made to suffer from Christian slurs." His Christian friends were surpised at the outburst, and the local Congregational pastor answered that in forty years he had never heard or read anything in Sunday School to warrant the charge that "hatred of the Jew is systematically fostered in Christian Sunday Schools." The minister asserted that the hatred comes from the streets: "The rabbi is mistaken. There is quite enough to stir his deepest anger in the outrages which are being heaped upon one of the noblest peoples, who God the father of us all, has ever appointed to dwell upon the face of the earth."[40]

The rabbi's anger may well have stemmed from the events that were taking place in Russia. The pogroms of Russia were of deep concern to the entire Denver Jewish community. Jacob Schiff, the American Jewish leader, had wired Friedman to collect funds for the Russian Jews. The rarely united Jewish community joined together and appointed the Reform rabbi chairman of the newly created "Central Committee of the Rocky Mountain Region for the Russian Jews." As chairman he spoke for the community at every possible occasion. At one mass meeting at the Temple the interior was dramatically "draped in black, with American flags draped conspicuously among the folds."[41]

A mass meeting of Christians was held, with the sympathetic *News* reporting that "A Jewish rabbi speaking from the pulpit of the first Baptist Church, and almost sobbing forth the soul cry of his down-trodden race in Russia, was the spectacle which presented itself to a large audience." At the end of his address he was recalled to the pulpit for a few more words, after which "Almost sobbing, he sat down, while the audience remained fixed and immobile."[42]

How to deal with the death and destruction befalling his people? Under the heading "The Decadence of Zionism," he wrote that America should assimilate all the Russian Jews. She would be compensated for the temporary disadvantages.[43] Until almost the end of his life, he refused to consider Zionism as part of the

Jewish heritage or even as a solution to the immediate terrors of anti-Semitism in Russia. When a friend who had been a fellow-student with him came to Denver to deliver an address in favor of Zionism, Friedman refused to let him speak at the Temple. He was so strongly anti-Zionist that when the Sokolow Zionist delegation came to Denver in 1922, the leaders of the celebration found it necessary to ask him not to interfere.

Years later, when he visited Palestine after the rise of Hitler, he was no longer so outspoken against Zionism, although he claimed to be more firmly "opposed to a nationalistic Jewish state" than ever. When he described the Hebrew University on Mount Scopus, he said, "There is something of which every Jew in every part of the world can be proud." At the same time he feared that "Jewish nationalism promotes Arab nationalism."[44] Despite this he minced no words in accusing Britain of betraying the refugee Jews.[45] A surprised community and the bewildered members of his congregation heard him address the Hadassah chapter and the B'nai B'rith College of Jewish Studies in phrases filled with praise for the Jewish achievements in Palestine.

There was no Anti-Defamation League in existence during the years in which he performed many of the duties later assigned to that organization. At the Central Conference of American Rabbis in Charlevoix, Michigan, he was appointed chairman of a committee to "stop the caricaturing of the Jew." Credited with starting the movement in 1907, he and Alfred Muller asked the Associated Press to eliminate the word *Jew* from the news service's stories when used in a descriptive sense. The B'nai B'rith and the Union of American Hebrew Congregations became interested in Rabbi Friedman's idea that "There is no reason why our religion should be used for press or profit." He then appealed to the theatre managers to stop the practice of ridiculing the Jews.[46] With the local B'nai B'rith lodge he labored to protect the "good name" of the Jews. The minutes of the lodge obliquely refer to the theatre owners on Curtis street (Denver's White Way) who ruefully, or graciously, pulled down a sign and canceled a picture that had offended the Jews.

He stood against prayers in the Senate addressed other than to the "Lord, Our Father," as violating freedom of religion; and against the admission of the Bible in the public schools, as violating the separation of church and state.[47]

As a man of strong convictions, it was inevitable that he was sometimes more successful than he wished. In minimizing the ritual, he had not drawn clear enough lines for his congregation to follow. In 1909, as the old year was slipping away, he asked his congregation not to give a New Year's Eve dance, since the holiday fell on a Friday night. The young people went right ahead. The newspaper account did not help matters by adding that the Orthodox rabbi had made the same request, to which his young people responded by holding their dance the following night.[48]

Adored by his congregation, Friedman was nevertheless, even by some of them, accused of being a snob. This is refuted by those least likely to come to his defense if it were true. As a young rabbi, he sought out the East European scholar Bernard Hurwitz, for advanced study in the sacred writings. The family never mentioned this, thinking that it would cast adverse reflection on the rabbi's knowledge. Years later, when Hurwitz was struck down by an automobile and taken across town to the Orthodox Beth Israel Hospital, Rabbi Friedman appeared early in the morning at his bedside. The surprised family murmured, "Rabbi, how nice of you to come!" In turn, the rabbi was surprised, "And not come and see my teacher?"[49]

In fifty years he unified his congregation, although it meant creating a wide schism in the community. When he died, many of his members who had never missed services rarely attended again, presenting the question, was it the love for Judaism, or the veneration of the rabbi that had brought them to the Temple while he lived? The members of the local American Council for Judaism justify their stand against Zionism on the basis of his teachings. A decade after his death, a newly created "Denver School for Reform Judaism," in 1955, was established, because "the Temple is no longer teaching the kind of Reform Judaism that we were taught as children. They are teaching too much Zionism and nationalism, rather than stressing that Judaism is a religion." The principal of the new school informed the *Intermountain Jewish News*:

> We will teach simple Reform Judaism exactly as it was taught at Temple Emanuel by Rabbi William S. Friedman when I was a girl. We will teach Prophetic Judaism—a Judaism for Americans. Especially in the early grades we will stress the spirit of Judaism, the love of one God and the worship of Him thru his ideals.[50]

From this school, in 1957, was formed Congregation Micah, the second Reform congregation in almost a century of Jewish life in Denver.

4

At first, Temple services were held on Friday night and Saturday morning, but soon the Friday night services assumed the entire Sabbath. The use of German was important to the founders. As late as 1883 a rabbi was requested "to lecture in German on Kol Nidre night."[51] As English replaced German, an English memorial prayer was introduced in 1886 to take the place of the *Kaddish*.[52] The Sabbath school, conducted on Sunday, gave instruction to the children of members and non-members. The latter paid a fee of two dollars a month for each child—in advance—and ten dollars to be confirmed. Until the Orthodox Jews had a Sunday School, it is said that their children began to straggle in, particularly from the West Side, where only Hebrew schools for boys were first organized. The instruction followed the Reform idea: "The children were taught prayers, and what it means to worship One God."[53]

Confirmation was as significant an event as high school graduation. At first it took place at the age of fourteen, but as the original seven classes were increased to ten, the ceremony began to take place at the age of sixteen. From childhood on, new generations of American Jews were taught by Rabbi Friedman to have a reverent attitude in the Temple in which pervaded the quiet and orderly atmosphere of a well-disciplined congregation.

Arrangements for death were provided for in the Constitution under "Last Honors to the Dead," and called for a benevolent committee to attend to the burial. At the expense of the congregation two suitable persons watched the remains of the deceased, if not contagious. A carriage was provided for the committee, and if requested, "the remains may be brought to the Synagogue and funeral services held there."[54] Floral wreaths, prohibited at Orthodox funerals, were placed by the B'nai B'rith at the graves of the lodge's deceased members at the time of burial.

Not until 1906 was there a Jewish undertaking establishment in the state. With the coming of the horse car, whole cars were chartered for the trip to the cemetery. In the 70's, when Denver was small and the lodge, the Temple, and most of the Jews were in the same neighborhood, B'nai B'rith members called special meetings at the lodge rooms and then marched in a body to the home of the deceased. The Tramway Company had a special hearse built when it converted to the use of cables. The company's line led to the cemetery, so that, until the coming of the automobile, funeral processions were, in part, conducted by the Tramway Company.

5

Out of the burial society had come the Hebrew Cemetery Association. Apparently the small group of Jews met informally under this name and that of the Hebrew Benevolent Society. While David Kline was said to have been the president of the cemetery association in 1867, there were no records to show that the group had a formal existence before May 7, 1871, when the Hebrew Benevolent Society was formed. The problem of the cemetery grounds had been a troublesome one, and the society had been put "to much expense buying and rebuying the property."[55] In 1871 Congress made a special grant of land to the city, and the society was formed so that the Jews could continue using their grounds.

In March, 1873, a petition appeared in the *News* reading:

> To the Mayor and Members of the City council: Your committee to whom referred petition of Julius Mitchell and others on behalf of the Hebrew Benevolent Society, that the city of Denver, in making the government entry of 160 acres for a city cemetery, do include in said entry of 160 acres the burial grounds of said society, consisting of 10 acres, and that the city, after that make a deed to them. Have had petition under advisement, and find that petitioners had rights prior to the city of Denver, and would recommend that their prayer be granted and the mayor be authorized to make a deed confirming the above named 10 acres to the Hebrew Benevolent Society for burial purposes upon their paying to the city treasurer, expenses incurred in obtaining government title.[56]

While the Hebrew Benevolent Association and the Hebrew Cemetery Association were the same group, articles of incorporation were filed under the latter name by David Kline, H. Z. Salomon, John Elsner, J. Gottlieb, and C. M. Schayer, on July 20, 1873.[57]

Other problems were added to those of their rights to the property. In 1884 the Jews asked that a pest house be removed from the cemetery, which was defiling their well-tended grounds. No matter how carefully the Jews kept their portion of the cemetery, Denver's eastward growth became so rapid that soon the cemetery was unwillingly surrounded by the irate residents of a fashionable section. In 1887 the Grand Army of the Republic removed the bodies of their members buried there. By 1890 only the Catholic and Hebrew sections remaind. The *Republican* reported that the Catholics were to take the matter up of moving the bodies from consecrated grounds.[58] That same year graves in the Jewish and Catholic sections were "violated." The Denver *Times* believed this to be the work of ghouls. It was discovered by the sexton of the Jewish cemetery. He had found one grave opened and the casket dropped, as if hurriedly, on the ground. The woman whose remains they had disturbed had "had a fear of ghouls, and had been promised a safe resting place." The *Times* also suggested that it might have been the "work of medical students, or neighbors who don't like burials."[59]

Even while it was apparent that they would have to give up the grounds, the Reform Jews continued using them for new burials for another two decades. In June, 1903, the Health Commissioner ordered the immediate cessation of burials on Capitol Hill and in the Catholic and Jewish cemeteries as a health measure. The objections of the residents was that the cemetery was not kept up, although "The Jewish cemetery is perhaps the most beautiful spot in the city, but the others abuse burials in used graves and piling of bones. . . ."[60] The B'nai B'rith minutes refer to burials in the Jewish Cemetery as late as 1910.[61]

While the old grounds were being used, the Temple entered into a contract with Riverside Cemetery for a Jewish section. David May, the merchant, purchased the first cemetery lot for $150.[62] Riverside was used for several years until the Temple negotiated for permanent grounds in the new Fairmont Cemetery, which belonged to the same organization as Riverside. The new grounds were named "Emanuel."

As soon as burial was halted in the old cemetery the unpleasant job of exhuming and re-interring the bodies began. An estimated 600 or 700 familes were involved in the transfer, which lasted from 1911 until 1923, when the grounds were sold by the Temple for a substantial figure. Most of the pioneers were re-interred in Emanuel, with the original tombstones placed over them. The Orthodox were taken to their cemeteries, although many of the oldest stones bear Orthodox inscriptions, at the very least "P'nee" (he is buried). These inscriptions, give way in the 80's to more modern stones on which there is little or no evidence of the religion of the occupant of the land beneath it.

Only Leadville, Colorado Springs, and Pueblo have Jewish cemeteries. In Trinidad, a section of the Masonic cemetery belongs to the Jews. From nearby Central City to Alamosa in the south and Durango in the southwest corner of the state, the bodies of Reform Jews were brought to Emanuel cemetery for burial.

6

Congregation Emanuel rapidly outgrew its first home. Again the women gave an elaborate week-long "Fair" in November, 1881,[63] to raise funds for a new building. Senator Nathaniel P. Hill sent a solid silver brick. Wolfe Londoner donated $200 for an inscription in a "Book of Life," and Governor Tabor was reported as spending his money freely. The women raised $3,500 towards the $32,000 temple at Twenty-fourth and Curtis streets, the uptown fashionable section. When the dedication took place the following year, the enthusiastic press devoted two solid columns to it and to the banquet tendered by the "Hebrew admirers of Dr. Sonneschein," who was brought from St. Louis for the occasion. The *News* reported:

> It is not flattery, it is downright truth to say that when the Jewish people undertake anything they always do it well. . . . The time when Hebrews are known chiefly as pawn brokers and second hand clothing dealers is past. . . . In many respects the Hebrew is being called the rising race. . . . They move with little friction and still less pretence. They have a high place in the history of the city and county government, and are adopted without question among the best metropolitan society.[64]

This was not quite true—Jewish names are not found in the annuals of the newly-formed fashionable clubs of the early 80's nor in the lists of those attending the most exclusive parties.

A fire in 1897 almost destroyed the building. The third home of the congregation at Sixteenth and Pearl was completed January, 1899. Six years later, it was again too small for its Reform congregation, the largest between Chicago and the Pacific Coast. This time the building was enlarged. After more than a half-century on the same spot, land was broken in 1955 for the congregation's fourth home, many miles southeast of its original home in downtown Denver.

In terms of wealth and importance, the Temple had its share of Colorado's millionaires and leaders. The roster included the familiar names of Simon Guggenheim, David May, Commodore Louis Beaumont, L. H. Guldman, Otto Mears, Max Schott, and I. W. Bernheim.

FOOTNOTES

[1]*The Rocky Mountain News*, both daily and weekly editions, was carefully examined for the word "Jew," from April, 1859 to 1863. Many copies are missing, particularly during the period of the fire and flood. The years 1863 and 1864, were also examined, but not so diligently.

[2]Town Record, Denver City, *op. cit.*, Dec. 26, 1859.

[3]*RA, op. cit.* Mrs. Sam Goldsmith, the daughter-in-law of Henry Goldsmith, and Mrs. Sam Bowman, his granddaughter-in-law, furnished the name of "Clara," the surviving baby. "Aunt Clara," as she was known, was the mother-in-law of Mrs. Bowman. The family tried to find the grave of Mrs. Goldsmith, but were unable to do so.

[4]*Republican*, "The City of the Dead," April 21, 1890. According to this article the land known as the "Capitol Hill Cemetery" was first used in 1869. There is no indication that the Jews used any other burial ground but this, which was known as the "Jewish Cemetery." They may have used the land before the non-Jewish population did.

[5]*JO*, Nov. 24, 1905.

[6]*RMN*, Jan. 11, 1862.

[7]Watters, *op. cit.*

[8]The Arkushes gave the date of their marriage as 1863. Marriage certificates in Denver begin with Index No. 17, Nov. 27, 1867–1917. Records prior to that were kept in the territory to which the particular section of the later-created state belonged. Only 12 marriages involving Jews are recorded. There is, however, an overlapping in the next volume, 1874-1880.

[9]*RMN*, Sept. 21, 1861. Adler is previously mentioned, May 6, 1861, as an endorser of the gold rate regulations.

[10]Denver Lodge, *op cit*. From Byers' address: "I see here to-night a Brother who taught me my first Masonic lesson, when I petitioned for initiation in Capitol Lodge No. 1, in Nebraska." This could only be Jacobs, since he was the only one of the three of the original Auraria lodge members present, and was originally from the Capitol Lodge.

[11]*RMN*, Sept. 21, 1865.
[12]*RMN*, Sept. 22, 1865, p. 4.
[13]*RMN*, Sept. 30, 1865.
[14]*RMN*, Nov. 25, 1865, p. 1.
[15]*RMN*, Dec. 5, 1865, p. 1.
[16]*RMN*, Sept. 21, 1866.
[17]*RMN*, Sept. 10, 1866.
[18]Samuel Kline, *Recollections and Comments.*
[19]*Ibid.*
[20]Emanuel minutes, I, Dec. 20, 1874.
[21]*RMN*, Sept. 30, 1875, p. 4.

²²Emanuel minutes, Aug., 1875.
²³*Ibid.*, Sept. 17, 1876.
²⁴*Ibid.*, Sept. 3, 1876.
²⁵*Ibid.*, July 1, 1877.
²⁶*Ibid.*, Oct. 7, 1877.
²⁷*AJY*, XXX, p. 178.
²⁸Brochure, 75th Anniversary Temple Emanuel, excerpts from minutes, Oct. 12, 1875.
²⁹*Ibid.*, Dec. 5, 1875.
³⁰*Republican*, July 5, 1901, p. 12.
³¹WmSF scrapbook.
³²*Glory that Was Gold*, Central City Opera Association, p. 111.
³³Denver *Post*, May 24, 1905; *Jewish Gazette* (N.Y.), June 11, 1905.
³⁴*Republican*, Mar. 19, 1890.
³⁵*JO*, July 22, 1904.
³⁶WmSF scrapbook, BMH program July 21, 1904.
³⁷There are several clippings in Rabbi Friedman's scrapbook on the subject of his opposition to missionaries visiting the city. However, this particular story does not appear. Interview, William Rosen.
³⁸*Republican*, Nov. 8, 1903; *Times*, Nov. 11, 1903.
³⁹*Post*, Oct. 19, 1937.
⁴⁰*JO*, Nov. 17, 1905.
⁴¹*JO*, Nov. 11, 1905.
⁴²*RMN*, Dec. 1, 1905.
⁴³*JO*, April 28, 1905.
⁴⁴*IJN*, Sept 3, 1937.
⁴⁵*Post*, Aug. 29, 1937.
⁴⁶*Post*, July 2, 1910.
⁴⁷*JO*, Feb. 22, 1907, July 26, 1907.
⁴⁸*Times*, Dec. 31, 1909.
⁴⁹As told by Ida Hurwitz and Mrs. David Pelton, daughters of Bernard Hurwitz.
⁵⁰*IJN*, July 15, 1955.
⁵¹Emanuel minutes, Oct. 4, 1883.
⁵²Emmanuel minutes, Feb. 10, 1886.
⁵³Interview, Mrs. Henry Schwartz, Jr.
⁵⁴Emanuel minutes, Apr. 14, 1878.
⁵⁵*RA*, p. 50.
⁵⁶*RMN*, Mar. 15, 1873, p. 6.
⁵⁷Art. Inc. No. 109.
⁵⁸*Republican*, Apr. 21, 1890.
⁵⁹*Times*, Aug. 22, 1901.
⁶⁰*Ibid.*, June 24, 1903.
⁶¹*Post*, Apr. 7, 1911.
⁶²Emanuel minutes, Apr. 21, 1896.
⁶³*RMN*, Nov. 6-22, 1881.
⁶⁴*RMN*, Sept. 4, 1882.

Gaining the "Needful"

1

It was inevitable that in the epidemics of "gold fever," the young adventurous Jews would contract the same ailment. However, after a brief search for the precious metals, the obvious needs of the miners hastened the recovery of most of the young Jews from the malady. These were the merchants who "grubstaked" many a miner and bought interest in frequently successful mines. Their search for gold was vicarious. Fitted by previous merchandising experience, it was only natural that most of them should take on the job of supplying the miners.

Like Abraham Jacobs, who moved his O. K. Store to Spring Gulch in the "richest square mile on earth," with its booming mining camps of Central City, Blackhawk, Nevadaville, Mountain City, and others even less temporary on the face of the map of Colorado, many of the Jewish pioneers brought their stores to the miners. Sometimes the procedure was reversed, as in the case of the Deitsch and Sonneberg firm, which moved its store from Central City to Denver, where, in 1862, their firm received a train of eight wagons of merchandise.

The movement from the "states," and from Denver and back to the mining camps was exceptionally heavy during the early years of settlement, with new names appearing on every stage list: L. Morris leaves for Buckskin Joe (a mining camp above South Park);[1] A. Sands and wife, and Miss Sands arrive, with Sands returning from a "five month sojourn in the eastern markets, and bringing out his lady and sister to make the city their abiding home."[2] On their way to Central City were Israel Wolfe, A. J. Poznanski, and J. Ringolsky.[3]

In providing the miners, the merchants were faced with an

important problem, the existing rates of gold dust, which was the principal medium of exchange. A public meeting was held in 1861 to establish gold dust rates.[4] For the varying quality of gold, the leading merchants set rates with Platte River gold commanding $20 per ounce, down to common, badly retorted gold at $12 per ounce. Fred Z. Salomon was on the committee in Denver and Abraham Jacobs on a similar committee in Central City. Reading the resolution in the latter town, Jacobs averred for the merchants, "on our sacred honor, we business men and mill owners set the following rates. . . ."[5]

The rates so set did not last long because the miners regarded the setting as an arbitrary decision.[6] But this exchange of business men, along with the Chamber of Commerce[7] in Denver, crystallized into business groups bent on improving financial conditions in the territory.

The merchants supplied the miners with clothing, staples, tools, and some luxuries. Jacobs advertised among his tools "very scarce eight-tined sluice forks." On exhibition he had a tempting incentive—a nugget of gold and quartz worth $166.30.[8] Such items satisfied the miners for a time. Their food consisted mostly of dried and processed items. Fresh vegetables were a luxury, not to be imported, but grown near the pioneer's home in the lower land of the prairie. In the high altitude of the mining camps, with the short growing season and rocky terrain, only a few vegetables could be grown. But who wanted to plant radishes and onions on top of the soil when under it lay tons of gold? The miners could wait until their pockets became better lined with the "needful."

The Homestead Act brought the settlers, with hopes of large scale farming. In Colorado, then as always, the major problem of existence was water. Only the mountains, blanketed in snow, represented a fairly dependable source. On the eastern plains and in the parks between mountain ranges, irrigation by ditch was the only method of bringing water to the growing crops. Leopold Mayer and Isaac Gotthelf joined with a few others in 1881 to create a large system of irrigation for the San Luis Valley—"the first large system planned on modern lines." The construction of the main ditch was called the "Del Norte Canal."[9]

Near the present site of Pueblo, the Goldsmith brothers and Simon Nathan tried farming. In Denver, Henry and Joseph Kline made an attempt at sheep raising. Joseph Kline was not one to stay with any one endeavor too long. According to his son,

S. J. Kline, his father had joined the Pikes Peak "boomers" in 1859, was in Montana in 1863, Cimarron (southern Colorado and New Mexico), in the 70's, Leadville in 1880, and Couer d'Alene in the 90's. Joseph Kline had met his wife in Munich, married her in the United States, and before 1861 brought his family from Leavenworth to Denver by mule train on a journey lasting twenty-five days. In Denver he was in business with various relatives and was elected to serve on the fourth city council.

His children were born in the different cities where he settled long enough for them to be born. The first child was born in Cincinnati; the second, Leavenworth; the third, Central City; and the fourth in Denver, followed by twins born on Yom Kippur in the same city. Whatever success he may have met in sheep raising was easily matched by his success in fatherhood. On the birth of one child, the local German newspaper commented: "That is right, Joseph, stock raising is the best business."[10]

Although a number of Jews engaged in farming, Jewish successes in the agricultural life of the territory were few. By the time of Colorado's fifth annual fair in 1870, in a lengthy list of firms awarding prizes for the best agricultural products, practically every Jewish firm was listed. However, only one Jew seems to have won a prize: H. Schayer, who won a diploma for the best keg of vinegar in his class.[11] Not until the coming of the land-hungry Russian Jews, who had been denied the right to own any land, were farming and cattle-producing to achieve importance in Jewish enterprise.

The Jewish professional men came slowly at first. Dr. Elsner and Dr. Heimberger were the earliest. The latter succeeded Dr. Elsner, with whom he shared an office, as county physician. Both men signed the charter creating the first medical society in the region. Although Colorado became the goal for the respiratory sick, with abnormal need for physicians, there appear to have been fewer than twenty permanent Jewish physicians in Denver at the turn of the century, and almost half that number of East European origin.

One of the most distinguished of the early doctors was Robert Levy, a nephew of Dr. Elsner. Born in Canada in 1864, he was one of the earliest of American-born physicians in the Jewish group. He was educated in Wisconsin and entered the University of Denver in 1879, where he received his B. A. degree. He completed his professional training at Bellevue Hospital Medical

92

College in New York. Upon graduation he returned to Denver in 1884, where he began a medical practice which lasted until 1945—exceeding the continuous practice of his uncle by more than five years.

Unquestionably one of the outstanding physicians in the state, Dr. Levy distinguished himself in the field in which he specialized, otolaryngology. For this purpose he took specialized courses in Berlin, Halle, and Vienna. As an authority in his field, he held chairs in the local medical colleges. He held various offices in five national medical associations, and the presidency of both the Denver and state medical societies. For the medical journals of the nation he wrote fifty-five articles using his research on the effect of tuberculosis on the nose and throat. A national figure in medicine, he treated many an illustrious personage, not the least of whom was President William Howard Taft.[12].

The doctor born in Europe found it easy to enter his profession in the West. In contrast the lawyers, teachers, and journalists who practiced in Colorado were almost all native-born or had spent their childhood in America. For the lawyers there was ample need arising from the interpretation of mining law and water rights. Descendants of pioneer German Jews, some of the Colorado-born attorneys reached the heights of their profession in the early 1900's, almost all of them serving in some civic capacity.

Many young Jewish unmarried women became teachers in the public schools, rising to the position of principals. It is strange that, in such a masculine society, so many of them never married but continued in their profession frequently until death.

As more and more newspapers began publication, trained journalists from the East entered the newspaper field. Some of them had university training; others rose from the ranks. Herman Silver, better identified with politics, was also manager of the Denver *Tribune*. Alfred Patek was a graduate of the University of Wisconsin in 1900. When he came to Denver that year it was as the managing editor of the Denver *Times*. Another, Jacob O. Heimberger, the adopted son and nephew of Dr. Heimberger, was educated at Jarvis Hall near Denver and at the state university. At Saguache, during vacation, he began to learn the newspaper business, and by the age of twenty-one was the advertising solicitor of the Leadville *Herald-Democrat*, one of the most influential newspapers in the state. Included in every change of ownership of the paper, he became its sole owner. At his untimely death all the stores and banks in the city closed and flags were flown at half-mast while Leadville mourned for the young editor. B. F. Zalinger, Mrs. Elsner's brother, known as "Nap" (for Napoleon) who learned the printer's trade as a child, later held the job of city editor on at least two Denver dailies. A sister, Jennie, was society editor on the *Republican*. There were several women on the newspapers, including Mildred Morris, who later worked on newspapers in the East.

In banking, only after success had been achieved elsewhere were directorates offered. In addition to Fred Z. Salomon, at least three German Jews were directors of banks: Meyer Friedman, David S. Lehman, and Louis Anfenger. Although the early Jews branched out into other lines, such as real estate and insurance, it was the store which kept many Jews alive—from the clerks to the shopowners. If a store was successful, it was enlarged and a branch store was opened in another boom camp. If an excitement died out, the entire town, with its Jewish merchants, moved to a more likely camp. Above all the pioneers were mobile. Only scores of ghost towns with empty, weatherbeaten buildings testify to the activity that took place in them.

Some of the stores grew to immense proportions, but great wealth came to only a few of the merchants.[13] One of these was L. H. Guldman, who opened stores in Leadville and Cripple Creek. These were never so successful as his Denver "Golden Eagle." Some of his success is attributed to his saving of an aged Chinaman from a pursuing mob during the Chinese riots. The grateful Oriental population (which was considerable at the time) traded at his store thereafter. He is also said to have stopped trouble for the banks in the Panic of 1907 by redeeming in gold coin all "cashiers' script" promissory paper.[14]

The Golden Eagle was far from being a fashionable store. But its fire sales, using a wealth of newspaper space in the Denver *Post,* and the possibility of buying bargain merchandise at low prices, made it one of the best-known stores in the city and Guldman a millionaire. Guldman's charities were many and varied. He helped endow the Rude Community Center and later the Guldman Community Center. He gave generously to, and helped build, Denver's first Orthodox Jewish general hospital and old folk's home, the Beth Israel. He was always generous to the constant stream of women who came to his store with such announcements as, "Guldmankeh, I need sheets for a poor family."

The stories of the successful German Jews are well recorded. Obviously there were many more who came to seek their fortunes as miners in the West and slipped away without a line written about them anywhere. Colorado has always had a transient population. As the local clergy frequently pointed out, "Preaching in Denver is like preaching to a procession."

Only when a story ended in tragedy meriting newspaper notice did the public hear of it. The Jewish benevolent societies never publicized the names of their relief list.

One such case was headlined in the *News* under "Yesterday's Suicide," with the comment that this suicide was different from the great number of suicides of the previous months. "Carl Heinig, a Jew who ran a small jewelry manufactory . . . and resided with his family on the 'Bottoms' far out from any regularly laid out street . . . in a shanty or shed . . . was found dead." In addition to his crippled wife, Heinig left "a boy of 14, right manly, a boy of 7, and by far the most intelligent of the lot a bright-looking little girl of 10. She is bright beyond her years as Jewish children so frequently are, and is the reed upon which the family leaned."

Heinig had had a good business in New York, but business reverses brought him to Kentucky, and from there, because of the metals in the West, he came to Denver. He finally saved enough to try mining and sank his money into a worthless prospector's hole. The mind of the man who had been steady, "thrift-and-industry-minded became affected. In his last effort he had melted $15 worth of gold and poured it into a glass vessel. The glass broke and the gold fell into the sand and was lost." The hapless man "took a paper, emptied it into a drinking glass," and before swallowing it, told his bewildered children, "It's good for rats."[15]

The Panic of 1873 was felt by the Jews to some extent, but no failures of any importance were recorded.[16] Not so the Panic of 1893, when the silver mines were closed after silver had been demonetized. All but a few of the merchants on Denver's Sixteenth Street were completely wiped out.

2

Among those Jews who became miners in the West was the Fifty-niner Simon Nathan, who had come directly from Leavenworth to California Gulch. The mine he owned in the area was so rich that, according to a granddaughter, "he took out the gold in hunks." After six years of mining, the family moved to a farm near Pueblo. Subsequently the mine he had opened and left became one of the richest gold mines in the Gulch.

Separating South Park on one side and California Gulch on the other is a range of mountains of magnificent beauty and of treacherous heights. To the Nathans it is still a cause for wonder that they crossed this range from Buckskin Joe to the Gulch with four tiny children and a cow.[17]

At its height, California Gulch numbered about 10,000 persons. This was Leadville's first boom—the search for gold. By the middle 60's the area had quieted and the population had dwindled to handfuls of stubborn miners. The second boom in the region, which gave the city of Leadville its name, was created by the carbonates, lead and silver. In the late 70's when it occurred, the precarious roads and trails were crowded with the optimistic prospectors, who came in such number that beds were rented for three eight-hour shifts in the largest of Colorado's boom towns. Many of them were seasoned miners. Others came directly from the East, with no knowledge of the region or of mining.

Leadville, still the dream of the placer miner with his pan, pick, and mule, was also the goal of the eastern capitalist with his satchel-carrying mining expert. A promising claim had been located in 1869, and re-located in 1877, named the A. Y. and Minnie mines. When its owner decided to sell, ready buyers were found in the persons of a man named Stevens and his partner, Levi Z. Leiter, who was also a partner of Marshall Field in Chicago.

Leiter was at home among the wealthy American and English capitalists who were investing in the west. His wealth and marriage brought him into the most exclusive social circles— one daughter was married to Lord Curzon and another to the Earl of Suffolk. On one occasion in Washington, he is said to have remarked to the daughter of the President of the United States, "I suppose you wonder, as do I, at seeing a gnarled little Jewish peddler being host to a table like this."[18]

Leiter's mining battles in Leadville were dramatic forerunners of many similar fights involving litigation and underground hostilities. Owning many subsurface rivers of metals, his investments were soon organized into the Iron Silver Mining Company, one of the greatest producers in the region. Leiter's association with the Leadville community was minimal, and many of the Jews neither suspected nor cared that Leiter Avenue, in the shadow of Colorado's highest peaks, was named for a one-time Jewish clerk.

The A. Y. and Minnie came into the hands of a Swiss Jew, Meyer Guggenheim, who was already successful as the owner of an embroidery business in Philadelphia. For $5000 he purchased a half interest in the mine, which took $25,000 to be unwatered. Within six months the mine was producing $100,000 a month. By 1890 the mines which produced silver and lead were valued at $15,-000,000. Although much of the metal was pure, it was necessary to find a cheap means of smelting it. In Pueblo the family erected a six stack plant, and the company there became the Philadelphia Smelting and Refining Company. This was followed by the giant American Smelting and Refining Company, which controlled the industry.

Out of the Guggenheim mining activity in Leadville, Pueblo, and scattered mines throughout the state, grew the vast Guggenheim metal empire from Alaska into South America. Four of his children were identified with mining, and one in particular, Simon, who served as a United States Senator from Colorado, was in fact a representative of the mining industry during his term in Washington. Simon, who remained in Colorado until his term as Senator expired, made some of the largest endowments to the state's universities and colleges in their history. His major gifts were to the Colorado School of Mines and Metallurgy, although each of the major campuses has a Guggenheim building which was endowed at the time of his election by the Republican silver legislature. The Guggenheim Pavilion at the National Jewish Hospital was also one of his many gifts to the institution.

Unlike Leiter, Meyer Guggenheim and his family were intimate with the Jewish community in Leadville and Denver. Meyer played pinochle with his co-religionists and was well-liked by them. Although he did not join the Temple or Synagogue in Leadville, his son, Simon, was a member of Temple Emanuel in Denver and a friend of Rabbi Friedman, who officiated at his marriage in New York.[19]

In Denver Guggenheim gave to the traditional synagogue, as well as the Temple, and helped the settlement work for the East European Jews with $500, promising to contribute ten per cent of all money raised in excess of $5,000. How the Jews regarded the

Midas in their midst is hard to determine. The members of the Temple were proud, of course, that one of their number was one of the few Jews to serve in the United States Senate. The Jews, like the non-Jews who were active in Democratic party politics, did not like him. The rest of the Jewish community was neither impressed nor displeased. In an emergency individuals or groups might turn to him for funds or political help, but otherwise they had little contact with him.

Between the eastern capitalists and the grizzled prospectors, were the scientific mining engineers. The sons of some of the Fifty-niners and later settlers became involved in all of the metallurgical processes. There was very little that was spectacular in this form of gold-seeking. Only when something unusual happened was attention focused on them. In 1904, one Jewish man was killed in a fall down the shaft of his company's mine.[20] The following year another prominent miner missed his footing and slipped into a stope, causing a rock slide which crushed and smothered him.[21]

3

Since the activity of Leadville was the busiest in the entire state, outside of Denver, for many years, it was natural that the town should attract the second largest number of Jews.

By 1878 there were at least seventeen Jewish families in Leadville. In the directories and newspapers of the following year dozens of Jewish names were added. With an eye open to the possibilities of mining, and a little or a lot of money invested in any one of a number of small mines, the permanent Jew nevertheless was principally engaged in merchandising. His businesses included restaurants, saloons, liquor stores, pawn shops, jewelry shops, watchmaking, book stores, real estate agencies, and clothing.

Life in the city above the clouds was difficult, principally because of the cold. Fires were kept going indoors in summer as well as winter. The air was so rare at 10,152 feet that even a common cold was dangerous, and pneumonia could well be fatal. The clothing stores were filled with woolens designed to protect against the bitter cold.

A small clothing store operator, David May, had come to Leadville from Manitou Springs, where he had gone to recover his health. May made a brief attempt at mining, which he gave up whole-heartedly when he saw the great possibilities of clothing the 30,000 inhabitants of one of Colorado's largest cities.[22] In September, 1877, he opened a frame and muslin shack,[23] with a stock of long red woolen underwear and Levi's, two items in great demand. It was not long before he replaced the tent-like store with a frame building and attracted, as a partner, Moses Schoenberg, the third son of Elias Schoenberg, the owner of Leadville's only theatre until Tabor opened his celebrated opera house.

The two other Schoenberg boys ran clothing stores. One was "Cheap Joe's," owned by Joseph E., and the other the "Boss Clothier," owned by Louis D. Schoenberg, or Louis D. Beaumont, as he was also known. When their sister, Rosa, arrived, May began a courtship which culminated in their marriage in 1889. During that year, May and his brother-in-law, Louis, opened their first branch store in Pueblo, and the following year, one at Irwin (later a ghost town) farther west in a new booming area. Other branch stores were opened in Glenwood Springs and Aspen. Schoenberg ended his partnership with May in 1885 and May continued in business under his own name.

After three years he made a spectacular entrance into the business life of Denver. May purchased a bankrupt store, hired a brass band, and paraded the streets to advertise his new venture. Within a few days he had disposed of his entire stock. Having met with such success, he sold out his Leadville store and concentrated on becoming Denver's leading merchant. Now joined by his brothers-in-law, Louis and Joseph, he began a highly personalized and prolific advertising campaign. There was no doubt of the future of the company. Four years later the May Company made its first national move, with the purchase of a store group in St. Louis, the Famous-Barr Department Stores. The firm was well on its way to becoming the nation's oldest, most prosperous, and most successful store group.

If May had any other business ventures, they have not been publicized. Yet during the time he was in Leadville, there appeared an item in a Denver newspaper to the effect:

> Fulton Market opens September 26. P. Schlesinger & Co. . . . Wholesale and retail butchers and manufacturers of koscher sausages, boneless pickle meats, tongues, smoked pickle breasts, salamy, goose and duck sausages. Weiner knock, French pompadour sausages, etc. Very respectfully, P. Schlesinger, D. May. [24]

May's financial success was due to his dynamic methods of conducting business. His social success came from his pleasing and generous personality. In Leadville, his store had been a popular spot. Leadville was, like Central City, a cradle for many of Colorado's millionaires, and May, like most of the Jews there, was on intimate terms with them, taking part in political activity along with them. In 1881, the young Republican merchant was elected county treasurer and served twice in this capacity in the Democratic stronghold. He was also asked to run for state treasurer, which he declined to do. In later years he refused the post of consul at Frankfort, Germany, offered him by President McKinley.

There was little doubt as to his religious convictions. He helped organize the Leadville Hebrew Benevolent Association in 1879, joined the B'nai B'rith lodge there and served on the building committee of Temple Israel. In Denver he was active in Temple Emanuel. With Rabbi Friedman and Edward Monash, another department store owner, he toured the East to raise funds on behalf of the new, but empty hospital, the Frances Jacobs Hospital. When it became the National Jewish Hospital for Consumptives, he signed the articles of incorporation and served as an active member of the board until his death.

May gave generously not only to the hospital but also quietly to his co-religionists when he knew their need. He did not limit his friendships to the Reform group, but belonged to the Synagogue as well. May was more interested in traditional Judaism than most of his contemporaries. When he first came to Denver, he lived with the Orthodox Goldhammer family on Osage Street. He hired the local *schohet*, Louis Schechter, to teach Hebrew to his eldest son. A son born in Leadville is listed in Dr. Elsner's *b'rith mohel* book.

May's brother-in-law, Louis Schoenberg, for his activity on behalf of, and gifts to, the French children orphaned by the first World War, was decorated by the French government, honored by the title of "commodore," and his name permanently changed to Beaumont, which had been an alternate name with the same translation. Beaumont set up a trust fund of $13,000,000, from which contributions to ninety-six Jewish and non-Jewish institutions have been made.

In addition, he gave a nurses' home to the National Jewish Hospital and established the Schoenberg farm and trades school in

Denver to raise produce for the hospital and to train patients for employment.

These men, despite their wealth and the resultant assignment to them of aristocracy by the community, kept their heads. They acted with such good will and decorum that although they left Colorado in the early part of the century, their good reputation remained.

4

The solidarity of the Jewish community in Leadville was an enviable point in the Jewish history of the state. In the Jewish group were German, Polish, Russian, Hungarian, French, and English Jews, as well as Reform, Orthodox, and indifferent. Despite the varied backgrounds, there were no snobbery and no resentment when some grew wealthy and others remained poor. Unlike the social life almost everywhere else, Jewish life in Leadville was united. Nor was the relationship of the Jews to the larger community any different. Their neighbors and friends were millionaires as well as "Cousin Jacks" (Cornish) and Welsh miners. Only the fashionable Assembly appears to have closed its membership to the Jews, who seem not to have regarded this as a snub.

The rigorous life and the common problems it created may have been one of the reasons Leadville became the "city of friendship" and a rugged Utopia for the Jews. In addition, Leadville was larger than most of the mining camps, and the loneliness that sickened many a young Jewish woman was absent there.

In this strange ice box on top of the world, lawlessness and bawdiness flourished side by side with respectability and culture. The gay 90's were at least as gay in Leadville as they were anywhere in America. Many homes were furnished in taste, discerning and expensive. Diamond-dust mirrors, crystal chandeliers, rich upholstery and elaborately carved furniture, were not confined to the millionaires. Many a Jewish home boasted as much. When David May bought a stock of expensive velvet brocade dresses, which an overloaded Chicago store could not sell, the booming mining town relieved him of them within a week at prices from $200 to $400 each.

By the 90's the newly rich had so much money they had to devise methods of spending it. The city's most spectacular project was the building of a fabulous ice palace in 1896, a massive structure designed after a medieval Norman citadel. The Jews took an active part in building the palace and in enjoying it. The promotional stunt, for that was what it also was, was built to last for a long time, but perversely 1896 was a warm year and in April the Ice Palace melted away.

From all over the country came tourists, businessmen, and honeymooners. Many an adventurous Eastern youth came to work in the mines during summer vacation. The register of the fashionable Vendome Hotel reveals in its pages the names of Jews from all over the region and the country.

Despite distances, poor transportation, and rugged terrain, it was possible, at least until the turn of the century, for any one Jew to know every other Jew in the state. Marriages linked the families of the early settlers into a complex genealogy that united the Jews for more than religious reasons. Leadville was one place where almost everyone had a relative. Very little intermarriage or conversion plagued the Jews there.

Where Jewish life struggled or was non-existent in the other mining camps, it blossomed in the high altitude. Jewish organizations appeared almost immediately. In 1879 a burial association, the Hebrew Benevolent Association, a B'nai B'rith lodge, and the Reform Congregation Israel were formed. Tabor, always a friend of the Jews, donated the congregation several lots on the corner of West Fourth and Pine, on "Millionaire's Row." The Temple, built in 1884, was a delight to young and old alike, with its arched ceiling decorated with twinkling stars. When the Orthodox group, Kneseth Israel, organized their congregation in 1892, Tabor gave them assistance so that they could purchase a church, which they converted into a synagogue.

In 1882 a cemetery was purchased from the Evergreen Cemetery Association. When the Temple was built, all of the cemetery property was transferred to the congregation, which was incorporated in 1887. The cemetery, shaded by stately pines on a mountain side, served the community and its descendants even after there was only a handful of Jews left in Leadville.

In 1880 the women organized their Hebrew Ladies' Benevolent Association for the purpose of helping the needy, whether Jew or Christian. The organization's elaborate balls were given for charity. The community was impressed not only by the *toilette* of the ladies, but the newspapers also made frequent comments on the Jewish concept of charity: "They do not give the names of those to be benefited, although very worthy, and would get even better attendance."[25] Purim balls and strawberry festivals were social highlights to which the entire community was invited, with the newspapers carrying complete description of the elegant apparel of the ladies. The women had reading and cultural clubs. The Reform Jews subscribed to the *American Israelite* and gave generously to Hebrew Union College and Cleveland Jewish Orphanage. Strangely, the charter of the first B'nai B'rith lodge there, Rocky Mountain Lodge No. 322, was forfeited and the lodge disbanded in 1881 "for having been neglectful of its obligations."[26] In 1903 a new lodge was proposed. Its formation was postponed to the following year because of a typhoid epidemic during which many lives were lost.

Jews remained in the city into the 30's, but Jewish life was almost over by the first World War. When the third and fourth periods of Leadville's life came there was no Jewish movement to the old camp. Only Max Schott, of the American Metal Company, who negotiated the purchase of the mines for the Climax Molybdenum company when "moly" became a vital material, was identified with the later periods of the region's life. In 1951, Miss Minette Miller, when asked for the Jewish community, said, "I am the Jewish community."

In Denver, and probably elsewhere, having lived in Leadville during its heyday became a form of *landsmanshaft*. The friendliness of any Jewish life in the west compared with that of Leadville comes off second best.

5

Most of the ugly, squalid mining camps, with their shacks and sheds, were set against backgrounds of alpine beauty. Few, however, compared with the beautiful setting of Aspen, at the foot of the Sawatch Range, across precipitous Independence Pass from Leadville. In 1949 Aspen was the scene of the Goethe Festival, bringing philospher Albert Schweitzer to the new summer culture seat, on his first visit to the United States. In winter the mountains above the town become a Switzerland for skiers. Hunting and fishing bring travelers to it in the fall and spring.

David Hyman, an eastern capitalist, may have never dreamed of the summer festivals or of the mountain sports when he crossed the range on snowshoes in 1880, but he was immediately impressed by its beauty, writing: "You could not help but exclaim, what a beautiful site for a town." Leadville was booming when Hyman was notified, "There is a tide in the affairs of men, which if taken at its flood, leads on to fortune. We congratulate you. We have drawn upon you at sight for five thousand dollars."

David Hyman's representatives had invested in seven and a half mines in the new area and immediately laid out a townsite of 320 acres, naming it Aspen. In later years, Hyman said, "The story of Aspen is the story of my life." According to the man who attended the birth of the camp, "Aspen was one of the most delightful mining camps in the United States, if not the nicest, and it attained a growth of some 12,000 inhabitants in the years '92 and '93, just prior to the Panic." In 1880 Hyman sold lots for as low as $10, which later were sold for as high as $10,000.[27] Hyman Avenue became the principal thoroughfare in Aspen.

Both Hyman and his wife Betty were very active in the charities in Denver. They are found making donations to the indigent sick,[28] getting the local bathhouse "to set aside one day a week for the wants of the Russian immigrants,"[29] and giving generously to the Jewish Hospital Association.[30] Hyman was a pallbearer at the funeral of Frances Jacobs, whose husband had invested in property near Aspen.[31]

When the question of his title to the Aspen holdings came up, Hyman asked his lawyers, the Colorado senators Henry Teller and Charles J. Hughes, whether his faith as a Jew would stand in the way of protecting his titles. "It was unanimously agreed that they would take care of the question of faith."[32]

The activities of another Jew in Aspen bear repeating. According to Muriel Sibell Wolle in *Stampede to Timberline*, in 1910, when Elias Cohn was the manager of two mines there, one of them became flooded. The pumps, covered by water, could not be put into operation to remove the water. Cohn suggested that deep sea divers be brought, who could dive into the shaft and put the pumps into operation again. Although the idea was ridiculed, his company agreed to send for two divers from New York, who were paid $100 a day, and who successfully put the pumps to work again. Again they became submerged, and again the divers were sent for. After starting them for the second time, the company purchased a diving suit and the divers trained a few miners how to use it and how to reach the pumps.[33]

In the towns which rose and then slumbered there are many

evidences of the Jews who lived there. In Aspen, the lovely mansion of Jacob Sands still stands. The handsome merchant as a bachelor, won the hearts of the ladies in the camps of Gilpin County. Even the beautiful Baby Doe, whose romance with Tabor shocked and fascinated the nation, looked with favor on Jake, when both of them were still in Gilpin County. One story of her life says that it was Jake who brought her to Leadville, where she met Tabor.[34]

6

Aspen lost much of her population, but was revived as a cultural and recreational center to which leading musicians and philosophers have been attracted.

Not all of the mining camps fared so well. Many of them, doomed to oblivion, are not even ghost towns. Dozens of picturesque towns, with equally picturesque names, served as the homes for many Jews in the late nineteenth and early twentieth centuries. In fact, Jewish names are found in practically every town in Colorado that ever had a post office.

In such towns as Tin Cup—where it is said that the cemetery had four separate knolls, "Community, Jews, Catholic, and Boot Division (for those who died with their boots on) "[35]—Buckskin Joe, Bald Mountain, Nevadaville, Hamilton, and Gold Hill, the Jews lived and worked sometimes for as long as the town was in existence. From most of the other towns, which did not become ghost towns, but lost most of their population, the Jews gradually moved away. Such towns included Silver Cliff, Alma, Telluride, Rico, and Crestone.

In the latter category belong the adjoining towns of Victor and Cripple Creek, in the mountain region above Colorado Springs. For a time this was the most important area in the state. When the Panic of 1893 had all but devastated the economy of Colorado, it was the gold of the Cripple Creek-Victor area that saved the state. It was there that Bernard Baruch spent a summer shoveling ore into buckets, and invested in a mine of worthless low grade ore.[36]

In these towns, which were business rivals, the Jews were a united group, with each town taking turns holding High Holiday services in the fall and sharing Sunday school sessions. Almost immediately after the important gold strikes had been made, the Denver secretary of the B'nai B'rith recorded in the minutes of

April 22, 1894: "Bro. Chas. B. Cohen reported that a new society has been started at Cripple Creek for charitable and social purposes, called B'nai Israel, of which he is president."

It is likely that this same society served as a congregation, which is said also to have been called B'nai Abraham. The group was never large enough to acquire a temple or synagogue. For the High Holidays a store was rented, and the religious Jews stayed overnight in the town in which services were being held, to avoid traveling on the holidays. The Orthodox, liberal by the standards of the period, had their kosher meat shipped from Denver. Many a Christian neighbor had chicken for a week-end when the fowl arrived too late to be koshered for the Sabbath.

One B'nai B'rith lodge served both communities. This successful lodge, in terms of interest and attendance, was Cripple Creek District Lodge No. 522, which was installed by the Denver lodge, October 13, 1901. The Cripple Creek lodge lasted until 1912, when the members took withdrawal cards. Seven of them then joined the Denver lodge.

As in Leadville, there was friendliness in the community, regardless of the Jewish settlers' origin. However, there was a shade of snobbery in the German Jewish group that was not found in the same group in Leadville. Perhaps the reason for this was that the larger community demonstrated similar feelings. There was in this mining camp a group of well-educated and wealthy engineers who had little to do with the ordinary miners.

The maximum number of Jews who lived in the mining camps was reached in Central City, Leadville, and Cripple Creek. In the other camps, there were so few Jews that any attempt at Jewish life was impossible. For the High Holidays the Jewish family could go to the closest town with a synagogue or temple. There were enough Jews scattered throughout the state that, from time to time, those Jews too far from the cities with congregations organized services for a large area. Thus, services in Gunnison were attended by Jews on the Western Slope. Sometimes towns in the same area took turns. In South Park, the Jews of Buena Vista, Fairplay, and Salida held services alternately, saving the participants the necessity of crossing a mountain range. During such services the Reform and Orthodox worshipped together.

7

One of the most frequently encountered names, as might be

expected, was Cohen. When these men were discussed, they were identified as "Fairplay Cohen" or "Georgetown Cohen." In Fairplay, Sam Cohen, who was born in Poland and came to Colorado in 1873, was one of the most popular members of the community. Deeply interested in the welfare of Park County, he helped by investing heavily in mining and by grubstaking many prospectors. There he donated a large section of land with picnic facilities which was known as Cohen Park. In addition to storekeeping, he had a thriving lumber business from which he supplied the railroad ties for the Denver and Rio Grande Western when its rails were being laid. Because of the esteem in which he was held, Cohen was the first Republican in the county to be elected to the state legislature in fifteen years.

Like most of the Jews who knew them, he was personally on good terms with individual Indians. One of his customers was the obese and unpleasant Indian Chief Colorow. The settlers were amused when Cohen displayed in his store a "biled" shirt made for the vast Indian.

In the town of Guffey, Sam Cohen's cousin, Gustave Cohen, held the office of justice of the peace. The "Georgetown Cohen" was Louis Cohen, a merchant in the picturesque silver mining camp. Georgetown, with its outstanding examples of Victorian architecture and its famous Hotel de Paris, rose from a rough mining camp to the elegance associated with European nobility. Many a silver king lived in the beautiful town, and several Jews lived there comfortably. A small park in the heart of town is named "Strousse Park," a gift of a Jewish merchant, S. Strousse, who lived there for a long period.

The Cohen of San Luis, and his partner Nat Nathan, were not well-known to the Jews of Denver. Both men operated general merchandise establishments, listed as "Louis Cohen & Co." and "Nathan & Meyer."[37] Both men served in the state legislature from Costilla county.

As a result of the Leadville boom, many Jews came into the state only to find the cloud city well-supplied with merchants. These late-comers fanned out into other likely places. One of these was Silver Cliff, where the Friedheim family opened a general merchandise store. Although Silver Cliff was the third largest town in the state at its peak, it never attracted more than eight or ten Jewish families. There was no Jewish organization, nor is it likely that services were ever held. The Friedheim children attended the Methodist Sunday School. As they grew up and the town's population began its decline to forty inhabitants, the Friedheims left for more likely places to make a living. Alfred Friedheim ventured into Telluride. When he lived in that mining camp, there was but one Jew there. The town boasted one church and twenty saloons. Although it seems that there were never more than two Jews in Telluride at any one time, the number of Jews who lived there at various periods in the 80's and 90's numbers at least a dozen.

In Grand Junction, the rich farm and orchard country, one of the earliest arrivals was Morris Strouse, a young German Jew. At the age of seventeen, he came to the United States and, after living in New York, southern Florida, New Orleans, and Chicago (where he traded for several years for a fur company, traveling into the "wilds" of Iowa and Nebraska), he tried Colorado. In 1861 he married the sister of S. L. Holzman, an early Colorado merchant, and through him became a kinsman to the large Sands family in the West. He was in Colorado when he heard of the townsite on the western edge of the state. With two friends he took a covered wagon west from Canon City. While his companions slept in the wagon, Strouse slept under it in a tarpaulin to protect him against the snow. He opened a clothing store in Grand Junction and built a large fur trade, buying deer and bear skins by the wagonload from the Indians. After a time he added wool to his purchases.

He was on excellent terms with the Indians and was a good friend of Chief Ouray and his family. Scores of Indians, who called the little merchant "my friend heap big little man" and who did business with him for more than forty-five years, attended his funeral. At his death at the age of ninety-three, the local newspaper obituary had a familiar ring:

> A picturesque and lovable figure passes from the life of the city and the western slope . . . not many of his race have ever left settled civilization to come into the raw new west . . . and too few citizens anywhere leave behind them the record of as blameless a life.[38]

It never seems to have occurred to the pioneers that the total number of Jews in Colorado was so small that if more than one Jew lived in every town and camp in the state at the same time, there would not be enough Jews to go around.

TRINIDAD

8.

The oldest congregation outside Denver in continuous existence is the Congregation Aaron in Trinidad. The history of this Jewish community, which built its temple on the old Santa Fe Trail, is an interesting example of the adaptability of the Jews to their environment, while retaining their Jewish identity, especially since all around it intermarriage was eradicating Judaism.

Where ornate and lavish Spanish cathedrals prevail, the simplicity of Colorado's oldest Jewish house of worship still in use is a sharp contrast to the culture of the southwest. Yet the romantic region influenced the Jewish life of the town, which goes back to the earliest years of settlement. There were very few white settlers in the area in the 60's when the first known Jew, a man named M. Wise, arrived in the early part of the decade. At least another six Jews arrived before 1870, and the first Jewish family was established in 1870 with the marriage of Isaac Levy. That year and the following, two young men (apparently miners) from Elizabethtown, New Mexico, helped complete a *minyan* for Yom Kippur. Four more Jews came into the region in 1872.[39] Between 1877 and 1880 the Jewish community numbered about fifteen Jewish families,[40] almost all of whom had come before the railroad.

When the first board of trustees of the newly incorporated town of Trinidad met in 1876, Sam Jaffa, who had been there for four years, was elected the chairman of the group. At the same time Isaac Levy was elected to the board. In the records filled with names of diverse origin, such as Jesus Maria, and Delos, Jewish names appear with frequency and regularity. When the Jewish community was large, the city council always had one or two Jews serving. They still took an active part in every phase of city life even when there was only a handful of them left. In 1952, at the time of his death, Gilbert Sanders, the leader of the Jewish community, was a county judge.

When the coal mining industry began its greatest activity, a B'nai B'rith lodge was chartered in 1878 with twenty-nine members. At the birth of Arthur G. Jaffa, in 1883, the Congregation Aaron with eighteen members was organized, and when the charter was signed, there were fifty-five names on the document. That fall the first services of the temple were held in the Opera House at two dollars a seat. That same year the first cemetery meeting was held. The Jews, who were prominent in the Masonic organizations in the city, bought two and a half acres of land adjoining the Masonic cemetery.

In 1887, Temple Aaron was begun. A Hebrew Ladies' Aid Society, which became the Temple Sisterhood, was formed in 1889, opening its fund-raising activities with a strawberry festival. In 1894 a cultural group, the Montifiore Literary Society, was founded.[41]

Jewish life flourished in the small city on the Purgatoire River. One of the reasons was the strong leadership it had from the first. Distinguished service to the state, to Judaism, and Trinidad was given, among others, by the Freudenthal family. Invited by the directors of the Congregation, Rabbi Leopold Freudenthal, a graduate of Heidelberg, accepted the rabbinate and served the congregation from 1889 until the date of his death in 1916. His record of ritual circumcisions is at the Hebrew Union Archives.

His sons' activities in Trinidad were many and varied. Sam, an attorney and state legislator, brought books into the city for its libraries, helped establish junior colleges throughout the state, and brought to Trinidad Colorado's first junior college in 1927. Alfred, a physician, gave liberally to his city during his life as well as after his death. The popular doctor, who accepted no fees from the poverty-stricken of the area and frequently gave them money instead, left half a million dollars in an unusual will.

To his attorney, Gilbert Sanders, he gave a nine-word will: "All of my estate I give to Temple Aaron." The money was used to establish the Alfred Freudenthal Memorial Trust Fund and Foundation, which assists the churches of twenty-four different denominations, service clubs, and goodwill efforts. Milk, glasses, books, and scholarships are given to needy children. The impressive list of beneficiaries of the Foundation has been helped by the interest alone—the principal of the foundation has never been touched.

From Trinidad came Joseph Jaffa, an outstanding lawyer. He served on the board of trustees of the Colorado School of Mines at the time Senator Guggenheim made his gift of $75,000 to the school. Leo Gottlieb, president of the Colorado School for the Deaf and Blind in Colorado Springs, for whom a building was named, was also identified with politics.

Unlike the population of the mountain camps, the Trinidad population appeared to be stable. During the years when gold and silver towns vanished, the coal town and Temple Aaron flourished. With 10,000 miners in the coal fields, there were as many as 550 Jews in the area before 1920. That year the Temple was modernized and steam heat and organ music added for the physical and spiritual comfort of the congregation.

But even coal mining was not an enduring industry. In the depression years that followed, Trinidad lost most of its Jewish population. By 1950 there were but seven Jewish families in the city, three of whom were descendants of the original founders of the congregation. In 1949 three anniversaries were celebrated for them by the Temple: the eightieth of Leo Gottlieb, the seventieth of Albert Moses, and the sixtieth of Gilbert Sanders.

Until his death, Gilbert Sanders was the "lay-rabbi" of the Temple. He gave weekly broadcasts over the local radio station for the Temple, acted as president of the Freudenthal Foundation, the Aaron Cemetery Association, and the Temple itself. He was awarded just prior to his death, the degree Doctor of Letters by Hebrew Union College. Like most of the Jews in Trinidad, Sanders spoke Spanish, and as an attorney he represented the Catholic Church in legal matters.

The civic and social life of the community continues as though it had a large Jewish community. The meeting rooms of all of the women's clubs belonging to the City Federation are in the Temple Aaron, which also sponsors an interfaith tea for the club women regularly. While Reform, the congregation never moved so far to the left as the Reform congregation in Denver. The women support Hadassah and attend the organization's functions in Denver. The United Jewish Appeal and other Jewish causes are helped by the Foundation. The Trinidad Jews refuse to let Judaism die. With the help of the Foundation, if, or when, Jews come to the little city again, they will find Jewish institutions waiting for them.

This was demonstrated during World War II, when the United States government brought into the area a prisoner-of-war camp, with sixty Jewish boys from Brooklyn to guard the indignant German prisoners. There was life in the Temple again, with the delighted congregation purchasing *yarmulkes* (skullcaps) for the Orthodox boys and arranging for the weddings of five of them while stationed there.

Not all of the Jews of the area are as interested in the Temple as the Brooklyn boys were. When invitations are sent to the Jews of the neighboring towns for the High Holidays, with distinguished speakers like Dr. Jacob Marcus, Dr. Abraham Cronbach, and its own former rabbi, Martin Weitz, few of them respond. The Orthodox prefer to go to Pueblo where there is an Orthodox-Conservative congregation. The others simply are not interested.

FOOTNOTES

[1] *RMN*, May 12, 1862.
[2] *RMN*, May 26, 1862.
[3] *RMN*, June 19, 1862.
[4] *RMN*, May 3, 1861.
[5] *RMN*, May 8, 1861.
[6] *RMN*, May 22, 1861.
[7] *RMN*, Oct. 26, 1860.
[8] *RMN*, Aug. 28, 1861.
[9] Jerome Smiley, *Semi-Centennial History of Colorado*
[10] S. Kline, *op. cit.*
[11] *RMN*, Sept. 23, 1870.
[12] Thomas E. Carmody, "Robert E. Levy," Reprinted from the Annals of Otology, Rhinology and Laryngology. Sept., 1945, Vol. 54, No. 3, p. 615.
[13] *RMN*, Aug. 24, 1879. In the long list of names of "Men of Means," and the amount on which each was taxed, the following appears:

"Appel & Co. $7,100
Albert Abel 5,980
S. L. Holzman 7,630
J. Holzman 6,750
A. Jacobs & Co. 7.300
I. H. Castor [Sic] 6,750
Wolf Londoner [Sic] 15,680
Julius Londoner 5,780
Edward Pisco [Sic] 7,000
S. Rose & Co. 10,650
Salomon Bros. 21,000
Wineman & Guldman 5,100
B. A. Wisebart .... 9,050"

[14] J. E. Smith, *op. cit.*
[15] *RMN*, Sept 12, 1882, p. 4.
[16] *JO, op. cit.*, Nov. 24, 1905.
[17] Interview, Mrs. Fred Meyers.
[18] Dixon Wechter, *Saga of American Society*.
[19] *JO*, Oct. 14, 1904. Also, Mr. William Guggenheim of New York married Amy Steinberger of the Metropole Hotel.
[20] *JO*, Nov. 18, 1904.
[21] *JO*, March 3, 1905.
[22] *RMN*, Sept. 13, 1925.
[23] *RMN*, Nov. 26, 1948.
[24] *RMN*, Sept. 24, 1881.
[25] *RMN*, Oct. 17, 1881.

[26] BB minutes, July 10, 1881.
[27] David Marks Hyman, "The Romance of a Mining Venture," courtesy of the American Jewish Archives.
[28] DPL clipping file, no source, Dec. 20, 1892.
[29] *Israelite*, No date, 1892. Wm. S. F. Scrapbook.
[30] *Israelite*, Dec. 4, 1894.
[31] *Republican*, Nov. 7, 1892.
[32] Hyman, *op. cit.*
[33] Wolle, *op. cit.*
[34] Caroline Bancroft, *Famous Aspen*, p. 39.
[35] Wolle, *op. cit.*, p. 184.
[36] William L. White, *Bernard Baruch, Portrait of a Citizen*.
[37] *Colorado State Business Directory*, 1881. The Meyer referred to may have been Ferdinand Meyer, a Jewish pre-territorial trader from New Mexico.
[38] *Grand Junction Sentinel*, Nov. 1, 1928.
[39] *JO*, Nov. 11, 1905, "Jews in the Country Towns of Colorado." Also Sol Jaffa on the Jews of Trinidad, David Gottlieb interview, State Historical Society, CWA, 1933, 1934.
[40] U. S. Census, 1880 lists at least 20 Jewish men in Trinidad.
[41] Temple Aaron Biblette, Nov. 11, 1949.

"Papa Had a Cold"

1

On the heels of the gold-seekers came the health-seekers. The same vivid blue skies and sunny days, the invigorating clear air that had stimulated the healthy miners like good wine, was the medicine for which the victims of tuberculosis rushed in as great a number as the Argonauts to the gold fields.

From the earliest days the community had been faced with the problem created by the respiratory sick, but the stigma attached to the disease was so great that it has rarely been documented. How many people came for their health and gave as their reasons the lure of the West—adventure or gold—will never be known. Even their descendants will say more often than not, "Papa had a cold, and the doctors sent him West."

It was apparent from the first that this was a community problem, but the individual sectarian charities tried to handle it for their groups alone. The Jewish group, burdened with the "normal" type of charity problems, was faced also with the long-drawn out disaster: the coughing, spitting, hemorrhaging sick.

Charity in the Jewish community had begun with the first burial and prayer society, out of which grew the more permanent Hebrew Benevolent Society in 1871. The next year the Hebrew Ladies Relief Society was formed under the leadership of Mrs. Delphine Cohen. The men and women worked together as early as 1876. Both groups merged into the Jewish Relief Society in 1900. Aside from local routine relief problems, the Jews throughout the state were called upon to raise funds for the Cleveland Jewish Orphanage, for the victims of the Chicago fire, the Central City fire, the San Francisco earthquake, and the various benefits for actors and musicians.

The Jewish group confronted another problem not met by the other charities. In 1881, the Jews of Russia were faced with annihilation. Not only were the Colorado Jews asked to raise funds for relief, but also they were called upon to take part in rehabilitating the immigrants who were coming West during the heat of the Russian terror. With all of the charity problems confronting the small group of Jews in Denver, it was small wonder that the president of the Temple sent out a warning to Russian emigrants not to come to Colorado.[1]

While Denver was receiving, with some aversion, the East European Jews, it was a far more reluctant host to the ever-increasing stream of respiratory sick. Medical opinion at the latter part of the nineteenth century prescribed the salutory effects of mountain climes. Denver, a mile above sea level, was believed to be such a place where a cure could be effected. In the East the doctors ordered the trip West. The indigent, who had no doctors, were well aware of the prevailing medical belief. They were encouraged by the Eastern charities—anxious to be ridded of their unwelcome dependents—with gifts of one-way tickets to Denver.

In the minutes of the B'nai B'rith are the names of the many sick brothers who came to Colorado. These presented no problem for the Jewish community, for the mother lodges of these men paid for their care. The problem was the indigent sick foisted on the Denver Jewish community. Angrily the lodge recorded in 1874, after the United Hebrew Relief societies of Chicago had sent an invalid to Denver without means:

> After considerable debate, during which the injustice and impracticability perpetrated by said and similar associations east, toward our Jewish community, which is comparatively speaking, poor . . . viz; sending to us such parties without first providing the necessary means for them, without which they cannot live, unless they become a heavier burden to us than we can stand. . . .[2]

the secretary was told to notify the Chicago charities of the sentiments of the lodge. But the stream of tuberculous increased. The lodge thought of curtailing its other contributions because, "Our geographical situation is such that we must be prepared at all times for such emergencies . . . calls for assistance from other places should only be responded to in extreme cases."[3]

The first attempt to solve the problem by the B'nai B'rith was recorded May 12, 1878:

> Resolved that a committee of five be appointed to correspond with all Jewish Congregations and Jewish secret societies in the United States for the purpose of assisting this Lodge to erect a building for sick and needy Israelites which are sent here from all over the United States to recover their health.

The problem was certainly not confined to the Jews. The words *consumption* and *tuberculosis*, when the latter word became the designatory word for the disease, were almost banned from the newspapers. They appear only seven times in the news columns of the *Rocky Mountain News* from the early 60's to the late 80's.[4] It was bad enough, the newspapers reasoned, that the hordes of sick were descending upon Denver; with any publicity the city would be deluged. With the hospitals of the state making no secret of the fact that they would take no patients for the treatment of "consumption," and private boarding houses becoming increasingly wary of their tenants, the charities of the city wrestled with the problem, which in the late 80's was impossible to ignore. Not mentioning the disease by name the *Republican* reported that, "The town is getting to be a sanitarium."[5]

At a meeting of the Associated Charities in Denver, October 29, 1889, J. S. Appel, the organization's president, introduced the hospital topic, and offered a resolution, "That the city of Denver be petitioned to appropriate $5,000 for the year 1890, toward support of a hospital to be erected by the Associated Charities." One woman guaranteed $10,000 toward the building of a hospital for the "contagious." Next a local bishop offered forty-eight lots on Berkeley Lake, under the care of the Sisters of St. Francis.[6] The Denver *Republican* editorialized on the bishop's generous offer, but did not approve its acceptance, preferring that the hospital be in the hands of the Associated Charities, so that "it could always be investigated and scrutinized."[7]

While the Associated Charities were debating and considering these proposals, the Temple Emanuel decided to submit to its membership the question of building a hospital for the use of the sick Jewish people of the country, "particularly those, who of necessity, are sent here to obtain the benefit of Colorado climate."[8] A mass meeting of the "Hebrew Citizens" was called for November 3 at the Temple to consider the erection of a hospital for the "Jewish sick of the United States."[9]

On November 15, the *Republican* carried the story of the adopting of a charter by a newly organized, "Jewish Hospital Association." Thus was proposed a hospital for the treatment of "zymotic" diseases, under Jewish management, non-sectarian, and for the purpose of alleviating suffering. The optimistic Jewish community of 500, and certainly not more than "800 Israelites," calculated how funds would be obtained. It was suggested that twenty-five persons pay $100 each. An estimated five hundred clerks would be asked to give $10 each, and with funds obtained throughout the region a total of $10,000 was expected. Almost immediately $5560 was raised. Committees were appointed to solicit donations in the East European Orthodox group in West Denver, in the rest of the state, throughout the nation, and from foreign countries.[10]

The community of Denver was pleased with the Jewish plan. The *Republican* commented in its editorial columns that it believed that the number of Israelites in the city was great enough to erect and maintain the hospital liberally, and suggested that others could copy Jewish charity.[11] In December, the Temple's Rabbi Friedman, who had been in the city three months, left for Trinidad, where he dedicated a new temple, and went on with Henry Frankle, the president of the Jewish Hospital Association, and Frankle's wife into the Southwest, where they raised $750 in Las Vegas, $550 in Albuquerque, $400 in Santa Fe. Back in Colorado they raised $1000 in less than five minutes in Leadville.[12]

The following April, the twenty-one most prominent Jews in the state, many of them leaders in the Temple Emanuel in Denver, filed articles of incorporation for a Jewish Hospital Association. Even then, the document did not mention the name of the disease for which the hospital was being erected.[13] In June lots were purchased, and that year ground was broken. After two years, the cornerstone was laid on October 9, 1892, amid "exercises attended by several thousand people of all denominations, and the cable and electric car lines were taxed to full capacity, while the route to the site was lined with carriages."[14] Finally the disease was mentioned by name when Rabbi Friedman described the scope of the hospital:

> As pain knows no creed, so is this building the prototype of the grand idea of Judaism, which casts aside no stranger, no matter of what race or blood. This institution was inaugurated for the treatment of consumption mainly, particular attention will be paid to these cases.[15]

The completed hospital was simply known as the Jewish Hospital. It was about to be opened when, in November, the "Mother of the Charities," Frances Wisebart Jacobs, died.

2

While the Jews, as well as the other religious and national groups, were battling their charity problems through their benevolent societies, a few visionaries among them saw that many of these problems were community-wide. Because there was already in the early 80's much overlapping in the way of services and financial help, these leaders believed that only by unified charity would the charity problems of Denver be solved. The name of one woman, the wife of an early pioneer, became synonymous with charity, and attained the highest form of recognition the state had to offer for her labors in the unifying and expanding of all charity work in Denver. This was Frances Wisebart Jacobs, the wife of Abraham Jacobs. In 1863 Jacobs left his partner, Benjamin Wisebart, in Central City, while he traveled the long pioneer route back to Cincinnati, where he married his partner's sister, and returned with his bride across the wilderness and into the frontier mining camp.

Through the years that followed, her husband's prominence and reputation for integrity, her brother's successful civic and political carrer, and her own commanding, yet amiable personality, were the basis for a hearty welcome into the most exclusive social circles in the state. Social prestige was not what Frances Jacobs sought. She seems to have lived quietly until the late 70's, when her children were out of babyhood. During these years the limelight was on her husband, whose activities took him throughout the state.

The indefatigable pioneer, whose movements have been described in the years of the gold rush, continued at an energetic pace. He moved his store from Denver to Central City and remained there several years, also investing in property in Golden, Georgetown, and Highland (seven miles south of Aspen). He inaugurated the Denver and Santa Fe Stage Line in 1867. For three years Jacobs carried the mail south at no charge. According to the *News*, "Few men would have carried it for so long without pay." The newspaper suggested that the citizens "get up a petition that Jacobs be properly paid for his past and future services."[16] His friend, Fred Z., circulated petitions for mail service throughout the territory. By Jacobs' stage line, which consisted of four Concord coaches, the mail was received in Denver from Trinidad in thirty-six hours, and from Santa Fe in four days. The established mail service, which he sought to replace, delivered the mail in a week from Trinidad, and ten days from Santa Fe. Nevertheless, he was unable to obtain a mail contract, and in 1869 he discontinued the unprofitable venture.

From 1865 to 1875, he had two clothing stores, one in Denver and one in Central City. A year after the Central City fire, he left the mountain town and thereafter concentrated all his efforts on his O. K. Clothing Store in Denver. Here, he again took an active part in non-partisan politics, and in charitable and other civic undertakings. His family took part on the reception committee welcoming President Grant to Denver in 1880, and he served as president of the Pioneer Association at the time of its Quarto-Centennial in 1884. Until his death in 1913, when he was the state's oldest Mason, he was a living symbol of the pioneer lodge.

Jacobs joined the B'nai B'rith lodge in Denver and became its president in 1881. That year the lodge voted for Mrs. Jacobs as one of the fifteen directors of the district for the Cleveland Orphan Asylum. Despite this, when Frances Jacobs died in 1892, her death was not mentioned in the minutes, nor were condolences sent the bereaved family by the lodge.

Tragedy struck the Jacobs family in several forms. The Central City fire left Jacobs' store in ashes with a loss of $50,000. In 1885 his clothing store in Denver failed. The crowning tragedy of the family was the loss of a son. Even before his wife's death in 1892, Abraham Jacobs faded into the background. In 1900 he was suspended for non-payment of dues by the B'nai B'rith lodge, although efforts had been made by the lodge to retain him for as long as possible. The man who was on the committee to draft a constitution for Denver, who had served on its first board of education, and who had been a symbol of moderation and good citizenship, at the age of sixty-nine was employed as a dump guard by the Board of Public Health and Safety.[17] At the age of seventy-nine he died leaving only his unmarried daughter, Evelyn, then principal of the 29th Street Primary School.[18]

Still he was not entirely forgotten. A few pioneers still reminisced about him, and one suggested naming a street for him. It was his wife, however, who reached Colorado's Hall of Fame.

An early item concerning Frances Jacobs is found in 1877 in the Denver newspapers. She was invited to sing at the Unity Chapel,[19] and later to recite "Shamus O'Brien" at the Maennerchor.[20] These, like her annual New Years Day receptions and other social activities, were directed towards fulfilling her mission, charity. Denver's charity work, although early begun, had not achieved its first charitable institution until 1872, with the Denver Orphan's Home, the city's first non-sectarian relief organization. The Jewish women had formed the Hebrew Benevolent Ladies Aid Society that year. As its president, possibly the second one, Mrs. Jacobs found not only that the problems were too vast for one organization, but also that they were not Jewish problems. She believed that charity was to come from everyone and to be given to any who needed it. While retaining her interest in the Jewish group, she began to work at all levels of civic charity, from the top, where her "elocutionary powers made her an attraction" and loosened the purse strings of the community, to the "bottoms," where she assumed the menial responsibility of disbursing the funds. Until the time of her death, she walked through the dust, the mud and rain, and the snow and ice, into the filthy, poverty-ridden shacks. There she was as likely to clean up a squalid home as to berate a "shiftless beggar, or a worthless, intemperate husband."[21]

The Ladies' Relief Society, formed in 1874, recognized her worth. She became an officer immediately and so served until the time of her death. Still there was no unified charity in Denver. The efforts were accelerated during the next decade. In 1881, Denver held its first charity ball,[22] which her family helped stage. From that time on there was a steady effort to combine and unify the charity work. By 1887, Denver had a population of 79,000, as compared to 4,759 in 1870.

The Ladies' Relief Society was an important force by the time it held its fourth public meeting at the Tabor Grand Opera House in 1887. More than 2000 came to the meeting, and many were turned away from the overflowing opera house. The twenty-two different charities were considered, and the idea already in the minds of some of them was formulated by Rev. Myron Reed and Father William O'Brien. The two men discussed their idea and "sought and found Mrs. Frances Jacobs, first vice-president of the Ladies' Relief Society, and a woman who shared their ideas. . . . These three formed a tri-unity, and the start toward the organization of Denver's charity." They were joined by Dean Martin Hart and another Catholic priest. Hart, who was from London, had some background in the English idea of federation.[23] Together these five achieved the first federation in Denver, The Charity Organization Society in 1887, and possibly, despite other claims,[24] the first successful plan for financing a federated charitable organization, through which teams of workers solicited men in different lines of business and other citizens to raise a set sum.

For fifty years, others than these five have been honored as the founders of the Community Chest in Denver. The most popular and recurring acknowledgment is to: "two Protestant ministers, a Catholic priest, and a Jewish rabbi." There was no rabbi in the group. Frances Jacobs was the "Queen of the Charities" and the founder of the forerunner of the Comunity Chest. The C. O. S., as it was called, became a federation of most of the philanthropic societies and institutions of the city. The Hebrew Ladies' Benevolent Society was one of the thirteen charter members Until her death, Frances Jacobs served as secretary of the C. O. S.

The organizations which joined the C. O. S. became better organized and more efficient in their charity work. For the Jews, however, the receipts could not possibly cover the amount that was needed. In 1889, the Hebrew Ladies' Benevolent Society received $1,200 from the C. O. S. That year it assisted 523 persons, or 150 familes, at an expense of $1,975. There was no abatement in the needs of the Jewish group, as the Jewish community kept growing with more East Europeans fleeing from Russia and leaving the sweatships of the East, where they had been stricken by tuberculosis. The C. O. S. allotment was increased to $1,800 yearly during the first decade of the twentieth century, still not enough to meet the abnormal needs of the Jewish community.[25]

Specifically the labors of Frances Jacobs took many forms. The newspapers recorded the activities, and eloquence, of "Mrs. A. Jacobs, the Queen of Charity Work," in championing the cause of little children. She had been so impressed with the Golden Gate kindergarten in San Francisco that she induced the citizens of Denver to establish the Free Kindergarten Association. As president of the Ladies' Relief Society in 1890, she explained the situation confronting the homeless women of the city, and made an appeal for an adequate home for working women in Denver. When the newspapers boasted of the eight-hour day under which men were working, Mrs. Jacobs urged the girls of the city to band together, form organizations, and make similar demands. She asked that the existing employment office, a filthy place, be cleaned up, that it be required to register every job to which a girl was sent, and that the girl know what wages she would get. From a moral standpoint, she wanted the office to act with responsibility, for too many girls had been sent to jobs that "ruined them for life." She told of little girls that she had talked to "of 12, 15, and up to 17 years of age, who knew more of the vices and immorality than I may tell you of in a lifetime."

At the same time she denied an accusation that the Ladies' Relief Corps discriminated against Catholics. In the previous two weeks, she had visited fifteen families, of which five were Catholic. "What can I do for you, in what way can we help you?" she said was the way in which the needy were approached, not with "What is your religion?"[26]

Collecting clothes for the poor at her home, investigating the charitable agencies, including the Newsboy's home, pressing for the establishment of relief homes for the sick and aged, was still not all she wanted to do. One of the things Frances Jacobs longed for was a hospital built for the victims of tuberculosis she encountered daily. Her pleas were made to the entire communiy, and she begged the newspapers to help her. On this score she met a stone wall. She continued to do what she could, stopping to help a hemorrhage victim on the streets, and calling the police surgeon. Frequently she had to call for her own doctor, whom she paid from her own purse.

In 1883 she sponsored a hospital benefit,[27] but her vision of a community hospital was to take another form. The Jewish Hospital was completed in 1892 at the cost of $42,000. That year, at the age of forty-nine, Frances Jacobs died.

Her death was a blow to Denver, to the towns outside the city which she had guided in their charity efforts, and to the National Conference of Charities and Corrections, where she had annually represented Denver. The funeral services were held in Temple Emanuel and were officiated by the rabbi and three leading Christian clergymen. Two thousand people, representing nine organizations and all departments of the city and state government, came to pay their last respects to her. The following week memorial services were held at the First Congregational Church, with addresses delivered by the governor, mayor, and the leaders of the community. The C.O.S. published a memoir containing most

of the words spoken about her, "as a token of its appreciation."
That Frances Jacobs was praised and loved was well-known, but on this occasion she was also defended of all the censure that had been whispered about her:

> Mrs. Jacobs had a wonderful gift in her power to deal with repulsive people. She was freed from all bondage of prejudice. It has been said that she was not fastidious nor particular in her tastes. But it was as hard for her as for anyone to live in daily contact with misery and want and uncleanness—only her heart was too full and her hands too busy to permit any natural feeling of disgust....
> Her keen sense of humor was a great help to her. Her nature was sunny. She saw the bright side of everything. She appreciated a comical situation. Her capacity to turn everything into a jest caused some people to misunderstand her....
> She had little time for the outward observances of religion. She cared little for creeds and ceremonies. Not the beliefs she held, nor the prayers she said, nor the day she observed, but the thing she did was her religion. Her faith was in deed and not in word.... She had seen face to face more people in trouble of all sorts than anyone in Denver.[28]

Denver was at its bawdiest and filthiest, and at a period of rapid growth, when Frances Jacobs laid the foundations for the charity work for the leading city of the region. She had accomplished this through her own credo: "How are you to have that sympathy for the poor, miserable creatures whom you meet? It is only by having a oneness with man and God."[29] She had given her life for charity. Overworked, her resistance low, she had taken cold, peritonitis set in, and she never recovered.

The deeply-moved communal leaders passed many resolutions. J. S. Appel, a co-worker with her in the Associated Charities, hinted at one proposal when he expressed his hope for the time "when, in our beloved Denver, that she loved so well, shall arise a structure over whose doors shall be inscribed, The Frances Jacobs Memorial Hospital." To her husband and daughter were tendered resolutions by the Women's Christian Temperance Union, of which she was an honorary member. To her daughter, the Girls' Benefit Club expressed their sympathies, "All . . . have felt her unswerving integrity and elevated character through the sterling principles of her daughter." One of the girls who signed the document was Mary F. Lathrop, who subsequently became the nation's first outstanding woman attorney.

The most significant resolution was passed by the Jewish Hospital Association, which had decided to name the newly constructed Jewish Hospital, "The Frances Jacobs Hospital."

3

Frances Jacobs' name was placed on the hospital building. It was not only a fine memorial to her, but considering her great popularity with the non-Jewish community, it would also bring in contributions to the Jewish non-sectarian hospital.[30] There is no way of knowing whether this would have been true. The next year was 1893, the year of the "Great Panic." There were no funds for hospitals in the almost bankrupt state. In 1896 Rabbi Friedman, David May, and Edward Monash (uncle of Sir John Monash) went east, but the three imposing young men were unsuccessful in obtaining funds. The hospital needed $15,000 for yearly expenses, and although Denver had raised almost three times that amount for the original investment, there were no funds from the nation.

The unfairness of the situation was voiced in the leading Denver dailies. Said one, "The distinguishing characteristic of the Jewish people is their loyal devotion to the sick and poor of their own race, but the Jews of Denver are doing a quadruple share of the work."[31] More and more frequently the Denver group approached the eastern charities, whom they reminded that, since they had sent the sick west originally, it was their duty to pay for the patients' maintenance through support of the hospital.

Ironically, the newspapers in which the words *consumption* and *tuberculosis* had been taboo suddenly began to dramatize the situation to the embarrassment of the Jews. One story, a month after Frances Jacobs died, carried the headline, "Toward the Sunset. From the Russian Steppes to the foot of the Rockies. The Rugged Journey of the Solomons from New York to Baltimore, Baltimore to St. Louis, St. Louis to Kansas City, Kansas City to Denver." The head of the family, a "consumptive," his lame wife, and their six children, aged one to ten, were too much for the Jews to care for, and according to the newspaper, the "Russian Benevolent Society threw up its hands." Said the newspaper, the society had to draw the line after so many such cases.[32]

The story was hotly refuted by Rabbi Friedman a few days later. The Hebrew Benevolent Ladies Society and a few interested individuals raised enough money to keep the family in Denver.[33] This, however, was only one case. How many Jews died and were buried in paupers' graves is not known. Only for a figure like poet David Edelstadt, whose body was buried in a pauper's grave, was a search made, many years after his death in 1896.

Finally the hospital association made a plea that a national organization take it over. First the directors of the national Council for Jewish Women studied the possibilities. While they were considering the proposition, the B'nai B'rith lodge in Denver presented the same idea to the national order. Six years after the hospital was completed, the B'nai B'rith opened the doors of the hospital, which it dedicated in December, 1899, as the National Jewish Hospital for Consumptives. Frances Jacobs' name was removed from the building. The mayor, speaking on the significance of the dedication, said:

> It consummates the work begun years ago by one of Denver's noble pioneer women, Mrs. Frances Jacobs, but on a broader and more extended scale than she had planned. While the "Frances Jacobs Hospital" will not exist in name, it will be a pleasure to know that out of her efforts has grown an institution, national in its scope, and dedicated to the humane and charitable work in which during her lifetime she so earnestly engaged.

As the hospital acquired more and more buildings, the original building was renamed in 1916 the William S. Friedman Building. Commenting then on the original change of name, a writer signed "H. C." wrote, "It might be said by a parity of reasoning by calling an institution international it would enlist aid from abroad or, to go further, and call it universal and thus invite interstellar contributions."[34] The building was torn down in 1948.

Frances Jacobs was not forgotten. The Board of Capitol Managers, of which Otto Mears was chairman, was deciding upon the sixteen outstanding pioneers of the state to be honored with stained glass windows in the interior of the gold-plated dome of the new state capitol building. Without dissent, and at the very time her name was being removed from the hospital, she was the only woman chosen for the honor.

The nineteenth century, the West, and the ancient concept of *tsdokoh* had produced a mighty figure. Another such figure, the embodiment of compassion, of Hebraic *rachmonis* would make such a mark in the twentieth century. Although he was in Denver before the century ended, much would take place before the community would be aware of Charles David Spivak.

FOOTNOTES

[1] *Jewish World Hamagid*, Vol. 26, 1882, courtesy American Jewish Archives.
[2] BB minutes, Oct. 11, 1874.
[3] *Ibid.*, Jan. 14, 1877, p. 252.
[4] The *Rocky Mountain News* is topically indexed from 1865 to about 1885 at the Western History Department of the Denver Public Library. Six of the references appear in the years 1872-5, and one in 1881. However, the advertising columns carry "cures" for "consumption" along with those for other diseases. *Times*, Apr. 25, 1892, "Koch's lymph" was advertised among other cures at the "Denver Sanitarium for Consumption." *American Israelite*, Apr. 2, 1891, reports that "Dr. A. J. Mauer has opened his hospital for consumptives." Courtesy American Jewish Archives.
[5] *Republican*, Oct. 29, 1889, p. 3.
[6] *Ibid.*, Nov. 5, 1889, p. 7.
[7] *Ibid.*, Nov. 6, 1889, p. 4.
[8] Emanuel minutes, Oct. 17, 1889 (from brochure).
[9] *Ibid.*, Oct. 20, 1889 (from brochure).
[10] *Republican*, Nov. 22, 1889.
[11] *Ibid.*, Nov. 16, 1889, p. 4.
[12] *Times*, Dec. 17, 1889.
[13] Art. Inc., Apr. 7, 1890. The board "reserves the power to exclude such diseases impedient to admit."
[14] Milton Anfenger, *Birth of a Hospital*, p. 17; *RMN*, Oct. 10, 1892.
[15] *Ibid.*, p. 17-18.
[16] *RMN*, Mar. 20, 1868, p. 1.
[17] *Denver City Directories*, 1900-1910.
[18] Records, Denver Public Schools.
[19] *RMN*, Mar. 10, 1877, p. 3.
[20] *RMN*, April 8, 1877, p. 4.
[21] *Memoir of Mrs. Frances Jacobs*.
[22] *RMN*, Oct. 28, 1881, p. 2; Nov. 11, 1881, p. 4.
[23] John C. Fleming, "Golden Anniversary of the Community Chest," 1887-1937.
[24] Abraham Cronbach, "Jewish Pioneering in American Social Welfare," *American Jewish Archives*, June, 1951, p. 51.
[25] *RA op. cit.*, p. 49.
[26] *Republican*, April 2, 1890.
[27] *RMN*, July 29, 1883, p. 3.
[28] *Memoir, op. cit.*
[29] *Ibid.*
[30] *Smiley, op. cit.* p. 776: "Her friends decided to make the hospital a memorial to her and contributed $8000 to its funds, and it is because of this that the institution is commonly known as the Frances Jacobs' Hospital." Her niece, Mrs. Theresa Jarecki says that while Mrs. Jacobs was alive she

obtained a great many contributions from Cincinnati before the building was completed. Her husband did not sign the charter of the hospital in 1890. However, according to the BB minutes he was sick at both the time of the preceeding and following meeting when the charter was signed.

[31] *RMN*, July 29, 1897, p. 5.
[32] DPL clipping file, Dec. 11, 1892.
[33] DPL clipping file, Dec. 20, 1892. See Mrs. David Hyman.
[34] *DJN*, June 23, 1916.

Benevolence, Brotherly Love and Harmony

1

There was nothing particularly "Jewish" about the social life of the pioneer Jews in the West. Since they were among those who brought Eastern manners into the raw frontier and were founders of the Masonic lodges and literary clubs, they were leaders in the early social life of the pioneer community. Just when a separate Jewish social life began is hard to determine. It may have been the result of the exclusion of the Jews from the social clubs in 1881, as will be described later, or it may have started with the establishment of their own private club possibly as early as 1876.

For recreation the Jews partook in the same activities as the larger community. As pioneers their lives were exciting enough, but they added hair-raising escapades into the unknown mountains, took boatrides down uncharted streams, and played boisterous tricks upon each other. With the coming of their women their hardships were softened. They attended the plays at the theatre on the Platte River, took part in musical and cultural programs, and gave banquets and receptions on all possible occasions. Outside Denver at least two halls were owned by Jews, the Schoenberg Opera House in Leadville and Wisebart Hall in Central City.

"Behind a pair of fast trotters," the young men and women went on sleighing parties.[1] They still attended the costume balls at the Turnverein after they were restricted from the fashionable clubs. The children were not overlooked. Many of them attended dancing school with the daughters of Denver's leading citizens. They, too, came in costume to the "Children's Carnival," not unlike those worn by their parents at the *Bals Masque*.

One of the most "elegant" social affairs ever held in early Denver was the opening of the Tabor Grand Opera House in

1881. The dress of the occupants of the various boxes was painstakingly described. In the lengthy list, profuse with the names of leaders of the state, were listed many Jews, including, "Mrs. A. Jacobs, black silk, diamond jewelry, cardinal flowers."[2]

Despite the vast distance to the East there was a great deal of travel, with the Westerners bringing back more young people on their return from the "states." Proudly, they showed them and Eastern visitors, the scenic wonders of the Rockies. The coming of the railroad stimulated more travel into the mountains and more visiting throughout the state. Certain spots seem to have been particularly popular with the Jews. Dome Rock, Meadow Park and Table Mountain (near Golden) were favorites for all-day picnics. Organizations and private parties brought their bands to play at the pavilions provided there. The never-ending parade of visiting celebrities was offered the thrill of the Georgetown Loop, the Moffat road, the Garden of the Gods and the Cave of the Winds. The scores of mineral springs throughout the state became fashionable gathering places.

In Denver there were "Moonlight Tallyho parties in the Columbia coach;"[3] rides in the Denver Horse Car, for those of lesser means, and the entertainment added by the creation of an amusement park on the shore of Sloan's Lake called Manhattan Beach. During the years of its existence there was a hotel on the grounds, a steamer on the lake, a theater seating 3,000, a zoo, roller rink, elaborate gardens and fountains, roller coaster, and a grandstand seating 2,000 alongside a large athletic field. When the theater burned in 1908 interest began to fade.[4] A mile to the north a new theater was opened in Elitch's Gardens, where the outstanding actors of America played summer stock. The coming of the automobile changed entertaining. The proud owners gave automobile parties for their groups and were on call to entertain delegates to the Jewish conventions held in Denver.

While the Jews were excluded from the "Sacred 36" who guided Denver's social life, and from most of the social clubs, the social registers published their names and the rosters of their clubs. There was no exclusion from the civic celebrations. They served on the committees welcoming U. S. Grant on his two visits to the state, for which not mere red carpets were spread, but silver bricks in Central City and Georgetown, and Brussels carpet in Denver. They attended a banquet for T. R. Roosevelt given by

129

the Chamber of Commerce in 1905. The Jews took a leading part in the "Festivals of Mountain and Plain" for as long as the celebrations were held. Wolfe Londoner was one of the festival's originators. No one appears to have had as lively a time as the "one-man convention and tourist bureau," who, as the perfect host, cultivated a southern accent for a visiting delegation of Mississippi editors. Also open to the Jews were the pioneer associations, which were closed to the Negroes and Orientals. These were the Sons of Colorado (pre-territorial) and the Territorial Daughters for those who had been in the state before 1876.

Purim balls were held even before the Congregation Emanuel was organized. As early as 1868, the *News* effused over a celebration, which was held "while the rest of the world was observing Lent." A later description of a Purim ball in 1879 tells that the dancers did not wear shop costumes, but contrived them at little expense. Mrs. C. M. Schayer, the wife of the lay-rabbi, came as Queen Esther, Mrs. J. Gottlieb as Pocahontas, her husband as a rooster and Isaac Gotthelf, up from Saguache to attend the legislature, in "domino." The ball was complete with a grand march, royal procession and movable scaffold. "Some of the mottos to the dances, which numbered 25 in all, were a trifle crude, but this was not noticeable.... The attendance was very large and included the majority of Denver Hebrew Society."[5]

2

The history of the Jewish clubs can be traced through the newspaper accounts of the Purim balls. Although the Temple also held similar celebrations, the Purim ball became a regular function of the social club. It is difficult to determine to which club goes the honor of being the first such club in Denver. When the opening ball of the season was given by the Standard Club in 1880, it was stated that this was the club's fourth season. If it is true that the later Progress Club was its direct successor, the Green Gables Country Club, which succeeded Progress Club, can claim a continuous existence as long as the state of Colorado, 1876.[6]

The Lotus Club (sometimes Lotos), not to be confused with the exclusive social club of the same name to which only one Jew belonged, was created in 1880. This was a new club composed of "some excellent gentlemen."[7] That November the club gave a ball at Walhalla, where many Jewish balls were given for at least a decade. On the east wall the word "Lotus" was inscribed in large letters with green vines around it. Seventy couples attended, "many going home after midnight."[8] There followed a year of *musicales*, balls, and literary entertainments "at their handsome quarters on Larimer Street." The Fifty-niner, Julius Mitchell, delivered the "Soliloquy of Richelieu" at one entertainment, which the newspaper reviewed as showing too much strength in the characterization, "but Mr. Mitchell's figure and face were fine for the part." On the same ambitious program the members heard a debate on women's suffrage.[9]

The following year, 1881, the Standard and Lotus Clubs consolidated. The latter club, which was composed of "a younger element of society," offered its rooms until the new building near the site of the first Temple Emanuel, on Nineteenth and Curtis, was completed.[10] The new two-story building, with its name "Standard" in white stone was the first social club to have "status."[11] The furnishings included six full sets of scenery, portraying scenes on the coast of Ireland for use on what was considered the "best appointed stage outside of the Tabor Grand Opera House." The club boasted ladies' parlors, a library, reading room, card room, billiard room, and bar, complete with oil paintings, steel engravings, stuffed chairs and cuspidors. "Elegant Collations" were served in the club, to which belonged "some of the wealthiest, most influential and highly cultured men of the city."[12]

The club had a six-year lease on the building, which it also rented to other groups. Before the lease expired a new and even more "elegant" club succeeded it. Progress Club was founded May, 1885,[13] and the following year moved into its location at Twentieth and Lawrence Streets. By 1890 the club owned its own building in a fashionable location at Twentieth and Lincoln Streets. At the end of the century the club had an annual income of $7500 and a membership of fifty.[14] Both increased sufficiently until the club was able to acquire a modern building on East Colfax and Williams. Here the club had a gymnasium, swimming pool, and the other vital appurtenances of the non-Jewish clubs in the city.

Until 1927 the most important social affairs of the Jewish community were held at Progress club. In the days when the *Jewish Outlook* had to define the word *choopa*[15] in connection with Orthodox Jewish weddings and describe traditional Purim festivities for its readers, the newspaper never found it necessary to define such words as *kermis*, dancing the *German*, or *domino*.[16]

Progress Club ended when I. Rude, the tiny tailor-philanthropist, purchased the building which became the B'nai B'rith-I. Rude Community Building. The members of Progress club purchased a magnificent estate southwest of Denver and organized a new club, Green Gables, similar to the family-type club of the non-Jews, in a verdant setting, complete with golf course, swimming facilities, and provisions for lavish entertaining.

There appear to have been more than one Young Men's Hebrew Association. The first "Y," as it was popularly known, made its first social venture in 1879, with the Purim ball described above. A founding date of 1886 is also given in a history which says the organization ceased to function as a result of the Panic of 1903.[17]

The "Y" was said to have been founded to furnish a home for young men, particularly strangers in the city. In 1889 it staged entertainments for the newly proposed Jewish Hospital. With the Temple's literary society, it gave "first rank entertainments."[18] For several years the B'nai B'rith and the "Y" held joint picnics, and in 1903 the latter suggested that it become an auxiliary to the B'nai B'rith.[19] In 1904 it was still the "only organization succeeding in bringing young people together."[20] What happened thereafter is not revealed, but in 1911 a Young Men's Hebrew Association gives the date of its founding as March 7, and points out that "In its short existence it has acquired its own club rooms and a library has been donated."[21] In 1901 another Young Men's Hebrew Association was founded by the East European Jews.[22] An orginization with this name met with another group, the Jewish Alliance, in 1912 to consolidate. Articles of incorporation were filed for a Young Men's Hebrew Alliance.[23] The organization was dissolved in 1915.[24]

The Harmony, Social and Literary Society was in existence in 1884. That year the club gave a Purim ball to which were invited both the Reform and Orthodox rabbis. However, since the Standard Club gave a ball that same evening, it appears that there was not enough room in Denver for two such clubs.

At the beginning of the vigorous campaigns for the establishment of Israel, another group, many of whose members belonged to Green Gables, decided it needed a city club. The mansion owned by the son of Senator Nathaniel P. Hill, which had been the scene of many of the entertainments of the Sacred Thirty-Six, was purchased. The newly created Town Club refuted charges that it was founded in opposition to Zionist elements in Green Gables by opening its doors years later to the pro-Israel Allied Jewish Campaign which held some of its fund-raising functions there. Plans for a second country club, Meadow Hills, began to materialize in 1956, while one of the non-Jewish country clubs quietly began to take in Jewish members.

Over the years the Reform group started a very few other organizations. The *News* reported in 1881 that "After a great deal of discussion and long promised effort, a dispensation was finally ordered for the establishment of a lodge of the Free Sons of Israel at this City." The initial initiation took place in the rooms of the B'nai B'rith. Dr. Elsner and David Kline, both founders and ex-presidents of the B'nai B'rith lodge, were chosen officers. The reasons for the formation of this lodge and how long it lasted are lost in the past.[25] There are references in the B'nai B'rith minutes to "other lodges," one of which was the "K. S. B."[26]

Other clubs existed solely to stimulate the intellectual life of the leaders of the Jewish communities. In Denver an attempt was made in 1906 to gather together a score of the outstanding "thinkers" of the state into a club, the "Maimonideans." The club did not last long. During its life it arrived at such conclusions that the Sabbath should be observed on Saturday, and that Jews could not properly have Christmas trees or exchange presents with each other.

The Denver Philosophical Society numbered in its membership several Jewish "intellectuals," some of whom served as officers. Rabbi Friedman belonged to the Antithesis Club, an even more select group.

3

In contrast to the social clubs of German Jews, the B'nai B'rith, while not wholly democratic in practice, had a set of ideals which it sought diligently to uphold. Following carefully the program of the national order, the Denver lodge added its weight to those who sought to face and solve the problems confronting the Jews everywhere.

The suggestion for the creation of a B'nai B'rith lodge, said to have been made in the insurance office of Louis Anfenger, was also related to another existing organization. On April 7, 1872, in the religious column of the *News* appeared the notice:

> The Hebrew Benevolent Society of Denver will meet at the hall of the I. O. Benai Berith on Sunday the 7th inst. at 3 o'clock p.m.

The newspaper on April 9 noted that the lodge was organized "last Saturday." This was the culmination of a week's activities. From the first until 1912, the B'nai B'rith was almost the sole voice of the Jewish community. Even when the community was divided in the early part of the twentieth century, the lodge room was the only place in the city where both sides of the divisive issues could be aired. The meetings were not always peaceful, friendly discussions. The minutes of many a meeting in which the Brothers had spent the greatest part of the morning rising to points of order, demanding apologies, and threatening to withdraw from office, end with the amazing closing signature, "Benevolence, Brotherly Love and Harmony prevailing. . . ."

When the lodge was a year old, "It was moved and seconded that this Lodge return their Charter. . . . After a spirited discussion the motion was lost. In the affirmative were F. Z. Salomon, A. M. Appel, B. Berry, Isidor Dietsch and Julius Londoner."[27] In the negative were David Mitchell, H. I. Weil, H. Schayer, John Elsner, M. Hattenbach, and A. H. Fleischer. By one vote the lodge kept its charter.

The lodge, with a little more than a score of members, met the appeals made to it with admirable generosity. The first appeal was to contribute to the mission of the American consul, and leader of the order, Benjamin Peixotto, in his efforts on behalf of the Jews in Rumania. Four months after the lodge was instituted, a committee raised $112 for the purposes.[28]

While increasing numbers of tuberculous sick descended on the Denver community, the lodge still contributed $75 for the "relief of Yellow Fever Sufferers in the South,"[29] made its annual Purim contribution to the *Alliance Israelite Universelle*,[30] sent $100 for the relief of the victims of the pogroms of 1881,[31] and made its regular contributions to the Cleveland Orphan Asylum.

The national organization kept the Jews of Denver, and of the entire state who belonged to it, alive to the needs of their co-religionists throughout the world. It also brought information and guidance to the conservative group in the West, which was always on the verge of becoming self-satisfied.

It was to the lodge that a Jew in distress was likely to turn first. The lodge acted on almost every issue involving the civil rights of individual Jews, as well as the entire Jewish community. One of the earliest tasks it took up occurred in April, 1874, when the *Rocky Mountain News*, which delicately referred to the Jews as

"Israelites" or "Hebrews," printed a story on "The Murder of Perry, by Fareber, the Jew."[32]

A few days later the newspaper reported that Fareber claimed that he had not committed the crime of murder, but of homicide, "which took place at my rancho at the junction of Sangre de Cristo and Abeyta Pass, in defence of my home and life. The deceased had a lot of money on him which I didn't touch." He claimed that he had tried to surrender, and asked for an impartial investigation.[33] He was jailed in San Luis. When the case was brought to the attention of the Denver lodge,

> Bro. Anfenger rose, and with a few appropriate remarks referred to the perilous condition of a co-religionist, Mr. Fareber, who was lying in jail in St. Louis [San Luis] Colorado under the charge of murder. Fareber had asserted his innocence and appealed to friends for assistance in obtaining a fair trial. Bro. Anfenger was not aware that Fareber belonged to our order, in fact, thought he did not. But it being one of the cardinal principles of our order to battle against prejudice and to vindicate justice, his opinion was that, our lodge should take steps to secure for our unfortunate co-religionist a fair and impartial trial, and to employ good available counsel for him. He did not wish in the least, and he knew it could not be the intention of our lodge, to shield anybody from justice, but the wise benefits which the law accords to every prisoner, should also be shared by Fareber, and that to accomplish, we ought to do all in our power.[34]

A committee was appointed, funds were collected, and a lawyer, E. L. Smith, was engaged to defend Fareber. The *News* carried the outcome of the case in August, "Fareber, the Jew, who murdered Perry in the Sangre de Cristo Pass was sentenced at San Luis last week by Judge Hallett to five years in prison...."[35] The minutes do not record whether the intervention of the lodge had "vindicated justice," or not. At the very least, while the newspaper still called him "Fareber, the murderer," the sentence he received absolved him of the crime of murder.

A similar case was brought to the attention of the lodge ten years later, in January, 1884, by Bro. N. Weinberger of Gunnison:

> asking cooperation in procuring suitable counsel in defending Mr. Prince of Irwin, charged with the killing of a man, it being claimed that Mr. Prince is a member of Achim Lodge No. 175 of St. Louis, and that the killing was done in self defense.[36]

The sum of $100 was appropriated to be used if necessary in defending the accused, and the lodge notified Achim Lodge to do more and remit at least $500. The Denver lodge heard a motion to engage Thomas M. Patterson, a leading lawyer, at $750, to defend Prince, and at the same time send out circulars to all lodges to contribute funds. A total of $112 was received from St. Louis, which was sent to Moses L. Block in Gunnison, to be paid to the attorney engaged.

While the lodge was working on his behalf, Prince committed suicide in July, leaving it to the Denver lodge to make all the necessary arrangements for the transportation of Mrs. Prince and the remains of her husband to St. Louis and to attend to her "wants and comfort." The St. Louis lodge reimbursed the Denver lodge for its expenditures.

A similar case is recorded in the minutes: the Denver lodge aided the Jews in Leadville and Aspen in helping protect the rights of another Jew, Israel Engel, accused of murdering his Jewish partner on July 8, 1892. An "Engel Fund" was formed in Leadville. In addition to a donation by the Denver lodge, two lawyers were appointed to make solicitations for the fund.

Over the years the results of the Lodge's intervention were frequently successful as well as heartwarming. One unusual problem was posed in the lodge room by

> Bro. Ballaban of Galil Lodge, Safed, Palestine, who requested the lodge to assist him to the end that this government instruct its representative in Turkey to protect his family which were in imminent danger of being assaulted by brutal officers, thanked the Lodge for the interest taken in his case. Bro. M. L. Anfenger having reported that the protection asked had been granted and that the American consul had been instructed to afford the daughters of Bro. Ballaban its protection.[37]

Two years later Ballaban wrote from Safed in Hebrew:

> Honored Sir:—
> With a heart filled with gratitude to the Denver B'nai B'rith Lodge, and to all its members, who helped me, I send greetings. You will recollect that nearly two years ago, I appealed to the brethern at one of your meetings, at the time when my family here were in danger of having my two daughters kidnapped by Arabian ruffians, the awful consequences that would have followed. Brother M. Anfenger wrote to Brother Hon. Simon Wolf at Washington, through whose in-

fluence the State Department sent a demand to the Turkish Government through its consul here to protect my family from those ruffians. I am grateful to you all, and to the United States Government, whose demand worked wonders, for from the day this demand came here, those persecutors and ruffians desisted from their horrible designs, and since then they are even in fear of raising their eyes upon my household.[38]

The enthusiastic membership was ready to have the letter published in the *B'nai B'rith News*, but was dissuaded by Milton Anfenger, who thought it not advisable because the result had been accomplished by Simon Wolf as a representative of the Union of American Hebrew Congregations, and not as president of the B'nai B'rith.[39]

These were extreme cases. There were a great variety of other cases, such as the problem of the ten-month old boy brought by his mother and the sheriff from Trinidad to the state Home for Dependent Children. The child could have been legally adopted, but the state would not transfer him to any other institution. For a year and four months a committee tried in vain to remove the child from the Home.[40] The lodge helped locate missing relatives and assisted local orphans in gaining entrance into the Cleveland Orphan Asylum. For some of them the lodge acted as guardian of their possessions, investing their money, which was turned over to them when they were of age.

Established and proposed charities, as well as social and literary societies, turned invariably to the lodge for its support, if not financial then moral. The B'nai B'rith contributed to the Council of Jewish Women's settlement work; donated to the Free Loan Society; gave generously for many years to the Hebrew School of Denver (although very few of the children of its members attended), took part in the discussions creating the Denver Sheltering Home; helped with contributions to the Jewish Free Kitchen in West Colfax in 1907-8; was ready to help the sufferers of the West Colfax flood in 1909, before the city came to the rescue,[41] and also helped the victims of the Pueblo flood in 1921.

Most important of the lodge's early accomplishments was its presentation to the District Grand lodge of the problem of the sick "consumptives" flocking to Denver and of the hospital which was unable to open for lack of funds. Through the Denver group's efforts the national board took over the hospital. The Denver lodge continued with financial support of the newly named National Jewish Hospital, even to the total exclusion of help to the Jewish Consumptives Relief Society. Through its efforts work was found for discharged patients who had decided to remain in Denver.

Also of great importance was the effort, later called "antidefamation," which the lodge had undertaken from its very inception, in protecting the Jews from libel and discrimination. As has been discussed, the lodge and Rabbi Friedman gained national recognition for their accomplishments with the Associated Press and the National Association of Theatrical Producing Managers in New York. On the local scene, the lodge sought to protect Jewish peddlers who were being daily attacked by the less refined element of the city.

Discriminatory immigration laws and Russian denial to American Jews to visit Russia were protested by the lodge at the instigation of the national order. Proposed by the lodge, a memorial passed both houses of the Colorado legislature unanimously.[42] As the gates of immigration began the swing to closing, the lodge increased the number of people it helped into the region. Removal Committees worked with the national Industrial Removal Organization, and later took part in the Galveston Plan to help distribute the immigrant Jews, who were being urged to leave the congested eastern seaboard.

With the support of the lodge the unification of the Jewish community through the Central Jewish Council in 1912 was made easier and came earlier than it would have had the lodge denied its support. Despite the opposition of Rabbi Friedman to the Council and the contemporaneous Jewish Social Service Federation, the lodge, the majority of whose membership acknowledged Friedman as its spiritual leader, unhesitatingly supported the unification.

Many of the Jewish communal leaders were leaders in the B'nai B'rith. In Denver the Anfenger family was synonymous with the lodge. Louis Anfenger gave a lifetime of service to the lodge, to the district, and to the National Jewish Hospital. His sons and sons-in-law were closely identified with the lodge, but one in particular was the symbol of B'nai B'rith in Denver until his death—Milton Anfenger.

The handsome young man was the fair-haired child of the Denver lodge. Representing the aristocracy of Denver Jewry, he was not afraid to mingle with the East European Jews and their descendants, and came out whole-heartedly in favor of a unified community. It was he who formulated the resolution supporting the first Jewish federation of charities.[43]

While not drawing so much attention as its other activities, the lodge not only participated in intellectual pursuits, but also led the way in organizing them. First the lodge began to include lectures at its regular meetings prepared by members on subjects of which they had more than passing knowledge. During the tragic years of Hitler's rise to power in the early 30's, the lodge mapped out a "College of Jewish Studies," designed to bring to the Jews the best thought in the region—Jewish and non-Jewish. The College, which was endorsed by every Jewish organization in the city, was led by rabbis, college professors, and educated laymen. There had never been anything so overwhelmingly educational in the life of the Jewish community before. It proved so popular, that, although there was always a financial deficit, new additions were made to the faculty each season, many of them nationally-known figures.

The last college was held in 1939. Even with outside contributions, the tuition of $1.00 for a series of four lectures was not enough to pay the expenses of the program. That year the B'nai B'rith paid the $250 deficit and no plans were made for a future college. For several years, while the second World War demanded most of the community's efforts, the lodge devoted little time to the intellectual pursuits. In 1945, the lodge inaugurated the B. B. Forum Series, inviting nationally-known speakers and artists. The series continued under the sponsorship of the lodge until 1949, when it was taken over by the Jewish Community Centers, which managed the lectures until 1953. In 1955 the men's clubs of the synagogues added their support in sponsoring a similar series.

When the lodge dropped the Forum Series, it began participating in an new program of the national order, by introducing the "Mountain States Institute of Judaism." Arranged as a yearly three-day retreat in the mountains, the Institute offers a faculty of outstanding figures on the American Jewish scene.

4

Contrary to later stories, the B'nai B'rith never denied its membership to the East European Jews. Isaac Epstein (an early miner from "Poverty Gulch") and Marks Amter, both of whom were founders of the Orthodox congregations, joined the young lodge. A few more Russian Jews petitioned until there were about a dozen members before 1900. Although no Jews born in East Europe ever held the presidency, there is nothing to indicate that they were not wanted as members. When the refugees from the pogroms became financially able, they were acceptable to the lodge. Nevertheless, many of them hesitated petitioning, fearing that, even if they were accepted, they would still be snubbed by the *Deutsche Yehudim*. Occasionally a brave soul joined the lodge, like Joe Washer of the Cotopaxi Colony who joined in 1898, and the Troyanskys of the Atwood Colony in 1903. The lodge gave Moses Troyansky six months to "enable him to learn sufficient English to understand the obligation."[44]

Not until 1916 and Jacob Lieberman, who was four years old when his parents brought him to Denver, was the presidency held by anyone not of German-Jewish stock.

For the later-comers, most of whom could not afford the Standard or Progress social clubs, the B'nai B'rith was a poorer man's club. The early lodge had at least one social event yearly: a Purim Ball, anniversary ball, or banquet and ball. There were memorial services for Jewish figures of international importance, and celebrations of birthdays of living great Jews. In 1884 the lodge made arrangements for a celebration of the 100th birthday of Sir Moses Montefiore. According to the minutes it was "moved and seconded that the Orthodox Congregation be notified in time of the Montefiore Celebration." The motion was lost.[45]

When the lodge acquired its own quarters in 1929, many rules were laid down against gambling on the premises. Nothing was said against card-playing, and this form of recreation filled the rooms outside the lodge room until the late hours. In 1939 the popularity of bowling was brought to the attention of the lodge,[46] which formed leagues with interested merchants sponsoring teams. Since B'nai B'rith membership is required of all bowlers, scores of men joined, thereby increasing the lodge membership from the largest in the order in 1905, with 435 members, to 2,250 in 1955.

A junior B'nai B'rith had been formed in Denver in 1924, for which Milton Schayer had written the ritual. At the same time the Aleph Zadik Aleph was formed in Omaha. The latter became the junior national order using Schayer's ritual. There were half a dozen young men in 1949, some of whom had been members of the A. Z. A. who wanted to join the B'nai B'rith, but would not join such a large organization. Previous attempts at forming a second lodge had been resisted. In 1942, Milton Anfenger had opposed the idea with, "We don't want any more of east side and west side grouping. We don't want any more of the schism of orthodox and reformed—a disunited Jewish community."[47] In 1949 the national president, Frank Goldman, came to Denver to install his son Edward as president of the new Mile High Lodge.

With three women's chapters in 1957, B'nai B'rith Girls, and the Youth Organization, B'nai B'rith affiliation is offered almost every member of the family.

5

During the panic year of 1893, Carrie S. Benjamin, who had been a delegate to the Congress of Women at the World's Fair in Chicago, came back to Denver so imbued with enthusiasm for the new Council of Jewish Women, which was being organized that year, that she organized the Denver chapter of the organization on her return.

In Denver, as elsewhere, the Council's work was philanthropic and civic. It came into being during the great wave of health-seekers and Russian immigration. The Council, interested in the welfare of both groups, tried first to interest the national Council in taking over the still empty Jewish hospital. For the immigrants, the Council's greatest efforts during the period were spent in settlement work in the new community growing up on the West Side and in West Colfax, as will be discussed later.

For themselves the women planned improvement programs in parliamentary law, physical education, study groups, and sewing circles. During the Spanish-American War the women donated bandages to the local relief societies working for the service men. The wives of the leading citizens were the leaders of the Council, and through the group's membership in the State Federation of Women's clubs, also participated in sponsoring or opposing legislation which affected them as women, or their families.

The programs after the meetings were musical and literary and greatly resembled those of the ladies' auxiliary of the Temple and later Temple Sisterhood, to which most of them belonged. So close was the relationship that when the third building of the Temple Emanuel was erected, the Council gave the congregation a check for $1000.

A junior section was formed in 1900 for boys and girls from fourteen to twenty. Literary and musical programs, debates and plays were given by the young people, most of the proceeds going to the Settlement House in West Colfax. In 1913, a Junior Council of Jewish Women was formed for girls. It had been many years before more than one name and address from West Colfax was listed in the senior Council roster. It was different in the Junior Council, where girls from the West Side, and soon West Colfax, were found as members and officers of the organization. The girls entertained at the local hospitals, and were very much in demand for "tag days" for Jewish and non-Jewish organizations. During World War I they sold thrift stamps and knit and sewed for the war effort. With the senior Council they tried to keep open the May Morris Home for working girls from 1925 to 1927. Denver was too small a city for this type of home, and the idea was abandoned.

FOOTNOTES

[1] *RMN*, Nov. 27, 1880, p. 5.
[2] *RMN*, Sept. 6, 1881.
[3] *JO*, Aug. 11, 1905.
[4] Harvey Jordan, *Program 1941 Regatta, Sloan's Lake*.
[5] *RMN*, Mar. 11, 1879.
[6] *RMN*, Sept. 26, 1880.
[7] *RMN*, Sept. 26, 1880, p. 5.
[8] *RMN*, Nov. 24, 1880, p. 4.
[9] *RMN*, Mar. 13, 1881, p. 2.
[10] *RMN*, July 27, 1881, p. 5.
[11] *RA, op. cit.*
[12] *RMN*, Oct. 31, 1881, p. 8.
[13] *AJY*, 1899-1900; Freidenthal goves the date as 1886, and *JO* as 1885.
[14] *Ibid.*
[15] *JO*, Feb. 22, 1907.
[16] *JO*, Feb. 23, 1906.
[17] *JO*, June 23, 1911.
[18] *RMN*, May 15, 1890.
[19] BB minutes, May 10, 1903, p. 394.
[20] *JO*, Jan. 1904, Vol. I, No. 7, p. 9.
[21] *JO*, June 23, 1911.
[22] Art. Inc., Colorado, May 10, 1901. Four names from West Colfax Orthodox community.
[23] Art. Inc., Colorado, Jan. 28, 1913.
[24] Dissolution of Corporation, Colorado, Jan. 29, 1915.
[25] *RMN*, May 24, 1881, p. 4.
[26] BB minutes, Aug. 13, 1882. Apparently "Knights of the Sons of Benjamin." The other group referred to is the "F. S. or I." the Free Sons of Israel.

[27] *Ibid.*, May 27, 1873; Jan. 25, 1874, David Mitchell "congratulated the lodge on the harmonious feeling . . . and said it was a pleasing contrast to . . . one year ago.
[28] *Ibid.*, Aug. 7, 1872.
[29] *Ibid.*, Sept. 22, 1879.
[30] *Ibid.*, Feb. 22, 1880.
[31] *Ibid.*, Feb. 26, 1881.
[32] *RMN*, Apr. 21, 1874.
[33] *RMN*, Apr. 21, 1874.
[34] *Ibid.*, Apr. 26, 1874.
[35] *RMN*, Aug. 11, 1874.
[36] *Ibid.*, Jan. 22, Mar. 25, July 27, Aug. 10, and Sept. 14, 1884.
[37] *Ibid.*, Oct. 13, 1907, p. 317.
[38] *Ibid.*, Letter incorporated, Sept. 1, 1909, p. 87.
[39] *Ibid.*, Oct. 10, 1909.
[40] *Ibid.*, Dec. 13, 1908, May 9, 1909.
[41] *Ibid.*, July 26, 1909. Th lodge authorized the president of the Jewish Relief Society to draw to the amount of $100 if necessary. However, Aug. 22, 1909, the city contributed $2000, Simon Guggenheim, $100 and $85 came from other individuals.
[42] *Ibid.*, Apr. 21, 1911, p. 221.
[43] *Ibid.*, Dec. 22, 1912, p. 363.
[44] *Ibid.*, June 23, 1903, p. 406.
[45] *Ibid.*, Sept. 28, 1884.
[46] *Ibid.*, Sept. 12, 1939.
[47] *Ibid.*, Oct. 13, 1942.

"The Hebrew in Politics"

1

When a list of local, state and national officials of Colorado was published in 1934,[1] covering the period from 1858 to that year, the list included the names of at least sixty-two known Jews, holding a total of 190 offices during the period. From a sampling of the names omitted in the index to the work—U. S. Senator Guggenheim, Mayors Wolfe Londoner of Denver, Mike Studinski of Pueblo, J. M. Sampliner of Grand Junction, and Jacob Chisdes of Sugar City; Justice of the Peace Gustave Cohen, and Denver's fire chief, Phil Trounstine—it is safe to assume that there were at least twice the number of Jews during the period holding public office than were listed in the index. Even were such a list complete, it would neither be a measure of the acceptance, nor of the popularity of the Jews, many of whom were successsful enough to win their party's nomination for office, although they were later defeated at the polls. In addition, there were many important figures in politics who turned down public office, although they were offered such honors.

Political leadership was not difficult to achieve in the pioneer period, when the Jews were identified with the "Law and Order" tickets. Their names were found in the early columns of the *Rocky Mountain News,* signing petitions for such diverse projects as prohibiting cattle from running through the streets, settling the question of mixed schools, investigating freight rates charged in the territory, and looking into the misappropriation of civic funds. In the earliest election near Cherry Creek, a Citizen's Meeting in 1859 elected Abraham Jacobs to serve on the first city council. Leopold Mayer followed him, serving three terms until 1864, when he left for the San Luis Valley. Joseph Kline, on the

144

fourth city council, completed an unbroken succession of Jews on Denver's earliest law-making body.

Among the important appointments in the early period, in addition to that of Territorial Treasurer Fred Z. Salomon, was the appointment by President Grant of Herman Silver as register of the Denver District and then his appointment as director of the mint; Abraham Lincoln's appointment of Julius Londoner as Postmaster of California Gulch, and later the appointment of Joseph Harrison as United States Postmaster for Denver.

Almost all of the early Jews were staunch Republicans. While the Jews who came into the territory at the end of the Civil War included men who had fought on both sides, the majority had been on the side of the Union. Colorado, which had supported the North, was Republican in national elections until 1888. For many years almost every successful Jewish candidate for public office, or appointee, was a member of the party.

Before Colorado achieved statehood, Benjamin Wisebart was elected to the upper branch of the territorial legislative council. While serving, he introduced bills permitting criminals to testify in their own defense, taxing the capital stock of national banks, and requiring judges of elections to count ballots in the presence of the voters. All of the bills were passed.[2] He also served several terms on the Central City council and was elected mayor of the "little kingdom of Gilpin County" in 1876.

Another early legislator was Edward Pisko, who was born in Austria. He arrived in the United States at the beginning of the Civil War. "Obeying the impulses of his heart, he proved his loyalty to his adopted country, by enlisting as a private in the 45th New York Volunteers."[3] With his regiment he participated in the battles of Chancellorsville, Gettysburg, and Sherman's march.

In 1876 he was elected by a decisive majority to represent Arapahoe county in the lower branch of the territorial legislature, where he introduced a bill on compulsory education, and a bill relieving property from taxation to the extent of any valid mortgages encumbering it, which was already subject to taxation in another form. Neither of the measures became part of the law then.

Pisko acquired a reputation for introducing the "prayerless" legislature, also called the "No Chaplain Legislature." He had convinced his colleagues that as "church and state were separate in this country, such services were unnecessary."[4] No prayers opened the territorial legislature during the session of 1875-6.

After his untimely death his widow, Seraphine, became a leader in Denver's charities.

2

It was to a practical joke Eugene Field, the poet, had played on him, that Wolfe Londoner credited his election as mayor of Denver in 1888:

> I am one of the few men who ever got even with Gene Field. It was near an election, and I had taken quite a prominent part in politics, in one instance, trying to influence the "Colored vote." Gene Field wrote an article, saying that I would present every colored voter who called at my store, with a watermelon. Fortunately I found a wagon of Georgia melons on Market Street and I passed them out.
>
> The next day I put an ad in the News that Gene Field wanted a watchdog, and set a time for owners to bring dogs to his office. At the appointed time there was a yelping and fighting and scrambling of dogs in Gene's office. He climbed on the table and screamed for help, while the owners of the dogs fought lustily with each other.
>
> To return to that watermelon incident. It placed me in high esteem with the colored people. At a big colored meeting, at which prominent Denverites spoke, I was introduced by the Negro chairman in this way. "We now come to a man who is the friend of colored people—speaks to us on the street, and treats us to watermelons. Tho' he has a white face, he has a heart as black as any of us."[5]

Londoner waged a difficult campaign. One newspaper accused the Jews of voting for Jewish candidates. The *News* published an answer under the heading "Hebrew in Politics" by a "Hebrew" who also took exception to the newspaper's claim that Londoner, as a Jew, was making a grand offer for the Negro vote. To this, "Hebrew" said that Londoner is making the offer as a Republican, and not as a Jew. "But then everyone in Denver knows that Mr. Londoner is not a Hebrew, except by descent. If he were by faith or heart he would not make such a degrading offer."[6]

Wolfe Londoner was forced by the opposition into running as a Jew although he had joined the Episcopalean Church. The votes throughout the city were discouraging, but in the Negro district there was a landslide of votes for him. Said the irrepressible mayor, "I never cast bread on waters, but watermelons on Denver's Ethiopia, and the scriptural promise may be true."[7]

Just what "degrading offers" Londoner made came out

during Londoner's term as mayor. A trial was held on the legality of the election, in which he was charged with violating the city charter. Every newspaper argued the case, with the *Republican* and *Times* claiming that he had been elected by a seventy-seven vote majority.[8] In 1891 the Supreme Court vindicated him personally. In March he resigned as mayor. The case set a precedent for later elections which were suspected of being fraudulently conducted.

Londoner's popularity suffered little because of the trials. Few people remembered either the trial or his resignation. Instead it was remembered that he had built the county courthouse without incurring a penny's worth of graft in the construction. The Jews remembered that he had been a Jew and appreciated his generosity to the various Jewish drives in the city. But most of all, he was remembered for the yarns he spun and the pranks he and his friend Eugene Field had played on each other and the community's leaders.

One of the best stories Londoner told was his discovery of an ancient and deserted metropolis in the mountains. The National Geographic Society found out about his claims, and Wolfe was almost shamed into leaving town as a fraud. Years later, when the cliff dwellings of the Mesa Verde were discovered, Wolfe righteously proclaimed, "That's the city I found."[9]

Whatever adverse criticism was made of him, he endeared himself forever to the newspapermen. In the basement of his fancy food store, he founded his "Cyclone Cellar," where reporters sought relief from the pressure of the outside world above them and were regaled with Londoner's stories and plenty of "ink," which was sold under a different label upstairs. Londoner claimed the name of the "club" was a misnomer, that the reporters met with a "cyclone" when they arrived at home. From the cellar grew the Denver Press Club, in which Londoner was an honorary officer throughout his life.

3

In politics the mutual exclusiveness of the "German" and "Russian" Jews, or of the Reform and Orthodox, played little part. Both groups staunchly informed the press and the public that there was no such thing as a "Jewish vote." How true this was may be judged from the claim of a daughter of Benjamin Wisebart, who, after having been defeated in his campaign for state treasurer, pointed out that he had been unable to capture the vote of the East European Jews in West Colfax. Even greater proof was furnished by the same Jews, when many of them voted in the 30's for a man who had been a Ku Klux Klansman in the 20's.

The Jews throughout the state voted according to their political conviction, and to a great extent to their contributing economic position. This did not mean that a "Jewish vote" was not sought—even by the Jews. One of the most successful men to try to win the Jewish vote for the Republican party was Amdeé L. Fribourg, who was adored by the East European Jews. In Colorado he followed the building of the railroads and the linking of the rail lines in South Park. There he prospected for gold. His unsuccessful search for the precious metal did not fulfill a prediction made to him by a fortune teller that he would handle "millions in gold," nor the sudden vision of an old Negro, who said to him, "Boss, there's dollar marks all over you everywhere." Instead the prediction was fulfilled by his appointment as weighmaster of the United States Mint. During the twenty-two years he served in the mint, every single grain of gold or silver that came in or went out passed through his hands. At one time during his tenure there was as much as $500,000,000 in gold bars in the mint.[10]

Fribourg served in the tenth legislature from Denver. During his campaign, he made a point of informing the voters, "If you vote for me, you are voting for a Jew." When William Jennings Bryan was running for office, Fribourg claimed that through his efforts a single precinct remained Republican, while the rest of the state voted Democrat. Fribourg was a great help to the immigrant Jews in Denver. He was a leader of the Hebrew Republican Club at the turn of the century, and incorporator of "The Jewish Protective Association," one of the purposes of which was to educate and Americanize "those of our members, who, though foreign born, have adopted this Free America as their home and the United States as their country."[11] The Fribourgs were also active in the Zionist movement and the West Colfax charities.

The popular politician proudly claimed that the Temple Emanuel was founded in the home of his uncle, Emanuel Block, and that before the Temple, *minyanim* were held in private homes. Nevertheless, most accounts agree that the congregation was organized at the home of Louis Anfenger, at the *b'rith* of his son, Milton. The Anfengers were active in the political life of Denver.

First Louis served in the house of representatives followed by his son Milton, who served two terms as state senator. After graduation from Stanford University, where he roomed with Herbert Hoover, he opened a law practice in Denver. As the owner of the Denver Bears baseball club from 1923 to 1932, he established a baseball stadium for the club, called Merchant's Park. The club was revitalized in 1947 and a new stadium built. Shortly before his death in 1952, he was honored by the sports lovers of Denver before a crowd of 4,568.

The Anfengers were Republicans. In 1952 a grandson-in-law of Louis Anfenger, Charles Rosenbaum, was named by the Republican governor to fill the vacancy of district judge. Into this Republican family, the brilliant young lawyer Philip Hornbein married in 1905. Hornbein became one of the outstanding Democrats in the state. A man of strong convictions and of great generosity, he earned the respect of all groups of Jews, and the love of the less affluent East European Jews.

Coming from an Orthodox Jewish family, Hornbein was a first generation American, was completely acceptable to the aristocracy of Denver Jewry, despite that fact that he was a founder of the Zionist movement in Denver, a champion of the Jewish Consumtives Relief Society, and not the least interested in the machinations of "society," although he is listed in the Denver Social Record. His brilliance as an attorney in preparing a case and his ability in presenting it earned him the admiration of the community.

After passing the bar in 1901, Hornbein became a law partner of Alfred Muller and opened his first office in Cripple Creek. He returned to Denver in 1902 just before the worst mining strikes in the history of the state, during which Governor James Peabody had declared martial law in Telluride, Trinidad, Cripple Creek and Victor. Peabody was a candidate for governor again in the election of 1904. His opponent was Alva Adams, who his party claimed had won by 5,000 votes. Adams, a Democrat, was sworn into office. But the Peabody supporters refused to acknowledge the election of Adams, and the case was brought before the Supreme Court. Before the election the Republicans had issued an injunction to stop the Democrats "from stealing votes." The Supreme Court bench on which sat three staunch Republicans, ruled that the Democrat election officials were guilty of contempt and that Peabody was elected governor. Seated by the legislature as governor, Peabody resigned within twenty-four hours and his lieutenant governor, Jesse F. McDonald, became governor of Colorado.

Hornbein was one of Colorado's seven foremost lawyers selected to defend the election officials. Although they too were charged with contempt, Hornbein's leadership in the Democratic party was secure. As a Democrat, he became intimate not only with the leaders of the party, but also with the inhabitants of the "Gas House District" along the bottoms, between Cherry Creek and the Platte River, which was Denver's First Ward, and the focal point of settlement. At the turn of the century, the bulk of the inhabitants of the neighborhood were immigrants, among them a large number of bearded Jews and Irishmen with thick brogues. When the Ku Klux Klan came to power many of the Irish Catholics of the "Gas House District" led the fight against the hooded order.

Hornbein took part in Mayor Robert Speer's first campaign and was his attorney during the period when the corporations were fighting the visionary independent candidate. He became chairman of the state Democratic convention and nominated his friend Edwin C. Johnson for governor in 1932 and Alva Adams for United States Senator in 1938. Because of his ability, his strict guardianship of civil rights, his humanitarian ideals as well as his position in the party, he was offered a district or supreme court judgeship by Governor Johnson, which he turned down.

The Democrats became more popular after the nation-wide spotlight was focused on the strikes in the mining country. Max Morris, one of the few Jewish labor leaders of Colorado, who was a vice-president of the American Federation of Labor, was elected to the state legislature for two terms. He died in 1909, while settling a controversy as secretary of the Retail Clerks' International Protective Association, which had its headquarters in Denver.

While there were Jews in both political parties on both sides of Cherry Creek, the popular notion of the rich and Temple Jews as Republicans, and the poor and immigrant Jews as Democrats, persisted for a long time. The generation of native-born Jews among the more socially acceptable portion of Denver Jewry made their own decisions in politics. From them came such leading Democrats as County Judge Ira Rothgerber and Walter Appel, the latter a third generation American from a leading Denver family. The East European Jews in the first decade of the twentieth century were ready for politics. Three Jews ran on the Republican ticket in 1904, which, by contrast, included millionaire Simon Guggenheim and an immigrant West Colfax merchant, Abraham Radinsky, who ran for the state legislature. The highest political office ever held in the state by a Jew was that of United States Senator by Simon Guggenheim, when he was elected by the state legislature. During his tenure the vote for the office was given directly to the people, and Guggenheim, known to all as a Jew, especially because of some of the vicious attacks made on him involving his religion, did not seek re-election. Few Jews had such high ambitions. As the cities grew larger, and the Jews began their movement away from the small towns, fewer of them were elected from the districts outside of Denver to the House or Senate. The days when there were enough Jews in the legislature to hold a *minyan* came to an end about the end of World War I.

FOOTNOTES

[1]Ben Draper, "Alphabetical Index to Officials of Denver and Colorado, 1858-1933."
[2]Vickers, *op. cit.*, p. 642.
[3]*Ibid.*, p. 547-8.
[4]*RA*, p. 7.
[5]Hill, *op. cit.*, p. 122.
[6]*RMN*, Nov. 6, 1881, p. 4.
[7]*RMN*, Oct. 23, 1891.
[8]*RMN*, Apr. 1, 1890, p. 4.
[9]J. E. Smith, *IJN, op. cit.*
[10]*IJN*, Apr. 4, 1929.
[11]Art. of Inc., Aug. 17, 1895. Just prior to the Panic of 1893, a Hebrew Protective Association took part in the "joyous Republican" parade, with 1000 voters in line. This seems to be a typographical error, inasmuch as the Swedish Americans are listed with 400 in line. *Times*, Nov. 11, 1894, p. 1.

"Extra"

1

Journalism in the West became as wild as the earlier region had been with the increase of the daily newspapers. The journalistic sins the press committed were many and grievous, but so far as the Jews as a religious group were concerned, they were forgivable. From the earliest years there was little or no anti-Semitism in the newspapers, although the publishers made a distinction between "Hebrews" or "Israelites" and "Jews." The former terms were used for the local groups, and the latter as a term of opprobrium, as in the San Luis killing, when the accused was referred to as "Fareber, the Jew." Sometimes an offensive remark slipped by the alert eyes of a publisher, and sometimes he did not know the remark was offensive. Only a word from one of the rabbis, or the B'nai B'rith, to the publisher, and a particular sin was not repeated again.

When the newspapers attacked an individual, as in the case of Ernest Morris and the Denver *Post,* the columns could be filled with the derogatory material, but of the man's religion there was not even a hint. Morris, who wrote a painstaking autobiography, *Gathering Much,* prior to his death in 1937, told not only the story of his life, beginning with his father's leaving his birthplace in Russian Poland in 1847 to seek his fortune in San Francisco at the age of thirteen, but also the story of the political life of the West. Most exciting was his account of his fight with the colorful journal and the surprising end to the story.

The Denver *Post,* in 1912, had branched out with the Sells-Floto Circus, to which it hoped to attract William F. Cody, "Buffalo Bill," who was already in partnership with Major Gordon William Lillie, "Pawnee Bill." Because of Cody's improvidence, it had been necessary for the two showmen to form a corporation under the laws of New Jersey, called "Buffalo Bill's Wild West and Pawnee Bill's Far East, Combined."

With Buffalo Bill in debt to the *Post* for $20,000, which he had borrowed, and with little likelihood of his repaying the money, the newspaper began to take over the combined show. Then Lillie turned to Ernest Morris for protection of his interests. After three years of litigation over the circus, in which Morris successfully established his client's rights to the property, the lawyer said that his name was banned from the newspaper.

A monster mass-meeting was planned for the eve of the draft registration for World War I, on September 12, 1918, at the city auditorium, in order to create enthusiasm for the military plan. Notices were sent to all of the newspapers in Denver to publicize the event. When the *Post* did not publish the notice, Morris, who was to preside at the meeting, made an appeal on the front pages of the two other dailies, saying that the *Post* had refused to publish the notices, adding "You do not need the Post to hold a patriotic meeting and fill the auditorium." According to his unpublished but well-documented book, the *Post* seized the opportunity to make this a big story. His name was back in the newspaper. A cartoon was splashed across the front page of the newspaper, with an accompanying story in which he was called a "skunk, rat, hun, and a relative to the Crown Prince." As similar stories appeared, twenty-three lawyers of the city volunteered to sue the *Post* on Morris' behalf for $375,000. The newspaper filed a counter-suit, charging that Morris had libeled it first in his appeal to make the mass meeting a success in spite of it and sued him for $150,000.

The newspaper's circulation had not suffered during the spirited fight with Morris, and this was a good time to call a halt to the whole business. One of the publishers called on Morris to make a financial settlement. Morris told him that he would not consider anything unless a retraction equal to the charges was made in the newspaper. The publishers agreed. Morris took no money for settling the case and proposed that, instead, the *Post* donate ten thousand dollars to twenty-three charities, with Morris selecting half of the beneficiaries and the *Post* the other half. Thus, according to Morris, each of the twenty-three lawyers had served one charitable institution.

Several years later the publishers came to Morris with a "meritorious" case against a Hollywood motion picture company, involving the rights to portray Buffalo Bill. The case never reached a conclusion. Harry Tammen, one of the publishers, was dying. After years of fighting, he asked the lawyer to serve as an honorary pall-bearer at his funeral.

During all of these battles the *Post* never once indicated that Morris was a Jew. Had the newspaper really wished to hurt Morris, it would have been only easy to do so through his religion.

2

While it was true that many of the newspaper's big advertisers were Jews, it was equally true that from the Jewish section, West Colfax, came the bulk of their "newsies" and on the editorial and business staff there were always Jewish employees.

The most important contact the Denver newspapers had with the Jews was through the newsboys. No matter what the policies of the newspaper on which they worked, in later life the many men who sold newspapers on the streets of Denver become almost maudlin when they remember the kindnesses they received from their employers.

This was especially true of the two newspapers which survived, the Denver *Post*, the "Big Brother" of the community, and the pioneer *Rocky Mountain News*. All of the highly competitive newspapers, who were constantly devising methods to increase their circulation, entertained their newsboys royally with lavish dinners, picnics, free stage shows, and movies. That this was good business did not in any way dim the loyalty of the newsboys nor of their immigrant parents, whose bread and butter was earned on the streets of downtown Denver. "Hustling sheets" was one of the mainstays of West Colfax, until the 30's when the radio made "extras" obsolete.

Before that when an extra edition was ready for the streets, the principal of Cheltenham school and probably the other schools in West Colfax would come into each room to ask the teacher to dismiss the newsboys for an immediate meeting. One of the Denver *Post* or *News* circulation managers would pick out from the assembled group the boys whom he knew to be the best young salesmen, and incidentally, the neediest, and load them onto a waiting truck. When an early morning extra was called it might be the father of one of the circulation managers who went to the newsboys' homes and had the eager parents waken their sons for their mission of disseminating the news. All editorial and reportorial sins were forgiven by the parents whose children were treated with kindness by the Denver dailies.

The Forms of Hatred

With relatively little anti-Semitism in politics, and even less in the newspapers, there was, nevertheless, enough to concern the Jews. The most obvious was the social barrier erected by the exclusive clubs in the early 80's. Just how this came about, and exactly why, remains a mystery. During the very first year of settlement in Denver, Fred Z. Salomon and Abraham Jacobs had led in the forming of the Auraria and Denver Chess Club and Literary Society which met in Jacobs' building, at the time a center for the more refined of the pioneers. When Auraria and Denver became one, the pioneer group changed its name to the Denver Chess and Whist Club, and later shortened the name to the Denver Club. The only objection to the changing of the name was, "It may be confounded with the 'Denver Club Rooms' . . . not at all similar in character."[1] Forty to fifty members held meetings in the "elegant" rooms over the New York Store (owned by Poznanski and Cohen).

In 1868, Isidor Deitsch was a director of the club, which was organized "on the same basis as the great clubs of London." At that time the Denver Club was a friendly group, concerned with having comfortable furnishings in its rooms and the leading journals and magazines to read, and was contemplating a grand inaugural ball, or "pic-nic."[2] In 1881 a new Denver Club was formed, to which professing Jews have never been admitted, yet the secretary of the club states that it is actually the same club, reorganized to correct certain difficulties the old club had encountered.[3]

The exclusion of the Jews from this club did not go unchallenged. On August 14, 1881, the *News* reprinted a full column story from the Leadville *Herald*, headed, "Proscribing the Jews." After many paragraphs of praise for the Jews, the writer concluded:

> With all these facts in view, is it not strange that in the United States, the home of the oppressed of all nations, that in Colorado, where every man who comes with a desire to work is welcomed, there should exist certain members of a club, composed professedly of gentlemen, who do not hesitate to attempt to close its doors upon a race, which has produced a Christ, a Moses, a Mohammed, and so many more of the greatest names in history. If the Savior . . . were to apply for admission would he be denied because of his Jewish parentage[?] . . . Yet admission is refused to men in this state who excel in culture, refinement, gentlemanly manners as well as ability and scholarship. The others . . . can scarcely construct a sentence but [have] sudden wealth. It is shameful.[4]

This, and the popular type of anti-Semitism, ascribing to the Jews a difference in behavior, offended the sensitivities of the thoroughly Americanized Jews. Such statements, as the speech of the president of the Chamber of Commerce at the Ladies' Fair at the Temple Emanuel, in which he stated flatteringly, that he would "never live in a town where there is no Hebrew church, for there there is no money," or a newspaper item that the people of Idaho Springs like the presence in their midst of a goodly number of Jews, for "as a great many think, wherever the Jews locate in business, it will be for the money and prosperity,"[5] caused the unaccepted Jews to scrutinize themselves for the cause.

The Council for Jewish Women, in a discussion, came up with the following comments: "We make for ourselves a voluntary ghetto," by the president and founder of the Denver chapter, Mrs. Benjamin, who pointed out the clannishness of the Jews at the cafes and summer resorts, and the evil effect of the exclusiveness, "separating us from other races." Another member thought, "We should marvel not at persecution but at toleration, considering how recent the ghetto life was." Still another member disagreed that the Jews were exclusive—instead it was the Jews who were excluded by hotels, summer resorts, or "any cosmopolitan place. No cultivation, beauty or charm, can outbalance being Jewish. It is a barrier." An optimistic soul ventured the opinion that "we must carry out our mission of bringing spirituality to the world by mixing and dropping class lines." Only one member declared, "We should be exclusive. It is not necessary to apologize for being a Jew."[6]

The press and the Christians also considered the matter gravely. The popular Unitarian minister David Utter, after making such statements as "It is the Jewish race, not the Jewish church that is disliked," and that the solution to the problem of anti-Semitism is intermarriage, which would be the cure within three generations, concluded, "But, if I were a Jew, I would take all the dislike in silence, and keep up the bars against intermarriage, just for the glory of belonging to a people with such a transcendant history."[7]

"The first public instance of Jewish prejudice" was recorded in the Denver *Jewish News* in 1916, when a hotel in Estes Park advertised, "No Jews or tubercular people admitted."[8] The tourist bureau of the mountain town refused to distribute the pamphlets of the hotel containing the restrictions.[9] Colorado was one of the early states in the union—and one of only seven[10]—to pass a law, March 30, 1917, prohibiting discriminatory advertising by hotels.

Of deeper concern in Denver was a dangerous form of anti-Semitism, which began in the first part of the century, with the Jewish peddler on his horse-drawn wagon as the target of violence. As the population of Denver increased, there were new gentiles who "did not know Joseph" nor cared that the Jews had taken an active part in the building of the community. The *Jewish Outlook* reported that "an old rag picker was set upon and beaten by some kind of Christian hoodlums." His clothes were torn, he was insulted, frightened, "and the poor little old rickety wagon, with its poor little load of rags was burned."[11] The son of an early *schochet* in Denver, John Schechter, remembers that he and his father were forced to wrap themselves in gunny sacks before they left for the slaughter house, to soften the blows of the rocks which were hurled at them as they drove, with the cries of "sheeney" ringing in their ears. A keg of beer accompanied them to work, for the workers would not allow Schechter to slaughter without the alcoholic "gift."[12]

Most tragic of all the crimes against the Jews was the Christmas day attack in 1905 on two Jews who were loading scrap iron onto a railroad car. They were set upon by a gang throwing bricks and iron bolts, resulting in the death of the two men. The two leaders of the gang received sentences which the Jews did not believe were commensurate with the crime. One received a sentence of four to six years in the penitentiary, and the other received seven months and fourteen days.[13] A year later two other Jews were murdered under similar circumstances and the two killers received sentences of a little longer duration.[14]

The life of the Jewish peddler was a precarious one, and the Jewish community worried for his safety. The B'nai B'rith lodge at the instigation of Alfred Muller appointed a committee to investigate the "persecutions of Jewish peddlers." The police department (with two Jewish men on the force) ordered its patrolmen to give the peddlers all the protection in their power.[15] Muller wrote letters to the principals of all of the Denver Public Schools to be read in the classrooms, explaining the pathetic position of the peddlers, and appealing to the American ideals of sportsmanship of the boys making the attacks.[16]

As disturbing as the attacks on the peddlers were, the Jewish community was troubled more by the attitude of the court. Justice appeared to be one-sided. When the *Times* reported in 1909 that a young Jewish boy was sentenced to five to ten years in the penitentiary for being a member of a "fence" gang guilty of petty larceny,[17] it was apparent that the court's sympathies were not with the Jews. His sentence was longer than that of the earlier killers.

The attorneys of the community were shocked in 1920 after a Jew was shot and killed in the barn behind his home in West Colfax. He and his brother were quarreling over a horse trade with another man, who shot both men and fled to El Paso, Texas. Brought back to Denver to stand trial for murder, the judge reprimanded the district attorney for filing a charge of murder and congratulated the defendant's attorney, whom the local Jewish lawyers accused of inciting prejudice during the trial. After the trial the judge shook hands with the defendant and congratulated him on receiving the verdict of "not guilty."[18] The Jews were outraged. At the B'nai B'rith lodge a committee was appointed consisting of Rabbi Friedman, Philip Hornbein, and Charles Ginsberg to decide whether action should be taken.[19] A protest was entered against the ruling of the judge and was circulated through the community for signatures. It is said that the offending judge's attitude was considerably changed thereafter.

There were at least three other unsolved murders of Jews in Denver, one termed an assassination,[20] another during a robbery,[21] and the third that of a man disliked because of his business practices. None of these was the result of anti-Semitism. Although the Jews and others agitated for the finding and sentencing of the murderers,[22] there was not the accompanying fear that anti-Semitism generated.

The kleagles and dragons of the Ku Klux Klan took over the state government January, 1925. Clarence J. Morley was inaugurated governor in the packed city auditorium, the only inaugural not held in the state capitol. Dr. John Galen Locke became the ruler of the invisible empire of the Klan in Colorado. Although the rise of the Klan was no surprise to the Jewish community, which had seen it coming for several years, the Jews of Colorado had no program to fight the regime. Worse, there was very little agreement among the community leaders on how to handle the frightening situation.

Milton Anfenger went directly to Locke to find out what the exact attitude of the Klan was. Since there was only one franchise in the city for a baseball club, Anfenger asked him what his standing was now, as the club's owner. He found Locke with a gun and dog at his side. The emperor greeted him cordially, reminding him that he had fought for Anfenger's election as Exalted Ruler of the Elks, and that he had signed Anfenger's application for the Consistory. He then gave him a check for $100 for a season box seat at the ball park, with the assurance, "Our fight is not against your people." The Klan, he said, was against the Catholics and Negroes.

Similar assurances were given to the Catholics, and perhaps to the Negroes. Some of the Jews believed, or wanted to believe, that the Klan was not against them. Others, who were gravely concerned, looked for champions among the white Protestants who were not involved, believing that "it would look better" if the Klan was fought by non-Jewish and non-Catholic spokesmen. There were also appeasers. The B'nai B'rith lodge in 1924 had made arrangements for an open meeting to which the Klan officials would be invited in their capacity as public officials. As one of the committee arose to announce the plans for the meeting, Charles Ginsberg moved "that no member of the KKK be invited to attend any meeting of our lodge." After a great deal of discussion, the motion was lost.[23] The issue came up again at the following meeting at which Ira L. Quiat presented a lengthy motion condemning the invitation of the hooded order to a public initiation as inconsistent with the principles and ideal of the lodge and that Ginsberg's protests were consistent and proper as a Ben B'rith.[24] Phillip Hornbein, in defending Ginsberg, suggested that the lodge members dress in white *kittel* (robe) for the occasion, as though it were Yom Kippur. The KKK "would hail us like long lost brothers." No open meeting for the Klan was held at the lodge.

At the Ex-Patients' Tubercular Home, however, Governor Morley was "given a spontaneous and hearty welcome." The Klan governor wrote a letter calling it "one of the most worthy charitable institutions in Colorado," and said that it deserved support throughout the United States.[25] In addition to the appeasers were the traitors. One Jewish and one Catholic lawyer worked for the Klan. When the majority of the district judges were Klansmen, either of these two lawyers had to be hired by the Jews or Catholics in order to receive any form of just treatment by the judges.

Not even a handful of Jews fought the Klan, but those few who did were leaders of such magnitude that they carried great weight locally and gave courage to the bulk of frightened Jews, particularly those who remembered the pogroms of Russia. Ira L. Quiat, "the silver-tongued" orator of the West Colfax settlements, was elected to the state senate in 1925 as a militant anti-Klan spokesman, against his opponent who ran as a Klansman. His subsequent re-elections until 1933, when he left politics, were a testimonial to his stand on the Klan, as well as his leadership in the Democratic party.

Charles Ginsberg took a militant stand against the Klan. Not only in the lodge, but throughout the city and at the state university, the colorful and uninhibited Jewish lawyer spoke out fearlessly against the white terror. Like Ira Quiat, whose parents immigrated after the pogroms, Ginsberg was a product of the Orthodox Jewish community.

Sol W. Horn, a businessman and government employee, who gave up his government job to fight the Klan, was not strictly a Jew. At a meeting of Negroes he was introduced by the chairman, who in extolling him urged the audience to hear him well for "He was born a Jew, is a Catholic in religion, and in complexion resembles the rest of us." Horn worked closely with the groups which were trying to break the hold of the Klan in the city government even before it rose to power in the state.

Great weight was carried by Phil Hornbein, who was not in the least frightened by the Klan. Offered protection by the ministers and organizers of the various meetings at which he spoke, he scoffed at the suggestion. He advocated an all-out legal fight to break the hold of the invisible but well-known rulers.

Before the Klan tightened its hold on the state, these four men had helped circulate a petition to recall a high local official. The Jewish leaders of the community were afraid to put their names on the petition, and did not do so until the Catholic leader, Father Hugh McMenamin, signed it. The greatest part of the fight was waged by the Irish Catholics, the Denver *Post*, the Denver *Express*, and a number of celebrated idealists, among whom was Judge Lindsey. Actually the demise of the Klan was its own doing. Corruption within the ranks broke not only the grip of the menace, but also the menace itself.

While many of the Jews were terrified, the Klan had not yet resorted to violence when it fell from power. The group's membership came from all walks of life, answering the varied appeals the kleagles made. Among these were the promises of social prestige, proclaiming the superiority and power of the white Protestant. There was the excitement of cross-burning, parades, a woman's drum and fife corps, and the important mystery surrounding the secret ritual. But most attractive was the economic boycott leveled against all firms other than Klan-owned or endorsed.

The Klan also made deep inroads into the Masonic lodges. For several years Jews were unable to join most of the lodges in Denver. There was little the Jews could do about the blackballs that came their way. Nevertheless, a red-headed ex-army Jew from a mining town in Colorado managed to get back at one group of Klansmen. Since he was not known as a Jew, he joined the Klan in Denver and attended the secret meetings, there learning who the Klansmen were. Back in his Masonic lodge, which accepted no Jews during the reign of the Klan, he attended every meeting and blackballed every single petitioner to the lodge who was a Klansman. The bewildered members could do nothing about the situation, and if they suspected who was dropping so many blackballs, they still could not understand why, for they never suspected that their most regular-attending member was a Jew.

After the Klan left the political and economic scene, there was a lessening of anti-Semitism, but the effect of the state's excursion into the wilderness of prejudice was not wholly eradicated. The B'nai B'rith and later the Anti-Defamation League fought all forms of prejudice, but they could not change the pattern of social life in Denver. They could neither change the policies of excluding Jews from membership in the fashionable clubs, nor could they thwart the beginning of "gentlemen's agreements" to keep Jews out of the exclusive neighborhoods.

Still, this was unimportant to most of the Jews, who had the desire and ability to get along well with their neighbors, just as they had in the pioneer community. Even the divisive Klan created a bond between those it sought to dishonor. Father McMenamin said in 1923, "I love you for the enemies you have made, for my people have made the same enemies."[26] The Jews had close friends among the idealistic leaders of the community. Particularly devoted were Judge Lindsey, Mayor Speer (the builder and beautifier of twentieth-century Denver), and J. Warner Mills, who resigned from the Denver Athletic Club because the members of that club did not permit Jews to membership.[27]

The courts rescheduled trials when participants could not come because of the Jewish holidays. After the Jews had been disfranchised twice in the history of Denver when elections coincided with the holidays, the city made provision for the Jews to mail in absentee ballots, so that they would not have to vote on a holy day.

In 1921, when anti-Semitism was reaching its height, the *Jewish News* in Denver reported a conversation Walter Appel had heard in the court of the justice of peace. The justice noted that the defendant was not in court on October 3, and asked if it was because the day was a Jewish holiday. The plantiff announced, "It doesn't make any difference to me."

> The court: It does to me. If this is a man's holiday, he can't come here.
> Plaintiff: Because of the Jewish holiday, I can't get judgment here. I thought we were all Americans here.
> Court: Just for that reason. We respect a man's religion.[28]

Interfaith activities took place at every level. In 1955 some Jews and Catholics felt that they had gone too far when a combined demonstration of the Passover and Communion service was staged in Denver. The Passover services had been successfully staged earlier in the small community of Rifle, where no Jews lived. The Anti-Defamation League in conjunction with the Denver Council of Churches sponsored the combined event. Although Catholics did not attend, and the program was denounced by some of the horrified Orthodox Jews, the more liberal Jews and Christians, as well as the delighted press, regarded it as a success, with the *Post Empire Magazine* devoting its cover and lead story to the services.[29]

Communal effort quiets the voices of the hatemongers as they appear from time to time. Denver's young Mayor Quigg Newton established a Human Relations Commission during his term. A Fair Employment Practice bill was passed by the state legislature in 1951 and strengthened in 1955.

FOOTNOTES

[1] *RMN*, Jan. 15, 1863.
[2] *RMN*, June 1, 1868.
[3] Telephone conversation with club secretary, July 5, 1952; Forbes Parkhill, "The Five Homes of the Denver Club," *Post, Empire*, Dec. 26, 1954 gives date of organizing as July 10, 1880.
[4] *RMN*, Aug. 14, 1881, p. 7.
[5] *RMN*, Nov. 21, 1881, p. 4.
[6] *Times*, Nov. 22, 1900.
[7] *JO*, Dec. 4, 1903.
[8] *DJN*, June 16, 1916.
[9] BB minutes, June 11, 1916.
[10] The others are Illinois, Massachusetts, Michigan, New York, New Jersey and Pennsylvania.
[11] *JO*, June 22, 1906.
[12] Ida Hurwitz papers.
[13] *Post*, Dec. 26, 1905; *JO*, Jan. 19, 26, Feb. 16, May 4, 1906.
[14] *JO*, Feb. 15, May 3, May 10, 1907.
[15] *JO*, Feb. 12, 1909.
[16] BB minutes, June 27, 1909, p. 59.
[17] *Times*, Mar. 6, 1909.
[18] *DJN*, May 5, 1920.
[19] BB minutes, May 9, 1920.
[20] Seymour Jarecki assassinated, June 30, 1904.
[21] M. L. Caplan killed during a burglary at his home.
[22] BB minutes, Mar. 9, 1908. Two years later Herman Strauss called the attention of the lodge to the fact that the proper officials were not as zealous as they might be in the case.
[23] BB minutes, Apr. 13, 1924.
[24] *Ibid.*, Apr. 27, 1924.
[25] *DJN*, July 30, 1925.
[26] *DJN*, June 28, 1923.
[27] BB minutes, May 26, 1907.
[28] *DJN*, Oct. 29, 1921.
[29] *Post Empire*, Apr. 18, 1954.

The Yiddish-Speaking Jews

1

There is not such a wide gap between the coming of the "German" Jews and the "Russian" Jews into Colorado as is popularly supposed. Not all of the pioneers of 1859 and 1860, nor those who followed them in the next two decades, were from Germany. Nor were all of the East European Jews—who came from Austria, Hungary, Rumania and Poland—Russian Jews.

Not the country of birth, and not the religious practices of these groups, constituted the barrier between them. The only one real difference was that the East European Jews spoke Yiddish as their daily language and the Central European Jews who knew no Yiddish, spoke German. Even the religious services of the latter group were conducted in German.

Like the German Jews, the earliest East European Jews—of whom there were more than two dozen in Denver when the 1880 census was taken[1]—came to Colorado, not in waves of immigration, but as individuals, and for the same reasons the Central European Jews came. Many a young boy, even like Otto Mears, crossed the ocean to seek his fortune. Economics was a large factor in leaving the Old Country for America before the pogroms of 1881. With Colorado as a goal, at the height of the search for precious metals, these early Jews may be counted with their co-religionists in their reasons for going West.

Another important reason advanced by many young men who left Russian Poland was to escape being drafted into the Russian army, which used military service to destroy Jews and Judaism. One such immigrant was Simon Block, who came to Colorado in 1868. Born in Suwalki, Russian Poland, where he had acquired a "fair"[2] education and entered the grain trade, he was ready for conscription just as the farm he had purchased was confiscated by the government. Block fled. In Colorado he began as a peddler, making the rounds of the mining camps. His niece, Lena Zalinger, married Austrian-born Dr. Elsner, and he married the widow of his Russo-Polish friend, Joel Gottlieb.

Another lure to the West was the crisp, clear air of the mile-high city bordered by lofty peaks. Thus, many a learned and pious man came west, where he could not hope to live in accordance with the laws laid down for him. This sacrifice was not made for the sake of gold, but for one of which Judaism approved—his health. One or more of these reasons can be applied to almost every East European Jew who came before 1881.

The first of one of Colorado's most successful East European families came with the pioneers. Alexander Rittmaster, like Block, also came from Suwalki. An escaped prisoner of the Crimean War, he is said to have settled in Central City in 1860. Seven years later he was joined by a nephew, Abraham Rachofsky,[3] who escaped Suwalki when Russian Cossacks invaded his parents' home. Rachofsky arrived in New York the day after Lincoln's assassination. Apparently Mrs. Rittmaster, who lived there in preference to Central City, helped in his first business venture, teaching him the words, "Glass put in." He saved enough money to invest in an unprofitable hoop skirt factory. From this he had only enough money left to take a train almost to Council Bluffs. On foot, he followed ox teams loaded with freight bound for Cheyenne. His meals were earned by gathering "buffalo chips" for the wagon train for use as fuel. His sleeping quarters were the ground. Arriving in Cheyenne with one dollar, he felt he could afford the luxury of a "nickel cigar." He stopped in a saloon, made his purchase, and waited for change. There was no change. From Cheyenne he walked to Pueblo, more than 200 miles. There he obtained work as a cowhand for eight months in 1867. His next walk took him to Central City, where he went to work for his uncle in the general merchandising business. Now his walking and tramping days began in earnest.

With two large canvas-covered bags and two telescope grips filled with merchandise, he began peddling to the neighboring camps in Gregory Gulch, Clear Creek, and beyond. He crossed steep passes, following the trails of the prospectors. Sometimes the packs were so heavy that he had to put on counter-weight. Even the strongest miners were said to have found them hard to lift.

If the mountain was too steep to descend with his wares, he would roll the packs down first. For his merchandise he received gold dust. Change was made in the precious currency, the miners and merchant trusting each other in its weight and quality.

Across the range from Georgetown are Handcart Creek, Handcart Gulch, and Handcart Pass. A descendant of one of the residents says:

> My father used to tell me of a Jewish peddler who used to take his handcart over the range as soon as the snow melted. There was no wagon road, just a trail, but it was a shorter route than the wagon road over Webster Pass. These passes led from somewhere near Grant over the Continental Divide and down to Montezuma. I know my father thought he deserved much praise for his ambition and hard work in bringing needed articles to the people of those isolated districts.[4]

The description could fit any number of Jewish peddlers.

Within a year Rittmaster and Rachofsky opened a clothing store in Caribou, in Boulder county, which was enjoying a silver boom. When the town was destroyed by fire Rachofsky had no alternative but to return to Central and start peddling again. This time he had an interest in his uncle's business, which became "A. Rittmaster & Co."

While he was building his own successful business and reputation, taking part in the building of the city's famed opera house, planting the first lilac bush in the Gulch, and subscribing to every civic improvement, Rachofsky kept his family in mind. He sent for his brothers, his sister, nephews, nieces, and cousins. The Rachofsky name began to appear on stores in almost every town on his peddling circuit. He brought enough relatives into Colorado to start what his family likes to call an early "chain" store. The chain had been strengthened when Rachofsky married the sister of Georgetown Louis Cohen. Other marriages as far west as Silverton linked the family and business ties. After conferring with the older Rachofskys, many of the young people decided that Poland had not treated the Jews so well that they should carry the foreign "ski" on their names. They changed their names to Ross, Rice, Rich, Rayor, and Ray.

After the Polish revolution and ensuing pogroms, the remaining Rachofskys fled from Poland to England. Abraham's sister, Mary Kubeski, who had hidden him in a forest before he came to America, left with her husband and three children for Manchester.

There three more children were born and the Kubeski name was changed to Kobey. Isaac Shwayder, whom the eldest Kobey daughter, Rachel, married in England, came to Central City, where he began peddling just as his wife's uncle had earlier. He was not joined by Rachel until two years later. The Christians who knew him were greatly impressed by his piety, particularly his restraint when a package arrived on *Shabbas,* obviously containing pictures of his family, which he had not seen for many months. Not until evening did he cut the string around the package. His in-laws, the Kobeys, came to Central later.

Abraham Rachofsky brought a *Sefer Torah* (scroll of the Bible) to Central City, where he conducted Orthodox services. When his son was ready to be *bar mitzvah,* he was sent to Alexander Rittmaster, now in New York, for the necessary preparation and ceremony marking his entrance into Jewish manhood. The Rachofskys joined the Temple in Denver. Mary and her family were pious, observant Jews. The only concessions she made to western ways was the discarding of the *sheitel* (wig worn by pious married women) at the insistence of her daughter on their way to America. Life in the mountains did not lend itself to the keeping of the minute traditions, but the Kobeys made every attempt. At first they had kosher meat shipped to them, but it arrived spoiled so much of the time that the family simply became vegetarians. Before Rachofsky built the first bath in town, preparations for the Sabbath included a trip to the mineral baths in Idaho Springs, a short distance by mine tunnel, but fifteen miles by the Virginia Canon road. This road, a narrow ledge zigzagging back and forth on the side of a wall-like mountain, is so frightening that Ulysses S. Grant, when taken over it, had to be reassured by the coach driver that he valued his neck as much as the president did his. The precipitous trip was taken weekly, and possibly more often, for no *mikveh* (ritual bath) existed in the mining camp.

The lonely, comfortless life was hard enough to endure, but the absence of young Jewish girls and women made it almost impossible for Mary Kobey. Her handsome sons attracted the gentile girls in the vicinity. When one girl voiced her determination to marry one of them, gentle Mrs. Kobey, in her broken English, pleaded desperately, "You don't want to marry a sheeney?"

As soon as they could, the Kobeys left the mountain camp for Denver. The Shwayders remained there a number of years as merchants and mine-owners. There was no Jewish house of worship in Central City at any time, despite the fairly large number of Jews who lived there over the years. Isaac Shwayder, who had been trained in Europe, acted as the rabbi for the mountain community, which was both Reform and Orthodox. He performed marriages for both, and served as cantor as well. Services were held in a store building. When the community became too small, the carpet department of Rachofsky's store served as a synagogue.

Few women earned the love and gratitude of so many Jews as did Mary Kobey, who became known as the "angel of mercy" in West Colfax. While staying in her daughter's home over the High Holidays, the woman, who was now a grandmother, heard that a Jewish woman had given birth to dead Siamese twins. The babies had been delivered by students of the Gross Medical College, who took them to the school to preserve and study. The young mother, an immigrant, was unable to stop them. When Mary heard the story she went directly to the College, where she explained that the preservation of bodies was contrary to Jewish law and asked that the bodies be returned to the family for proper burial.

Since she had studied midwifery she decided that there was a real need for her in the poor Jewish community growing up around the Platte River. Over the protest of her children, who felt she was too old to engage in such strenuous work, the small, friendly woman, whose English was liberally sprinkled with Yiddish, became the most welcome sight to the young women of West Colfax.

Her husband, Samuel Abrum, also known as A. S. A., was listed as rabbi of Agudas Achim, the Lithuanian synagogue on the Platte River, as well as a scribe for the community, which needed an expert hand to repair and write sacred documents. As was the case with most pious men, he had very little money, and was not in a position to disapprove his wife's project. Not only was it a good deed, but whatever she brought home would also be helpful.

Working alone, or calling in a doctor for a difficult case, she is said to have had "a healing power" that had the women clinging to her. Actually she was a conscientious woman who cared for the mothers as though they were her own daughters. In one case where she had delivered a normal child, the mother called her again to deliver another. When she arrived she found that the child she had previously helped bring into the world was not walking. After she delivered the baby, she took the older boy to a clinic where the offending ligaments were severed. For ten months she examined the child faithfully, until she was certain that he would walk normally. Many such stories are told about her—how she never completed her job with the delivery, but sometimes stayed on with the family, caring for the new baby and mother and helping the father. Her own children were in the capable hands of her daughter, Rachel Shwayder, who helped rear her brothers and sister, along with her own large family.

When Mary was faced with difficulty in delivery, she called in Dr. Morris J. Krohn, a young physician in West Colfax. Krohn married her granddaughter, Florence, who, after they were married, studied midwifery, so that she could take much of the unpleasant work of cleaning up off his hands. Dr. Krohn delivered more than 2,500 babies, a large portion of them to Jewish immigrant mothers.

Mary and A. S. A. lived near the little synagogue close to the Platte. As they grew old their children and grandchildren became concerned and asked that they move into the Beth Israel Old Folks Home. The couple refused, but they finally consented to be moved into a house near the Home. Despite the fact that the house had running water, instead of a pump in the kitchen, and other similar conveniences, Mary was pining for something. She was happy again when her brother then bought her a cow.

When she died in 1921, after living in Denver for thirty-three years, she left seventy-four descendants. In 1955 there were 189 descendants, eighty-eight of whom were from her daughter Rachel. By comparison, her brother, Abraham, left nine. With all of her brothers' and cousins' descendants, the Rachofsky-Kobey-Shwayder family is one of the largest Jewish families in the state, and one of the oldest, beginning with Alexander Rittmaster in the early 60's.

The musical talent of A. S. A. and Isaac, both of whom had cantorial training, was found abundantly in the Shwayder children. A neighbor, Wilberforce Whiteman (father of Paul, the "King of Jazz") was director of music in the Denver Public Schools when the Shwayders were living in West Denver. Recognizing the ability of the children, he brought Jesse Shwayder to St. John's Episcopal Cathedral, and at the age of nine the boy's solos delighted the congregation. Soon the children were singing throughout the city, especially in great demand by the churches everywhere, except at the Temple Emanuel, where Jews were not in the choir. Jesse was also a violinist and started a dance orchestra while he was still in high school. Liebe, a pianist, played with Ossip Gabrilowitsch in the Detroit Symphony. Florence, a contralto, directed the choir at the Messiah Lutheran Church. Hannah, in addition to singing on the radio and in local opera, later became a soloist at the Temple and director of the congregation's music.

The Shwayder family struggled in West Denver. Their little grocery did not always bring in enough money to provide for the large family. The grocery was sold for a second-hand furniture store, which was no more profitable. Jesse saw the plight of the family clearly. "Pa," he decided, "we're going to auction off the store." A retail luggage store was opened, where Jesse was so successful that the manufacturers of one line brought him to their headquarters in New York. A year later he returned to Denver, and in 1910 he opened his own luggage factory. The whole family worked in the factory, the younger brothers varnishing trunks, sweeping, and running errands. From this factory grew the largest luggage factory in America, Shwayder Brothers, with the famed Samson label.

2

Russia, under Alexander III, supplied a terrifying reason for further immigration into the United States and even Colorado. That country, in 1881, embarked on a vicious plan to rid itself of the Jews. One third were to be slaughtered, one third to be converted to the Greek Orthodox church, and the remaining third to be expelled.

The bulk of Russian Jews came to the eastern seaboard of the United States, where the Jewish leaders saw that congestion would create more problems. Colorado, far from the crowded East, was one of the places deemed suitable for the immigrants. From this same group other Jews came later after they had contracted tuberculosis in the eastern cities.

There were also idealists in this group, the advocates of social justice, and the followers of the *Haskalah*, "The Enlightenment." Racing for America, they had before them the vision of land, of farms, and of stock which they could own for the first time in a long period of their history. Dearer still was the prospect of full citizenship—especially the precious right to vote in a free election.

Purely personal reasons played their part. An apostate in the family spelled such disgrace that it was impossible to find suitable matches for the unmarried young people in the family. Sometimes the reason was economic, in that while there was money for food, there was not enough money to dower a bride. *Yichus,* or prestige, played such an important part in marriages, that most parents would be heartbroken to permit the marriage of a child to one of inferior position, particularly in learning. Rather than remain a spinster, many a young girl left for the Golden Land, where she needed no dowry and was free to marry anyone who asked her.

Living in tenements in the East and working in sweatshops, the immigrants were no closer to working the land than they had been in Russia. The Hebrew Immigrant Aid Society (HIAS), well aware of the plight of the newcomers, formulated plans to settle them throughout the country, preferably in colonies. The reaction in Denver to such plans was not warm. In 1882 the president of Temple Emanuel sent out a warning to Russian immigrants not to come to Colorado:

> Twenty-one immigrants have been sent to us. The travelling expense for each of whom from New York amounts to $420. To this we added enough to enable them to live for a short time, and to send some of them back to New York, $500. Altogether close to $1,000. This sum has enabled us only to find a place for one man to sell his merchandise in a public square. When later on he will have to pay for this privilege himself, he may not be able to support himself any longer. Of the above mentioned immigrants, two shoemakers and two peddlers may be able to make a living. The best thing for the rest of them, and for ourselves, is to send them back to New York.[5]

Despite his warnings, the Russian Jews came to Colorado. From one unsuccessful colony begun that year came a descendant who was to occupy the presidency of the same temple from which its ex-president had issued his warning. The same year of the above warning an opposite attitude was reflected in *Hazefirah*:

> (A New Group of Immigrants in America)
> Compared to the wretched exile in Paris, how well off are our brethren in Colorado, USA, who have congregated there and found all they need. Now they are considering that man does not live on bread alone. They wish to observe their religion, and since they do not have a Sefer Torah and other necessities, therefore we turned to Rabbi Hildesheimer in Ber-

lin, to give them spiritual assistance as he has already done while they spoke to him in Berlin. Their letter of request was printed in the Jewish Press, and we are sure that our brethren in Germany will soon come to their aid.[6]

3

The pathetic condition of a group of Russian immigrants in New York, the ideals of the HIAS, and the ambitions of a Portuguese Jew in Colorado, combined to weave a colorful story that is endlessly retold in Denver.[7]

With funds supplied to a great extent by Baron Maurice de Hirsch, most of the Russian immigrants came directly to New York. One group, bound together through marriages and *landsmanschaft*, and said to have had farming aspirations, came to Michael Heilprin, then the brilliant guide of the HIAS program for agricultural colonization in America. He was considering sending the group to Oregon, when an offer was presented to him which would solve the problem of settling these sixty-four persons from Volhynia, Kiev, and nearby Russian provinces.

The offer was made by Emanuel H. Saltiel, a Portuguese Jew, with a reputation as a successful mining man. In addition, he manfactured concrete building material, as many oval trademarks on the sidewalks of Denver testify. (Incidentally, this appears to have been a family project. A John T. Saltiel filed a patent, June 9, 1903, for a process of manufacturing artificial stone. The ingredients consisted of "tallow, or suet fat, three dozen finely crushed eggshells, and vinegar, boiled together and cooled. To this was added powdered granite and glass, grit, pebbles, clinkers, etc.")[8] Among his investments were two mines near Cotopaxi, between Salida and Canon City.[9] As the story is told in Denver, the Leadville boom was at its height and throughout the state there was a heavy demand for miners. Saltiel could not, or would not, meet the competitive wages resulting from the heavy demand for labor.

Active in many of the Jewish organizations in Denver, he was informed on the Russian Jewish situation in the East. He is thought to have decided to bring in his own labor supply. As a wealthy and generous westerner, he made an irresistible offer to settle a colony of Jewish farmers on his lands, promising houses, barns, sheds, furniture, household equipment, tools, seed, cattle, horses, wagons, and a year's supply of feed for the animals. All of this for $8,750. The colonists were to raise $1,250 to cover the cost of rail transportation to his property. The HIAS approved $10,000 from the Baron de Hirsch Fund. Although there was no reason to suspect deception, the organization, nevertheless, sent a young lawyer to Colorado to investigate the area. He was never heard from again by the HIAS.

Here there are two versions to the story. The most popular one, related by the immigrants and their descendants, is that the prospective farmers, most of them bearded *Chassidim*[10] (members of a pious mystic sect), journeyed into the strange land. Their train took them close to the awesome Royal Gorge, through deep, dark canyons and past the barren rocks of the region. If their spirits were lifted at the sight of the strips of green along the river of the Arkansas Valley, they soon fell. They arrived in Cotopaxi May 8, 1882, where they found that the farms they had been promised were eight or ten miles south of the town. Instead of twenty houses and five barns they found twelve small, poorly constructed cabins, most of them without chimneys, doors, windows, or stoves. Instead of 160 acres in each of the twenty divisions, the land they were to till rose high onto the rocky soil of the ridges around the canyon, virtually immeasurable. Not even a road or well was provided. The most abundant source of water was the flash flood common to the region—more devastating than almost all of the other elements.

According to Flora Jane Satt, a descendant of the patriarch of the colonists, Henry (Gold Tom) Thomas was the prospector who filed the claim of the discovery of the Cotopaxi Lode, which he named after a Spanish Andean volcano. In her description of the Jews' arrival at Cotopaxi, which was given her by Charles H. McCoy, McCoy added that Gold Tom was shot and killed on the steps of the Cotopaxi Hotel by A. Hart on May 23, 1883. A different version is told by Hart's descendants.[11]

E. Samuel Hart was living in New York when he was asked to supervise the trip for the immigrants going to Colorado. He left his family behind while he made the trip with the colonists. His wife and children came out on the next train. According to a son, Josiah C. Hart:

> I saw Gold Tom get shot. He was on the porch of the store across the way from our store. I was on our porch when a man by the name of McCoy came out of our store and saw Gold Tom and shot him. That was all there was to it.[12]

E. Samuel Hart's son, Myer, was sheriff of Cotopaxi at the time. Saltiel and Hart were cousins—Saltiel from South Africa, Hart from Thelma, England. The Harts lived behind the General Store until 1884, when they left for Chicago.

The popular version continues with the fact that the immigrants could speak no English, Saltiel no Yiddish. The colonists could only believe that Saltiel had made an error. In June they decided their first need was a synagogue. In their first letter to the HIAS they requested a *Sefer Torah* (lending credence to the item in *Hazefirah* that it was this group that made that request). When they received the scroll it was housed in an abandoned cabin behind the General Store, the first and only synagogue in Cotopaxi. Two weddings were performed that summer.

The pleasant Colorado fall compensated for much of the colonists' hardships. Winter was an almost unendurable contrast. The potatoes which should have been ready for harvest were frozen, and one colonist noted that the potatoes he had planted were better than those which had grown in the barren soil. Without fuel, adequate clothing or ammunition for their European guns, the terrified colonists faced the frightening winter with its begging Indians, and roaming bears. Penniless, they had to make their puchases from the general store on credit.

There was no choice left the men but to go to work for Saltiel in his mines, four miles away. For their labor they received $1.50 for the day shift and $2.50 for the night. Their wages were not cash, but vouchers which they could use at the general store. By now the colonists began to believe that they had been victimized, and that the dream of an agricultural colony was as remote as ever. The men left the mines and found work in Salida digging trenches for the Denver and Rio Grande Railroad, which graciously gave the *Chassidim* their day off on Saturday so that they could keep what was sacred to them—the Sabbath.

By the second year they were sufficiently familiar with the region to send delegates to Denver for aid. In the meantime their appeals to the HIAS led the organization to send Denver investigators to Cotopaxi. All accounts vary concerning how they effected the rescue of the group. Apparently there were many persons in Denver who were deeply concerned by the plight of their co-religionists. Help of various kinds came from both the German Jews and the East European Jews. The Hebrew Ladies' Benevolent Society was credited with helping the colonists from the time the first group was brought to Denver until the group was formally disbanded in June, 1884.[13]

Having been a part of the Cotopaxi Colony became a badge of *yichus,* just as helping rescue them became an honor. Two members of the Orthodox synagogue in Denver, Rabbi Solomon Arager, Marks Garbarsky and a Mr. Schayer (probably Charles Schayer), were remembered by the colonists as being particularly attentive to their needs. Adolph Weiner is said to have helped them so much that he was almost financially ruined.[14] Later one of the Orthodox groups named a lodge after him.

It must not be supposed that the spirits of the colonists had suffered during these two rigorous years. They were *Chassidim,* and were not only cheerful, but even gay. One of the colonists had a music box as well as the ability to perform sleight of hand tricks. "Katerinchick," as the colonists called him, amused them during the long winter evenings. The holidays were celebrated in true *Chassidic* style. For the Passover, when the colonists were unable to obtain registered Passover flour, some of the men traveled to Salida. There in accordance with the laws of the *Shulchan Aruch,* they picked every tenth sack of flour for use in baking their matzos.

Mrs. Satt points out that the colony had wasted almost three years on the wretched land when they could have chosen their land from the public domain and acquired it by homesteading. But the years of hardship and the tragedies of burying two newly born babies and a young child did not stop them from making the new country their home. Nearly all of the members of the colony remained in the state or nearby, many of them continuing with great success in farming, stock-raising, and allied fields.

4

Fifty years after the Cotopaxi Colony had disbanded, Dr. Charles D. Spivak and Dr. J. M. Morris wrote an account of the colony for "the Future Historian of Jewish Agricultural Colonies in the United States." The article concluded: "That, for reasons inscrutable, most of the colonies were planted on land which was unfit for cultivation."[15]

Whereas this was true of Cotopaxi, it did not apply to the Atwood Colony, which organized more than a decade after the first Jewish colony in Colorado. If the Atwood colony is regarded as a failure, it should not be because it was planted on unfit land, for it was located on the rich land of the Logan Valley. There were

Frances Rose (Rosenzweig). Courtesy Dena Kalischer.

Dickinson Library. Photo by author.

Knesseth Israel. Photo by author.

David Spivak stained glass windows for BMH. Photo by author.

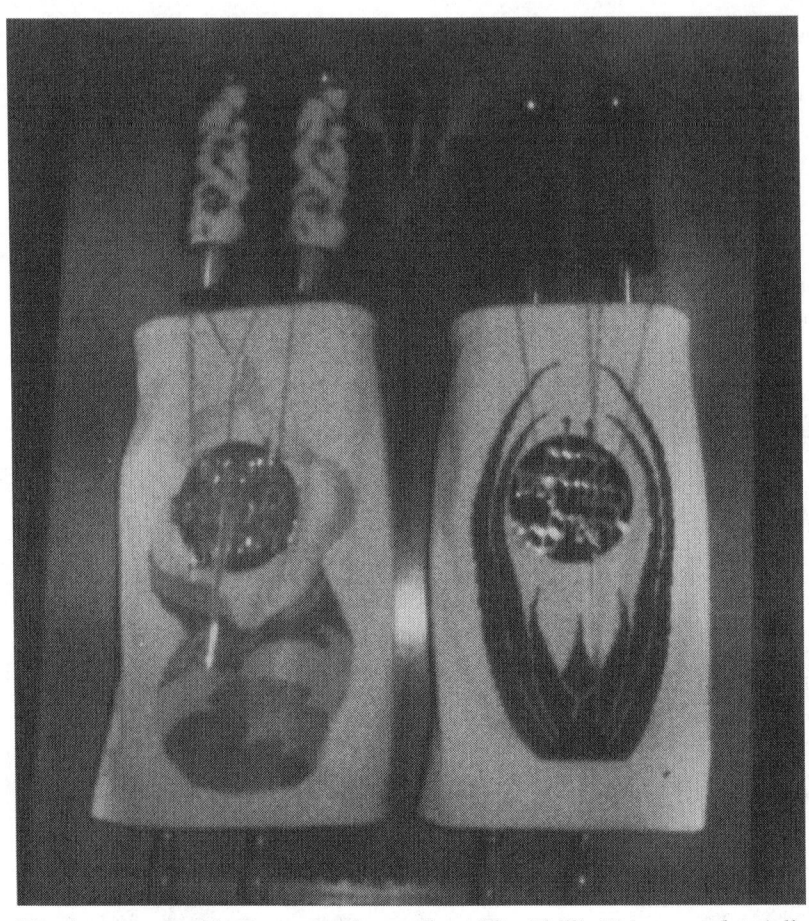

Torah covers at Air Force Academy chapel by Phillis Kantor and Arielle Miller-Timen. Photo by author.

Paul and Fannie Pepper Libert on Edgewater farm, 1917.

Looking west, Zera Israel, Gardenschwartz grocery, Palm Theater. Photo by author.

A. Z. Salomon's Dry Goods (1886) at 16th and Stout Streets, Denver. Courtesy of Bob Fuller.

Sixteenth Street, 1938. Paul Libert collection.

Babi Yar Park. Photo by author.

North High students paint Prime Minister Golda Meir's home. Courtesy Esther Cohen Strauss.

Stained-glass portrait of Chief Justice Edward E. Pringle of the Colorado State Supreme Court. Photo by Mark N. Kiryluk for *University of Denver Law*.

other factors which destined the colony to come to an end three years after it was organized.

Unfortunately the story of the Atwood Colony appears never to have been recorded. As it is told here, it is pieced together from four, frequently conflicting, accounts by former colonists, and from the minutes of the B'nai B'rith lodge which became involved in the colony's affairs.

In 1891 the national B'nai B'rith requested the Denver lodge to report a plan for the systematic distribution of Russian Jews throughout Colorado. A proposal was made to the lodge by T. C. Henry, a prominent irrigation man and land developer. Although the lodge minutes[16] do not reveal his plan, subsequent events indicate what his suggestions were.

According to Mary Fine Fishman, who at sixteen was the colony's secretary, a group of sweatshop workers, tailors, and small businessmen, who had met at *landsmanshaft* gatherings in Philadelphia, had heard that there was land in the far west suitable for farming. All of them were poor and had suffered greatly in the Panic of 1893. They met together in 1894 to discuss what possibilities there were for them to form a colony and acquire land. Mrs. Fishman relates that a member of the group, a Mr. Silver, was sent to Baron de Hirsch with the idea of the philanthropist financing a colony. Since the Baron had established the fund named for him in New York in 1891, with the purpose of aiding immigrants in establishing themselves throughout the United States, the delegate was surprised that the Baron refused.

Thereupon, the group, most of whom could neither speak nor write English adequately, sent Mary to her school teacher asking that she write an advertisement to the effect that a "group of twenty-five families want to be settled on farm land." The advertisement brought responses from California and Colorado. The Colorado answer came from T. C. Henry, who may have envisioned just such a project when he made his proposal. Silver, the delegate, was sent to investigate the Logan Valley in the area around Sterling, land Henry had under contract.

Finding the land favorable, and the price of three or four dollars an acre within its means, Silver notified the group in the East of these facts. Two groups of men left for Atwood to organize the colony, the first coming into the region by way of Galveston, arriving at the site in March, 1895. Louis Fine was chosen director of the colony. Together with Henry, the men made all of the living arrangements and outlined the agricultural plans. Henry alloted the cattle, horses, and lumber. In addition, one ex-colonist reported that Henry was to supply flour and potatoes for six months. Although all accounts agree that he carried out his part of the agreement, he could not meet the demands of the group from the first.

The land was excellent, the neighbors not only sympathetic but helpful as well, and the prospects appeared bright. Despite this by September more than half of the colonists left. A look at the composition of the colony offers a partial reason. Four distinct groups joined the Atwood Colony. They came from Philadelphia, New York, Argentina, Baltimore, and New Jersey and represented all parts of Eastern Europe. There was even one who had been in a Palestinian colony. He was known in Atwood as "Yankel Koloneist." It is said that the colony included about sixty families, and about 300 individuals. Apparently there were too many bachelors for a stable community. The respectable members were shocked by the behavior of the "roughnecks" with whom they had to work and live. Some of the bachelors who shared a cow with a family demanded an equal amount of the milk, no matter how many children the latter included.

Religious dissension rent the community further apart. The young people were confused and anxious to drop the burdensome ritual. Some of the group kept the Sabbath and others did not. Many of the elders wore beards and held religious services daily to the annoyance of the non-religious element, which was additionally disgusted with the necessity of having kosher meat shipped by wagon or rail to the colony. Poultry was shipped from Atwood to Denver to be slaughtered and then shipped back. The kosher chickens were thrown from the freight cars to the waiting colonists. The first complaint was voiced when some of the members found that they were more than a hundred miles from Denver. When a son was born, one family took the baby to Denver for the *b'rith* and remained there. After breaking their first Yom Kippur fast with watermelon, the food in greatest abundance, most of those who had a trade either left for Denver or returned to the East.

Some of the ex-sweatshop workers had to be taught such elementary facts as how to hitch a team of horses. To make it more difficult, the hundred horses sent in by Henry were said to have been broncos which took a year to break, but the colonists had to farm with them immediately.

Before he died, Meyer Forman, an ex-colonist, was interviewed by Dr. Morris, whose notes[17] give a different version from that of Mrs. Fishman. According to him, one response to the colony's advertisement came from the Bevan Company[18] of Colorado, offering agricultural land to the prospective settlers to be paid for in small installments. Eighteen members contributed the sum of ninety dollars to their delegate, not Silver, but a man named Yedevitz, who left for Colorado early in August, 1894. His reply by letter was that "Everything is of the finest, good land, wonderful opportunity." But, "His report was not so optimistically received as it was given." Many of the members expressed doubts, and asked the delegate to return with a detailed report. Forman, who had been a farmer in Bessarabia only the year before, was impressed. He decided to investigate before the delegate returned. He arrived in Denver in 1895. The notes are not clear, but apparently the first delegate was not delighted to see him.

With an interpreter, a "Mr. Itzkovitz, a native,"[19] Forman appeared at the Bevan Company where he was given a "cool reception." Mr. Bevan refused to deal with him as an individual. Forman was then referred to J. S. Appel, who referred him to Rabbi Friedman. The rabbi showed interest, and in turn introduced Forman to attorney Alfred Muller, at the time a highly respected communal leader. Through Muller, Forman met Henry, who took Forman to the available land. Both agreed that the 6500-acre tract was sufficient for the hundred families. According to Forman, and contradicted by the other accounts, Henry then went to Philadelphia, where he made arrangments to finance the colony, the funds for which were sent to the district attorney in Sterling.

Among Forman's memories were the visits by Dr. Spivak and Solomon Bloomgarden (Yehoash), who came to visit and eat watermelons; the kind treatment by the non-Jews, especially in Sterling, where "they were offered everything they needed" when Shavuouth came, and that some of the men worked on the railroad rather than on the land.

These accounts are augmented by that of Nathan Schwartz, who came with his father, older brother, and brother-in-law to the United States in 1894 from the forest country near Kremenitz.

His father, Samuel H. Schwartzburg, was holding a twenty-five year lease on the equivalent of 7800 American acres when the family was forced to leave everything under a new law, and to flee because a relative, an electrical engineer, had participated in the assassination of one of the Czar's cruelest aides. The act was so serious that 10,000 *rubles* were offered for his capture.

Schwartz says that when he arrived, there was nothing but a still "of a mind to go onto the land." In New York where men were getting about three dollars a week as pressers or coat makers, his eldest son fell sick while working and attending college at the same time. Schwartzburg bought into two Jewish colonies in New Jersey. Both failed. It was then that the family saw the Fine group's advertisement. Schwartzburg invited the Philadelphia group to his home at 98 Suffolk Street in New York. There a decision was made to send three delegates to Colorado.

Schwartz says that when he arrived there was nothing but a railroad station sidetrack called Atwood, and that the first house was built of sod. Schwartzburg bought his own land, separating himself from the non-observant and rowdy element as soon as possible. His son, Nathan, who shortened the family name, believes that what doomed the colony was the conditions resulting from the Panic of 1893. With alfalfa worth two dollars a ton, the colonists burned the crop. Eggs sold for ten cents a dozen, and all the colonists could do with the abundant watermelons, cantalopes and muskmelons was eat them. Nevertheless Schwartzburger remained with his land, meanwhile homesteading more in the state. His sons worked in Denver during the winter, while he built his herd of thirty-two head from one cow.

The fourth account, offered by Louis Rossman, who was a child in the colony, consists of his memories of the tanks of fresh milk brought to the colonists in Galveston by local Jews. He remembers arriving in Atwood where there was nothing but prairie and waiting stacks of lumber. The Rossman's house was the last one built, and until a building was set aside for worship, it served as the *shul* (synagogue), housing the *Sefer Torahs* and a cantor named "Naphtali."

According to Schwartz, Henry drew up a contract to allot each family sixteen acres of land and the privilege of buying up to sixty acres, at either $38 or $42 an acre. The three and four dollar acres he believes was for dry land. Each family was to put $90 into the colony, $50 to Henry and $40 for traveling expenses. The land was owned by Henry and no deeds were drawn up.

It is possible that the de Hirsch Fund helped several individuals or even one or more of the four groups that constituted the colony. It was the Fund that came to their rescue. The final developments are taken here from the 1896-7 minutes of the Denver B'nai B'rith lodge.

5

In July, 1896, Dr. Spivak, as a guest ot the lodge, reported that he had received inquiry from a society in Philadelphia asking about the advisability of sending a colony of Russian Jews to Colorado to settle on farms.[20] Since the Atwood colony was under way, there is a chance that this inquiry came from one of the four groups of colonists who may have come out later. However, because Dr. Spivak knew Louis Fine in Philadelphia, and visited the colony during its existence, the matter is puzzling.

Two months later, "Bro. Muller made a speech on the condition of the people in the Atwood Colony, who he said were in a starving condition."[21] Their condition was so bad that a committee was appointed and a special meeting was called.

It was decided to restrict an appeal for aid to the colonists to the city of Denver.[22] After the sum of $45 was raised and sent to the colony, the committee was instructed to write to the trustees of the Baron de Hirsch fund and ask for assistance for the colony.[23] While the lodge was raising money for the colonists, the Jewish community was confronted with another problem—the colonists who had moved to Denver. In December the *Republican* published a news item:

> Arapahoe County [to which Denver belonged]
> Will Sue Logan County for Support Given
> The expense to the county occasioned by the Jewish colony sent here from Logan County will be charged to that county, and if not paid, Arapahoe will sue for the amount expended on the colonists.

Logan County insisted that it was not its responsibility, but several of the ex-colonists had already said that the county had given them aid in order to move to Arapahoe County.[24]

The lodge considered giving some of the money raised for the colony to the ex-colonists, but decided against it.[25] In April the Atwood committee received $2000 from the Baron de Hirsch fund, and paid $100 to "receive the Townsite of Atwood."[26] From the money they received, the committee bought 680 acres of land. The deed was made out to the Atwood committee. At the same time the committee bought twenty-five cows and 70,000 shingles for roofing the homes of the colonists.[27] In June "the $2500 of the Baron de Hirsch Fund had been disbursed."[28] In September the Fund sent another $750 for the colony.[29] In spite of all this help, a year later, December 11, 1898, the minutes record:

> The interest on the land is unpaid and there are no funds to pay it. The committee has written to the Baron de Hirsch committee advising them to pay the mortgage and own the land. They answered that they will not invest any more money in the Atwood Colony, but will turn it over to the Lodge.

At the following meeting the trustees of the lodge reported that the land was sold for taxes. The lodge decided to sell its equity in the land.[30] Almost the last minutes on the subject of the colony, August 13, 1899, record that "Bro. Troyansky and others of the Atwood Colony are desirous of buying the land which had been sold under the mortgage, but cannot get a good title unless the lodge relinquishes the privilege of redemption."[31]

The Troyanskys were not discouraged by what had been called a failure. One of them brought a letter to the lodge, addressed to the Jewish Agricultural and Industrial Aid Society of New York, and written by the professional and business men of Sterling:

> They invited this Society to investigate that neighborhood for a colony of Jewish immigrants, and promised a hearty welcome to those who may be located there. They spoke in the highest terms of those Jewish colonists who formed the original Atwood colony, and who have remained there, and who have prospered. They believed that these people would lend all the aid possible to such new arrivals.

This was 1903, when the terrible pogroms of Rumania had been unleashed against the Jews:

> Bro. Trojansky, one of the original Atwood colonists, then spoke upon the subject, and expressed the hope that the B'nai B'rith would take this matter up, as he believed that to place the persecuted brethern on these lands, would make them self-supporting with very little aid. [32]

It was in this region that Simon Fishman turned the first sod for wheat, and from which he took his bride, Mary Fine, to Kansas, where he became the "Wheat King."[33] A half-century later, one of the heartiest welcomes ever expressed by the Sterling community was to a group of visiting Israeli cadets in 1955. No deliberate attempt to win the hearts of the gentiles would have been more successful than the everyday behavior of the Russian and Rumanian Jews.

6

Cotopaxi and Atwood were not the only attempts at Jewish colonization in Colorado. A reference is made by Martin M. Weitz to a second attempt by the Cotopaxians to form a colony, "with the intention of farming near flourishing Greeley, but this was a failure and abandoned."[34] It is likely that there were others, but like the story of the Kiowa colony,[35] they have not been recorded.

Moses Rosen, locally called "Moishe Techetener," after the village in Volhynia from which he came, arrived in Colorado after 1881, with his young son Peretz, who died shortly afterwards. Since he was an intimate of the colonists of Cotopaxi, and on his first trip to the region came with some of them, his family believe that he went first to the colony, and seeing the lot of his *landsleit* moved to Pueblo. During the Panic of 1893 he returned to Europe where he remained for two years, until he could convince his wife, whom the rabbi told a divorce was preferable to following him to the irreligious New World, that she could live a pious life in Colorado. In the meantime his younger brother, Ephraim, came to Colorado in 1890 and sent for his family in 1894. Both families lived in Pueblo and then moved north to Denver.

Ephraim, who hungered after land, was excited about the possibilities of homesteading, but living in the wilderness as a lone Jewish family did not appeal to him or his wife. He solved the problem by inviting nine other Jewish families, enough to form the required *minyan* of ten for religious services, to join him in his plan of forming a volunteered colony. With the maximum loan for such purposes, $500 from the Baron de Hirsch fund, he gathered the group together to form a semi-co-operative colony in Kiowa, on the plains southeast of Denver.

The ambition of the group was to farm and raise stock. Unfortunately it lacked the funds to meet the prices of the period. Coal, at three dollars a ton, was too expensive. The colonists found it cheaper to burn corn. Moreover, this colony was faced with a problem which had not confronted the other colonies. There the neighboring gentiles had been sympathetic and helpful. The Kiowa colony was surrounded by the ranches of wealthy breeders of purebred cattle, who were afraid that their prize stock would become enamoured with the scrub cattle of the Jews. They simply eliminated the Jews' animals.

In disgust, all but Rosen returned to Denver. He remained on his homestead until 1921. At the same time he maintained a home in Denver, to which his wife came for *Shabbas*, the holidays, and on those occasions when she had to help their kinsmen and *landsleit*. In the Denver home, several marriages were arranged, employment was found for new immigrants, and when one "enlightened" couple decided not to have a *b'rith* for a baby son, the Rosens and their neighbors hired a *mohel*, baked delicacies, borrowed the baby and celebrated the ceremony in the Rosen home.

The differences between the two brothers, Moses and Ephraim, are an illustration of the divisions taking place in the American Jewish community. Moses lived in Denver, content with his life of junk-peddling, the *Chassidic* synagogue (to which he had brought the 200-year old family Torah), the *chevrot*, (brotherhoods), and the neighborhood charities, particularly the home for wayfarers. He could wait for the coming of the Messiah to effect the return to Zion. Not so Ephraim. He was an early and passionate Zionist. Finding a group whose ideals were like his own, he joined them in founding the first Zionist synagogue in Denver.

7

The Jewish colonists were people of definite ideas. They had come into the West so that they could live close to the soil. Not all of the East European immigrants who followed were of the same caliber as the colonists who remained in the West, but they were forced to adhere to the standards set by their predecessors. As individuals, very few of them attained recognition in the larger community, but they successfully transmitted their ideas if not their Orthodoxy to the next generation. So strong was the contrast between their lives under the Czars that they followed strictly the rules laid down for them by Judaism and Americanism. The reputation they earned for Denver as "kosher" was spread throughout the world. Most of them took part in bringing their less fortunate kinsfolk, *landsleit* and total strangers out of Eastern Europe.

8

After the National Jewish Hospital for Consumptives was opened in 1899, the local organizations again turned to the problem of immigration. Even before the Kishinev pogroms, the Denver B'nai B'rith appointed a "Roumanian Refugee Committee" to assist with immigration. The minutes of September 9, 1900, record that:

> three of the Roumanian immigrants have arrived here and that they have procured work for them in the Hospital, and that they have written the C.G.L. [Constitution Grand Lodge] President to send six more.

The Grand Lodge sent out representatives to describe the "lamentable condition of the Ghetto Jews of New York,"[36] and to plead for help in relieving the congestion on the Atlantic coast.

A pleasant young man, Maurice Caplan, was appointed by the national lodge in the interest of "Ghetto removal" to place refugee Jews in small towns. When the Kishinev massacre broke out, the lodge had received ninety-seven persons from New York and Rumania in the first six months of 1903.[37] The committee's name was changed to the "Committee for Modern Immigration."[38] The lodge did not give financial assistance, but helped the Industrial Removal Office in New York with investigations and the enrolling of guarantors for the immigrants.

Caplan was killed by a burglar in 1906. A new agent, the poet Solomon Bloomgarden, was appointed to work with the Galveston office of the IRO. He was commended "for his conscientious, untiring and economical administration of his work." Reaching into his own thin pockets to help the pathetic newcomers, he gave an inkling into how the immigrants were treated:

> I feel that we have a just right to enter a vigorous complaint in regard to the way these people are handled on the trains, being side-tracked or held over from twelve to fourteen hours somewhere on the road. In addition to the inconvenience suffered by the passengers, this office has been put to expense and discomfort, the agent being compelled to be at the depot at unreasonable and unusual hours, with no results.[39]

In the decade following Kishinev the lodge helped bring at

least 822 immigrants to Colorado, most of them from New York and Rumania.

FOOTNOTES

[1]In the U. S. Census, Arapahoe County, eighteen definitely known Jewish families are listed, giving as their birthplace countries in East Europe. There are even more names of single young men.
[2]Vickers, op. cit., p. 341; *Jewish Voice*, Sept. 18, 1891, reports that he came "from a talented and renowned family," and had a "sterling command of Hebrew and Talmudic lore."
[3]Irma Rice Mayer, "Sketch of Abraham Rachofsky," Central City *Register-Call*, Nov. 24, 1939; interviews with Anne Rachofsky Wittelshofer, daughter of Abe Rachofsky; Mrs. Dora Kay, daughter of the Kobeys; Mrs. Hannah Berry, daughter of Isaac and Rachel Shwayder; Rose Cour, Denver *Monitor*, Nov. 17, 1954.
[4]Correspondence, Mrs. Elizabeth Roller.
[5]*Jewish World Hamagid, op. cit.*
[6]*Hazefirah*, 1882, p. 342, courtesy American Jewish Archives.
[7]Mosa Heller Hoffman, *IJN*, Sept. 15, 1954; Dorothy Roberts, "The Jewish Colony at Cotopaxi," *Colorado Magazine*, July, 1941; Flora Jane Satt, "The Cotopaxi Colony," master's thesis, University of Colorado, 1951; Dr. Charles David Spivak and Dr. J. M. Morris, *IJN*, Oct. 15, 1925; Martin Weitz, " 'Chassidim' in Colorado," *Year Without Fear*, p. 96-99.
[8]*Post Empire Magazine*, Nov. 28, 1954.
[9]*Colorado State Business Directory*, 1881. Under Cotopaxi listing, Saltiel advertises: "Gold, silver, copper, zinc-blende and carbonate ores; mica, crude sheet, and pulverized; feldspar, rose and crystal quartz &c. Branch office, Leadville, Placer and Denver."
[10]Satt says they were *Maskilim*. Prevailing opinion is that the bulk of the group were *Chassidim*.
[11]Interview Robert M. Hart, and Hart family correspondence. Mrs. Satt refers to A. S. Hart in her thesis.
[12]Letter, Josiah C. Hart.
[13]*RA, op. cit.*, p. 48-9.
[14]Satt also lists G. S. Kohn, A. Strauss, L. Witkowsky (Whitney).
[15]*DJN, op. cit.*
[16]BB minutes, Sept. 27, 1891.
[17]J. M. Morris papers.
[18]The Bevan Company is listed as handling real estate in only one issue of the Denver City Directory, 1895.
[19]Not listed in the city directories during this period.
[20]BB minutes, July 12, 1896, p. 20.
[21]*Ibid.*, Sept. 27, 1896.
[22]*Ibid.*, Oct. 18, 1896, p. 33.
[23]*Ibid.*, Oct. 25, 1896, p. 34.
[24]*Republican*, Dec. 8, 1896.
[25]BB minutes, Nov. 8, 1896, p. 36.
[26]*Ibid.*, Apr. 25, 1897, p. 62.

[27] *Ibid.*, June 3, 1897.
[28] *Ibid.*, June 27, 1897, p. 72.
[29] *Ibid.*, Sept. 27, 1897, p. 82.
[30] *Ibid.*, Dec. 25, 1898, p. 145.
[31] *Ibid.*, Aug. 13, 1899.
[32] *Ibid.*, June 28, 1903, p. 406.
[33] Simon Fishman scrapbook.
[34] Weitz, *op. cit.*
[35] Interview, William Rosen.
[36] BB minutes, Sept. 8, 1901.
[37] *Ibid.*, July 12, 1903, p. 409.
[38] *Ibid.*, July 26, 1903, p. 412-3.
[39] *Ibid.*, Dec. 18, 1907, p. 331-3.

Acceptance and Rejection

The year 1881 saw a change in the course of Jewish history. In Colorado, far from the pogroms in Russia, the beginning of the large wave of East European immigrants came just when the fashionable clubs were being organized and a new social class was being carved out of the newly-rich westerners.

This development was a sharp contrast to the attitude of the brave pioneers who had crossed the Great Plains, sharing their adventures and struggles in the lonely and wild new country. With this pattern of friendliness in the larger group applying to them, the Jews would certainly not permit themselves the luxury of snobbishness within their own group. The early Jews from Russia and Poland became members of those institutions later identified as German and Reform. Jews from widely separated places in Europe lived close to each other in Denver and the mining camps, engaged in partnerships, and frequently were tied together by marriage. In addition, there was a small group of German Jews who preferred Orthodox Judaism to the new Reform.

The Colorado Jews were still smarting at their exclusion from the newly-formed social clubs, when their penniless, threadbare brethren from Russian began to arrive. If they were not delighted with them, they could not be blamed too much. An old claim that the most respectable Jews remained in Russia was not without justification. For, while there were many immigrants of refinement, there were also many coarse young men of little learning and less acceptable conduct. Too many of them represented a noisy and disorderly generation which had cut itself from its roots in Europe but was not yet adaptable to the new soil of America. Even while some shuddered at the new responsibilities thrust upon them, most of the Jewish community was ready to plunge into the difficult tasks before it.

Effecting the rescue of the Cotopaxi colony taxed the Jewish community almost to its limits and consumed several years. With this fresh in their minds, it was no surprise to the Jewish community when Rabbi Friedman told the mass meeting called by the "American Committee for Ameliorating the Conditions of the Russian Exiles," in 1891 that their job was not to bring in additional refugees, but to Americanize those already here.[1]

During the next decade his thinking on the problem changed, to the extent that he said, "We may as well stop talking about enacting more rigid emigration laws to prevent their coming. Shall we let that piteous appeal for help fall on deaf ears; that cry that comes from the heart of the Russian Plains. I tell you we cannot, for the Jew is one."

Rabbi Friedman made this statement in an address before a meeting of the Council for Jewish Women, while he was in New Orleans in 1903. The women were discussing child labor and other current American problems, when the rabbi burst out with, "Let us wash our own faces." To him it was more important to consider the problem of the Russian Jews. He told the women,

> We, who are the cultured and refined, constitute the minority . . . we shall be judged by the majority, by the Russian Jews, by the children of the Ghetto. . . . What a powerful weapon your influence can become in a Jewish community, in lifting up and educating and civilizing the Russian Jews. In 50 years from now, or less, they will far outnumber us. Their children will far outnumber your children, and your children, though educated, cultured, refined, wealthy, will find themselves in the majority and judged by the Russian Jew.
>
> Yet . . . statistics show that no one has better powers of adaptability than the Russian Jew. At school his child learns English much faster and speaks it more plainly than the children of the German Jews; they outstrip them in the course of studies, they are going to go ahead if we help along, without patronizing them, and if we do [not?] they will get ahead without us. . . .

The rabbi told the membership that Council should confine itself to working for the Russian Jews, as it was doing in Denver, where he had directed its activity for the past twelve years, and where the women were going into the homes of the Russian Jews "in the right way."[2]

The Council carried the bulk of the Americanization program in Denver, although the B'nai B'rith and Temple gave their unstinting aid. Their inescapable job was settlement work. A free kindergarten was opened on the east side of the Platte in 1890[3] and in West Colfax in 1891. Night schools with Americanization classes,[4] a settlement house, a "Mission Sunday School,"[5] and even provisions for free baths were organized in the decade before the turn of the century.

Mrs. Seraphine Pisko, then the leading woman in philanthropy, was impressed with the conduct of the settlement workers, "Young men and women who had come to scoff remained to pray. . . . They now declare that the happiest hours of their lives are those spent with these marvelously interesting and lovable children of recent immigrants." She commented on the "spiritual passion" the workers met in "these, who are after all, the rock, which is the foundation of the House of Israel." The Orthodox newcomers were assured that their traditions would not be taken from them.[6]

Immigration created a variety of concerns for the older settlers. A principal one was finding jobs for the foreign born Jews, the healthy and the sick. The Denver B'nai B'rith lodge drew heavily on its outstate membership for jobs in mines and ranches. The lodge's employment committee worked closely with a similar committee at the National Jewish Hospital.

A new problem, one that the historic people had never faced before, grew out of the broken and displaced communities in the strange new environment: juvenile delinquency. The East European parents could not cope with their children, not only because of the different environment, but also because most of them were sick and physically unable either to provide for them or to discipline them.

The non-Jewish community was suffering to a larger degree from the same problem. Denver's famed Juvenile Court had been established by Judge Lindsey. With his help, the Jewish organizations mapped out effective programs for combating the evil. Jewish officers were appointed to keep the youngsters in line. The settlement house opened evening club rooms with the city's prominent men and women conducting classes. The Jews supported the Juvenile Improvement Association and helped the Association's newsboys' club at a time when eighty per cent of the newsboys were the children of the Jewish immigrants.[7]

Juvenile delinquency reached its height before World War I.

At the same time, some of the former trouble-makers were justifying the community's earlier interest. In 1921 one boy who had been in trouble entered Harvard, and another, Georgia Military Academy. At its height there were never more than seven or eight boys at the State Industrial School at a time and most of the trouble the boys had caused was in the form of vandalism.

The German and Temple Jews felt a strange pride in the immigrants, even in the delinquents. They quoted Judge Lindsey who said that "of all human beings he had contacted the children of the recent Jewish immigrants are the most fascinating."[8] He was so enthusiastic over the "wonderful intelligence of the Russian Jewish children" that he set aside $200 from his lecture fund for a more adequate settlement house for West Colfax.[9] They consoled themselves with his statement, that, "on the whole, I believe their are fewer Jewish boys in Court in proportion to other nationalities as shown by our records, and they are always responsive and appreciative of kindness and assistance."[10]

The "ghetto" in West Colfax came in for favorable comment by the older Jewish community: "This quarter is probably unique as a ghetto district, inasmuch as it has no large buildings or overcrowding. It is made up entirely of small houses, with plenty of air and Colorado sunshine for each."[11] Even the *Chassidic* synagogue received favorable comment during a visit by "a renowned *maggid*' to the "largest ghetto in the Rocky Mountain region." In spite of stifling air and squalid surroundings, lack of decorum and order, there was still an uplifting spirit of which the writer approved and suggested that "Reform Judaism should not degenerate into cold Unitarianism."[12]

The more prevalent rumblings in the older community also reached the *Jewish Outlook*. The Russian Jews were warned to do things as citizens and not as Jews, and not set up a *Judengasse*. Every time the activities of the more boisterous and pugnacious Jews appeared in the newspapers the Temple Jews were embarrassed, particularly when the stories concerned squabbling in the synagogues. There was also animosity against the "parvenu, about two years out of the ghetto, who may have received charity to commence their style."[13] When the Temple Jews became frightened at the rise of the immigrants, the learned young Dr. Philip Hillkowitz reminded them that "The uncouth beard may hide a sage deeply versed in Talmudic lore."[14]

Even if the German Jews had been ready to accept the immigrants socially, the newcomers were not all of one mind to be accepted. While they received the help of the *Deutsche Yehudim* gratefully, they disapproved of the form Judaism had taken at the Temple. One may even wonder if the immigrants even regarded their benefactors as Jews, since most of the Jews who came in the 80's and 90's regarded themselves as founders of the Denver Jewish community.

As for their children, after the boys had beaten up their instructors and were ready to accept what they had to offer, they seized the opportunities to develop their talents and take part in social activities of which their parents had never heard. In the early part of the century the settlement workers referred to "Russian Jews, Polish Jews and American Jews." To be American Jews like the workers was the goal of the young people, who were quickly Americanized, and were accepted as part of Denver's Jewish community.

After regaining their health, or disappointed by the lack of economic opportunity in the west, large portions of the immigrant group left Denver. Those who remained adapted themselves to the community, without sacrificing their piety, and certainly not their existence as a separate group.

Matters would have continued in this way, with a gradual integration of the children and younger people among East European Jews into the Jewish community as was happening elsewhere. But the health problem forced an important issue and caused a deep split in the community. By 1905 the Temple, B'nai B'rith, and the National Jewish Hospital closed their ranks tightly against a common enemy. The East European Jews all over America, pressing for leadership, were endorsing Zionism, and social ideals far too strong to please the conservative Reform Jews. Worst of all, in their own Colorado the newcomers were building an institution that might rival the older community's precious National Jewish Hospital for Consumptives.

FOOTNOTES

[1]Emanuel minutes, Nov. 8, 1891 (brochure), question brought to attention of congregation; BB minutes, Aug. 23, 1891, p. 286.
[2]WmSF scrapbook: New Orleans *Picayune*, Mar. 3, 1903.
[3]*American Israelite*, Nov. 20, 1890. First kindergarten for "Poor Jewish children" opened "last Monday in Shomro Emuno synagogue" Nov. 5, 1891, second school in West Colfax. Courtesy American Jewish Archives.
[4]BB minutes, Dec. 8, 1895.

[5] The daily newspapers referred to the first settlement as "The Colfax Mission House," *Times*, June 26, 1899.
[6] Seraphine Pisko, "Denver's Jewish Settlement Work," *JO*, Jan. 5, 1906.
[7] *JO*, Apr. 7, 1905.
[8] *JO*, Jan. 5, 1906, *op. cit.*
[9] *JO*, Oct. 23, 1908.
[10] *JO*, Jan. 19, 1904.
[11] *RA, op. cit.* p. 8.
[12] *JO*, Jan. 6, 1905.
[13] *JO*, Jan. 15, 1909.
[14] *JO*, Feb. 12, 1909.

West Denver, "Brooklyn," and West Colfax

1

On the west banks of Cherry Creek, where the pioneers had built their homes and stores, and where Denver was created, new faces appeared as the pioneers prospered and moved eastward to the new fashionable streets, particularly Champa and Curtis, as the town grew into a city. The newcomers were mostly Irish and German, with an ever increasing number of Jews fleeing from the pogroms. At no time did this section, known as "West Denver," or the "West Side," become exclusively Jewish, even in the area of four to six square blocks where most of them lived. At its height, this section, the heart of which was Eleventh Street, was perhaps eighty per cent Jewish, but there was so much movement to and from it that it is difficult to estimate the number of Jews who lived there.

West Denver included all of the area between the creek and the Platte River. Although there were Jews on the very banks of the Platte, they were not to be found across the river in "No Man's Land."[1] There some of the most prominent men in the state had built mansions, while scattered squatters lived in shacks where they chose. One of the first Jews to live on the west side of the Platte was Isaac Goodstein, who came to Denver about 1878 from London after fleeing from Russian Poland. He joined his brother-in-law, Philip Rosenthal, who owned the Swansea Smelting Works[2] and the Denver Rolling Mills.[3]

While peddling on his wagon, Goodstein came to a beautiful section on high ground, across the river, where he stopped to talk to a man who was moving out of what appeared to be a comfortable house. Goodstein asked him who owned the place and was told that he did not know, but that Goodstein and his family were welcome to move in. After moving in the Goodsteins located the owner, who told them that they could live there without paying rent, asking only that they pay for the use of the well on the property. Later the family, happy with the pleasant section and friendly neighbors, purchased the house, which included an acre of land and necessary barns, for $400, and paid $35 for the well.[4]

Although the section was called No Man's Land until 1891, there were many wealthy families living there. Dr. William Buchtel, brother of the governor of the state and son-in-law of P. T. Barnum, owned a summer home, "The Villa Grove" (close to the section known as the Town of Barnum). From the small schoolhouse, which all of the children as far west as Sloan's Lake attended, came some of Denver's leading doctors, lawyers, and a governor of the state.

The Goodsteins lived in the neighborhood for thirty-seven years, while it became exclusively Jewish and the citadel of Orthodox Judaism in the region. Another early inhabitant of the section was Joseph Tobias, who had first settled along the river, where he had spent one winter with his family in a pitched tent when his junk business was not too profitable.[5] Although a large part of the Jews moved east from West Denver when they could afford to, a more pious group crossed the Platte to find their homes.

Cutting through the section was the "Golden Road" (branching off near the Platte to Morrison) leading from Denver to Golden. In 1891 the section on the south side of the road was incorporated as the Town of Colfax. The other side of the road was the Town of Highlands. When Colfax became a town, its business section, in the very heart of the town, seceded from Colfax and took for itself the name of Brooklyn. This area, nine and a half blocks in length and two and a half blocks in width, numbered 300 inhabitants.[6] With most of the business houses of Colfax in Brooklyn, many interesting and complicated problems arose. The Denver *Republican* claimed that they were unique in the history of city government. Both towns levied taxes on the area which included the town hall and post office. When police officers of both towns patrolled the street, the question was, "which one should be arrested for impersonating an officer?"[7]

Finally Brooklyn "threw in the sponge,"[8] and became merely Golden Avenue in the town of Colfax. During its brief life, a Benjamin Silverman was elected trustee of the town,[9] and in a subsequent election Abraham Goodstein turned down a similar office.[10] In 1891 Joseph Tobias built a "block" on the well-traveled avenue at a cost of $6,000.[11] The following year the *Republican* reported that "a Jewish wedding was held at Colfax Hall."[12]

When the Cotopaxians were brought down from the mountains, the Jewish community was confronted with the problem of housing them. The Goodsteins and others kept them until houses could be found for them. United action turned up some shacks along the river. As soon as they could, the majority of the colonists settled permanently, not in West Denver, but in West Colfax, close to the river. These immigrants did not follow the pattern typical of most cities, moving into the vacated homes of their wealthy brethren, but created a new Jewish section, which according to the January 1, 1904, issue of the *Jewish Outlook* numbered about 400 families or 1650 individuals.

In 1897 Colfax was annexed to Denver. Golden Avenue became West Colfax Avenue. The eastern half of the same street, which had been known as Hartman Avenue, became East Colfax. Later the long street cutting through Denver became part of U. S. Highway 40, bisecting the United States. In Denver, West Colfax meant the Jewish community located from the banks of the Platte to Boulevard F (now Federal Boulevard). As immigration, removal from the east, and the continuity of health-seekers swelled the West Colfax population, it began to expand westward street by street—not always with the approval of the non-Jewish population —until the strip along the avenue to the county line became solely Jewish. For at least thirty-five years, half of the Jews of Denver lived in West Colfax, and it is likely that half of the Jews of Colorado lived there until World War I.

2

For many years the home of Shul Baer Milstein, the patriarch of the families that had formed the Cotopaxi colony, was the center of the new community. Milstein as the leader of the *Chassidim* was not only the foremost religious figure, but also the leader of West Colfax philanthropy. In this he was joined by the most picturesque figure in the community, his sister-in-law, Hannah, who was better known as "Chana de Gabbiteh" in West Colfax. Her primary interest was the various poor families for whom she collected food, clothing, and funds. No one ever accused her of being shy. Day in and day out she accosted everyone she met with "Nixnootz, tremp. Gib, gib!"[13] Woe betide anyone who did not give. She scolded them mercilessly bringing in the family's genealogy—good or bad—to make her point. Nevertheless, she never divulged the names of those she helped. When she brought aid, it was to the back door so that the family would not be shamed.

In addition to the individuals who engaged in charity, the immigrants organized their own aid associations. Even before Colfax was annexed to Denver a group of women organized the Ladies' Hebrew Relief Society in 1895.[14] The society, the purpose of which was "collecting and distributing aid to the poor, sick, and suffering" in the community, was capitalized at $1000 in 1000 shares of $1 each. Although the principal place of aid and the business office was West Colfax, a number of women on the east side of the creek were officers. A year later the Jewish Ladies' Aid Society was organized "to alleviate the sick and distressed and to assist the poor people of the Jewish faith."[15] These women, who are said to have started the society in 1892, were almost all members of the later Beth Ha Medrosh Hagodol, which was organized in 1897.

The residents of West Colfax were taxed to their limit in keeping the needy and sick in their homes. An *Hachnosas Orchim* (home for wayfarers), also known as the West Side Jewish Sheltering Home, was opened about 1905 on Fourteenth and Canosa Court, close to the synagogues on that corner. When the West Denver Talmud Torah ceased to function as a school about 1937 the building was used as shelter.

West Colfax differed from the *shtetli* (small East European village), which had been composed of one national group. There were Jews from every *goobernyia* of the Russian Pale. In addition to the Old World system of *yichus*, the social-religious prestige which placed rabbis and scholars at the top and shoemakers, tailors, and draymen at the bottom, in this small community *yichus* was based also on the country—even city—of origin. This was a very complex hierarchy, for one might be on top by virtue of learning, but looked down upon for coming from the wrong town. In West Colfax the Lithuanians were at the top and the Galitzianer (Galicians), who were of small number, at the bottom. The Ashkenazi-Lithuanians referred contemptuously to the *Chassidim* as *chynucks* (fanatics). The "westernized" Jews of the community ridiculed the dress of the *Chassidim*—which consisted of knee-length black silk frock coats, large brimmed black hats, sometimes trimmed with fur—and their full-bearded faces with uncut earlocks.

One family clan from Brest-Litovsk, who had been glaziers, were dubbed the "Glazerlach." This family was so prolific that intramarriage almost erased the system of *yichus* along the Avenue. When one patriarch of the Glazerlach died the newspapers reported that he had left eighty grandchildren and 250 great-grandchildren. The "glassies," as they were called when the Jews became more familiar with English, married into every stratum of the Denver Jews, from that of the pioneer aristocratic Temple through each synagogue and national group. Almost every family that remained in West Colfax from the first World War to the second became related through marriage to one of the large families of West Colfax like the Milsteins or the Goldberg-Glazerlach.

In time the terms which had been used slightingly—*Chynuck, Rotner, Galitzianer, Ostrover,* and even *Litvak* (Lithuanian)—carried no stigma. The descendants came to use these terms as honored distinctions, and the grandmother who had sighed at a marriage she regarded as a misalliance, learned to shrug and say " 'S America." *Yichus* was permanently pocketed as the new generation found the materialistic values of the non-Jewish community more to their tastes.

3

There were still other groups of which to disapprove, and of which to be disapproved by. One was the unfortunate sick from the sweatshops. The stigma of having tuberculosis earned one the label of *catootnik,* especially if the victim of the disease happened to be a socialist or other form of non-conformist to the existing community. In this group, some of the members of which had been among the intellectuals who had tried to break the cruel vise of the Czar's official and unofficial government, were mostly ex-factory workers of the East Coast. It mostly was a transient group, small in number but highly vocal.

There were, however, close ties that the Orthodox community was quick to recognize—the common love of Yiddish, the philanthropies in which they worked side by side, and the fact that a "Jew was a Jew," regardless of his religious belief, or lack of it. Even at the *gnossiniks'* most irreverent act the Orthodox Jews, while horrified, could not suppress a chuckle.

According to one local legend, a *gnossinik* left his home on Yom Kippur morning, telling his wife, who was not too familiar with his activities, that he was on his way to the synagogue. With *tallis* and prayerbook under his arm, he went, not to the synagogue, but to a room engaged by his friends for playing cards on the holy day. Entering the room, an expression of indignation covered his face, and he reprimanded the players: "Gentlemen, I'm surprised. Playing cards! And without a tablecloth." He unfurled his *tallis* and covered the table. The game proceeded, but the entire community knew about it.

Only the baser element desecrated the Orthodox Jewish religion. For the most part, the group was interested in education and philanthropy, especially for the sick. Their chief contributions were in the establishment of the Yiddish school and sponsoring concerts, lectures, and plays. By 1917 there were enough of them to form an *Arbeiter Ring* (Workmen's Circle) and acquire a building, the Labor Lyceum, in West Colfax. This they considered the only educational center in West Colfax, to which they "invited men of prominence to spread the light of civilization in the 'Ghetto' of Denver that is West Colfax."[16]

This lofty attitude did not enhance their popularity. None of the Jews of West Colfax thought of the Jewish section as a ghetto. Moreover, piety did not preclude enlightenment. The Jews of West Colfax sneered back at the "liberals" and accused them of practicing "free love." Yet, it is surprising, if true, that there was proportionately less intermarriage among the children of this group than there was in the group of Orthodox Jews. To the chagrin of the leftist group, some of their children gradually moved back toward the religious life. They, as well as their parents, later became Zionists, and with the establishment of the Jewish state, and the Democratic party taking over most of their goals of social justice, there was nothing left for the group but its cultural life—to read Sholom Aleichem and Peretz—in which they were joined by the rabbis and Orthodox Jews.

4

Because there were no factories comparable to those of the large American cities, there was virtually no Jewish labor movement. With the exception of a Journeymen Tailors' Local in 1916,[17] which was created when twenty-six per cent of the patients at the Jewish Consumptives Relief Society belonged to the needle trades,[18] there is no other mention of a Jewish trade union in Colorado.

The small shopkeeper had no need to worry about strikes, and the Jewish peddler decided his hours and working conditions.

Although peddling was the main support of West Colfax and West Denver, the early Jews engaged in many other occupations. In the census of 1880, the following occupations are listed by the vanguard of East European Jews: Two iron dealers, a salesman, huckster, buttonholemaker, pawnbroker, three tailors, a watchmaker, liquor dealer, miner, widowed dressmaker, dry goods dealer, and a "preacher," David Cohen. On the West Side, where there were many hotels and boarding houses, one such residence listed ten laborers born in Russia of Russian parents. None of their names was particularly Russian or Jewish: Herman, Graff, Baker, Schofman, Berry, Snider, Kriser, Schaffer, Borge, Gunder. Nearby another boarding house listed four railroad workers, ranging in age from eighteen to fifty, with equally enigmatic names: Waston Anton, B. Simmerman, Anton Boruch, and Vana Shuman, also of Russian birth. Since there were very few Russians in the region during this period, there is a possibility that these men were Jews, but none of these names is subsequently found in connection with any Jewish group.

There were also a number of young Hungarian Jews who had come, unburdened by families, to seek their fortunes in the West. These foot-loose young men were to be found throughout the state, from Poverty Gulch in Cripple Creek to the mining camps of the San Juan. One young Hungarian, Sam Butcher,[19] came to Colorado about 1875 as a railroad worker and miner. Working in Leadville and Cripple Creek, he became an expert hardrock miner and mastered the difficult art of blasting. His experiences were typical of the period on the frontier: meeting a bear in a cave, which he killed with a knife; escaping from an Indian attack on a wagonload of settlers in which everyone but he was massacred; and working among Jew-hating miners. He never revealed his religion to them. At one time when there was a German with a hooked nose in the group, the miners decided he was a Jew, and gave him a merciless beating. Butcher's identity was revealed in Leadville, when his miner friends told a tailor there that Jews never soiled their hands with a pick and shovel, preferring to live off the miners. The tailor replied that Butcher was a Jew. The surprised miners, who already liked Butcher, decided that it made no difference to them what Butcher was.

Many of the Jews who were peddling in the early 80's are not listed in the Denver city directory, principally because there was no need for an address. Most of them were single, or had left their families in Europe until they could send for them. They found peddling most profitable in the mining camps and farming communities. In Colorado, as it had happened throughout the country, peddling became the principal occupation of the Jewish immigrants. But there were two particular considerations to explain the preponderance of peddlers in the state and especially in Denver, not quite as applicable to other places. So long by-passed by the railroad and boosted for its climate, the capital city was kept from becoming a smoke-filled manufacturing city. There were no factories large enough to employ the great number of immigrants, and there was not enough demand for the skill of the shoemakers, tailors, tinners, and other craftsmen.

The many who came for their health wanted outside peddling in the much-publicized climate. Added to this was the valid reason given by Mrs. Pisko at a mass meeting of the C.O.S. in 1900, "that the Jewish Sabbath was a cause of much poverty among the Jews who would not work at a trade on that day. For this reason many skilled workmen do nothing more remunerative than peddle bottles."[20]

The new immigrant took his savings, if any, or borrowed money from the Hebrew Free Loan Society or from a less formal free loan in West Colfax established by the earlier East European immigrants. With the loan he bought a horse and wagon and left for the mining camps or the country. He sold merchandise and bought a variety of things from the farmers or miners from calves to junk. Sometimes the purchase of cattle took him directly into the livestock industry. Other times, he saw land he could own by homesteading. By 1903 an estimated forty East European Jews had won their land.[21] Many Jews became farmers and ranchers, later specializing in stockraising, breeding, and cattle finishing. In Denver the Jews began to play an important part in the meat-packing industry and as processors of the wool, hides, and other by-products of cattle and sheep. The large salvage houses—rag, waste paper, and bottle firms—were also the end result of the junk-peddling business begun by the peddler with his horse and wagon.

In merchandising, the immigrant shopkeepers did not attain the success of the founders of the early department stores. Although their shops were smaller, the owners made a living and earned the respect of the community. Their stores became familiar sites in every town in the state. Many of those who specialized in jewelry or furs were successful with their luxury items in the region where millionaires were made overnight in the rich mining camps. One grocery firm, founded by the Jacob Miller family, achieved national recognition for its chain of super-markets.

As Anna Hillkowitz wrote in 1905, in America "engaging in trade has ceased to be a stigma. A business calling is as honorable as any profession."[22] In the East European Jewish community, however, the highest profession a man in America could attain was a career in medicine, with the law following a respectful distance behind.

At first there were far more physicians of East European origin in the Jewish community than there were lawyers, writers, or other professional men. Obviously, not only was there a demand for doctors, but also it was a universal profession, which did not require a native accent. In the Denver community some of these men earned not only local but also national recognition. Among them were the true humanitarians of the period. The names of those who had achieved prominence as early as 1905[23] includes: Adolph Zederbaum, M. Kleiner, Charles D. Spivak, Philip Hillkowitz, M. J. Krohn, Sol Ringolsky, Emanuel Friedman, Oscar Shere, and I. D. Bronfin. A list given by Dr. Spivak in 1924 on the "Contributions of Colorado Jewish Physicians to Medical Literature" lists twenty-six physicians, many of them of East European origin, as contributing from one to seventy-one articles each, or a total of 362. According to Dr. Spivak's findings, the average contribution of a Colorado medical author was 6.5, and of a Jewish one was 7.4.[24]

For many years very few East European Jews achieved wealth. Even their sons who followed them in merchandising were only able, at best, to earn a comfortable living. Life was relatively easy in Colorado, for while labor had made little progress in the state, particularly in Denver, and wages were low, expenses were also low. Many of the Jews owned their own homes even before the depression of the 30's. During the depression, life was not easy, but Colorado did not suffer as did the highly industrialized sections of the country. Even then, the poorest families among the Jews were able to free their children to "work their way" through college.

The life of West Colfax was circumscribed, but it was happy. New troubles, as compared with the Old World sadness and fear, weighed less heavily on the immigrants. When times were bad, or when the flood of 1909 left $50,000 worth of damage one Sabbath, these hardships could be easily overcome by those who had experienced the pogroms.

Dr. Maurice Fishberg, in Denver on a health study, presented his description of West Colfax in 1904:

> A walk in this neighborhood reveals a most peculiar condition of affairs. It is the most curious "Ghetto" I have seen in the U. S. or Europe. All the houses are of brick, are mostly of one story. . . . Although not paved the streets are fairly clean. They are not obstructed by stands, push-carts, wagons and other paraphernalia, which we are wont to associate with Ghetto streets. The homes of the poor living here are as a rule tidy and clean, nothing like the overcrowding seen in Jewish quarters in New York or Chicago. The environment here looks more like that of the average small western town than like a Jewish district of Europe or America.[25]

FOOTNOTES

[1]*Republican*, Jan. 1, 1892, p. 13, col. 4.
[2]*RMN*, Oct. 17, 1880, p. 4, col. 4.
[3]*RMN*, Nov. 25, 1880, p. 4, col. 3.
[4]J. M. Morris interview with Isaac Goodstein. Interview, Sarah Greenblatt, his daughter.
[5]"Pioneer Jew Describes West End Birth," *West End Press*, Aug. 24, 1934.
[6]*Republican*, Jan.1 1892, p. 13, col. 1-4. Art Inc. No. 4752, Dec. 10, 1891.
[7]*Ibid.*, Mar. 10, 1892, p. 6, col. 4.
[8]*Ibid.*, June 12, 1892, p. 20, col. 6.
[9]*Ibid.*, Jan. 6, 1892, p. 6, col. 3.
[10]*Ibid.*, Mar. 18, 1892, p. 6, col. 4, refers to "A Goldstein." Mrs. Greenblatt believes that her brother Abraham Goodstein was meant.
[11]*Ibid.*, Jan. 1, 1892.
[12]*Ibid.*, June 26, 1892, p. 17, col. 4. Says contracting parties were "Miss Anne Korch and Mr. Sam Grimes." The bride's name was Karsh.
[13]Esther Gamzey, "Chana de Gabitah's Appeal," *IJN*, May 8, 1952.
[14]Certificate of Incorporation No. 7099, Jan. 21, 1895.
[15]Report of meeting, Record No. 10647, Nov. 3, 1897.
[16]*DJN*, Nov. 20, 1924.
[17]*DJN*, Feb. 4, 1916; Feb. 26. 1916.
[18]*DJN*, Feb. 4, 1916.
[19]Interview, Jacob Butcher.
[20]Denver *Times*, Oct. 9, 1900.
[21]*RA, op. cit.*, p. 8, col. 3. *RMN*, Feb. 13, 1884, p. 6, col. 3.
[22]*JO*, Nov. 24, 1905.
[23]*Ibid.*
[25]"The Jewish Consumptive in Denver," *JO*, Nov. 4, 1904.

Minyanim and Congregations

1

The Jews had a universal failing best expressed by the venerable story of two Jews on a desert island who built three synagogues, one for each of them. The third? "That's the one we don't go to."

The Orthodox Jew, who spent most of his free waking hours in the synagogue, regarded it as another home. How the services were conducted and who the other worshippers were was, therefore, important. Temple Jews and outsiders were often horrified by the familiar and sometimes boisterous ways in which the Orthodox conducted themselves in the synagogue. The Orthodox countered that they were not strangers "in their Father's house."

Minyanim and congregations were organized, split, disbanded, reorganized, and consolidated with such frequency that it was possible during one period of a quarter-century to worship in a different synagogue every year.

Early Orthodox worship is virtually unrecorded in contemporary accounts. Thus, the frequently contradictory history of the first *minyan* by Sigmund Friedenthal, written in 1908, is the only source giving the earliest date of Orthodox religious activity.

> In 1877 the first permanent Orthodox Minyan was formed in the city. It marks the beginning of a separation between the different forms of worship. The Orthdox contingency received several valuable additions to their number at about that time, whose names should be mentioned. They were Elias Menkus, Joseph Solomon, Leopold Bamberger, Marks Amter, H. Plonsky, Marks Garbarsky, and Solomon Arager.[1]

Who composed the "Orthodox contingency" is not revealed, but most of the names mentioned as "valuable additions" to it did not come to Denver until a year or two later. However, there are enough names of known Orthodox Jews in the city in 1877 to lend credence to Friedenthal's statement. For many years the leading figure of the Orthodox Jews in the entire state was the successful shoe merchant, Henry Plonsky,[2] who is credited with organizing the first *minyan* immediately upon his arrival in Denver. Polish-born Plonsky was forty-three years old[3] when he arrived in Denver from New York. He had been in the United States since 1851, and was as Americanized as any of his German- and Prussian-born co-religionists. Very popular and active in all groups, he was one of the signers of the articles of incorporation for the Jewish Hospital and took part in the various celebrations at the Temple, where his son-in-law Henry Frankle was the congregation's president and a founder of the hospital. The short, elderly gentleman, carrying a gold-headed walking cane, whose dignity was tempered with warmth and friendliness, was well loved by all of the early East European Jews with whom he visited and frequently played cards.

Meeting above the rooms over his shoe store on Larimer Street, the first *minyan* appears to have been first known as the Chebra Ahavey Emuno. On the death of A. L. Friedenthal the *News* published on December 30, 1879, a resolution signed by Dr. Elsner, L. Loeb, and Philip Rosenthal.

In 1880 when there were more than two dozen East European Jews in the state—most of them Orthodox—the *minyan* became a congregation. According to the articles of incorporation[4] at a meeting of the congregation Ahawu Emuno on July 5, Plonsky was elected president; Gus M. Levy, vice-president; J. Friedenberg, secretary; J. Solomon, treasurer; and J. Amter[5] and J. Eppstein,[6] trustees.

For the next few years the congregation was listed in the city directory as Ohawi Emune and Ohava Emuno, and described as an Orthodox Jewish Congregation at 375 Larimer, Plonsky's business address, according to the early system of numbering.

When Congregation Emanuel sold its first temple at Nineteenth and Curtis to a private party, December 15, 1881,[7] it was rented or leased to Ohava Emuno for use as a synagogue. About then Solomon Arager, a rabbi and a *schochet* by profession, was brought to Denver from San Francisco by the Orthodox Jews. He was hired as the first rabbi of Ohava Emuno, which he served for two years.

The daily newspapers devoted a great deal of space to the holidays of 1883. After reporting the services at the Temple, which the *Republican* estimated were attended by 600 persons,[8] the newspaper described the Orthodox services as "not less beautiful and probably more imposing," the peculiar sight of the audience praying with covered heads and with the "tales" around the shoulders of the male worshippers.[9] The *News* reported that the largest[10] crowd attended Ohava Emuno. After Yom Kippur services, the *News* described them for their readers as "exceedingly solemn and impressive," that prayers were chanted in a loud voice, with beating of the breast and solemn gestures. In all the reporter found the services "strange and impressive." The *Republican* described the "scathing" sermon of the congregation's second rabbi, M. Klinkowstein, about Jews who denied their religion.[11] Much of the sermon was directed at "our so-called radically reformed brethren" and those who kept their stores open "this sacred Sabbath of all Sabbaths, and who don't want it known they are Jews."[12]

The *News* observation that the largest crowd had attended Ohava Emuno is interesting. According to Friedenthal, Plonsky, who joined the Temple Emanuel in 1878,[13] started his own congregation because he was dissatisfied with the service there, which permitted much latitude in the exercise of the "varying degrees of orthodoxy and liberality."[14] Whether or not the Orthodox Congregation could attract more than 600 persons, it is true that many of the German Jews were Orthodox. Such families as that of Susie Saly, the sister of the noted German historian, Heinrich Graetz, kept German from becoming synonymous with Reform.

After four weeks of committee investigation, resulting from charges that Rabbi Klinkowstein had eaten pork and smoked on the Sabbath, the rabbi was found guilty on June 1, 1884, by a vote of 21 to 18. On June 13 the minority published a resolution in the *News* protesting the methods of the investigation and the balloting. The resolution was signed by twenty-seven members, headed by Henry Plonsky, "late president," who tendered their resignations to the congregation. They were answered two days later in the *News* by Charles Lasky, president; M. Garbarsky, vice-president, and J. Solomon, treasurer, who appear to have remained with the congregation. That same month the rabbi left Denver.

Susie Saly's son-in-law, Hyman Saft, was the next rabbi of Ohava Emuno. He had studied at the short-lived Rabbinical Seminary in Philadelphia. He arrived in Denver with his wife, Bertha, and four children in 1879. The next year he offered to become the rabbi of the Temple, which accepted. He withdrew the offer.[15] In the 1885 city directory he is listed as the rabbi of Ohava Emuno.

Thereafter it seems that Ohava Emuno was without a rabbi. For almost a week before the High Holidays of 1885, the *News* carried an advertisement, headed in large Hebrew letters:

> The Congregation at the corner of 19th and Curtis wishes to inform the Hebrews of Denver and surrounding country that they have a new and able minister. He comes with the best of references from the city of New York to officiate at Rosh Hashanah, which falls on the 10th and 11th, and Yom Kippur on the 19th of September. Seats at J. Solomon's, 413 Larimer; M. Garboski's, Blake and 15th St.[16]

Apparently the rabbi did not materialize, and an address was delivered by Leopold Bamberger on "The Five Objects Placed in Sir Moses Montefiore's Coffin at His Desire." This was the last year the synagogue was mentioned by name in the daily newspapers.[17]

In the same column advertising the services at Ohava Emuno, a small note announced that the "Rev. J. Potashinsky invites all Israelites to attend the New Year services at Warren's hall, 285 Champa." Seats were on sale by the rabbi or S. Block. Just who this group was, if it was new in 1885, or was a splinter from Ohava Emuno, remains a mystery. One can only guess from the fact that Potashinsky was the rabbi that it was an ultra-orthodox group of worshippers he was to lead.

The city directory continued to list Ohava Emuno at the Curtis address until 1889, when the name of a new congregation appeared, Shomro Emuno. It would seem that Shomro Emuno succeeded Ohava Emuna. But this was not so, although there are very few clues as to what actually happened. One clue is the name "Shomro Emuno," meaning "those who observe (or guard) their religion." "Ohava Emuno" meant "those who love their religion," and because the founders of Ohava Emuno later established a more liberal congregation, it is most likely that the Shomro Emuno group wanted a stricter synagogue. Two congregations had come from the Orthodox *minyan* of 1877. Friedenthal said that "Congregation Shomro Emuno was organized in 1877."[18] At least one of those identified with the *minyan* was a signer of the articles of incorporation of Shomro Emuno on August 28, 1887.[19]

Plonsky is said to have returned[20] his congregation to the rooms above his store. At least four public halls were used for services on *Shabbas*, the holidays, *bar mitzvahs*, and weddings. Lincoln Hall on Fourteenth and Larimer was the most popular. According to the *American Israelite,* June 9, 1892, "The Orthodox Congregation, Rodof Sholem, has been organized, with Mr. Henry Plonsky as president."[21] Friedenthal says that Plonsky was "dissatisfied with the manner and methods of worship in the then existing orthodox congregations."[22]

Rodof Shalom (those who pursue peace), was incorporated October 14, 1892. It gave as its object: "to cherish, perpetuate and uphold the belief in one God, to perpetuate the cause of true Judaism, to provide suitable grounds and erect thereon a suitable building or buildings for the worship of God in accordance with the above faith."[23] The trustees were Henry Ornauer, who was born in New York of Austrian parents; J. S. Dreyfuss,[24] who was born in Germany; and Marks Amter, born in Courland, who had been in Denver for more than twenty years.[25] All three were well-known men in the Jewish community, and were representative of a group later referred to by the Orthodox Jews of West Colfax as *"halbeh Deutsch"* (half German).

One puzzling note is introduced in the minutes of Temple Emanuel, May 18, 1886:

> ... that a committee of conference, consisting of three members of the Board be appointed to confer with a like committee to be appointed by Congregation Rodef Zedek [those who pursue justice] relative to the consideration of the subject of consolidating the two congregations.

Rodef Zedek is never mentioned again. Since the date in the minutes is close to 1887, when the building of Ohava Emuno was sold, it may be that in the years between Ohava Emuno and Rodof Shalom, the first and the same Plonsky congregation may have been in continuous existence.

Again Rabbi Hyman Saft[26] was engaged as rabbi of the Plonsky synagogue. According to Friedenthal, the congregation gained in influence and membership. "A religious school was established, the first orthodox one in the city, and did excellent work." Rabbi Saft was superintendent of the school, in which he was assisted by at least two German Jews. The Panic of 1893 interrupted the progress of the congregation. Rabbi Saft left Denver, and the group worshipped without a rabbi.

One man who remembers Plonsky's activities is Walter Appel, who as a child lived next door to the Orthodox leader. Plonsky stopped to chat with his neighbors one afternoon when he came home in an especially jubilant humor. "I don't need a monument when I die," he told them. "I have today established the Beth Ha Medrosh Hagodol." This date Appel believes to have been about 1895. The date of acquiring a synagogue building was not far off. Fire all but destroyed the Temple Emanuel on November 5, 1897. A month later the Beth Ha Medrosh Hagodol was incorporated, and the congregation purchased the Temple property. For the second time Plonsky's congregation moved into the home of the first Jewish congregation in the state. The synagogue was dedicated in 1898.

The following year a rabbi, R. Farber, was engaged.[27] He is said to have made many innovations, one of which was the confirmation of boys and girls. He remained two years. In 1902 the building was again damaged by fire, and after being rebuilt was rededicated. That same year Rabbi Charles E. Hillel Kauvar was brought to Denver. Although the congregation was most frequently described as Orthodox, from its very beginnings as Ohava Emuno there was strong evidence that it was a conservative synagogue. Plonsky, while more ritual-minded than the Reform Jews, was not as strict as the Orthodox religion demanded. His name was found at dinners were non-kosher food was served, such as the one tended Dr. Sonneschein in 1882. No Orthodox Jew would have sat at a table where other Jews were eating oyster and creamed chicken. Also Ohava Emuno and Rodef Shalom had been served by Rabbi Saft, whose daughter says that he was Conservative.[28]

Whether or not the Beth Ha Medrosh Hagodol, or as it is better known, B. M. H., called itself Orthodox, in practice it was not. Men and women sat together, priestly blessings were given by the rabbi, and women stood for the *Kaddish* (mourner's prayer). Obviously, the *Chassidic* Jews would not attend services at the B. M. H., but the issue was unlikely to arise. The building on Twenty-fourth and Curtis was still in a fashionable section. Not until the East European Jews of West Denver became more prosperous and more Americanized did they join it.

From the time he was elected president of Ohava Emuno until his death in 1920 at the age of eighty-three, Henry Plonsky was president of his synagogue. He had chosen Rabbi Kauvar from the Jewish Theological Seminary instead of taking a European rabbi. As he told his congregants, "I am bringing you a *rebbele*, who will be able to teach your American children according to their times."

Fifty years later there was still a question whether the congregation was Orthodox or Conservative. One of five rabbis in the 1950's, Ephraim Bennett, a graduate of the Jewish Theological Seminary, according to an article in the *Intermountain Jewish News* in 1954:

> ... delivered an outspoken series of Friday evening sermons in which he defined his beliefs that Conservative Judaism should be flexible to preserve the ceremonial beauty and spirit of the ancient tradition, while modernizing Jewish law in accordance with modern Jewish life in America. This position brought an open clash with the half-century tradition of orthodoxy at BMH, against which he was not able to prevail.[29]

This was answered a few weeks later, after 300 names had been signed to petitions demanding that Rabbi Bennett stay at the B. M. H.:

> The Beth Ha-Medrosh Hagodol Synagogue, in its fifty-five years of existence, has been governed by a clearly defined constitution and by-laws, and Article II of the Constitution states: "The purpose of this organization shall be to cherish and promote Orthodox, traditional Judaism." In this spirit the Religious services in the B. M. H. Synagogue have adhered to Orthodox practices and customs as recognized throughout the Orthodox Jewish world.[30]

There had been a split in the B. M. H. in 1911, which will be discussed later. After Rabbi Bennett and the discharge of his successor, there was a second split in the synagogue when a number of its members formed the second synagogue in Colorado called Rodef Shalom. Almost at the same time, July, 1956, the B. M. H. ceased to be a member of the Conservative United Synagogue of America.[31] The next rabbi, appointed in March, 1957, was graduated from the Orthodox Yeshiva University.

2

In West Denver, the congregation Shomro Emuno built its synagogue on the east bank of Cherry Creek, so close to the temperamental stream that the building began to sink almost at once. The Cherry Creek Shul, as it was called, used the building from 1889 to 1898, when it was given up, not only because of its poor footing, but also because of the congregation's inability to keep up the mortgage payments. Services were held thereafter in rented halls and store buildings. Some of its membership had moved east with Henry Plonsky's congregation, and at least two of its incorporators were living in West Colfax. At the same time, another group was also holding services in a store building.

The two groups under the new name of Shearith Israel (remnant of Israel) became one, dating the birth of the congregation as 1899. Services continued in a hall until 1903 when the congregation purchased a small but attractive church at Tenth and Lawrence. Several men of the congregation remodeled and repaired the building converting it into a synagogue. A measure of its success was that no new congregation appeared in West Denver after it was housed. As a permanent congregation, with its own Talmud Torah, it flourished for as long as there was a Jewish neighborhood in West Denver.

The building of Shearith Israel is said to be the oldest church building in continuous use in Denver. It is also the oldest synagogue building in continuous use, for although it has no regular congregation, it is used by the businessmen in the area, especially for *Yizkor* (memorial) services on the festivals. An amusing note regarding the synagogue is its listing for many years as the "Chariot of Israel." This was a better transliteration of the Hebrew name than some.

Around the fall holidays more information regarding the Denver synagogues could be obtained from such national publications as the *Jewish Voice*, along with contemporary descriptions of Jewish life. A columnist "S" estimated in 1891 that there were 1000 Jewish families in Denver, who on the holidays attended services "from the aristocratic Temple to *The Minyan Shteibel*." He described the latter as

> held in atticked loft, reached by means of a ricketty ladder from a slimy alley, adjoining a back slum, and patronized morning and evening daily by devout, long-bearded, longer pahessed Jews; often Jewesses, with the inevitable sheitel conspiciously displayed. We have in Denver a congregation composed solely of Chassidim, reminding one of a Shaker congregation.[32]

That year a "fine decorous service was conducted by a young, though celebrated chasan, Rudolf Funk of New York Conservatoire" at Clinton Hall, who was said to be connected with the "West End Synagogue."[33] Rabbi Funk found favor with the columnist for his "old fashioned Hebrew melodies, piety, and gentlemanly bearing." The Jews had a choice of nine places in which to worship, of which five were "permanent" in 1891.

One of them was Anshe Amunah, which was so crowded that "some men had to go in the ladies' gallery, to the consternation of the unofficial lady guardians." The writer reported that at only one synagogue other than the Temple was a sermon given. This was at the Fifteenth Street Bickur Cholim, whose preacher was given as Rabbi S. Arager. The writer was impressed that Rabbi Arager delivered a sermon on Yom Kippur on the same text and theme as Rabbi Friedman did at the Temple. By now Rabbi Arager was listed in the city directory as the pastor of the Chebra Kadish "church," and since articles of incorporation had been filed for a Chebra Kadish O. Bickur Cholim, it is apparent that the Chevra Kadisha and Bickur Cholim were one synagogue, as well as a group for performing their traditional functions which will be discussed later.

"S" had more than community news to impart. He had two stories to tell, which he claimed originated in Denver: On the steps of a synagogue during the closing of Yom Kippur services at *Neileh,* Leyeh asked Peshinky whether she thought that God would forgive her her sins, to which Peshinky replied, "Go, go, Layeh, you fool. If we were to pray a whole night and day like this to a robber or highwayman, he would take compassion on us. Surely God is no gazlon!" [34]

The other story dealt with a father who was informed of his son's rowdyism during the services and reprimanded him for not staying in the synagogue, to which the boy replied: "Little boys half as old as I are inside saying *Yizkor* and *Kaddish.* Whose fault is it?" [35]

This is perhaps the first touch of Yiddish humor to appear in the annals of Colorado Jewish history.

3

In the last decade of the nineteenth century the movement towards unification of the small synagogues west of the Platte had begun. Not so in West Colfax, which was growing with every trainload of immigrants and respiratory sick. There the most rugged form of Jewish individualism was under way. After the Cotopaxi colonists were brought down from the mountains, most of them attended the West Denver synagogues, although one of the men of the colony, Joe Washer, became a trustee of the B. M. H. The bulk of the colonists, who belonged to the Milstein family, held their own religious services and organized their own *Chas-*

sidic synagogue, Zere Abraham (descendants of Abraham). They met informally for several years after organizing in March, 1887,[36] first in a member's home and then in a rented house. Articles of incorporation were filed in 1889. In 1892 the congregation was sufficiently well established to file a record with the city, certifying that "... Rev. Israel Britwar is engaged as rabbi of said congregation and do hereby request to be admitted to perform all the marriage ceremonies according to the Hebrew Law."[37]

In 1901, the congregation was ready to give up its *shteibel* (small prayer house used by *Chassidim*) and began to build a synagogue on the same site on the banks of the Platte River where it crossed Golden Avenue and met Larimer and First Streets. The daily newspapers reported that "75 members, all Russian Jews in the Colfax Colony" were building the house of worship themselves and estimated the cost of the building at $4,000.[38] The new brick synagogue was dedicated October 28, 1901, with Rabbi Friedman delivering the principal address. The building, which seated 200, included a woman's gallery on three sides of the room, a *mikveh*, room in the basement for a *cheder* (schoolroom) and a chapel for daily services, which was promptly put to use for prayers and the reciting of psalms for the recovery of William McKinley.[39] Rabbi Martin Weitz describes the river called "flat" by the French explorers and the life around it:

> a low stream handy for *tashlich* (New Year purification) ... a life-cycle about a *schul* ... a *cheder* ... a *mikveh*, a cemetery, petty trading, and the future ... there was the large *Chassidic schul* on the banks of the Platte; there was and still is, a *Chassidich Rav* (rabbi) .... the joyous outpouring of *tephillah* (prayer), and pounding, at times, of imploring hands and earnest bending and bowing in liturgic meditation; there was and still is the donning of the white *kittel* (gown) and black *gartel* (belt) on high holidays.[40]

The impetus for the communal walk in which West Colfax marched in its holiday best to *tashlich* was gone when the Zere Abraham congregation bought the Labor Lyceum for a synagogue in 1938.

Although Zere Abraham served all of the *Chassidim*, it did not number among its congregants all of its friends and relatives. The large Glazerlach family clan from Brest-Litovsk organized their own synagogue almost on arrival. This was the Congregation Mogen David (Shield of David), better known as the Glazerlach Shul. As the Milstein name dominated the *Chassidic* synagogue so the Goldberg name was identified with Mogen David synagogue. The group is said to have received help for its first building from Louis Miller, one of the earliest Jews in Denver to own a junkyard, who gave several immigrants their start in their own salvage yards. The congregation appears to have been organized in 1885 at the home of Rabbi David Radinsky. Subsequently the house was purchased by the congregation and rebuilt.[41] The little synagogue was directly behind the large rag salvage building owned by the rabbi's son, A. D., who took for his firm its emblem, a *mogen David*. The synagogue was one of two in Denver to boast its own *mikveh*. For the ritual bath, its members claim, it took 500 stone jugs to keep the water hot enough to use. During the flood of 1909, when the synagogue stood in eight feet of water, it is said some of the worshippers constructed canoes and "paddled to see if all were well. Some even managed to pull anchor, and climbed inside to *dovin*."[42] Others, who did not belong to the congregation, remember when *matzos* were baked there one year. It was a community project to which all of the children came to watch the experts stipple and perforate the dough with sharp pieces of glass. Before World War II there were not enough men in the neighborhood to form a *minyan*. Most of the congregation had joined other synagogues. The building stood empty for many years until it was torn down about 1953.

In West Colfax the Lithuanians were regarded as the intellectuals among the East European Jews, while the community felt they were much too pompous. Although many of them had come before the colonists, there were not enough of them in West Colfax until 1891 to incorporate their own synagogue. This congregation, Agudas Achim, also held its services close to the Platte River in 1893 until it purchased its own building there in 1903.[43] The congregation disbanded about 1937, when its remaining members joined the next Lithuanian synagogue, Zere Israel.

A newcomer to West Colfax attended the services of one of these three synagogues until he found nine more kindred souls to start another *minyan*, then congregation, and then, if they could afford it, their own building. Many of the men who worshipped together disbanded before they could form a congregation. Most of the homesick newcomers looked for *landsmen* not only because they might know them but also to hear the familiar accents of the Old Home in prayer. It was not difficult to start a new group. There were always dissatisfied members in the existing synagogues to make up the necessary *minyan*. In the changing memberships of the congregations there must also be considered the issue of *coved* (honor). To some, being an officer was important enough to start a congregation.

Of the congregations which survived, one of the longest in duration was the Tiphereth Israel (Glory of Israel) which brought together men from many parts of Poland. The congregation was incorporated in 1901 and lasted until 1943, when the few remaining members disbanded and joined other synagogues.

The height of independence in early West Colfax was reached in 1900 when Israel Chatz (Kortz), organized his own synagogue, which was known in the neighborhood as "Chotsky's shul." The synagogue lasted for at least twenty years, during which old-timers say that Chatz was so anxious to have the synagogue well-attended that he bribed his neighbors with whisky to come.

The Zionists are said to have started their own congregation in 1903. [44] These men left the other synagogues where their relatives and *landsmen* prayed, to be with those of similar ideals. Many of them were intellectuals, or at least secular-minded enough to take a deep interest in world affairs. Their synagogue is said to have been more peaceful than any of the others.

With the immigration from Rumania at the turn of the century and after the pogroms of Kishinev, there were enough Rumanian Jews to organize their own synagogue, Yad Achaas (One Hand). Meeting in a vacant lot, the group held services in a tent for several weeks, before beginning construction of a synagogue on Fourteenth and Canosa Court. This short street, no wider than an alley and entered from the Avenue, boasted three synagogues on one corner.

From one short-lived synagogue grew another. This was Kesher Ohava (Union of Friends), which was formed from the dissatisfied members of the other existing congregations, with a mixture from Brest-Litovsk, Ostrov, and Kowel. The congregation met in a store, behind which was the residence of two of the incorporators. The congregation was incorporated in 1906. [45] A year or two later the Ostrover took over the building for their first synagogue, the Beth Jacob.

4

One of the largest groups of *landsmen* in Denver were the former residents of Ostrov in Poland. It is said that their first synagogue, the Beth Jacob, was organized in 1903. However, the first document recorded by the group was for the Ostrover Kranken Unterstizung Verein, July 31, 1907. The following year an affadavit was filed with the city of Denver for the Ostrover-Baizyon-Kiv Congregation.[46] This puzzling name, which should have been phonetically recorded as Ostrover Baiz Yonkiv or, Anglicized, Beth Jacob, has been perpetuated by innocent recorders.[47] The congregation had a turbulent history, which involved practically every Jew in West Colfax. Connected to the large Hebrew School, Yeshivas Etz Chaim, was a synagogue, where one of the rabbis had been insulted. There was a split in the group, with the offended Lithuanian members withdrawing to start their own synagogue and school a little more than a block away. That this was done for spite is obvious because of the name given the new synagogue and Talmud Torah, Yeshivas Toras Chaim, and because of its location at the time when the movement away from the neighborhood had begun.

The building was under way when it was suggested that the Ostrover, who had outgrown their building, and over which the city had built a viaduct, should join the new synagogue. By building together they could acquire a better structure. There were many who knew that the plan would never work and warned against the proposed merger. But the optimistic members blissfully explained how they planned to pray together. The Lithuanians, who prayed Ashkenazi, would conduct services one week, and the Ostrover, who followed the *Chassidic*-Sephardic prayerbook, would conduct the services on the alternate week.

Considering the temperament of both groups, it came as no surprise to the community that the new congregation in its new building exploded at once. The Ostrover, whose Polish accent amused the Lithuanians, claimed that the latter snickered while they were conducting services, and mimicked their "nee-nee-nee" pronunciation. The Ostrover were not ones to be ridiculed. Fighting broke out in the synagogue. The horrified Jewish community, particularly the Temple Jews, were deeply embarrassed by what was going on in West Colfax, especially when the police had to be called to keep order during Passover services.

After lengthy litigation, the Lithuanians withdrew from the building and built their own synagogue, Zere Israel Nusach Ashkenaz (again too close to the older neighborhood). I. Rude gave them a large sum to get the building started. The Ostrover kept the Yeshivas Toras Chaim building until after World War II, when they sold it to a furniture company and built anew a half-mile west, under their original name, Beth Jacob.

After the fight in the synagogue, feelings in West Colfax were strained. The Ostrover and Lithuanians of that generation never forgave each other. The Lithuanians continued to regard not only the Ostrover but also the Polish and Hungarian Jews with contempt. They were irritated by the *Chassidim* whom they accused of being "fanatic hypocrites," wearing transparent garments of holiness. In turn the Polish Jews accused the "Litvaks" of being sanctimonious show-offs, in addition to being "very stingy."

5

There were enough Jews from other towns near Ostrov to organize their own congregations. One such group came from Rotno, Volhynia. In 1904 they organized their synagogue, Congregation Keheleth Jacob. The group purchased a store building on West Holden Place, where services were held until 1946, when most of the old members had died and there were no longer enough for a *minyan*. The building was sold to a business firm for $600 or $700. An attempt was made to communicate with the Jews of Rotno, to send them money, *Sefer Torahs*, and other religious articles. They received the reply that all of the Jews of Rotno had been wiped out. The books and scrolls were turned over to the Knesseth Israel congregation, and the money is still held by a member of the original Rotner congregation.

Jews from the town of Matzov, Volhynia, were attending services at the Ostrover synagogue, Beth Jacob, when they decided at *Hakofas* (procession with Torahs) on Simchas Torah night to organize their own *minyan*. The group repeated the ceremony and rented a room on West Colfax in 1910. Joined by a few Jews from Kowel, they were able in 1913 to purchase a "shack" on Fourteenth and Canosa Court, which they fixed up as a synagogue, Beth Israel Anshei Matzover Chevra Volin. They prayed there until 1921, when the Rumanian congregation moved into its new building a mile west. The Matzover purchased the Rumanian synagogue and remained there until World War II. Thereafter the religious books were turned over to the new Yeshiva, and the group scattered throughout the West Colfax synagogues. One of the members of the old congregation, Ben Samett, who lived near the county line, found there a large neighborhood without a synagogue. He built his own synagogue, incorporated as the Boruch ben Isaac David and known as Samett's Shul. He had planned to continue it as the Matzover Shul, but there were not enough *landsmen* left to warrant the use of the name.

A very independent man, he financed the synagogue himself and was able to establish one of the few synagogues in Colorado where there was no disagreement over ritual, pronunciation, or any of the myriad of subjects that Jews find to argue about in the synagogue.

A new congregation, Knesseth Israel (Congregation of Israel), was organized by members of some of the waning congregations in 1907. Meeting in a home across the street from the then new Dickinson branch library the congregation grew until it was able to purchase the home and erect a new building on the site in 1910. It was known thereafter as the Hooker Street Shul.

With the building of the viaduct over the older section of West Colfax and the movement "up the hill," no new congregations were organized below Federal Boulevard. The Rumanian congregation Yad Achaas built a new synagogue a half-mile west of Federal Boulevard in 1923, which was for a decade the farthest west of all the synagogues in Denver with the exception of those at the Beth Israel Old Folks Home and at the Jewish Consumptives Relief Society.

6

After settlement work came to an end, the neighborhood clubs and young people began agitating for a community center. A group under the name of the Denver Hebrew Institute [48] began collecting nickels and dimes for a building in the swelling neighborhood. By 1925 the group had enough money to buy lots on West Colfax and Meade for $6,000. The following year, a group of women, organized as the Beth David Sisterhood, decided that the old Talmud Torah on West Fourteenth Avenue was too far from the center of population, and that a new Hebrew school and social center was needed for upper West Colfax. With the help of a Beth David Brotherhood formed in 1928 a concentrated campaign began. Reminding the residents that "About eleven years ago, a fortune was sunk into a *shul* [the Ostrover synagogue] which was supposed to be a Talmud Torah . . . "[49] the Beth David Hebrew School and Center pointed out the pressing need for classrooms. The Denver Hebrew Institute, which had not been happy with its name because it "sounds like a Talmud Torah,"[50] gave up its identity and merged with the Beth David groups in the newly named Denver Hebrew Educational Alliance. The new group, using the lots on Colfax and Meade—although the women already had lots on Newton Street—began building its school, which was also to house a synagogue. The colorful Hebrew names associated with synagogues were not even considered for the combined synagogue and school, which was completed in 1932 as the Hebrew Educational Alliance, and referred to in Denver as the Alliance.

The Alliance never became a recreational center in the sense in which the neighborhood clubs had intended, but its Talmud Torah became the most thorough in the city. Very soon the congregation ranked with the Temple and B. M. H. as one of the leading congregations of the city. With its establishment, unity was felt for the first time in West Colfax. Whatever feelings its members had on ritual or *landsmanshaft*, as parents they overlooked the divisive forces in West Colfax and concentrated on furthering the interests of the Alliance. The tide away from Torah was stopped in West Colfax, although almost a generation was lost in the transition.

Both the congregation and the Talmud Torah had outgrown the building before World War II. In 1952 the city's handsomest and most modern synagogue was completed in upper West Colfax a block away from Sloan's Lake.

7

In East Denver, where the Orthodox and Conservatives had only the B. M. H. to serve their religious needs, the congregation grew rapidly as large numbers of Jews continued to move away from Cherry Creek, or trickle in from West Colfax. Plonsky's *shul* was split in 1911. The *Jewish Outlook* did not "see fit to notice the controversy," and the stories that are told are still charged with emotion. The only facts are that, the year before, a twenty-four-year-old cantor, Jacob Schraeter, was chosen from forty-eight applicants. He was hailed with delight and described as a baritone, the son of a concert leader in the royal opera house in Hungary. The next year a large group, many of them Hungarians, with Schraeter as their leader, left the B. M. H. At the same time the B. M. H. called a special meeting for January 22, 1911, "to amend the Charter and by-laws of the constitution of the corporation

B. M. H. and enlarge the scope of congregational activities . . ."[51]

The secessionist group formed their own congregation Oheb Zedek (Those who love Justice), which met in halls and used the El Jebel Shrine for the holidays, until it built a synagogue on Twenty-second and Marion Streets in 1920. By 1925 it was called the second largest Orthodox congregation in the city. Actually, the men and women sat together, although a balcony was provided for the more Orthodox women. The depression of the 30's terminated the life of Oheb Zedek. The congregation was having difficulty keeping its building, which is said not to have been constructed strongly enough to carry the weight of its roof. At the same time the handsome new home of the B. M. H., which had left Twenty-fourth and Curtis Streets in 1921, was in dire straits, facing foreclosure of its mortgage. Oheb Zedek gave up its building and returned to the mother congregation with all its assets, including a membership of 400, thus helping to save the home of B. M. H.

When the B. M. H. moved to Sixteenth and Gaylord Streets, a prize location as the farthest east of all the Denver congregations for about thirty years, the old building was purchased by the remaining Jews in the area. With the held of I. Rude, a new congregation was organized under the condition that it be named for his father-in-law, Joseph Mandel. The newly formed congregation, Beth Joseph, remained with its diminishing membership in the building until after World War II. The handful left sold the old Temple - B. M. H. - Beth Joseph building and purchased lots on Eighth Avenue and Holly Streets in a totally new section to which Jews were moving. The old members called for a meeting to build a new synagogue. They were joined by a small number of young married couples who took upon themselves the extremely difficult task of interesting enough people to start a new synagogue in a new section. Building to meet immediate needs first, they began construction on the Talmud Torah and social hall, and not on the synagogue until 1955. The handful who reorganized Beth Joseph had the satisfaction of seeing it become so desirable that several years before it had a synagogue it was one of Denver's "big four" congregations.

In the post-war population movement Jews have s p r e a d throughout the city and around it. While they can use the synagogues at the Ex-Patients' Sanitarium, the American Medical Center (the J. C. R. S.), or National Jewish Hospital, these institutions once on Denver's outskirts are not conveniently located. In 1956 a new congregation, Beth Am, was formed by southeast Denver residents with the idea of building a Conservative synagogue.

FOOTNOTES

[1]*RA, op. cit.*, p. 8, col. 2.
[2]The Plonsky name appears for the first time in the city directory, 1878, as "S. Plonsky (L. Schiff & Co.) 343 Larimer." This name does not appear the next year, but does in the minutes of Temple Emanuel. There was also an "S. Plonsky" in Utah, where Henry Plonsky made several trips.
[3]1880 Census. Friedenthal says he was born in 1830.
[4]Certificate of incorporation, July 5, 1880, No. 411, Denver. Missing: election of trustees, Sept. 23, 1881, No. 576, Denver and articles of incorporation, July 15, 1880, No. 2847, Colorado.
[5]Although J. Amter is given this must be Marks Amter. So poorly are documents written, that when Amter married Julia Saft, the marriage certificate gave her name as "July Sept."
[6]Both Julius and Isaac Epstein are listed in the city directories prior to 1878.
[7]Abstract of title as given by Jesse B. Smith, Landon Abstract Co.
[8]*Republican*, Oct. 2, 1883, p. 10, col. 3.
[9]*Republican*, Oct. 3, 1883.
[10]*RMN*, Oct. 3, 1883, p. 4, col. 3. "Largest" may be an error. There is no indication that there was a third group.
[11]*Republican*, Oct. 11, 1883, p. 8, col. 8.
[12]*RMN*, Oct. 12, 1883, p. 2, col. 1.
[13]Emanuel minutes, July 24, 1878, "H. Plonski" reported favorably; Sept. 13, 1881: "A. Plonsky" applies and is elected a member. Either an error "A" for the similar "H" or for Adeline Plonsky, his wife, although the city directory of 1881 lists "A." and not "H." The 1880 census lists Henry and Adeline Plonsky.
[14]*RA, op. cit.*, p. 13, col. 13.
[15]Emanuel minutes, Oct. 17, 1880.
[16]*RMN*, Sept. 1, 2, 4, 7, 8, 9, 1885.
[17]*RMN*, Sept. 11, 1885, calls the synagogue, "Chava Emuno."
[18]*RA, op. cit.*
[19]Art. of Inc., No. 2726, Denver.
[20]According to Mr. Smith of Landon Abstract, the Temple sold the Nineteenth and Curtis property to Catherine Slockett, Dec. 15, 1881, for $8,000, who sold it to Michael Finnerty, Jan. 21, 1887. It was leased Sept. 21, 1888 to Zang's Brewery. According to the Denver tax assessor, a new store building was erected on the property in 1891.
[21]Courtesy American Jewish Archives.
[22]*RA, op. cit.*, p. 33.
[23]Art. of Inc., Oct. 14, 1892.
[24]U. S. Census, 1880, listed as J. S. Dreifus. Also in BB minutes and dailies as Dryfuss.

[25] Amter married Rabbi Saft's sister Julia, Aug. 14. 1870. See n. 5 above.
[26] *Republican*, Sept. 22, 1892. Saft conducted Orthodox services at 1747 Arapahoe.
[27] *RA, op. cit.*
[28] Interview, Mrs. Jacob Olcovich.
[29] *IJN*, April 15, 1954.
[30] *IJN*, May 29, 1954.
[31] *IJN*, Mar. 22, 1957.
[32] *Jewish Voice*, Oct. 9, 1891.
[33] *Ibid.*
[34] *Ibid.*, Nov. 6, 1891. Hebrew, "brute."
[35] *Ibid.*, Oct. 25, 1891, *Yizkor* and *Kaddish* are memorial prayers.
[36] *RA, op. cit.*, p. 34, col. 2.
[37] Art. Inc., Aug. 20, 1889; Jan. 6, 1892.
[38] *Republican*, Apr. 27, 1901.
[39] *RMN*, Oct. 28, 1901.
[40] Weitz, *op. cit.*
[41] *ICA*, Inc. Oct. 25, 1896, No. 9211.
[42] *IJN*, Oct. 11, 1951, p. 10, letter by Max Goldberg.
[43] Art. Inc. Nov. 19, 1891, No. 4739; *ICA*, purchased frame building, 1903.
[44] *ICA;* City records: Dorshei Zion Society of Denver, No. 21572, Mar. 23, 1909.
[45] City Records, 193-576; Kesher Ohavo Society, Aug. 15, 1906.
[46] Affidavit, Mar. 31, 1908, No. 508-264.
[47] *ICA* lists it as "Ostrover Baizyon Kiv."
[48] *DJN*, May 14, 1919.
[49] *IJN*, May 24, 1928.
[50] *DJN*, Jan. 15, 1925.
[51] *JO*, Jan. 6, 1911.

The *Shtetl* in Denver, Colorado

1

In transplanting the life of the small village of Eastern Europe to American soil certain traditional institutions were obligatory. Of these, those created for burial had to meet an abnormal demand. Death accompanied the health-seekers, many of whom lost their battle to the tubercule bacillus. The pioneers' cemetery east of Cheesman Park was used by the Orthodox Jews until the early 90's when it was obvious that burial would be stopped and a mass removal likely. The Orthodox established their own cemetery in 1892. There may have been an attempt to unify burial in the Jewish community. According to the *Jewish Voice* in 1891, the United Hebrew Cemetery Association was described as "an unusual amalgamated independent body" to which any Hebrew, Orthodox, *Chassid*, or Reform, could be brought.[1]

Under that name the Orthodox Jews purchased the grounds of a previously incorporated cemetery, Rose Hill,[2] northeast of Denver. About that time, a burial society with the traditional name of Chesed Shel Emeth (True Lovingkindness) was formed by the Orthodox Jews to bury the indigent dead. The society, which was in existence as early as 1896,[3] raised its funds through dues, balls, picnics, and outright donations. By December, 1899, the bodies of eighty-six poor were buried.[4] The organization remained in existence until as late as 1906, when a group of men in West Colfax, apparently unaware of the existing society, organized another Chesed Shel Emeth. The older group had provided for more than 400 free burials[5] when the second society was formed. The new group adopted the additional name of West Side Benevolent Society.

The existing cemeteries were used by the Chesed Shel Emeth

until 1908, when the society purchased twenty acres on the Golden Road, a few miles west of the four-year-old J. C. R. S. and almost in the shadow of the Rockies. The burial bround, called the Golden Hill Cemetery, was cut into two parts by the highway. On the upper portion, it is said, were buried the bodies of the patients of the sanitarium, so that they could not infect the "healthier" dead in the lower half. Golden Hill's dead were not only those of the sick or destitute. Many of the West Colfax community who had no ties to the Rose Hill cemetery were buried there, among them its rabbis and scholars as well as the members of the Workmen's Circle.

Both Rose Hill and Golden Hill are strictly Orthodox cemeteries, following such customs as arranging plots so that a married woman is buried between her husband and another woman, and burying suicides and victims of violent death apart from the rest of the underground community.

The Beth Ha Medrosh Hagodol established its own cemetery association in 1904. These grounds, called Mount Nebo, were opened in Aurora. After World War II the expanding town erected a water tank on the property and ordered that portion of the cemetery condemned. In ensuing litigation the rights of Mount Nebo were protected.

To these three cemeteries were taken the bodies of the Orthodox Jews which were exhumed from the old Jewish cemetery. In 1890 the *Republican* had guessed that "As to the Hebrews, they may raise some objections to the removal, but it is hardly thought they will make any fight in the matter."[6] No protest seems to have been made, although there are few exceptions in which a body once buried may be disturbed. The exhuming and re-interring was a painful task, leaving a bitter memory for those who sometimes found only a few bones of a loved one. Those Orthodox whose dead had been buried without coffins were never convinced that all of the remains were removed. Certainly not all of the dead were exhumed from the entire cemetery. In 1955, when the grounds were being excavated, two workingmen admitted that they had uncovered bones at the six-foot level and above.

The Chebra Kadisha O. Bicur Cholim was formed in 1887 with the purpose of holding religious services and aiding the poor and sick. The function of a *Chevra Kadisha* is the preparation of a body for burial—according to the prescribed Orthodox rules—for the poor. The purpose of a *Bickur Cholim* is to help the sick and needy living. As has been recorded, the group also met as a congregation with Rabbi Arager.

Jews dying of tuberculosis, "far in excess of the local poor," created a need for shrouds so great that a Ladies' Shroud Society was formed in 1900. The members supplied shrouds, coffins and carriages for the thirty to fifty deaths among the poor each year, "thus insuring a decent burial to the poorest." The success of that society was refreshing in the field of organized charity and has rarely been emulated. From its dues and sales of shrouds the treasury grew so large that dues were no longer required in 1905 and the society donated, from its surplus, gates to Mount Nebo, *Sefer Torahs* to the existing two sanitariums, and money to the Jewish Relief Society.[7]

2

How the early Jews managed to eat kosher food before the coming of Rabbi Arager is a mystery. It is said that some ate non-kosher meat but eschewed the products of swine. There may have been others, like Philip Rosenthal, who was educated in the procedure and slaughtered his own chickens omitting beef from his diet. Others are known to have become vegetarians. With the coming of Rabbi Arager, it was possible to observe the Jewish laws, for he acted as a *schochet* and *mohel* as well. Under him, and with the guidance of Marks Garbarsky, the Jewish community had all of its vital institutions. In addition to those mentioned Garbarsky organized the Mo'os Chittim (money for wheat) so that the Jewish poor would have matzo, meat and wine for the Passover.

The Garbarskys were a lovable family. Garbarsky is said to have walked blocks out of his way on the Sabbath in order to avoid embarrassing those Jews who kept their shops open on the sacred day. His daughter, Tena, was one of the most popular of Denver's young people. His son-in-law, Dr. Sol Ringolsky, was the physician of Thomas Walsh, the mining millionaire and father of Evalyn Walsh McLean. Mrs. Garbarsky, who was not impressed either by Walsh's money or his magnificent estates, was highly concerned with the activities of "poor Mr. Walsh's stomach" of which she could give a detailed account. She was a modest but strong-minded woman who let Tena talk her into only one change: she substituted for her dark wig a gray one as she grew older. Most of the Orthodox women wore wigs; few of their daughters did.

With the Jews who fled from Russia and those who came for

their health, came the Jewish Law. There was never again in the city a shortage of rabbis, *schochtim*, cantors, or teachers. A kosher butcher shop was opened in West Denver, which shipped meat throughout the state. Too often the meat arrived spoiled or too late to kosher for the Sabbath. Kosher bakeries followed. Although the women did much of their own baking, the baker's oven was invaluable to the women with huge pots of *cholent* that had to remain overnight in a low oven to please the exacting taste of the discriminating housewives. On Sunday the baker made up for a whole week's business. His clientele reached into the mountains and country, where the Reform as well as Orthodox hungered not only for bread but for delicacies as well.

The non-Jewish traffic in the streets kept West Denver from achieving the spirit of *Shabbas* that enveloped West Colfax. Along Golden Avenue, West Colfax became the *shtetl* in Eastern Europe. The streets were almost empty, as the Jews promenaded to their synagogues. After luncheon on their way back to study at the synagogue, they stopped to chat, sitting on the benches provided in front of the stores along the Avenue.

Before the holidays, activity increased, especially before the Passover. An early advertisement for "Passover Bread" appeared in the March 10, 1884, issue of the *News*, announcing that matzos "will be baked this year by Mr. Samuel Leach, Union Steam Bakery, under the co-joint superintendence of the minister Rev. M. Klinkowstein and the shohet, Mr. Arager."[8] By the turn of the century there were dozens of places—stores and homes—where Passover food could be obtained.[9] The most picturesque provider of Passover food was the lanky A. Wongrowitz, the early *shamus* (overseer) of the Temple. He threw in his most important commodity at no charge: a full and accurate account of every event in the Jewish community. While the community was small there was no need for a Jewish press. "Wongy," next to the kitchen stove, with a sip of wine, never omitted a bit of pertinent gossip.

Almost until 1900 there was only one *chupa* (marriage canopy) in Denver. When Emanuel Herskowitz, the popular baker, was to be married in 1892, the time of the wedding had to be arranged so that Sam Grimes could be married the same day under the same canopy. Very few wedding were held in the synagogues. On the West Side, Lincoln Hall was used most frequently when the wedding party was too large to hold at home. In West Colfax there was a choice of halls. But if it was summer and the wedding party was large, Bloomfield Park, complete with Japanese lanterns and orchestra, was the favorite place. Bloomfield Park can be considered part of the *shtetl*, although there is some doubt as to the religion of its owner. Bloomfield, who was an Englishman, explained to the Goodsteins (the early West Colfax Jewish family) that he was not a Jew, but that he had Jewish ancestors. Not only was the park the locale of social functions, but Bloomfield also kept tanks of fresh fish, a necessity for the holidays if not for every *Shabbas*.

Traditional societies, *chevrot*, devoted to Talmudic study may have appeared immediately with the synagogues. The first one to incorporate was the Chevro Mishno in 1891[10] on the West Side. At least one of its members had been in the first Orthodox *minyan*.[11] Later each of the synagogues organized its own. Most of the *chevrot* studied the Mishnah of the Talmud and a few studied *Shass*, a more advanced portion of the Talmud.

There was a Society Linas Hachesed (Justice Stays Overnight) at the Tiphereth Israel synagogue which provided "watchers" to stay with the sick and give aid to its members. A similar society, Linas Hazedek (Kindness stays over night), was organized at the Knesseth Israel. The two merged when Tiphereth Israel disbanded. Another mutual benefit society was incorporated in 1904 as Ahaves Achein Verein (Society of Brotherly Love) but surrendered its charter in 1909.

There seem to have been but two groups formally organized for *landsmen*. The first was the Oestreicher Kranken Unterstzungs Verein, composed of a small group of Galicians, incorporated in 1905.[12] It did not last long and was absorbed by one of the most aggressive of mutual-aid societies in Denver. This was first known as the Ostrover Kranken Unterstitzung Verein in 1907. A decade later its name was changed to the Ostrover Young Men's Benevolent Association, with membership open to everyone. The group raised a $3,000 free loan fund for *landsleit* who fled from the Nazis to Israel.

Many lodges of the national fraternal organizations were formed by the East European Jews. The first seems to have been the Baron de Hirsch Lodge No. 171 of the Independent Sons of Abraham in 1885 at which meetings were conducted in Yiddish. The lodges were social but also offered valuable insurance benefits.

In West Denver the Hungarian Charity and Pleasure Club[13] held most of its functions at the West Turner Hall. Picnics were held in country spots, one of which was Brand's Grove, which was reached by horse and wagon and later by a few Fords. Goulash was served, Hungarian music played by a gypsy violinist, and singing and dancing filled out a day of "pleasure." World War I stopped the activities at the Turnverein and the club was not revived.

The Yiddish theatre made its appearance in 1909 with visiting troups. There were two "nickel" shows on Golden Avenue, which were well attended, especially on Friday night. Tickets were purchased in the morning so that there would be no exchange of money on the Sabbath. These were the Alpha and Pellish's Hall. As the westward movement began another theater, the Lyric—later the Palm Theater—was built above Federal Boulevard. The Lyric was both a motion picture theater and playhouse. One troup, whose leading man was the idol of housewives, returned year after year. In addition to these, Goldhammer's Hall was used for organizational meetings, debates, and lectures.

Another form of recreation in which the Jews as well as non-Jews participated was the Russian hot baths. The first bathhouse was built next to the Avenue. In the 30's a similar bathhouse was built farther west. Both provided *mikvehs* after the synagogues no longer had the facilities.

The love of hot water, particularly mineral water, is one of the luxuries the East European Jews of Denver rarely denied themselves. Jewish women sometimes spent weeks at such places as Idaho Springs and Manitou, which were dropped for more fashionable places like Glenwood Springs as transportation improved. A few venturesome souls tried Hot Sulphur Springs and Salida. Many of the finest springs in the mountains were ignored because there was no social life around them.

The number of small social clubs organized by the young people was infinite. Several of them joined the League of Jewish Youth in 1920, which included the Menorah Society at the University of Denver. The agitation for club rooms continued long after Bloomfield Park became the I. Rude Community Center, and lasted until an old mansion was purchased farther west by L. H. Guldman for use as a community center. The Guldman Center had a hectic and not always adequate program for the neighborhood, but it was the first successful effort to bring the community of West Colfax together for recreation. After World War II the Jewish Community Centers were formed. The Guldman center was used as its

West Branch and the I. Rude-B'nai B'rith building as the East Branch. The Centers purchased a mountain ranch and organized a winter ski program.

3

Marks Garbarsky is credited with establishing the first Hebrew School or Talmud Torah in Denver.[14] Although there is no record of which school this was, religious instruction is mentioned in connection with the early synagogues. There was a Talmud Torah connected with the Cherry Creek *shul*, Shomro Emuno. After it merged into Shearith Israel, the new congregation formed a Talmud Torah in 1906. Within five months the school was teaching Hebrew to sixty children, of whom thirty-nine were taught without charge. The school raised funds through social activities. Although it was in precarious straits most of the time, it successfully instructed a large group of boys during the height of Jewish life in West Denver.

With the encouragement of Simon Wolf, the national president of B'nai B'rith, who was in Denver in the fall of 1904,[15] the Denver Hebrew School was established. At first it was supported by the B'nai B'rith, the Council of Jewish Women, Temple Emanuel, the B. M. H., and the Western Council of Zionists.[16] The following year Rabbi Friedman withdrew his support. The B'nai B'rith continued its financial support, and from time to time had a committee report on the school's activities. Alfred Muller, on the subject, expressed his opinion that there was a far greater need for an English school and settlement work in Colfax than a Hebrew school.[17] One member, representing the lodge at a school examination, reported back that "he took it for granted that the children acquitted themselves well in Hebrew, but what impressed him most was the lack of discipline."[18]

For a brief time the school held its classes downtown. Then, in order to cut expense, it was moved to the B. M. H. synagogue, where it continued under the same name until 1952, when it was renamed on the fiftieth anniversary of Rabbi Kauvar's ministry in his honor.

When Oheb Zedek was formed, the new congregation established its own Hebrew school and Sunday school, on the same pattern of the schools at the B. M. H., although the religious school seems to have been organized by Rabbi Friedman.[19]

The *Jewish News* pointed out in 1915 that more money and

brains was spent in West Colfax on education than in all of Denver put together. There extremes met. The secular Yiddish School, the Zionist Hebrew School, and the Orthodox Talmud Torahs were all part of West Colfax.[20]

Since the schools on the east side of the Platte were too far for the children of West Colfax to attend daily, the first independent school was organized in 1910 by thirty-five families who named it the Yeshivas Etz Chaim (School of the Tree of Life) or the West Denver Hebrew School and Synagogue. The following year it was moved into a new building on a pleasant residental street a block away from the Avenue and close to Federal Boulevard. Classes in the school, which was known simply as the "Talmud Torah," were provided for girls as well as boys. More than a full generation of Denver's Jews were instructed there.

At first the methods of maintaining discipline were harsh. The boys who were ferruled or spanked not only received no sympathy at home but sometimes were given more of the same. Gradually the gentler methods of the public school began to appeal to the parents as well as the children. Later education involved no physical punishment. The Talmud Torah which was to rival it a block away, the Yeshivas Toras Chaim (School of the Book of Life), actually conducted classes for a brief time. The establishment of this school did not break the Talmud Torah, although it did weaken it. The movement up the hill and farther west was the factor that ended the school which had no neighborhood to serve.

There were also several less successful attempts to educate the children. The Zionists opened a school with instruction in Hebrew for girls as well as boys. In 1928 the Rumanian Congregation Yad Achaas briefly attempted to hold classes as a branch of the Talmud Torah. In addition to the Talmud Torahs an attempt was made to organize a "modern Conservative Sunday School" in 1926, and an effort to unite all of the Hebrew Schools into "one great Hebrew Institute" called Agudas Evriah.[21] For the children living closer to the county line, private teachers were employed. In the 30's Hebrew classes leading to *bar mitzvah* were organized in the home of Dr. David Friedman and conducted by him, his father and brother. The classes were referred to as the "Upper West Colfax Hebrew School."

The completed building of the Hebrew Educational Alliance in 1932 meant not only a modern synagogue, but also a modern school. The healthy effect of the institution was that whether or not the residents joined, their children were enrolled in the Talmud Torah and Sunday school. The Jews who had been so adamant about the use of the Sephardic ritual in their synagogues listened proudly to their grandchildren pray according to the Ashkenazi ritual. The Alliance with its Talmud Torah operating on a schedule of three sessions a day, Sunday School, children's Sabbath services, and *Oneg Shabbat*, devised the most ambitious program for Jewish children in the city.

Just before the start of World War II a day-school, the Yeshivta, was built on West Fourteenth and Quitman Streets. The community was not ready for such a venture at the time. Disagreement among the members, lack of funds, and the war itself kept the school from materializing. The Yeshiva became another of the small synagogues in West Colfax. In 1953 there was sufficient interest to organize the Hillel Academy, the first Jewish day-school in Denver's history. It started modestly with a kindergarten and first grade. Each year another class is added. When there are six complete grades and the school has its own building, Hillel shall have attained its goal.

An entirely different type of school was the Yiddish School organized in 1914.[22] Although it was said that no religion was taught in the school, Dr. Spivak insisted that through the Bible stories, the significance of feasts and fasts, and the love of the Jewish people and their religion, the study of the Yiddish language was serving a religious purpose.[23] The school had a difficult time and closed briefly. In 1917 when the branch of the Workmen's Circle was chartered in Denver, a similar school was opened. This school lasted until the end of 1923.

After the death of Dr. Spivak, a tiny building was erected in his memory in West Colfax where part of his library was placed. The building, Spivak Institute, was dedicated in 1934 but was used very little for educational purposes because of its size.

Various groups were started for the study of Hebrew by adults, including an Agudas Dovri Ivris in 1919.[24] After the formation of the state of Israel, modern as well as Biblical Hebrew gave an impetus to several study groups. Classes in both were taught at the larger synagogues.

4

The immigrants took full advantage of the night classes conducted by the Council for Jewish Women. Denver's unique Emily

Griffith Opportunity School also played an important part in the educating and Americanizing of the East European Jews, most of whom regarded the school with reverence. There were many women who could not leave their homes for the classroom. Some of them taught themselves to read and write English. Others accepted the help of the teachers sent out by the Christian churches. Once the teachers understood that the missionary phase of their teaching was wasted they concentrated on the English lessons. Some of these women were the first American Christians the immigrant housewives met. The lessons became social events, for which the Jewish women did a little extra baking. The friendships that came out of these lessons may be counted among the successful interfaith activities in Denver.

The prize of American citizenship was sought through at least two organizations, the Jewish Protective Association in 1895, and the West Denver Citizens' Club, organized in 1906 with 573 members studying for their citizenship papers.

Even before Colfax was annexed to Denver, a group filed articles of incorporation in 1894 for a Hebrew Library Association with literary and educational objectives.[25]

When the Dickinson Branch Library, through a Carnegie loan, was built in West Colfax, it became one of the most popular spots in the entire section. For many years the various Jewish organizations held teas, meetings, and story-hours in the building. During the years when the neighborhood about it was solely Jewish, the librarians who served it claimed that it had the highest book circulation among the branch libraries in the city. When the westward movement took the bulk of Jews out of the area around the library, circulation dropped so low that the library was sold in 1954 and replaced by a "bookmobile," stationed between Colfax School and the Alliance.

5

Where most of the institutions created by the Jews were traditional necessities, the hiring of a rabbi was a luxury. Although there was no lack of congregations, there was never enough money properly to pay a rabbi in most of them. There was, nevertheless, no lack of rabbis, for respiratory disease or weakness brought many of them West. In their number were a few internationally-known men who managed to find a synagogue or synagogues to serve.

The lot of the rabbis was not an enviable one. Not only were they underpaid, not only was their learning unappreciated, but also a few of them were actually publicly shamed. In addition there was a source of friction between the Ashkenazi rabbis and the *Chassidic* rabbis over the merits of their respective traditions. Their followers argued the merits of their rabbis and brought the same cases to each for their opinion. One story recalls a source of strife between the two camps.

Many of the Jews were cattlemen, who drove their cattle into Denver, tied to the back of their horse-drawn wagons. Since the horses knew their way home, the owner was not always present to control the speed of the horses. The question was raised: since the Bible said that a horse and ox should not be yoked together, what of the reluctant cow that was being pulled ahead by the horse who decided the tempo of travel at the other end of the wagon?

The question was posed to the two rabbis, one Lithuanian, the other *Chassidic*. One said "permissible." The other, "positively contrary to Jewish law." While letters were sent East and to Europe to determine who was right, the Jews began to do battle in West Colfax. Although this was one of the beginnings of the celebrated Ostrov-Litvak antagonism in the neighborhood, nobody seems to remember if, or how, the question was settled.

The Lithuanians claimed that their rabbis in Denver were the greatest of all. Certainly such a man as Rabbi Elias (Elya) Hillkowitz, who came to Denver in 1890, was deserving of all the respect that was shown him by the entire community. Rabbi Hillkowitz was born in Rutwan, Kovno, Russia, and educated in the Yeshivas of Woloczin, Zhitomir and Kovno. He was ordained by the chief of the Russian rabbinate, Rabbi Isaac Elchanan, and served as a rabbi for the first time in Pickeln, Kovno. During the troubled years in Russia, he left the rabbinate for commercial pursuits, in which he acquired some wealth, but, driven from village to village, he lost it and came to the United States. In Cincinnati, the stronghold of Reform Judaism, he founded the first Orthodox synagogue and thus became the dean of that city's Orthodox rabbinate. Asthma brought him to Denver in 1890, and the following year he returned east to bring back his family. His son Philip, who was studying medicine at the University of Cincinnati, came to Denver in 1897.

In Denver Rabbi Hillkowitz was immediately recognized as the dean of the city's Orthodox rabbinate. When a dispute arose or a doctrine needed expounding, the other rabbis called in Rabbi Hillkowitz, whose word was accepted as the final one. He served the community without compensation until his death in 1906.

The Hillkowitz home was one of the few truly cultured centers in the city. There many illustrious travelers of the period, whether Jew or gentile, could be found. The sick and poor newcomers to Denver asked for the rabbi as soon as they arrived in the city. They were given as warm a welcome as was given to the visiting foreign consuls or European rabbis. The entire family was deeply interested in the problem of the health-seekers. When the J.C.R.S. was incorporated, it was Rabbi Hillkowitz who suggested the Talmudic words for its famous standard.

Among the rabbis of whom the Lithuanians boasted was the small-statured Rabbi Idel Idelson. Idelson was identified with several West Colfax synagogues and was one of the earliest board members of the J.C.R.S. Unfortunately, neither his scholarship nor his unswerving honesty was appreciated in Denver, particularly by the butchers. After helping found the first Talmud Torah in West Colfax, he left Denver for New York.

For a number of years when the dozen synagogues of West Colfax had very little money, two rabbis had them divided almost equally between them. One was Rabbi Isaac A. Braude, who more or less represented the Ashkenazi and Lithuanian congregations.[26] Rabbi Braude, who was born in 1884 in Lithuania, was educated in the Yeshivas of Telsiai, Mates, and Woloczin. When ordained, he became the rabbi of Girtezole, Lithuania.

In 1906 he fled to the U. S. by way of Siberia, Korea, and Japan. He first came to Denver, where he served until 1922. He then served in Dayton and Bridgeport. He returned to Denver in 1927, where he remained until his death in 1932.

Thousands attended the last rites for the rabbi, and to that time it was the most impressive funeral ever to take place in West Colfax. The police deflected the Sunday traffic from West Colfax, while the funeral procession marched from synagogue to synagogue on West Colfax. All of the rabbis of Denver, Cheyenne, and Pueblo spoke words of praise for the rabbi, and all of the city's cantors sang the prayers for the deceased. The *Jewish News* that week said that similar scenes had been enacted in Eastern Europe, where a chief rabbi was accorded such honor. In Denver, the gentiles exclaimed that they had never seen anything like it. Neither had the young American generation of West Colfax.

Rabbi Braude stood with "unashamed fervor" for traditional Judasim.[27] He was not afraid to "assail the Jews who neglected the Sabbath." In Yiddish he denounced the mothers who took advantage of Saturday bargains in the downtown stores.

Rabbi Ephraim Zalman Halpern who served the half-dozen Sephardic-praying congregations, contemporaneously with Rabbi Braude, was also unafraid to express unpopular opinions on the lack of observance of Jewish life. His presence added *Chassidic* color to Jewish ceremonies.

Before Rabbi Halpern left Denver, in 1923, he helped organize a League of Mercy to help both individuals and existing institutions. He made his home in Palestine, where he became the director of the Yeshivah Chaye Olam and Yeshivah Torah Veyirah, religious colleges in Jerusalem. In 1954 he returned to Denver for a brief visit, while on a tour of the United States "to popularize the cause of family purity in Israel,"[28] at the request of the chief rabbi of that country.

Rabbi Halpern was succeeded by Rabbi Yehudah Leib Rosenblum, who came to Denver in 1924 and was the rabbi for the Zere Abraham and Knesseth Israel congregations until his death in 1941. A learned man, he wrote many unpublished works of Responsa and commentaries on the Talmud. Rabbi Rosenblum proposed a Shomre Shabbas league in West Colfax, and both he and Rabbi Braude planned to canvass the homes to enroll members.[29] If *Shabbas* was neglected in West Colfax, there was little hope that it would be observed anywhere in Denver.

After the death of Rabbi Braude, a gifted *tsadik* took over the Lithuanian congregation. He was Rabbi Judah Leib (Louis) Ginsburg, who was born in Latvia in 1888. Rabbi Ginsburg studied in the Yeshivas of Lamz and Mereh and was a student of Rabbi Chaim Grozinski. As a young man, Rabbi Ginsburg held the post of *Rosh* (head) of the Yeshiva Eischckik, and three years later a similar post in Reziza. During World War I he was compelled to live at Yaraslavl, where he served as rabbi. While the Russian Revolution was in progress, many attempts were made to bring him to the United States. Through the intervention of Dr. Joseph Rosen of the Agro-Joint Committee, he was allowed to leave.

His first book, *Hebrew Ethics and Rights*, was published shortly after his arrival in the United States. In Denver he wrote a four-volume commentary on Talmudic and Midrashic interpretation of the Five Books of Moses, dealing with the ethical teachings of the Jewish rabbis. Much of his writing was begun while he was a patient at the J.C.R.S. After he left the sanitarium and took the Zere Israel congregation, which could only pay him a pittance, the love of the entire Jewish community was showered upon him in the form of a fund which was established so that he could continue his two-volume work, *Ethics of the Mishnah*. Not only did the Orthodox and Conservative Jews love him and his equally saintly wife, Eta, but also Rabbi Friedman of the Temple was said to have been one of those who actively supported him.

His writings included *Yalkut Y'hedah* (Gatherings of Judah) a five volume commentary; *Musar Ha Mishnah* (The Ethics of the Mishnah), and a book on the *Ethics of the Fathers*. During the last years of his life he had started to write the Ethics of the Prophets under the name *Musar HaNeviim*. The demand for his books was so great that the edition originally printed in Dwinsk, Latvia, in 1933, was immediately reprinted in St. Louis. His works are used in congregations and *yeshivas* throughout the United States, and are quoted for his original comments on the ancient religion. In 1944, his wife, Eta, to whom he had dedicated his last book, died.[30] Little more than a year later the rabbi died, leaving a large fund, of between $8000 and $9000, to have his books reprinted in Israel.

From the amount of money in the fund it is apparent that the Rabbi used very little for himself, yet his home was one of the friendliest and most hospitable in the city. There were always five or six guests eating with him, while his fragile wife served them. His genius did not prevent him from being one of the most easily approachable men in the community, and his pleasant wit made everyone comfortable with him. Of his literary style, one critic wrote: "he turns the dry passages of the Torah Cohanim . . . into a golden chain of sparkling gems."[31]

6

The list of rabbis who minstered or lived in Denver is long. A few were just right for their congregations and served for decades. Others came and left with the seasons. Only a handful became synonymous with their congregations: Rabbi William S. Friedman, more that fifty years with the Temple; Rabbi C. E. H. Kauvar, emeritus after fifty years with the Beth Ha Medrosh

Hagodol, and Rabbi Manuel Laderman, celebrating a quarter of a century with the Hebrew Educational Alliance in 1957.

When Rabbi Charles E. Hillel Kauver celebrated his fiftieth anniversary as rabbi of the B. M. H. in 1952, full pages were devoted to his life in the daily newspapers. During the celebration he was praised for his many activities—for most of which he had had to battle the stronger and earlier Jewish community. Among these were the Denver Hebrew School, the Central Jewish Council (of which he was the first president), the Jewish Consumptives Relief Society, and his very active part in the Zionist movement. At a mass meeting during the Kishinev pogroms, Rabbi Kauvar reminded the community that "When some of us wanted a Zion for the Russian Jews, it was said there was no need of a Zion, there was America: But every Jew has not his America."[32]

Rabbi Kauvar gained respect from the non-Jewish community through the Denver Ministerial Alliance and as an educator. He was the second rabbi to hold a university chair in Colorado. While Rabbi Friedman was teaching at the University of Colorado, I. Rude asked Rabbi Kauvar for a fitting commemoration of his son's *bar mitzvah*. The rabbi suggested Rude endow a chair in Rabbinic Literature at the University of Denver. The rabbi was named a full professor teaching the course he had suggested.[33]

Rabbi Kauvar was born in Vilna in 1879. He came to the United States as a child and was educated at the City College of New York, at Columbia University, and as a rabbi at the Jewish Theological Seminary. The synagogue in Denver was his first pulpit.

Another first pulpit for a rabbi was also the first pulpit in the congregation. The Hebrew Educational Alliance was successful in its first attempt at finding a suitable rabbi, with Rabbi Manuel Laderman. The tall young rabbi was the first native-born rabbi in West Colfax, with a religious background pleasing to the elders, and a modern American approach of which the more difficult younger generation approved. He came with just the proper amount of firmness to unite the West Colfax community and prevent the bickerings in his synagogue that had broken up so many others. In addition he became a great source of pride to his congregation and the entire Jewish community. His presence, sought after by many non-Jewish groups at all levels, resulted in so much radio and television time, that when he suffered a heart attack in 1953, Bishop Fulton Sheen, speaking in Denver, said he was the summer replacement for Rabbi Laderman.

Both the rabbi and his chic wife, Bess Laderman, have extended their interests into the larger community, where Mrs. Laderman is a leading patroness of the Denver Symphony. On the national scene the rabbi has held office in the Rabbinical Council of America, the Union of Orthodox Congregations, and the Mizrachi Organization of America. Named a European director of an affiliate of the Joint Distribution Committee, he took a year's leave of absence to help with the rehabilitation of the European Jews after World War II. Rabbi Laderman was born in New York and was ordained by the Hebrew Theological Seminary of Chicago in 1932.

Paralleling Rabbi Laderman's ministry, although for a shorter period, is that of Rabbi Daniel Goldberger, who holds his first pulpit as the first rabbi of Congregation Beth Joseph. Like Rabbi Laderman, the tall young man, who came to Denver in 1951, is a graduate of Hebrew Theological Seminary. He, too, has captured the attention of the Jewish and non-Jewish community.

Several of the West Colfax congregations have as their religious leader Rabbi Zalman Shmuel Shapiro, who came to Denver in 1933, after serving congregations in Chicago for twelve years. The rabbi, who was born in Minsk and educated at the Yeshivas of Baresov, and Minsk, was warmly greeted by the Jewish community, and his suggestions for Talmud Torahs, for a united rabbinical supervision of the slaughtering of meat, and for closer supervision of *kashruth*, were politely received, but for one reason or another never followed. Scrupulously honest, he refused to give his endorsement to any food products. To him come housewives with doubtful-looking chickens, and to him are brought complicated questions of Jewish law, such as those involving divorce. In 1955 he completed a book on homeletics, *Halacha* and *Responsa*. The rabbi's congregations are the Yad Achaas, Beth Jacob, Shearith Israel, and Benjamin Samett's synagogue.

West Colfax's oldest synagogue, Zere Abraham, has as its rabbi, Shloime Twerski, of the celebrated *Chassidic* family. Rabbi Twerski, in traditional *Chassidic* dress, with a university degree in psychology from the University of Chicago, is an answer to the critics of *Chassidism* who regarded the movement in Judaism as out of place in America. His carefully organized addresses and excellent diction surprise non-Jews and Jews with preconceived ideas as to the *Chassidim*. On Simchas Torah and Purim Jews converge from other synagogues to the Zere Abraham and his home to celebrate the holidays in joyous *Chassidic* style.

The rabbi for the Yeshiva and for Knesseth Israel is Rabbi Chaim Davidovich, who was born in Hungary and studied at Yeshivas in Tresburg, Scatmar and Budapest, and at the University of Buffalo. He served as a rabbi in Buffalo before coming to Denver in 1945. In addition to his congregations, he is the director of religious education at the National Jewish Home for Asthmatic Children. Following some trouble with the rabbinical endorsement of the slaughtering of meat, Rabbi Davidovich took over the supervision of all of the meat in the city which was to reach Jewish tables.

One figure, who was not identified with the Orthodox congregations but who made a deep impression on them, was that of Rabbi Herbert S. Friedman, who held the Temple Emanuel pulpit for nine years. His overseas experience with the Joint Distribution Committee, his service as a wartime chaplain, and his dynamic qualities of leadership marked him as not long for his congregation. After serving as a rabbi in Milwaukee, he assumed leadership in the United Jewish Appeal.

All Denver rabbis—exclusive of military chaplains—who have congregations belong to the local rabbinical council. The council's principal and perhaps unique achievement has been the agreement among the rabbis, with the help of the Anti-Defamation League, since 1939, not to perform weddings in any public hall, limiting these events to homes, synagogues, or private Jewish clubs.

A number of rabbis, born and educated in Denver, serve throughout the United States, but only one, Martin Weitz, has held a pulpit in Colorado. Among them are the Reform rabbis Sam Koch, Maurice Zigmond, Ernest Trattner, William Braude (son of Zere Israel's Rabbi Isaac Braude) and Abraham Klausner and Orthodox rabbis Melvin Rushnevsky and Israel Turner.

FOOTNOTES

[1] *Jewish Voice*, Oct. 9, 1891.
[2] A Rose Hill Cemetery Association was incorporated in 1890, but all the names on the document are non-Jewish. Art. Inc. Sept. 4, 1890, 639-267.
[3] BB minutes, Mar. 8, 1896, p. 3.
[4] DPL clipping file, Dec. 12, 1899.
[5] *JO*, Mar 24, 1905.
[6] *Republican*, April 21, 1890.

[7] *RA*, p. 49, col. 3.
[8] *RMN*, Feb. 21, 1885.
[9] BMH Bazaar program, 1905, in WmSF Scrapbook: seven groceries and butchers, one kosher restaurant advertised. All but one had a telephone.
[10] City records, Dec. 2, 1891.
[11] Elias Menkus.
[12] Art. Inc., Nov. 17, 1905.
[13] *JO*, June 26, 1906, fifth annual picnic.
[14] *RA*, p. 14, col. 3.
[15] BB minutes, Nov. 13, 1904, p. 79.
[16] *JO*, Nov. 11, 1904.
[17] BB minutes, Mar. 12, 1905, p. 110-111.
[18] *Ibid.*, June 10, 1906, p. 215.
[19] *DJN*, Jan. 14, 1920.
[20] *DJN*, Mar. 2, 1915, p. 10.
[21] *DJN*, Sept. 22 and Oct. 16, 1916.
[22] Morris papers, minutes *Yiddishe National Radical Shule, May, 1914*, Interview, Bernard Rose.
[23] *DJN*, June 11, 1915. In an editorial on "What is a Radical?" Dr. Spivak wanted the name changed.
[24] *AJY*, Vol. 22, p. 323. (1920-21).
[25] Affadavit of Inc. No. 6409, Jan. 18, 1894.
[26] *AJY*, *op. cit.*, Rabbi Braude, seven synagogues, Rabbi Halpern, six.
[27] *IJN*, June 24, 1932.
[28] *IJN*, Apr. 8, 1954.
[29] *IJN*, April 4, 1929.
[30] Interview, A. B. Cohen.
[31] *West End Press*, Jan. 4, 1935.
[32] *JO*, Nov. 17, 1905.
[33] *IJN*, B. M. H. Golden Anniversary Edition, Mar. 25, 1948, p. 15.

"The Tents"

1

The National Jewish Hospital for Consumptives, dedicated in a blaze of publicity in December, 1899, for several reasons could not begin to cope with the flood of sick at its doors. The hospital would accept only incipient, curable cases. Because patients were accepted only after arrangements had been made in the city from which the victims of tuberculosis came, it could only serve a limited number of the afflicted. A third and important reason was that the institution was not kosher. The rate of tuberculosis was high among the displaced Orthodox Jews in the east, many of whom would not even apply for admission to an institution where milk was served with meat. The problem of 154,000 people dying every year from the disease, and those afflicted with it, ten times that number, was more than the nation, and certainly Denver, could solve.

Calling themselves "The Immigrant Brotherhood of Consumptives," the Jews like the non-Jews, descended upon Denver, but because of their indigence, upon West Denver and especially West Colfax. The situation was described by Dr. Maurice Fishberg in the *Jewish Outlook*:

> . . . that a great proportion are here for their health is evident from their external appearances. . . . Most of these hungry-looking individuals do not present the general appearance of the average denizen of the Ghetto, not as busy or active as Jews generally are . . . standing around discussing weight gained or lost, new "cures," reading Yiddish papers. It is a city of rest not of activity as Ghettoes usually are.[1]

Dr. Fishberg said that room and board were from $6 to $9 a week, and pointed out that the sick must have air, food, freedom from care, and must be lively, cheerful, and happy. "No one ought to come here looking for work. Those without money perish"[2]

But the sick were desperate. Every train brought more and more of them. Men died on the downtown streets, and it became a common sight to see someone sit down suddenly on the street curb, and fall hemorrhaging into the street. The newspapers which had been so silent on the subject earlier, and then praised the Jews when the hospital opened with its first patient, a Swedish girl, continued to praise the Jews, especially for the fact that in tables and reports no mention of religious denomination was made by the hospital, and that "Hebrews do not predominate in the list of patients."[3] At the same time they described the cases where Jews with tuberculosis had starved to death.[4]

The older Jewish community, which had established the hospital, was furious, and the *Jewish Outlook* rose to the defense of the Jews. While one such newspaper story was not in accord with the facts, the periodical pointed out that

> this is, however, a case of wrongdoing by those who send helpless dependents to Colorado. The Jewish Relief Society can never hope to gather enough money to maintain the constantly increasing number of consumptives *with their dependent families* who daily come to Denver of their own volition, or by the mistaken motivations of their unjust friends.[5]

Again and again the hospital begged the eastern cities to look after their poor and sick, and not to make of Denver, which numbered less than 6,000 Jews, a dumping ground.

In West Colfax daily collections were made and "the red bandanna, *fatchule*, the symbol of old-fashioned Jewish charity was very much in evidence."[6] Half of Denver, and half of the Jews, it was claimed, were "ex-tuberculars" or had to care for sick members of their own family. Now they found what seemed to them to be all of the sick of the land on their doorstep.

The "lungers" decided to take the matter into their own hands. At a meeting on October 31, 1903, a group of men met together in a store building in West Colfax "to organize a Society for helping the poor Consumptives in this town who are badly in need of help." The list of men, most of them who were recovered or on their way back to health, was repeated in the history of the institution by Dr. Spivak:

> Mr. Benjamin Diamond, a tinner, and fair Hebrew scholar, who "spits strawberry juice" presided; Henry Cohen, a clerk,

who was elected secretary, an intelligent well-read young fellow with a cheerful disposition . . . Louis Shapiro, cigar-maker; Jacob Cooper, tailor; David Bernhardt, furrier; M. Levinger, musician; L. Wolf, tailor; J. Millstine, photographer; E. Aidelman, wagonmaker; Louis Bornstein, a silk weaver; David Kaufman, actor; Benjamin Wittenstein, a furrier; H. Heublum, a painter.

In addition, the names at the first meeting included Morris Yasness, Max Siegle, Jacob Fischer, Herman Katz, Harry Elbroch, Louis Levin, and M. Hyman.[7] Years later, it became customary for almost every prominent Jew to claim, if he was interested in the institution, that he was a founder of it. In a sense this was true of every resident of West Colfax, but the early minutes do not reveal the names of most of these claimants to the honor.

This first group chose for itself the name of Denver Charity for Consumptives, with Louis Shapiro as treasurer. A hat was passed that evening, and $1.10 was contributed. It was suggested that "we should appeal to the Rich people for aid, for all those poor consumptives who are badly in need of help." At the next meeting, a week later, the word "charity" was removed and the name changed to The Denver Appeal Society for Consumptives. A collection brought in $2.35.[8] Two more meetings were held. With dues set at five cents a week, $1.85[9] and $1.70[10] were collected.

A mass meeting was called for December 12, 1903, at the Tiphereth Israel synagogue in West Colfax, with Joe Washer presiding. The hall was so jammed that there was no standing room left

> and for once the orthodox custom of dividing the sexes did not prevail, nor did the rabbis protest. The addresses were so appealing, that the audience broke into a lament as poignant as that as in olden days on Tisha b'Av at the recital of Kinoth.[11]

A committe was appointed and the name Jewish Consumptives Relief Society adopted. At the first committee meetings were present Washer, A. Goodstein, Joseph Jaffa, and Doctors Zederbaum and Spivak. Jaffa was elected chairman and Spivak secretary.

To the next board meeting were invited the leaders of the Jewish community, particularly those connected with the National Jewish Hospital, including Rabbi Friedman. The guests made it clear that they were against soliciting aid from the outside, "since such action may bring a great number of consumptives to Denver." Dr. Spivak disagreed. It was his opinion that "increased demand for aid, as a result of an influx of consumptives, would also increase the sources of income."[12] Only Jaffa, of the Temple members, remained with the new organization, and was elected its president.

Another mass meeting was called in January, and the total collection since the first meeting was brought to $369.15. It had been the plan of the group to wait until there was $2000 in the treasury before making an appeal out of the city This was changed by an editorial in the *Jewish Outlook*, edited by Rabbi Friedman, saying that the Jewish Relief Society was in straits, that the town was flooded with tuberculosis, and asking that a "national society for Jewish consumptives be formed at once."[13] The board sent a letter to the *Jewish Outlook* stating that an organization, as outlined in the editorial, was already in existence. An appeal to the nation through the Jewish press was ordered to be sent out immediately, subject to the approval of President Jaffa. Jaffa, who was against the establishment of a hospital and wanted the work of the J.C.R.S. restricted, resigned.[14] Dr. Philip Hillkowitz was elected president.

The press and propaganda committee, to which Dr. Spivak invited his friend, Yehoash, began to function immediately. In Denver, the first to answer the plea was the Pride of Denver Lodge, Independent Order B'rith Abraham, which enlisted the aid of the national organization, which assessed a two and a half cent per capita tax. The Workmen's Circle followed. With the help of the Yiddish press, and its pleas from editors Abraham Cahan, Johann Paley, Leon Zolotkoff, and the poet, Morris Rosenfeld, ladies' auxiliaries and tributary societies sprang up almost overnight throughout the country. The English press followed closely and the Denver organization became nationally-known even before a hospital was begun.

For $5,000 twenty acres of land for a sanitarium was purchased in Jefferson County, a fifteen-minute walk from the end of the carline on West Colfax. Dr. Zederbaum donated the funds for the first edifice—a tent—in memory of his father, Alexander Zederbaum, the founder of the Hebrew journal in Russia, the *Hamelitz HaMaili*. Other tents were named for the I. O. B. A., Workmen's Circle, Theodore Herzl, the names of two to be auctioned off at the dedication, "if deemed proper."[15] A frame building was put up at the same time and the Jewish Consumptives Relief Society was ready for dedication, September 4, 1904.

The almost instant success of the new institution was due to the idealists it attracted. The National Jewish Hospital had as its supporters the wealthy Jews of America—in the Temple Emanuel alone, there were several millionaires. The J. C. R. S. was founded with the nickels and dimes that the hard-pressed Jews of West Colfax sacrificed, and the roll for breakfast that an Eastern shopworker gave up for a sick person in Colorado.

Among the many ardent workers for the institution was the son of Rabbi Hillkowitz who suggested the Hospital's motto from the Talmud, "He who saves one life is considered as if he had preserved the whole world." Dr. Philip Hillkowitz served the sanitarium as its president until his death in 1948. He was one of the leading pathologists and bacteriologists in the American Medical Association. Locally he held chairs at the medical colleges and served on the staffs as pathologist of four hospitals, and captain of the medical corps during World War I. Despite his vast knowledge of many subjects and his linguistic ability in fourteen languages he was an extremely modest and quiet man. He was appreciated by the non-Jewish community which changed local and state medical conventions so that he would not have to appear on High Holidays or at places where Jews were not normally permitted. With his passing —he suffered a stroke while presiding at a meeting where he was having difficulty with some of the members of the board of the J.C.R.S.—the last of the young selfless idealists, whose love for mankind had built the J.C.R.S., was gone.

During the years when the J.C.R.S. was new and was meeting violent opposition from the National Jewish Hospital, his sister Anna, who was a librarian at the Denver Public Library, took a leave of absence to travel for the institution as its first field secretary.

It was a thrilling day for these workers and for all of West Colfax when, close to the front range of the Rockies, the first six tents were opened to the first seven patients four days after dedication. The "tents" as the J.C.R.S. was called, became one of the most welcome sights in the West. Many a Jew, healthy or sick, exclaimed as he did on entering his synagogue, "How goodly are thy tents, O Jacob, and thy dwelling places, O Israel."[16]

2

The supporters of the National Jewish Hospital for Consumptives, remembering the prolonged labor in giving birth to the original free tuberculosis hospital, looked with fear and anger at the new venture launched by the East European Jews. The *Jewish Outlook*, the hospital's organ, sharpened its comments against the J.C.R.S. and its officers. One barb was directed at a Jewish physician for the institution, "who says only a few Denver Jews are against the J.C.R.S. His frantic attempt to leap into prominence, build up a reputation on the J.C.R.S., having proved abortive, he will again leap into his accustomed obscurity."[17] Since the three major offices of the institution were held by outstanding physicians in the community, any of the three may have been meant.

The *Outlook* gave as its reasons for opposition: "What if Denver does not want any more tuberculars and closes its doors and opposes erection of sanatoria, and what if people want no more of this, especially if the sick are mainly Jews?" Aside from the fear that the city would be over-run with sick Jews, an editorial the next week pointed out that the ninety-bed hospital cost $40,000 a year, and that another hospital would duplicate its work. The writer said that he regarded the whole thing as a calamity, and signed his name, William S. Friedman.[18]

The rest of the older community agreed. Ten prominent Jews were interviewed. Their opinions were: "The Centennial state shall not be turned into a Lazaretto"; "as visionary as draining the ocean," urging disbandonment and return of money already collected; Dr. Elsner voiced the opinion that physicians cannot attend the incurable without remuneration for too long; another believed that the institution should be in New York. Only Dr. Spivak, who was also polled, said that "It supports a definite demand and neither duplicates nor encroaches on existing organizations." He believed that first, by sheltering and feeding the destitute consumptive, the J.C.R.S. work would be a prophylactic measure, especially for those discharged as cured from other hospitals; that there would be no overlapping, since the emergency cases to be taken to the J.C.R.S. would not be admitted anywhere else; and that it provided for residents of Denver who become incurable.[19]

The battle continued not only in Denver, but also in the Jewish press of the nation. The *Outlook* claimed that the seven leading Jewish publications in America disapproved of the idea of the J.C.R.S.[20]

In answer to the many charges against the new institution, Dr. Spivak wrote in one national magazine: "We exist, we are here to stay .... There are institutions here for the rich sick and for the poor well, but what are the poor sick to do?" Low mortality records, he said, were not the ambition of the institution, but to realize the "pure sentiments of humanity," so that for every case that dies, and some must, the last days on earth would have been made comfortable.[21]

The officers of the J.C.R.S. were not bashful. They went directly into the strongholds of the "National's" supporters in the United States. Dr. Kate Levy of Chicago in *Jewish Comment* in Baltimore, particularly angered the National Hospital's supporters when she said that the National Jewish Hospital had originated with a "Jewess of Denver" [Frances Jacobs]. Writing in the *Outlook* Dr. Moses M. Collins said that the hospital was founded by Rabbi Friedman. Also he said that the statement that no Russian Jews would be admitted to the National was untrue and that ninety per cent of the patients were Russian Jews. He added that "Tuberculars need milk and meat. It is not true that Russian Jews view with loathing 'unkosher foods'."[22] The J.C.R.S. denied that it made any such charges,[23] but went right ahead seeking aid from the National's supporters. In Cincinnati Dr. William Hillkowitz approached the *American Israelite*, Mrs. C. D. Spivak spoke at the Chicago Council of Jewish Women where the national president, Hannah Solomon, promised to work for a per capita tax,[24] and Dr. Emil G. Hirsch wrote an article for the Chicago *Reform Advocate*, commenting favorably on the work of the society.[25]

Turned down repeatedly by the local B'nai B'rith lodge in its requests for aid, the J.C.R.S. turned directly to Samuel Grabfelder, the national president of the National Jewish Hospital, who wrote to the J.C.R.S. that the institution was doing a good and noble work, and that he was "anxious to become a contributor to the J.C.R.S., and furthermore that he is perfectly willing to join any movement toward the formation of a Central organization that would help stamp out the dreadful plague."[26]

FOOTNOTES

[1]Maurice Fishberg, *JO*, Nov. 4, 1904. The residents of West Colfax did not refer to this section as a "ghetto" and it is doubtful if any of them ever thought of it as one.
[2]Fishberg, "Life of Consumptives in Denver Boarding Houses," *JO*, Aug. 12, 1904.
[3]*Times*, May 16, 1902.
[4]*JO*, Jan. 1, 1904.
[5]*Ibid.*

[6] *DJN*, Oct. 22, 1915. Dr. Spivak gives the origin of the Yiddish word as the Italian *fazzoletto*. He makes this statement many times. Others do not recall the bandana.
[7] JCRS minutes, Oct. 31, 1903.
[8] *Ibid.*, Nov. 14, 1903.
[9] *Ibid.*, Nov. 21, 1903.
[10] *Ibid.*, Dec. 6, 1903.
[11] *DJN*, July 5, 1922. The article appears to be written by Spivak.
[12] JCRS minutes, Dec. 23, 1903.
[13] *JO*, Feb. 12, 1904.
[14] JCRS minutes, Apr. 7, 1904.
[15] *Ibid.*, Aug. 8, 1904. The fifth tent was named "B. M. H. Sunday School" before dedication.
[16] *Thirty Years of Saving Lives*, 1904-1934, JCRS Brochure.
[17] *JO*, June 10, 1904.
[18] *JO*, Apr. 15, 1904.
[19] *JO*, Apr. 22, 1904.
[20] *JO*, May 6, 1904.
[21] WmSF Scrapbook. Reprint from *New Era Illustrated* Magazine, Oct. 1904; JCRS minutes, Sept. 29, 1904, ordered 1000 reprints.
[22] *JO*, Oct. 7, 1904.
[23] JCRS minutes, June 11, 1904. Secretary sent letter to find out origin of "malicious rumor that the JCRS had officially denounced the NJH for making its inmates eat the flesh of swine."
[24] *Ibid.*, Oct. 11, 1904.
[25] *Ibid*, Apr. 1, 1905.
[26] *Ibid.*, Nov. 25, 1905.

Papa Spivak

The greatest single blessing that the Jews afflicted with tuberculosis in Denver, and perhaps throughout the country, ever had bestowed upon them, came to Denver after the Panic of 1893 in the person of a vivid red-headed young man, Charles David Spivak. He was no ordinary man, but excelled in many fields and made his mark as a brilliant physician, lexicographer, professor, editor, Hebraist and Yiddishist, Talmudist, Zionist, Socialist, but most deeply as the beloved humanitarian, "*Tateh* (Papa) Spivak."

Chaim David Spivakofski was born into an Orthodox Jewish home in Krementschug, Russia, on December 25, 1861, to Samuel David and Deborah Adel (Dorfman). His parents gave him a Hebrew and uncommonly thorough secular education, so that for the rest of his life he had a deep understanding of the problems that faced his people and mankind historically and contemporaneously. He was alive and young during the years when the Jews were subject to the vicious, ugly fury of the Russian government, when they were beaten, tortured, raped, and literally thrown to the dogs. As the terrible ax of the Cossacks was about to be swung into the neck of the Jews, Spivak began to study how the people could lift the evil hand of the Russian court and the dreaded Cossacks. He refused to believe that this terror was the Jewish lot and thus had to be accepted. In his studies be became a socialist, reading books forbidden by the government, and undertaking the publication of a small revolutionary paper.

According to his friend Abraham Cahan, Spivak fled Russia, not only because of his political activity, in which he had been apprehended, but also because of his strong feelings that as a Jew he had to do something for the Jewish future. As a member of the Am Olam (Eternal People), an organization of Russian Jewish immigrants who hoped to establish Jewish colonies in America, he is said to have come with the second group of Am Olam. He and a friend had planned to join a colony of Russian settlers in Oregon in order to apply their ideas of co-operation and living close to the soil. The colony was never organized and Spivak went to work in a New York factory for six dollars a week. From there he went to Maine where he worked in a wool mill.

His own aspirations and abilities led him into the field of medicine. Through the aid of friends he entered the Jefferson Medical College in Philadelphia. During his student days he was active in communal work in Philadelphia and began his writing in the Yiddish and Anglo-Jewish newspapers. The young man who had arrived in New York in 1883 was graduated with honors in 1890. In the years that followed he took post-graduate work at the University of Berlin, and returned to Philadelphia, where he married Jenny (Eugenia) Charsky, a well-educated young woman, in 1893.

Spivak was well on his way to prominence in his field. He was named chief of the clinic of gastro-intestinal diseases in the Philadelphia Polyclinic. In communal life he had begun to satisfy his longing to improve Jewish life. He was elected president of a group who sought responsibility and recognition for the East European Jews in the short-lived Jewish Alliance of America in Philadelphia, February 15, 1891. The plan came to nothing then but fifteen years later the idea came to life in the American Jewish Committee. Spivak's career in Philadelphia terminated abruptly when his wife's health demanded that they leave the East.

In Denver he was immediately recognized as a leader in his field of medicine, and upon his arrival in 1896 he was invited to become a lecturer on diseases of the gastro-intestinal tract in the local medical college, as well as professor of anatomy and professor of medicine.

Dr. Spivak always carried a pencil and paper with him. Out of his memoranda-stuffed pockets came his plans. One of his earliest, presented to the Denver and Arapahoe Medical Society, was his Union Catalogue Plan, to make available all of the medical journals and books in the city. All of the physicians were to turn over lists of the printed matter in their possession, and one complete list was to be compiled—exclusive of the works available in the public medical library. The master list thus obtained was to be kept by the library. Included in the information was the name of the physician in whose office a volume was to be found, and the hour of the day when it might be consulted.

The plan was hailed with enthusiasm, and the *Journal of the American Medical Association* suggested that the plan be followed by other large towns and cities. Queries came from all parts of the country asking for his advice on how to build similar libraries. Not only his articles on the subject, but also his own publication, *Medical Libraries*, which he edited from 1898 to 1902, carried his name throughout the medical world. In addition to the five volumes of the series, he compiled a large portion of the material for *Coloradoana*, a commemorative volume on the fiftieth anniversary of the Colorado Medical Society, which contained a list of the writings of Colorado physicians from 1871 to 1921. The article in the *Jewish Encyclopedia* on physicians was also written by Dr. Spivak. At the Denver Medical Society Library, where the published writings of local physicians are filed, his file bulges with reprints.[1] Although these are technical writings, they are enjoyable reading.

In his private practice he was an instant success, but he was greatly dissatisfied with the lack of treatment offered the tuberculous in the state. He made a request to an officer of the unopened Frances Jacobs Hospital that the building be put to immediate use. It distressed him to see the $40,000 building empty of anything save rats, but the officer firmly refused to listen to any proposition Spivak had to offer. Thus, when he was called to address the first mass meeting organized by the "lungers" in West Colfax, he found the field that was waiting for his enthusiasm and ability. This was a mighty task in an entrenched community, and one which required the co-operation of all the Jews, not only of Denver, but of the whole nation—appealing to the finest ideals of Judaism—*tsdokoh* for saving lives.

This ideal attracted just such professional men as Spivak, each of them with a lustrous name of his own. Doctors Zederbaum, Hillkowitz, and later Dr. Oscar Shere and Dr. I. D. Bronfin, were men whose brilliance was matched by their love for suffering humanity. The struggle was great, but so was the joy in working together for such a goal. Equally pleasing to Dr. Spivak was the list of founders, the humble men whose idea it was to help others overcome the disease as they had. On every occasion he repeated their names and saw to it that no individual was glorified by the labor of the entire group, but that each was credited wherever possible for his sacrifices and efforts. He never let it be forgotten that the J.C.R.S. was conceived in lower West Colfax, and that its birth was attended by the Yiddish-speaking Jews of America.

Spivak became the secretary of the organization, and his painstaking minutes reveal the idealism of its officers. Most of the board meetings were held in his office, where he and his friends, Yehoash and Jacob Marinoff, the writer of Yiddish humor, wrote the bulletins, press releases, and other publicity for the fledgling institution. To them were added Philip Hornbein, the lawyer; Henry Cohen and Mrs. Edgerton, the picturesque couple—he a labor lawyer and son of the founder of the Hebrew Ladies Benevolent Society and she his teacher and devoted friend—and, of course, all of West Colfax.

One of the first suggestions adopted was that no member of the board should hold any pay position in the J.C.R.S.[2] Another was that no one should be paid for soliciting funds, be it salary, commission, or expenses. This was the opinion of Henry Cohen, who believed that "the J.C.R.S. must remain unique in this respect as in all others," and that to pay a commission would lower the high standard the society had set for itself.[3]

The Press and Propaganda committee branched into its own publication, *The Sanatorium,* of which Spivak was the editor from 1907 until his death. On the staff of the bi-monthly were Yehoash and Marinoff, as well as writers who were patients at the J.C.R.S. Such a publication was far from the ordinary propaganda released by similar institutions. Humor and human interest stories filled the columns, and the poetry anonymously attributed to "Lungfellow" might have been penned by any one of a talented crew.[4]

As the J.C.R.S. became a permanent institution and the new American generation grew up, Dr. Spivak was ready to realize an early dream. By 1912 he was able, with the help of others like himself, to create Denver's Central Jewish Council. The *Kehillah* was organized on August 26, 1912, with two delegates from each of the thirty-two Jewish organizations in the city.

The following year he had a new project, editing the Council's newspaper, the *Denver Jewish News.* As its first editor he brought to the newspaper the same readability and Yiddish humor he brought to all of his writings. No one knows just how many articles he wrote under a variety of pseudonyms for the Yiddish press as well as his own newspaper. Publicity was not his goal.

Spivak's writings brought him more than local and national

fame. In 1911, with Yehoash, he wrote a Yiddish dictionary, containing all the Hebrew and Chaldaic elements of the Yiddish language, illustrated with proverbs and idiomatic expressions. He helped Yehoash with the popular Yiddish translation of the Bible. Thus it was that when he was appointed and accepted the difficult mission of the first medical commission to Poland for the Joint Distribution Committee, he was hailed by the Jews of East Europe not as the physician or social worker, but as the co-author of the Yiddish dictionary.

The mission to Poland was one for which he was not physically fitted. Most of the group, under military discipline, were young men able to withstand discomfort. Dr. Spivak was the oldest of the group, but he protested against any special consideration and refused to serve in any capacity but as a private. He became the *tateh* of this group, just as he had been to his patients, advising them, sharing their troubles, and, of course, conducting the *seder* on Passover for the group. When a particularly difficult mission was to be undertaken, he insisted on going, although not only hardship but also danger was involved.

His physical well-being was not disturbed by the mission, but his soul was. He came back to describe the tragic conditions he found. Poland was in the throes of a typhus epidemic. There was no food, no clothing, no sanitation, few hospitals, and little equipment. Dr. Spivak investigated, collected data, and made suggestions:

> This is a government function and must be done on a scale way beyond our resources . . . . No matter what measures may be undertaken, no matter what means are used for the improvement of sanitation, without the co-operation of the people, little will be accomplished. What Poland needs most is not only a program of sanitary equipment, bathing facilities, etc., but a program of Health Education.[5]

From devastated post-war Europe he brought back 20,000 letters to be delivered from the East European Jews to their relatives in the United States. He helped arrange the removal of 250 orphaned children to Canada, with the blessing of the Canadian government.

In the national life of the Jews of America he served as a member of the executive committee of the American Jewish Committee from 1914 until his death in 1927. He was a delegate to the American Jewish Congress, a member of the national board of directors of the Zionist Organization of America, and a national officer in the various Jewish conferences on health and communal activity.

No Orthodox rabbi defended the laws of the Torah and Talmud with more zeal than did the doctor, whom the socialists and radicals claimed as their own. He never separated science from the Bible; rather, he would prove a scientific point through the use of the sacred writings. At the same time that he endorsed the *mikveh*, to the chagrin of the "intellectuals," he endorsed autopsy to the displeasure of the pious Jews. His belief that the Bible had withstood the test of time led him to examine all new ideas in the light of the ancient laws and customs.

While he worked for a better world, he also worked for Zionism, which could not be said of most of the liberals of his period. When the Jews of the city organized its most magnificent reception in the history of the community for the Nahum Sokolow delegation, it was Spivak who carried most of the responsibility for the arrangements. When his friend, Leon Zolotkoff, the editor of the Chicago *Jewish Courier*, was vacationing in Colorado at millionaire Spencer Penrose's mountain home, Spivak was there with him, having a huge time setting up a constitution and writing the laws for a Jewish state in Palestine, more than a quarter of a century before the 2000-year-old dream came true.

As a writer and as a speaker, he was impressive. His students published an outline of his lectures in 1900, a tribute rarely extended to professors of medicine. A bibliography of his known 150 published writings, broken into five parts, was published in the January, 1928, issue of *Medical Life*. The titles of his writings reveal the many subjects in which he was versed.

I. Medical History: Thirteen articles, including such titles as "Menstruation," in which he makes special reference to the views held by the Talmudists, and which was the prize thesis at Jefferson Medical College in 1890; "Medicine in the Bible and Talmud," for the *Jewish Encyclopedia*; his important "Post Mortem Examinations Among the Jews—An Historical Sketch and a Plea to Jewish physicians"—important because Spivak believed that human remains could be used for study without violating the Jewish law; "Hebrew Prayers for the Sick," and "Longevity according to Hebrew Lore and Tradition."

II. Medical Bibliography: Six articles, and the five volumes he edited of *Medical Libraries*.

III. Technical Medical Writings: of which fifty-three are listed, many of which were based on his study and treatment of gastrointestinal disorders and of tuberculosis. Into these articles he put his theories of rest and proper eating. Even the titles reflected his humor, such as the one, "The Whistle in the Stomach. Who Blew It First? A Question of Priority."

IV. Non-Medical Writings in English: In fifty-one aritcles his subjects and titles range through many subjects which interested him, including "Jewish Colonization in America," "Photography in Russia," "A Plea for Home Industry from a Medical Point of View," "A New Vocation for Russian Jewesses," which dealt with nursing, "Jewish Journalism in Denver," "Food and Drink of Ancient Hebrews," "The Jewish Conception of Peace," "Morris Winchewsky, a Biographical Sketch," "Rabbi Hirschberg, He Does Not Like Yiddish," and a "Plea for Jewish Banking in Palestine," which he dedicated to the memory of Dina Zolotkoff.

V. Non-Medical Writings in Yiddish, Hebrew and Russian: The twenty-seven articles were similar to those in English and included: "Jewish Laws Compel Woman to Keep Her Body Clean," "Go Wash Your Hands." At least nine articles on how life may be prolonged, a favorite theme of his, and using illustrations from the Prophets, Solomon, the Psalms, and the Talmud to strengthen his view.

As a speaker, he was an attraction in the community. Once a year he gave an address at the B. M. H. synagogue, and whenever possible he gave speeches in Yiddish, which delighted the adults and impressed the young members because of his ability to give the address in Yiddish without using one word of any other language, and even more because of his wit and humor.

He paid dues to every synagogue, and spent the High Holidays in the B.M.H. Every Passover he brought home another set of dishes for the holiday. At the J.C.R.S., the patients looked forward to the *seder* over which he presided, and which ended in a *Chassidic* joyous note. He is said to have been angry but once in his life, and he was never other than informal and friendly. In his busy life he found the time to write more than a million letters, to play chess with cronies all over the city, and to study a page of *Gemarah* with a patient. He was vastly different from the professional social worker of his day and certainly from that of a later date. He always sided with the patients to the distress of the administrators of the hospital, loving and pampering them as though he were, in truth, their "Papa."

In the summer of 1927, shortly after the death of his beloved friend Yehoash, he found that he needed an operation, which he described to Isaac Rivkind of the Jewish Theological Seminary:

> They ripped my abdomen open, inspected my gall bladder, took out 613 stones as befits a pious man [the 613 commandments] sewed up again all the "thirteen things" and now I am more in this world than in the other! I hope by the grace of God, that next week I will be at home; I am still weak.

Spivak never went home. During the operation he was found to be suffering from cancer of the liver. Despite his pain, his concern was not for himself, but for others. "Death does not alarm me. I have not the courage to write Flora [Yehoash's widow]." Taken to a sanitarium in New York, where radium was being tried, he spent his time making plans for his family and his people. At first he had intended to give his entire library to the University in Jerusalem but changed his mind, because he felt that his obligation to his wife preceded the giving away of any of the meager wealth he had.[6] After his death, Mrs. Spivak had barrels of his books shipped to the University.

He dedicated his life to mankind while he lived. After his death he gave most of his body to medical science. Fate decreed that his theory of longevity would not apply to him—or he had lived his crammed lifetime in less time than if he had not been Spivak. In his last days in New York he outlined his will to Rivkind, making very clear his command that his corpse should be used for scientific purposes. "Why should bodies rot in the earth, when they can enrich medical knowledge and bring usefulness and rescue to the world? Why should non-Jews disgrace and dishonor their dead when the Jews do not? If, on the other hand it is not a disgrace, shouldn't the Jews take part in this practice?" Spivak knew well the difficulties of the Jewish medical students.

The instructions in his will were:

> After my body has been dissected, the bones should be articulated by an expert, and the skeleton shipped to the University of Jerusalem, with the request that the same be used for demonstration purposes in the department of anatomy.

Lest there be a misunderstanding as to where his love lay, Spivak ordered that the complete funeral be carried out according to the most Orthodox customs. He asked that those parts of his body which remained be buried in the Workmen's Circle plot of the

Golden Hill Cemetery, where his patient's bodies were also buried. Like Sholom Aleichem, he is said to have said, "I will enhance them. They will enhance me." His will provided that the chapter of Psalms customarily read on the burial day be read at his bedside, and that while the Hebrew was being read, Yehoash's Yiddish translation should also be read. There would be no eulogies, and the entire funeral was to be as simple as that of any of the friendless sick he had known so intimately.

Spivak returned to Denver and died on October 16, 1927. Rivkind said, "The death of Spivak marks the loss of a *lamed vov* (one of the thirty-six upon whom rests the world), a saint, as Yehoash called him."[7] His remains were buried next to David Edelstadt, in the cemetery between the J.C.R.S. and the mountains whose splendor he had admired, and whose magnificence he had matched.

Dr. Spivak's legacy to humanity cannot be evaluated. Many people lived to bring into the world their own children because, no matter how full the J.C.R.S. was, he always managed to scrape up a cot from some source and to squeeze it into the brimming hospital. The Russian Jew proved that the East European Jews were capable of assuming responsibility, and that experience was not a prerequiste in establishing life-saving institutions. He was happy to overlook petty differences in order to unite the Jews into strong central groups, always democratic in policy and action. Simply presented, he left many guides to those that followed who wanted to keep Judaism alive and healthy in a democratic America.

Some of his private research was original and invaluable, such as his survey of all of the cemetery records of the Jews in Denver, which he carefully checked in order to ascertain the principal causes of death among his people.[7] A similar study of his patients at the J.C.R.S. was designed to reveal which employment brought the greatest number of tuberculous to the institution.[8] One of his most interesting projects was a computation of the weight of the various members of the human body. A large tank of water was placed on his back porch. For fifty cents a newsboy would thrust a limb into the water, then submerge himself, while Spivak's son-in-law, Herman Strauss, measured the displacement of the water and computed the weight of the limb.[9] Not only did the scientific experiment have value, but also the various newsboys' mothers had cleaner sons.

The fatherly doctor left a highly respected family in the community. The young woman he married in 1893 was honored as a "Representative Woman of Colorado" for her work in education.[10] She studied at Columbia and Pennsylvania University, took her degree from the University of Denver, and later studied at the Sorbonne. In Denver she was a member of the Why club composed of twenty-one brilliant women, including Ruth Bryan Owen and Mary Elitch Long.

From this union there were three children. David, who died as a young man, won national acclaim for his portraits and landscapes. Deena, the oldest daughter, attended the University of Colorado and married a young professor of engineering there, Herman Strauss. The third child, Ruth, married Dr. Joseph Wolfe. Her interests took her into little theatre work.

To all children he was also a *tateh*. He had the opportunity of playing with only one grandchild. Frequently he would borrow Deena's baby, Adele, for a ride, promising to return her shortly. Instead he would be found at the J.C.R.S., where he fondly watched his patients playing with the baby on the lawn. One day her parents decided to follow Papa Spivak. They found the grandfather driving back and forth across a set of tramway tracks, just to make the "flivver" bounce and the baby giggle.

FOOTNOTES

[1]*DJN*, July 24, 1924. Lists number articles written by physicians. Spivak says 70 was the most written by any one.
[2]JCRS minutes, July 30, 1904.
[3]JCRS minutes, Dec. 13, 1904; Jan. 11, 1905; *JO*, Aug. 30, 1912: when the daily papers praised Dr. Spivak for serving without pay he corrected the statement, because just that year—after eight years without pay—he had begun to accept a salary.
[4]*The Sanatorium*, XII, Oct., Nov., Dec., 1927, memorial issue.
[5-6]Isaac Rivkind, *ibid*.
[7]*DJN*, Oct. 18, 1922. According to Dr. Spivak, 3650 Jews died in Colorado in the previous twenty years. The principal cause of death was tuberculosis in all its forms, then pneumonia, followed by heart disease and cancer.
[8]*DJN*, Apr. 10, 1925.
[9]Denver Medical Society, reprint in Dr. Spivak's file. It is said that he earned national recognition for this research, *Sanatorium, op. cit.*
[10]J. Semple, *Representative Women of Colorado*.

Tsdokoh Expanded

1

Once the Jews of America recognized the enormous task faced by the small Jewish community of Denver, the two institutions created to stem the White Plague, the National Jewish Hospital for Consumptives and the Jewish Consumptives Relief Society, were assured of nation-wide support. The health-seekers poured into Denver, bringing with them two new problems: what to do about the children of the patients in the hospitals, and what to do with the patients who were discharged, but still incapable of earning a living in competition with healthy men and women.

Since both problems were faced by both institutions, the community was able to unite sufficiently to find a solution. The most prominent members of the community, representative of the Reform Temple, the synagogues, both hospitals, and the leading organizations, met at the home of Mrs. J. N. Lorber in West Colfax in 1906 to discuss the advisability of establishing a Jewish orphanage in Denver.[1] The following year, with the support of all of the Jewish organizations in the city, the committees investigating the need reported "that it is contemplated to found a Sheltering Home. They expect to start small and grow."[2] After a mass meeting in January, 1908, enough money was raised to purchase an eleven-room house in West Colfax near Cheltenham school.[3]

The need for the Denver Sheltering Home was great, not only in terms of compassion for the children of the sick, but also because juvenile delinquency was becoming an overwhelming problem to a people who had never faced it before. One of the objects of the "Home" as it was called in West Colfax, was to prevent Jewish children from turning up in the detention home. The organizers of the Home were given permission by Judge Lindsey to give the Home the first chance to rehabilitate first-time offenders. Before the Home was established, many Jewish children had been placed in non-Jewish orphanages, where they learned nothing of Judaism and were taught principles antagonistic to their religious tradition. Another sore point to the community was that "we didn't care for our own."[4] Although not all animosities were set aside for this community project, nevertheless help came from both the elegant homes on Capitol Hill and the humble ones on the west side of the Creek. New communal leaders rose from this group, among them Bessie Willens, whose efforts were later extended into the women's Bickur Cholim, formed in 1915, and into other organizations.

Fire destroyed the first Home in 1914. The children were housed nearby for two years while a building was constructed. Shortly after it was occupied, a diphtheria epidemic broke out in the Home, and the well children had to be moved. The need for a hospital building was met in 1918. This was followed by I. Rude's donation of a dairy. Other early gifts included a girls' dormitory, central heating plant, and laundry. In 1920 the Home became a national institution with offices in New York and Denver. The name of the institution was changed to the Denver National Home for Jewish Children in 1926.

From the first the children of the Home could agree with Sholom Aleichem's Mottel, "How good it is to be an orphan." They were adored by the community, which sometimes sacrificed its own luxuries and those of its children, in order that the children at the Home would have only the best. A band was organized for them. They were given music and dancing lessons, a thorough Hebrew schooling, and picnics and outings. The children who lived at the home were a credit to the community. They were popular with their classmates in the public schools and their manners were a source of pride to both the east and west side of Cherry Creek.

As the White Plague began to recede and new ideas in treatment no longer proclaimed climate as the primary cure for the disease, there was a decreasing need for the Home as a shelter. Although there were always children in the Home because of death, divorce and poverty, the need for the institution as a refuge decreased as birth rates declined. With the great demand for adoptive Jewish children there was no need for an orphanage in Denver.[5] The home, with its excellent facilities for children, changed its scope, and after World War II became the Jewish

National Home for Asthmatic Children, under the original leadership, and still headed fifty years later by its first president, Mrs. Lorber. Admission is non-sectarian, although a Hebrew school is provided for the Jewish children. Under its roofs are housed asthmatic children from all sections of the country and Israel, receiving expert medical treatment for asthma. For those children from broken homes, the "Foster Home" plan is used in Denver.

As a preventive measure, a small and unusual institution was opened in West Colfax, not by the Jewish community, but by the Denver Public Schools. This was Cheltenham Annex, a short distance from the elementary school by that name. Popularly known as the "open-air" or "fresh-air" school, the building was designed for children in the early grades whose parents had tuberculosis, and who were themselves underweight and appeared undernourished. Regular classrooms were held on the first floor. On the second a special room was so designed as to permit the maximum of fresh air to reach the children. Only when the weather was exceptionally bad were classes held downstairs. The children wore special woolen hooded garments to school. Hot lunches were served, and time was allotted for rest periods.[6]

2

Not all of the patients who were "cured" at the two national hospitals wanted to return to their former environment. Not only they, but their doctors as well, still credited the Colorado climate and wide open spaces with their patients' recovery. At first the B'nai B'rith and the National asked the guarantors who had sent the sick to Denver to agree to defray the expenses of the ex-patients who were ready to leave Colorado, or to furnish sufficient means for them if they were to remain, so that they would not become charges of the community. But employment had to be found for them, so committees were organized by the lodge and hospital, calling on the Jews of the entire state to help.

A later historian claims that:

> In practically all cases the object of charity was a non-resident of Colorado—a health seeker from another state—and the burden became so weighty that in 1908, the legislature attempted to pass a law to prevent indigent tubercular from entering the state of Colorado.[7]

The only contemporary account in the *Jewish Outlook* in 1909 makes it appear that the problem was brought into focus by the smouldering antagonism of the National Jewish Hospital to the J.C.R.S. The front-page story was headlined "County Commissioners Threaten to Deport Pauper Health-Seekers." The report blamed the "Tent Hospital" which it said was the only institution inflicting public charges on the county. Despite these charges, the daily press continued to laud the institution and cited it as an example of "broad, sympathetic charity."[8]

So great was the number of sick in 1910 that the Denver Tramway Corporation ran trolley cars only half-enclosed, "to satisfy health-seekers' whims about plenty of fresh air."[9] There were by this time several sanitariums conducted by other religious and private organizations, also attracting non-Jewish tuberculous in the region.

A small group of Jews recognized their responsibility. It is commonly believed in Denver that in 1908 they formed the Aid Association for Ex-Patients of Denver Sanitariums. The minutes of the B'nai B'rith, June 26, 1910, record: "A request was received from the Mutual Aid Society of the J. C. R. S. Ex-Patients, asking to help them carry on their work, either by donation, or to help them sell Picnic tickets." The minutes record that $5.00 was donated.

Articles of incorporation were filed by the "Aid Association of the Ex-Patients of the J.C.R.S." January 17, 1911. Three years later the Aid Association for Ex-Patients of Denver Sanitariums was filed with the secretary of state. The latter document carries almost the identical list of names as incorporators, indicating that it was the same organization from the first.

It is popularly claimed for the creation of the association in 1908, that "by this step, efforts to defeat the proposed legislative measure were successful."[10] The immediate objective was to care for those discharged from the hospitals because the time limit of their stay had been reached, for those who needed further treatment—to rehabilitate them—and for those not quite ready to plunge into the struggle of earning their daily bread, so that they "will again become self-respecting and self-supporting citizens." Since these people were non-residents of Denver, they could not apply for relief. At first food, rent, and medical needs were covered by the association. The society also acted as a free loan society. Many an ex-patient borrowed money to buy a horse, wagon, and peddler's license, and started humbly collecting rags and bottles.

In 1916 a five-acre tract in Aurora, just east of Denver, was purchased. On the land, previously used as an orchard, stood a large farmhouse which was converted into a home, offering shelter to ex-patients, as well as medical treatment. The institution, which formally changed its name to the Ex-Patients Tubercular Home in 1927, was said to have completed the work of the hospitals in the recovery of the patients. It provided for its beneficiaries vocational training, first on the premises through a "vocational therapy industrial school." Lacking funds to bring the variety of instruction required to meet the abilities and interest of the ex-patients, the institution then developed a program enrolling the ex-patients in schools and colleges in the area.

Colorado was no longer the mecca of the tuberculous as new drugs and new theories, which no longer ascribed to the climate any particular healing quality, were advanced. The institution, like the Children's Home and later the J.C.R.S.—which became the American Medical Center, expanding its program to care for cancer patients—changed its name in 1955 to the ExPatients Sanatorium for Tuberculosis and Chronic Diseases. In 1957 a proposal to convert the Ex-Patients into a non-sectarian national mental hospital was under consideration.

3

In less than two decades the Jews of Denver had organized four national institutions—from the National Jewish Hospital, which had opened its doors in December, 1899, to the Ex-Patients Tubercular Home, first organized in 1908. From the 500 Jews in the city when the first was conceived to the 5,800, or less, in 1907, many of them sick themselves, the young community had led the way in the nation in caring for the sick on a non-sectarian basis. In the process of organizing these institutions for the sick of the United States, the Jewish community of Denver had been so busy tending its neighbor's vineyard that it neglected its own. Once the nation took on the burden of supplying funds for the institutions, the Jews of Denver began to feel released from much of their obligation. Facilities for the permanent community in health and recreation were meager.

The Jews began to talk about facilities for the older people and the sick as early as 1914, but no steps were taken until 1917. A Moshav Z'kenim society was organized and by 1920 there were enough funds to open the Beth Israel Old Folks Home in West Colfax. With the help of I. Rude, who gave the land, and L. H.

Guldman, who contributed $50,000, a hospital, known as the Beth Israel Hospital, was built next to the home for aged. This was an Orthodox institution, and was supported by the Reform Jews as well as the Orthodox. One of the members of the Temple, when asked why the Reform Jews took an interest in the institution, replied, "I was born and raised a Reform Jew. We can go to any institution in the city, but there are those who cannot. I, as my brother's keeper, am thinking of them."[11]

The hospital almost closed its doors later, and the *Jewish News* blamed the board of the hospital with, "they and their families turn up their noses at it, and do not go there when they are sick."[12] After World War II ended, a hospital was built in Denver at which no one, Jew or gentile, would "turn up his nose." Named after General Maurice Rose, the son of Orthodox parents, who, as a young man, had associated with the young people in the Jewish community, a two-million-dollar hospital was built in Denver after a nation-wide publicity campaign which brought Eddie Cantor to Denver to a $1,000 plate dinner, and for which the cornerstone was laid by General Dwight Eisenhower in 1948.

The community was able to cope with the problems of the sick and aged. For the latter a handsome building was built close to the Beth Israel Hospital facing Sloan's Lake and the Rockies. Other needs, particularly cultural and recreational, were not met so easily.

FOOTNOTES

[1]*JO*, Sept. 13, 1906.
[2]BB minutes, Nov. 10, 1907, p. 321.
[3]*Ibid*, May 24, 1908, p. 370.
[4]*DJN*, May 23, 1923.
[5]Art. Inc., Denver Sheltering Home, July 17, 1908, Sec. of State. Also articles of incorporation were filed Dec. 14, 1910 for a "Jewish Orphan Asylum." The same signatures appear on this document.
[6]Interview, Ben Blumberg.
[7]*DJN*, April 2, 1925.
[8]*JO*, Aug. 2, 1912, from Sunday *Post*.
[9]Souvenir Edition, *As-U-Go*, June 30, 1950 (Denver Tramway Co.).
[10]*DJN, op. cit.*, Apr. 2, 1925.
[11]*DJN*, Aug. 2, 1923.
[12]*IJN*, May, 1927.

The Muller Scandal
and the United Community

1

The breach between the "German" Jews and the early East European Jews before the conception of the J.C.R.S. was only as wide as Cherry Creek, and as shallow. The town was small and all the Jews seemed to know each other quite well. In many respects the early East European Jews in West Denver were a link between the *Deutsche Jehudim* and the Russian Jews. Many families who could afford it belonged to both the Temple and the Plonsky congregation. The early East European Jews were Americanized as quickly as their co-religionists, and they were hardy souls who were not afraid to share the rigorous life of the frontier. Intermarriage between the two groups was common with Jews from Russia marrying the daughters of Orthodox and Reform German Jews.

Even the establishment of the West Colfax Jewish community was not a divisive force in community relations, although there was no mutual social life shared between it and the Temple community. Both groups had to work together during the period when persecution reached its height in the Kishinev pogroms. From this community of interest, as we have seen, came the Central Committee of the Rocky Mountain Region for the Russian Jews in 1905. This committee, formed in the offices of Dr. Zederbaum, chose Rabbi Friedman as its chairman. After the Christmas day murders the committee's machinery for fund raising was used for the families of the murdered men. It was logical that out of this committee should grow an organization for future communal activity. While it lasted it performed a limited function in protecting Jewish interests. There had even been a suggestion as early as 1904 that the nine Jewish charities should be federated. Mrs. Pisko, who proposed the idea, pointed out that the Jews of Denver had been pioneers in city wide charity organization.

But the Central Committee and federation suggestion were submerged in the deep community rift which had resulted from the vague plans of the small group of men in a store building in West Colfax, materializing into the Jewish Consumptives Relief Society.

The German Jews forgot their refinement and began to attack not only the J.C.R.S. and its leaders, but also many of the East European or Orthodox ideals. On the side of the German-Reform group was a handsome and popular lawyer, Alfred Muller, who achieved prominence in all of his activities. He served not only as president of the local B'nai B'rith lodge but also as president of the District Grand Lodge. In communal affairs he served on the city's Associated Charities, and on the Juvenile Improvement Association. Most significantly, he was the secretary of the newly-opened National Jewish Hospital for Consumptives, and for his work on behalf of the hospital he was not only honored locally, but also was a delegate to the National Conference of Jewish Charities. To what he had to say, the older community listened carefully and proudly. When he reported the conditions in the Atwood Colony to the B'nai B'rith lodge, a committee was promptly appointed to investigate. As a member of the Central Relief Committee he brought to the attention of the B'nai B'rith lodge the treatment of Jewish peddlers and gave his time and efforts to protect them.[1]

Neither before nor after, was the Jewish community so shocked as when it learned, mostly through newspaper headlines, that the charming lawyer had died suddenly, leaving behind a deficit of $75,000 in the coffers of the National Jewish Hospital.

How Muller died—one legend has it that he placed a wax dummy in the coffin in his stead and escaped to South America—or what he did with the embezzled funds, are still mysteries. Ernest Morris and Joseph Jaffa, two of the leading Jewish lawyers in Denver, were assigned the task of unraveling the facts, which Morris set down in his autobiography.[2]

It had been the duty of the secretary, Muller, to deposit all of the hospital funds with the institution's treasurer in New York. Not all contributions which he received personally ever left his hands. This was petty pilfering compared to his other actions.

The hospital had borrowed a large sum of money from a Denver bank, giving in return a note signed by Muller and Samuel Grabfelder, the institution's national president. When the hospital was ready to pay the note, the money was sent to Muller, who kept the money and signed renewal notes payable to the bank over his own signature and the forged signature of Grabfelder.

Checks he received to pay Denver merchants for food and supplies he handled similarly, forging the endorsements and keeping the funds for himself. He told the local merchants that the funds for payment were tied up in the East, and that they would have to wait for their money. In addition, he purchased land for the hospital and reported that the purchase price was greater than the amount he had actually paid, keeping the difference for himself. He embezzled even the funds set aside for the patients to cover their return trip transportation from the hospital on their discharge.

When the discovery was first made, there were some suggestions to hush the whole matter, as it might be harmful to the hospital if the story were publicized. Grabfelder disagreed: "I am determined that no guilty man shall escape." Jaffa and Morris had Muller's assistant arrested. The expert penman made a partial confession, admitting that he had disguised his handwriting and falsified the books on Muller's order. Feelings did not run as high against him as they had against his deceased employer. Philip Hornbein offered to defend him. With twenty-seven charges brought against him by the District Attorney, the wretched man took a fatal dose of poison on the eve of the trial, "thus taking a change of venue to a court invisible."

The hospital was able to recover a little more than half the amount stolen. The leading officers of the institution made contributions to restore to the hospital the entire balance. Both of the investigating lawyers, Morris and Jaffa, became members of the hospital's board of trustees, and Morris' sister-in-law, Mrs. Seraphine Pisko, was elected secretary of the hospital.

2

Unpleasant as the story was, nevertheless it appears that it contributed toward the unification of the Jewish community in Denver. Apparently unrelated events, viewed in retrospect, led to the forming of the first Central Jewish Council in Denver. The minutes of the B'nai B'rith lodge record almost all of the events of major significance in the communal life. From them the story can be pieced together.

When Dr. Spivak came to Denver, he was already a member of the order in Philadelphia. He came to the Denver lodge as a visitor soon after his arrival, but did not present his petition for several years. Between the time of his arrival in Denver and his petition, the J.C.R.S. had come upon the scene. On March 13, 1904, Joseph Jaffa, who had been asked to serve as president of the infant J.C.R.S., introduced a resolution at the lodge:

> That Denver Lodge No. 171 IOBB appropriate the sum of $100 to the society, with the conditions that the sum of $1900 be subscribed and paid into the treasury of the society from other sources first; that the society accept members selected by the BB to the board of trustees, with the same power as any of the other members of the board.[3]

A committee was appointed by the lodge to investigate and report to the lodge. At a following meeting the committee reported:

> We attended a meeting of the Directors of said society and are of the opinion that the promoters have no definite plan outlined for the work of the society, nor does there seem to be an unanimity of opinion among its directors. We are led to believe they intend to organize for the purpose of caring for incurable consumptives and to make its scope a national one, as they have sent appeals broadcast over the country. Such an organization can do a great deal of good to suffering humanity and a great deal of harm to Denver, to its citizens and its Jews. We are of the opinion that it will not be possible for this society to get sufficient money to do effectual work, and that it will ultimately fail. We do not favor a donation at this time by the lodge.[4]

Within the lodge were members of the board of the J.C.R.S. Although the minutes do not describe the temper of the discussion, the hour became so late that consideration was postponed and a special meeting was scheduled. When the report came up for approval on April 24, the approving votes, representing the supporters of the National Hospital, were more than twice those whom they opposed at the new institution—fifty to twenty-one.

Dr. Spivak had not yet petitioned the lodge. Early the following year, 1905, his friend, Dr. Philip Hillkowitz, asked for information on how Dr. Spivak could obtain a withdrawal card from his Philadelphia lodge.[5] In April the petition was submitted and rejected. Until the death of Muller and the ensuing scandal, the question of donating funds to the J.C.R.S. was regularly brought to the lodge and voted down, and the petition of Dr. Spivak was regularly read and rejected. At the same time more and more of his friends were being accepted into the order. Ironically, the tents which had been erected to care for incurables from the length and breadth of the land were caring for members of other B'nai B'rith lodges.[6] Nevertheless the lodge refused a donation. Debates became more intense in the lodge, and charges became more and more personal.

But the J.C.R.S. supporters were persistent. In 1908:

> The motion to donate $50.00 to the J.C.R.S. was then taken up and Brother Muller took the floor to speak on the question. During his remarks Bro. Phil Hornbein rose to a point of order claiming that Brother Muller's remarks were not germane to the question, and that he had no right to attack any person who was not present to defend himself.[7]

There is no doubt as to whom Muller had attacked. Dr. Spivak was again rejected in September.

Muller died August 1, 1911. There were no resolutions pasted into the minute book eulogizing him as there were for every other deceased member, including his assistant.[8] The following spring Dr. Spivak petitioned the lodge and was elected.[9] He was given the unusual honor of being asked to give a short talk.[10]

3

By 1910 the leaders of the Central Committee felt its scope should be enlarged. The B'nai B'rith minutes report that a communication was received:

> From the Relief Committee of this city requesting that the Lodge send two members with full power to act to a convention to be held Sund. Jan 8 at 8 p.m. at Switzerland Hall, 1418 Larimer St.

The minutes add that the committee then representing it in that body would be continued.[11] The meeting was held with about sixty delegates present, representing every charitable, fraternal, and social organization in the city. Rabbi Kauvar was chosen chairman of the meeting. According to Meyer Friedman, the B'nai B'rith delegate, "Much talk was indulged in, but no one seemed to have a clear idea of what was to be done, or how it should be done."[12]

Early the next year one of the members of the lodge read a

lengthy paper on "The Necessity of a Kehillah." As an illustration of disunity, he used the two Jewish hospitals, "one supported by the German and wealthier Jews, the other by the West side and poorer Jews."[13]

The idealistic leaders of the Denver Jewish community could not wait for the natural amalgamation that would take place as their children grew up. The Central Jewish Council of Denver was organized, in part a successor to the first committee, but with the status of *kehillah* (Jewish community), as its founders fondly called it, one of the few in all America to endure.

The Council became permanent in October, 1912, with delegates from thirty-four organizations, including every synagogue, lodge, and society in Denver. With the encouragement of Judge Meyer Sulzberger, Dr. J. L. Magnes, and Louis Marshall, the Council attracted on its executive committee fifteen acknowledged community leaders representing the Reform, the Orthodox, and a small group of intellectuals who were not identified with any religious faction in Judaism. Conspicuous by his absence was Rabbi Friedman, although at least half of the committee included members of the Temple, and all but Mrs. Pisko were members of the B'nai B'rith.

The constitution adopted by the Council set forth its purposes "to further the cause of Judaism, and to promote concerted action by the Jews of Denver in respect to all matters of Jewish interest." At the same time the Council was to be "absolutely non-political, non-partisan" and was not to engage in any propaganda of a partisan political nature, nor interfere with the autonomy or religious principles of a constituent organization.[14]

From the newly-created Council came immediate action. A month after the constitution was adopted a mass meeting was called to arouse the Jews of Denver to take action on the massacre of Jews in the Balkans. The following year the idea of publishing a Jewish newspaper in Denver was presented and accepted by the Council.

The suggestion, presented by Dr. Spivak and Meyer Friedman, to the Denver B'nai B'rith lodge to sponsor the Big Brother movement, came from the Council in 1915. The issue of religion in the public schools was raised in 1916. The Council adamantly opposed to the idea, claimed for itself part of the success in the defeat of its adoption in the city.[15] Through the Council the governor of the state proclaimed January 27, 1916, as Jewish War Sufferers' Day. The night before the Council had called for a mass meeting, which was held in the city auditorium, and raised $24,000 for the cause.

From May 8, 1919, to December 9, 1923, no annual meetings were held and the Council was considered dormant. Yet, during those years activity had not ceased. In 1921 the Council gave its support to the American Jewish Congress and appointed delegates to represent Denver and Colorado at the Philadelphia Congress. It was the leadership of the Council, which made the arrangements for the spectacular and memorable visit of the Sokolow delegation in 1922. For the victims of the Pueblo flood in 1921, the Council, helped by the local Jewish agencies, raised $24,000 for the relief of the flood victims.

The Council when it was "rejuvenated" in 1925 had a balance in the general fund of $122.54 and $1747.22 in the Colorado Relief Fund. It leased the *Jewish News* to its editor and publisher for five years. The investigating and giving of credentials to *meschulachim* (charity collectors) was systematized. The Council helped the Ohio tornado sufferers, brought about the peaceful settlement of a problem created by two Jewish children placed in a Christian home, and formulated plans for a community drive for worthy causes, among which was the taking of an "authentic, thorough statistic of the Jews in our city." A plan was considered to create a subsidy for the outside charities in order to do away with the *meschulachim* entirely. During the decade that followed, the Council permitted no collections in Denver unless authorized (nevertheless heavily-bearded gentlemen appeared regularly on Sunday mornings in neighborhoods where there was only one Jewish family in the block). The Council endorsed or protested legislation affecting the Jews, gathered data from the Jewish cemeteries, and regulated the sale of sacramental wine during Prohibition.

The Council was not the Jewish charitable organization for philanthropy, but its emergency fund was used during the Ohio River flood calamity in 1937, and for a loan of $200, which was repaid, to start the preliminary work for an Allied Jewish Drive in Denver—the forerunner of the later-day annual campaign. Through the efforts of the Council, the immediate and urgent problem created by Hitler was met locally with the formation of the Denver Coordinating Committee for Refugees, with an appropriation from the Council of $100. The flexibility of the

Council was evident when the Emergency Trust Fund was diverted in 1938 into a Free Loan Fund to be used for the purpose of saving lives of those fleeing from countries of persecution. Even the Denver *Jewish News,* always in a precarious financial state, was in fairly good condition.

Overseas welfare problems were beginning to become of paramount importance as World War II loomed ahead. Dr. J. M. Morris, the Council's leading officer for thirty-five years, reported that in 1936 a definite plan had been submitted to set up a Jewish Welfare Fund in Denver to include all causes of Jewish concern, whether national or international.[16]

In 1941, a representative of the West Central State Regional Conference, a division of the Council of Jewish Federations and Welfare Funds, made a survey of the Jewish community organization in Denver. The survey, made by Charles I. Cooper, recognized what the Jews of Denver had long known,

> That because the most useful and energetic citizens of the Jewish community are preoccupied with the national health agencies, the needs of the local community are being overlooked, and the agencies for the service of their immediate neighbors are allowed to remain in a state of neglect.[17]

Before considering the rest of the Council's history and its dissolution, attention should be given to trace the history of the charity organizations that served Denver from the time the Council was formed in 1912.

4

Simultaneously with the establishment of the Council the same group made its first attempt at federating the Denver Jewish charities. In October, 1912, a committee was appointed by the Council to devise a practical method of collecting and disbursing philanthropic monies. The previous spring, Garfield Berlinsky of Cincinnati had been selected by the National Conference of Jewish Charities to make a study of the Denver picture. In Denver Berlinsky made an apparently exhaustive study of the complex problem in the nation's "dumping ground." He visited the various organizations and offered his suggestions, one of which was that the city's Jewish charities be federated.[18]

The following year, with Berlinsky's report accepted, the Jewish Social Service Federation of Denver was formed, with Berlinsky as its director, and offices in West Colfax. Early in March,

1913, the National Jewish Hospital asked the local B'nai B'rith lodge for its regular contribution. The lodge, which was making a monthly contribution to the Federation, referred the hospital to the Federation.[19] At the same time the United Jewish Charities of Cincinnati filed complaints through the National Jewish Hospital against the Denver Federation.[20]

Rabbi Friedman's name had not appeared in the Central Jewish Council. It did not appear in the rolls of the Federation, which was understandable and was in keeping with the growing attitude of nation-wide institutions, which did not want to go to Federations for their funds. The situation became so unpleasant locally that in November, 1915, a pamphlet was published "at private expense by justice-loving Jews," entitled *The Story of the Opposition of the National Jewish Hospital for Consumptives to the Local Jewish Charities of Denver.*

The pamphlet was not only a defense of Berlinsky against the accusations made against him and the methods he advocated, or that therefore the federation idea was a failure, but also stated that the real cause of Denver's problem was

> that by reason of the location in Denver of two national Jewish hospitals for consumptives, Eastern communities literally "dump" their worst and heaviest burdens upon this community and create a NATIONAL PROBLEM too great for local handling. These communities believe ... that their contributions to the hospitals entitle them to send dependents here.

The Federation had attempted to place the burden of support upon the cities "responsible for this inhumane treatment of the poor."

At this action, the National Jewish Hospital, Berlinsky claimed, began its overt opposition to the Federation. The eastern cities had threatened withdrawal of support of the hospital

> unless the hospital management forced an opening through which they might continue to send their dependent consumptives and their families to be supported by the Denver local community, or, in the absence of local support to die in Denver of starvation and neglect.

In turn the pamphlet accused "the management of the National Jewish Hospital of conniving, with other cities, to defeat the plans of the Denver Federation to procure support from the cities responsible." After three years of life, the Federation ceased to exist.[21]

The Federation had not been a success. The problem of national agencies versus federations was becoming acute, not only in Denver, but also throughout the country. A Jewish Aid Society was formed by the Temple Jews. The Federation group formed the Jewish Social Service Bureau, adding to their ranks the Free Loan Society and Jewish Ladies Aid Society, both of which gave up their names. Meetings were held in the same building the Federation had used on Federal Boulevard.

After months of disruption and arriving at a seeming impasse, the appearance of Boris D. Bogen, of the National Conference of Jewish Charities, at a mass meeting, stimulated a new impetus for unification. The existing aid societies merged in the formation of the Central Jewish Aid Society at the end of 1916.[22]

This group, no longer opposed by the National Jewish Hospital and its friends, carried the burden of Denver's Jewish charity for many years. The Society had struggled to raise enough money to carry on its projects. With the help of the B'nai B'rith it had helped the children of the poor by arranging for summer camping programs, and exhausted its funds carrying the burden of the unemployed during the depression. It was finally dissolved into the Jewish Family and Children's Service in 1954.

5

Only the most optimistic souls in the community envisioned the day when the National Jewish Hospital and the J.C.R.S. would not be at each other's throats. Several changes had taken place in the program of both institutions. The National had installed a kosher kitchen in the 20's and opened a "preventorium" for children. Both institutions had grown to great size by the time the depression began to create new difficulties in fund-raising. Representatives of the four national institutions in Denver met to formulate a plan for the joint collection of maintenance funds for the four organizations.[23] In 1934 the four institutions and the Jewish Consumptives Relief Association of Los Angeles tried to work out a joint fund-raising plan to cut down the expenses of separate communal campaigns. In Denver the first United Campaign was held in 1932 for the J.C.R.S., the Ex-Patients, and the Beth Israel Hospital, and in 1934, the five institutions, called the Council of National Jewish Agencies conducted the United Appeal. By 1936 the joint campaign became the United Health Appeal and so remained until World War II, when the city's Community Chest, temporarily called the War Chest, took the entire United Health Appeal for the Denver institutions into its beneficiaries.

6

During the same period the community carried on an annual campaign for "outside causes" under the name of the Allied Jewish Appeal, which was not a permanent organization but was reconstituted each year "from among the recognized leaders of the Jewish community." The greatest portion of the funds raised went to the United Jewish Appeal. By 1942 it was apparent that "onetime giving" was an unrealistic slogan. The Allied Jewish Council of Denver was organized, among other reasons,

> To unite the Jewish Community for the purpose of making one centralized appeal, collection, and allocation of funds to Jewish causes which have a justified claim upon the community for support, and to eliminate frequent and separate appeals and solicitations in the community: it being understood that the UNITED HEALTH APPEAL is considered a non-sectarian city-wide appeal.[24]

The Central Jewish Council was still in existence when the Allied Jewish Council became a permanent organization. A joint meeting was called in 1945 by both organizations. To the delegates, Dr. Morris offered, for their deliberation and decision, the question of whether they wished to form a new organization, to rejuvenate the existing Central Council, to fuse, or to coordinate their activities.[25]

It was not an easy decision to make, nor an easy task to contemplate the unification of the community. Neither board was anxious to assume the responsibility of representing or uniting the estimated 4,800[26] Jewish families in Denver. Nevertheless, the Allied, which had emphasized fund-raising and not broad policy-making —although its constitution made provision for the latter—had acquired prestige and skill in fund-raising. For this reason, principally, it was decided after three years of consideration, that the Allied, and not the older organization, would be the voice of the Jewish community. In 1949 the Central Jewish Council, after thirty-seven years of service, was dissolved[27] in order to make way for the Allied Jewish Community Council. One of its last acts was to settle the "Jewish Hospital Controversy"—whether Denver needed another Jewish hospital in addition to the Beth Israel in West Colfax. The Jewish doctors were particularly anxious to establish such a hospital, and were successful in creating enough of both community and nation-wide interest to build the General Rose Memorial Hospital.[28]

In 1950 the first general assembly of organizations was called by the Allied Jewish Community Council.

FOOTNOTES

[1] BB minutes, June 27, 1909, p. 59.
[2] Ernest Morris, "Gathering Much, An Historical Narrative."
[3] BB minutes, Mar. 13, 1904, p. 28 and 29.
[4] *Ibid.*, Apr. 10, 1904, p. 35.
[5] *Ibid.*, Feb. 12, 1905, p. 103.
[6] *Ibid.*, Apr. 26, 1908, p. 361.
[7] *Ibid.*, June 28, 1908, p. 374.
[8] *Ibid.*, Dec. 10, 1911.
[9] *Ibid.*, Apr. 14, 1912.
[10] *Ibid.*, Apr. 28, 1912.
[11] *Ibid.*, Dec. 25, 1910, p. 184.
[12] *Ibid.*, Feb. 11, 1911, p. 199.
[13] *Ibid.*, Feb. 11, 1912, p. 295.
[14] J. M. Morris papers. Constitution Central Jewish Council, Nov. 7, 1912.
[15] *DJN*, Nov. 12, 1915, protest against Gary School system of released time for religious instruction; *DJN*, Apr. 2, 1925.
[16] J. M. Morris papers, Mar. 26, 1939.
[17] *Ibid.*, Charles I. Cooper report; Oct. 8, 1941.
[18] BB minutes, Apr. 14, 1912. Federation incorporated Mar. 17, 1913.
[19] *Ibid.*, Mar 9, 1913.
[20] *The Story of the Opposition.* Courtesy American Jewish Archives.
sumptives of the Local Jewish Charities of Denver. Courtesy American Jewish Archives.
[21] *DJN*, Dec. 1, 1915, dissolved.
[22] *DJN*, Dec. 12, 1916.
[23] J. M. Morris papers. Minutes of the meeting of the Special Committee of the Conference of National Institutions in Denver. First meeting Mar. 16, no year given.
[24] Constitution, as published in the Council's *Blue Book*, 1943.
[25] J. M. Morris papers, Aug. 22, 1945.
[26] *Ibid.*, Cooper report.
[27] J. M. Morris papers, Special meeting, "The Dissolution of the Central Jewish Council and the Disposition of the *Intermountain Jewish News*," May 29, 1949.
[28] *Ibid.*, papers, correspondence, Feb. 7, 1945.

The Jewish Press

The *Jewish Outlook*, the first periodical for the Jewish community, appeared September 15, 1903, as a monthly. Its founder and business manager was twenty-year-old Samuel Priess (Price). With its second issue, the magazine became a weekly, for which Rabbi Friedman wrote the guest editorial. After the first two issues the rabbi became the editor and Dr. Moses Collins of the National Jewish Hospital the treasurer and in a few months Priess was no longer connected with the paper. The publication was unmistakably the unofficial organ of the Hospital, coinciding with the birth of its hated rival, the J.C.R.S. The editorial policy, which was not always in good taste, was strongly anti-Zionist and anti-traditional Judaism (which was excitedly denounced as the spawning ground of socialists and atheists). Although the *Outlook* was everything but a unifying force in the community during its early years, its publishers conscientiously opened the columns "to every variety of Jewish opinion."

After four years the periodical was sold to Ben Rosenberg. Rabbi Montague N. A. Cohen of the Temple Emanuel in Pueblo became its editor. In 1909 Jacob J. Lieberman joined the staff. With others hopeful of communal unity, the publication became an ardent exponent of the *Kehillah* idea, as it neared the end of its life. The periodical changed hands again in 1911; in 1912 publisher Aaron Rachofsky resigned; and in 1913 publication ceased.

The Jews were without a paper until February 26, 1915, when the first issue of the Denver *Jewish News*, published by the Central Jewish Council, appeared, with Dr. Spivak as its editor. The doctor not only wrote most of the material in its columns, but also solicited subscriptions for the newspaper as well. He and Milton Anfenger reached into their own pockets for several years to keep the paper going. As late as 1920 they had not been repaid the money they had advanced.[1] The first two volumes of the newspaper extant contain evidence of Dr. Spivak's genius for orderliness in the form of an index at the end of each year's publication.

The newspaper was then turned over to Victor Neuhaus, who was one among many of the interesting people and leading lights of the community who served on it. Despite the apparent support of the community, the financial condition of the newspaper was always shaky. In 1925 the name was changed to the *Intermountain Jewish News* to cover the larger region and receive support from outside Denver.[2]

In 1943 the publishing of the newspaper was taken over by professional men. Robert S. Gamzey, who had not only a degree from the University of Colorado School of Journalism, but also eleven years of experience on the Denver *Post,* and Max Goldberg, an advertising man, became its publishers. The weekly, the official organ of the Allied Jewish Council, was turned over to Gamzey and Goldberg by the Council, which removed itself from the newspaper business entirely. Increased circulation and advertising made it possible to increase the attractiveness of the newspaper. Under Gamzey, the verbosity and vagueness of the earlier issues disappeared. More news and information were packed into its columns, earning for Gamzey national recognition, and for his subscribers a more cosmopolitan point of view of matters pertaining to Jewish life.

The other publications which appeared and vanished in Denver included a monthly journal by Arthur J. Kirschstein, a former editor of the *Jewish News*. The publication, the *Western Jewish Advocate,* was started in 1929, and lasted until his death in 1942. The fourteen-year-old Martin Weitz began a newspaper career as the editor and publisher of the *Rude Park Tribune* in 1922. His first issue, which sold for two cents, contained four ads, had a circulation of 250, was literary in character, and "covered the international scene." Weitz was left with a deficit of $15.00, but continued the newspaper for four issues. In his solicitation for ads, the owner of a neighborhood theatre, who did not care for handbills, agreed to advertise in the *Tribune's* successor, the *Comet,* with a circulation of 1000 copies. With three more theaters, it became the *Comet Circuit,* running eight pages, one of which was in Yiddish. With its collapse in May there was a gap until November, 1923, when Weitz introduced his *Western Jewish World*. After reporting the marital troubles of a local couple, the young editor was forced to apologize[3] and retire from the newspaper business upon the insistence of his parents who believed that his schooling was more important than his journalistic career. The editor of the *Intermountain Jewish News* agreed to fill all of Weitz's subscriptions. According to Rabbi Weitz, "This was not exactly a merger, but it did permit a few hundred names to be added to the roster of the Intermountain Jewish News."[4]

A more serious attempt to establish a newspaper for West Colfax was made by Ben Blumberg, a former editor of the *Jewish News*, with a weekly called the *West End Press*. The newspaper, which was started in the bleak days of the depression in 1934, lasted for more than a year, during which time it covered everything of interest in West Colfax.

FOOTNOTES

[1] Milton Anfenger papers, courtesy Robert Gamzey.
[2] Oct. 14, 1925.
[3] *West End Press*, Sept. 14, 1934.
[4] Letter from Weitz to Gamzey.

Zionism

Just how early the Zionists first met together is not known. The first volume of the *American Jewish Yearbook*, 1899-1900, lists the "Chovevei Zion" with Meyer Feirstein as its first president.[1] By 1903 there was a B'nai Zion, Junior B'nai Zion, and possibly the beginnings of the Zionist synagogue, the Dorshei Zionist Society of Denver.[2] During that year a mass meeting was held at the B. M. H. to support the proposed purchase of Palestine from the Turkish government. The optimistic leaders were reported as believing that "on account of the present financial conditions, the purchase will be easily effected." The audience was urged to purchase stamps for use on letters, by the young Zionist leaders Philip Hornbein, Dr. Hillkowitz and Rabbi Kauvar.[3]

That fall another mass meeting of the B'nai Zion, with Hornbein presiding, was called on the occasion of the opening of the Sixth Zionist Congress at Basel, Switzerland.[4] With increased immigration Zionism gained in strength in Denver. Jewish National Fund stamps were sold in Denver in 1906 despite attacks against the sale by the *Jewish Outlook*.[5] The fall of 1908 and the next year saw a strong Zionist movement taking place not only in Denver but in the state. With the visit of A. H. Fromenson, who was cordially received by the B'nai B'rith as well as by the synagogues and Zionist groups, "Zionism made many friends at that week's meetings."[6] Dr. John Elsner's home was the scene of an elaborate reception for the lecturer, where Rabbi Friedman, who had said that week that "Palestine was sterile and only fit for Jews to die in,"[7] tangled with the Zionists. In the months that followed the Dorshe Zion Synagogue was incorporated,[8] a branch of the Order B'nai Zion was organized, and the Colorado Council of Zionists was formed. At least five Zionists from Colorado Springs, representing that city's

Zionist organization, attended the Council mass meeting in Denver the last week of the year. One of them read a personal letter from Dr. Herzl to Dr. Max Nordau.[9] In October, 1915, the movement was extended with the first meeting at the B. M. H. of a newly formed Mizrachi of which Bernard Hurwitz was elected president.[10] On December 17, 1915, the Denver *Jewish News* reported:

> A successful meeting of the Denver B'noth Zion was held at the home of Mrs. N. Block Sunday afternoon. The Denver organization will join the Hadassah Circle of New York.

At the time Mrs. I. J. Kolinsky was president of the B'noth Zion. Early the next year, at a meeting of the group, a report of Hadassah activities was read, and in April, 1916, the newspaper reported that Hadassah was to resume its activities at the home of Mrs. Kolinsky. The B'noth Zion was not mentioned again. By 1918 Hadassah membership reached 200. Shortly after, the group's president, Mrs. J. Marcus, died in the flu epidemic, and it is said that the chapter almost died, too. The chapter was reorganized under Mrs. Belle G. Kauvar, and thereafter grew steadily,[11] reaching a membership of 1,800 when the State of Israel was created.

Except for a group of Jews at the Temple, most of the Denver Jews (including the liberals), supported and attended the receptions and programs for the Sokolow delegation in 1922. The Jewish community had never before sponsored such an event. The arrangements began months before. Those in charge asked for help from Samuel Untermeyer in interesting the Denver Reform Jews in the *Keren Hayesod* (Foundation Fund), for which the whole celebration was staged. The delegates—Nahum Sokolow, Professor Otto Warburg, Colonel James H. Patterson, and Dr. Celina Sokolow—were met at the railroad station and were taken to their hotel in parade formation through downtown Denver. Dr. Spivak presided at the crowded city auditorium over a meeting addressed not only by the delegates, but also by state and city dignitaries. Denver passed its quota of $15,000 for the *Keren Hayesod* that night, and the following morning the total was more than $22,000.[12]

One of the most interesting aspects of the Zionist movement was its early involvement of children and young people. In 1908 there were three young people's groups and the Zion Hebrew School. Until 1928 there were some half-dozen changing groups of all ages. One active group, the "Stars of Zion," had a baseball team and held at least one debate with the Denver Junior Council at the Temple, over whether "Zionism is beneficial to the Jewish race." The judges, Senator T. M. Patterson, J. Hornbein, and Dr. John Elsner, awarded the laurels to the Zionist team.[13]

In 1928 the Zionist Council of Denver included the Poale Zion, Junior Hadassah, the Jewish National Fund, and the Young Judaea group, which with two other youth groups replaced four earlier clubs. Later the Zionist Organization of America (which reached a membership of 635 in 1948), the Women's Mizrachi, the Pioneer Women, and the Farband were added.[14]

Zionism brought forth many communal leaders. One of these—possibly the most generous philanthropist other than I. Rude—is Adolph Kiesler, who has given tens of thousands of dollars to various causes. To Israel his contributions have run into the hundreds of thousands of dollars. Through his judicious gifts, he has created good will for Israel locally, as for example his gift of a $10,000 Israeli bond to the University of Denver, which later honored him with the degree Doctor of Letters.

FOOTNOTES

[1] *AJY*, Vol. I, 1899-1900.
[2] *ICA*, Entry 16. The first time name appears, *JO*, July 22, 1904.
[3] *Republican*, May 11, 1903.
[4] *JO*, Vol. I, 1, Sept. 15, 1903.
[5] *JO*, Aug. 3, 1906.
[6] *JO*, Jan. 8, 1909.
[7] *Ibid.*
[8] Art. Inc., Denver No. 21572, Mar. 23, 1909.
[9] *JO*, Dec. 10, 1909, Dec. 31, 1909.
[10] *DJN*, Oct. 15 and 29, 1915.
[11] *DJN*, April 25, 1925.
[12] J. M. Morris papers. BB minutes, Jan. 26, 1922.
[13] *JO*, Feb. 12 and 19, 1909.
[14] *IJN*, Jan. 19, 1928.

The Jews outside Denver

1

Some observations about the Jews of the tiny towns of Colorado are in order before discussing Jewish life in the larger towns. One of these is the obvious problem of intermarriage which went hand in hand with being the only, or one of very few Jews in a town. The ubiquitous German Jewish traders who left Santa Fe for the north may have remained Jews during their lifetime, but the women they married were not, and their descendants were non-Jews who removed themselves as far as possible from anything Jewish. Of the seventeen white men between Santa Fe and Saguache in 1857,[1] it appears that most of them were Jews, but Judaism ended with them. In their case there were no Jewish women in the area to marry, but the same thing happened to the Jewish families who lived in the southern part of the state—except Trinidad. Those who remained saw their children intermarry and the end of Judaism in their lifetime.

Of course, there was intermarriage in the frontier town of Denver, but it was not so overwhelmingly widespread. How the Jews felt about it is not revealed in the newspapers, unless the stories in the social columns of the day meant parental approval. There appears to be only one early case where the reaction of an angry parent was strong enough to reach the press. This occurred in 1871, when the daughter of Solomon Nathan and her gentile suitor were married by a Christian minister. When the outraged father met the minister at a Denver bank, he attacked him. The minister claimed that the girl had threatened to go away with the man out of wedlock if he refused to perform the ceremony. Nathan pleaded temporary dementia and was fined forty dollars for the assault.[2]

The early pioneer or settler who was as thoroughly educated in his religion and in Hebrew as he was in secular subjects was able to transmit very little of the former to his children. The only formal religious education his children received was through the Sunday school of the most liberal Christian segment, preferably the Unitarian Church. Invariably the adult who grew up with this background says that his religion consists of the Golden Rule, sometimes adding the Ten Commandments. There is even an overtone of pride when he states that he was brought up as a heathen.

Still it is possible, as is claimed, that there was less intermarriage among the first generation of pioneer German Jews throughout the state than there was in the corresponding generation born to East European Jews in the city. If this is true, it is because the Jews knew each other intimately when the population was small, and because when the business opportunities died they left for Denver, where they joined the large Congregation Emanuel. Where they remained, intermarriage was inevitable, and even if the first generation found Jewish mates, their children, whose whole world was the gentile community, did not. The first generation's desire to continue Judaism had faded. Their children in the city or at the state's colleges had little to do with Jews, and affiliated with non-Jewish fraternities and sororities.

Where the Jew of Europe was embarrassed if he had to admit that he came from a village, and was inclined to deny it, the children of the pioneers were proud of coming from the mining camp or farming community and regarded it is a distinction that most of their associations were with non-Jews. Sometimes the German Jew felt resentment when the Russian or Rumanian Jew moved into "his" town. The newcomer was accused of having the "worst Jewish attributes," particularly that of clannishness. But the East European Jew was no different. Soon he, too, was looking critically at newcomers to be sure they would be acceptable to the gentile community. This attitude of "it won't look good to the gentiles" set for him an exceptionally high standard of business ethics and social niceties. It came from the assimilationist, anxious to please, and from the pious Jew, who took seriously his role as "a light of the nations."

2

There is one puzzling aspect to Jewish life in the country towns. Why were services held in some and no attempt made in others of comparable population? There were always a sizable number of Jews in the San Luis Valley. Although scattered, they could have held regional services as the Jews of South Park or around Gunnison did. Also Alamosa, the county seat, was a sizable community compared with those where joint services were held. Yet, it appears that there was never any Jewish religious life in the community worthy of mention.

The "first" Jewish wedding in the San Luis Valley was said to have been held in October, 1892, and was performed by Rabbi Friedman, for Anne Slavick of Alamosa and Henry J. Irmas of Kansas City.[3] During this period the Frank family lived there, and are best remembered in Denver for the trout which they shipped north. Later a man moved to the Valley who became a leader in the region, and although interested in Judaism, did not form any religious life for the Jews there. He was Albert Luria Moses.

A member of the famed Sephardic Moses family of Georgia, he was the son of William Moultrie and Penina Septima Moses. He came to Colorado as a young man. In Buena Vista he read law and was admitted to the state bar in 1891. First a deputy clerk in Chaffee County, then an attorney in the District Court in Mineral County, he became the district attorney for the Twelfth Judicial District of Colorado in 1909, and judge of that body by special appointment in 1930. Married to Rosa Nunez in 1885 in San Antonio, the family made their home in several towns and mining camps in the state before moving to Alamosa. In 1899 he joined the Denver Lodge of B'nai B'rith, but he was unable to attend meetings. According to the minutes of the organization, March 13, 1910:

> Bro. A. L. Moses, Creede, Colo., remitting his dues, and stating that, being the only Jew in Mineral Co., he cannot do much toward securing new members for the Order; nor does he like to send a photograph as requested, as he has never been in the lodge room since initiated, and he feared some member may inquire, "Who is this fellow, I have never seen him in this lodge room?"

He was also the Alamosa County Chairman for the Jewish Relief Campaign. As were most of the members of his family, he was buried in Emanuel Cemetery in Denver.

3

The East European Jew met the same cordial reception in the

mining camp and country town as his German co-religionist did, sometimes at the same time, sometimes many years later. He was just as active in the civic life of the community and held perhaps as many civic offices. He, too, might be the first person in the town to have a bathtub or piano. Perhaps the chief difference between the two was the greater desire of the East European Jew to leave the rural or mountain district for a larger Jewish center. Invariably, he was more religious, ordering his meat from Denver, taking his infant sons to the larger Jewish community for circumcision, or having a *mohel* brought to the town, and sending his children to Denver to relatives, where they could get a Jewish education and meet youngsters of their own faith. These Jews were to be found throughout the state, as single young men, or heads of families working to provide a home for families still in Europe. Young men, like Abe Flacks, "Abe the Tailor," made every mining camp in the state, sometimes in groups and sometimes alone.

Perhaps a representative family which began its life in Colorado in a small town was that of Dr. Abraham M. Blumberg. Blumberg was born in Courland in 1873 and was smuggled out of Russia to avoid the concentration-camp type of military conscription ordered there for the Jews. He came to Philadelphia, where he enrolled, at the age of twenty-one, in public school with the small children, and in night school with "the wild Russians." Rather than work in the sweatshops he put his knowledge of Hebrew to use as a teacher in a Talmud Torah, where he fell in love with one of his Sunday School students who was only twelve years old. He asked her to wait for him and entered the medical school of the University of Baltimore.

On graduation he received the customary offers extended by wealthy and indulgent Jewish fathers to acquire a doctor for a son-in-law. At the time $10,000 was a great deal of money to offer a young man without a practice. But Blumberg turned down such offers and became engaged instead to his former student. By now he was underfed and run-down, as well as poor, and the prospects of competition in the big city were not to his liking.

He left for Colorado, where he had family in Denver, and after looking over the cities and towns in the state found the minute town of Seibert, with its cowboys and ranchers, to his liking. In the town, with its five or six houses and saloon, he sought out the druggist. "We want you," he was told by the men.

Blumberg insisted on telling all present what he thought they ought to know. "First, I want you to know I'm a Jew, and if you have any antipathy toward me for this, tell me now. If not, I'll treat you right. I never want to hear the expression, 'the Jew.' Secondly, you know I am young. My fiancée is in the East. How can I bring her here? Where will we live?"

"We'll build you a house," he was assured. The men donated the lot, wood, and labor, and built a comfortable house for the doctor for which he paid, partly outright and partly by deducting his physician's fees for the treatment of those who had contributed.

The family kept kosher in Seibert. Meat and bread were shipped twice a week by express train from Denver. A *mohel* came from Denver to perform the *b'rith* when the first baby boy was born. On that occasion, the neighbors actually came to see for themselves if Jewish babies had horns at birth. After the Blumbergs had lived in Seibert for a year, a delegation from the county seat, where the political convention was being held, came to waken the family with the news that they had nominated Blumberg as coroner of Kit Carson County.

Life was comfortable for the family and the community was friendly. The citizens were ready to run the doctor for mayor, when the family decided that thirteen years of being the only Jewish family between Denver and Kansas, and seeing only Jewish peddlers and cattle dealers occasionally, was long enough. For the reason almost all Jews left their small towns, the Blumbergs left Seibert: the children were growing up. The family moved to Denver, where the doctor opened his office in West Colfax. The Blumbergs were typical of a large part of the West Colfax Jewish population consciously concerned with Judaism and their duties as Americans. From the family have come educators and journalists. One daughter, Mrs. Albert Solomon, served as president of the state Parent-Teachers Association.

4

Occasionally an advertisement appeared in the Denver papers for religious help, sometimes for a teacher, a cantor, *schochet*, or all three. These might come from an isolated Jew in a town like Walsenburg,[4] or from one of the college towns like Fort Collins.[5] There the Congregation B'nai Zion was attempted in 1921, but there was not sufficient interest or money in the town where the state agricultural college is located to sustain a congregation.

In Boulder, the home of the state university, services were held regularly and at least two congregations were organized as they were needed. The first, Adath Zion, was formed in 1905.[6] A second congregation, Anshe Emuno, was organized in 1919,[7] with the encouragement of the Denver Jewish community. However, Boulder, but thirty-five miles from Denver, apparently did not need the congregation as badly as some of the other towns. With improved transportation it was more satisfactory to go to Denver for services and a social life than to try to build one in a small community.

Efforts to form a congregation were more successful in the agricultural community of Greeley, where the Orthodox Jewish community formed the Congregation Beth Israel in 1925. The community is augmented in the winter by Jewish students at the state college, which has no Jewish fraternities as do the two other northern college towns. The same congregation, with additional members from its second generation, built a new synagogue in 1954.

There appear to be no other Jewish services in Colorado, except for Grand Junction, which, with the impetus from the uranium industry, had a large enough Jewish community in 1955 to start planning a synagogue. For the fall holidays that year, Paul Laderman, the son of Denver's Rabbi Laderman, was invited to conduct services.

5

When Simon Nathan came down from his mines in California Gulch to Beaver Creek in the Arkansas Valley, there was no town on the site of the old Fort Pueblo. After two years of farming and cattle ranching, he established the first clothing store in 1867 in the little town behind the stockade. He kept his farm for at least one more year, then devoted himself to his store.

Life behind the stockade was far from safe. The Nathan's baby daughter was kidnapped by Indians and returned only after she had been ransomed by the Nathans. When the men and boys had to leave to round up their cattle, Mrs. Nathan, on more than one occasion, had to crawl to the barn to milk the cows, and return to the house the same way, somehow dragging the filled milk pail after her.

Nevertheless, the Nathans thrived on this life. With the execption of a child who was burned to death, all of the young Nathans grew to adulthood, and the adventurous second generation spread into others of Colorado's small cities, Alamosa, Durango, Silverton, and Telluride. Around the Nathans grew much of Pueblo's life. Where they first camped, the city's leading department store, owned by another Jewish firm, was founded. It was the Nathan family who brought the first bathtub into the area, a tin affair which was the delight of the community which came first to admire it, then waited for an invitation to use it. The Nathan's daughter, Rebecca, was in the first high school graduation class of 1884. When she was sixteen the family had a piano shipped out for her, which arrived by ox-drawn covered wagon.

The Nathans were a conspicuous couple in the community, not only because they were there early, but also because of Nathan's generosity. After he retired he devoted himself entirely to charity. He imposed upon himself the task of visiting and helping the poor, which assumed such proportions that Mrs. Nathan "almost lost her mind." Believing that a person should get what he asked for, Nathan soon had to be dissuaded from giving so much. When he had given all of his money away, he gave his house to a poor woman, to the chagrin of his family. Until the very end he made daily reports to the local associated charity office. The Nathans were founders of the Reform Temple Emanuel in Pueblo, but this in no way prevented Simon Nathan from making a generous gift to his friend, Henry Plonsky, for the founding of a traditional synagogue in Denver. As far as Nathan was concerned "a Jew was a Jew."[8]

Another family of Fifty-niners settled in Pueblo in 1872. They were the Goldsmith brothers, Abraham and Henry, and their families. They, too, made a valiant attempt at ranching, after similar attempts in the middle west, and after homesteading in Denver on the site of Denver's tramway loop. After being flooded out three times in Denver, the brothers filed claims on the Arkansas, three miles from Pueblo. The very first deed ever handled in Pueblo was that of Henry Goldsmith, which was placed in the cornerstone of the courthouse when the building was erected.

The Goldsmiths were never too successful in holding their land. Even in Goldsmith subdivision in Pueblo, 125 of Henry's lots were condemned for a right-of-way by the railroad, and Goldsmith took what he could get for his virtually confiscated property. Abraham, his brother, moved to Trinidad and then Las Vegas, New Mexico. Both brothers were in a runaway accident, which resulted in Henry's death and crippled Abraham, who died in 1887 and was buried in the Congregation Aaron cemetery in Trinidad.

The West was truly wild when the Jews who built the community arrived in Pueblo. Aside from the frightening Indians, the loneliness of the prairie so affected many of the women that at least one almost died of homesickness. The small group of German Jews, without a congregation, were completely without ties. Some made an unsuccessful attempt at Jewish ritual, blessing the candles on Friday night, and during the Passover, using two sets of dishes, one for meat and milk. During the balance of the year any attempt at more was impossible.

As soon as there were enough Jews, a store building was rented for the holidays. For several years all of the Jews prayed together. Actually, the German Jews, without a congregation until the end of the century, were not so far from traditional Judaism as their brethren in Denver. The Goldsmith's in-laws, the Newmans, taught their children to pray in Hebrew, and were acutely distressed by their children's lack of knowledge of Judaism.[9]

With the impetus given the previously agricultural area by the new smelting and metallurgical processing plants of the Guggenheims and others, there were by 1895 a sufficient number of Jews to organize the first congregation. In Pueblo it was not the Reform but the Orthodox congregation which was first organized. For five years all of the Jews of Pueblo worshipped together as a congregation, called B'nai Jacob.

For the holidays of 1899, the forty or fifty Orthodox families combined with the Reform Jews of the city for services at the St. James Hotel. To conduct the services a local man, and a rabbi from Denver, were placed in charge.[10] The Denver rabbi was an extremist even in the very Orthodox community in Denver. In rebellion, his own son became a Protestant minister. This was the last time the united group ever met together. The following month the Reform group formed Congregation Emanuel, and the following year its new temple was dedicated by Rabbi Emil Hirsch, the leading Reform rabbi of Chicago, who called it "a jewel box." The congregation paid for its building, which was valued at between $8,000 and $10,000 within two years.

After the division, there was little or no spirit of unity between the two groups. Only the Associated Jewish Charities and the B'nai B'rith lodge contained members of both groups. Of the former, the work done seems to have been more than adequate for the small number of Jews. The organization collected funds from only the Jews, but disbursed monies to all needy.

The first B'nai B'rith lodge was in existence as early as 1886, when it was known as Twin City Lodge. In 1895 the charter of the lodge was revoked for non-payment of various contributions and for failure to make reports.[11] A new lodge was instituted in 1901.

Snobbery was the greatest divisive force in the Jewish community. In Pueblo the Reform group never became as anti-Zionist as their brethren in Denver, so that cause, which was so important to the north, could not be blamed for the breach in the community. The division was even manifest in burial. In the Jewish section of the old North Side cemetery, the first Jewish burials had been made. Later the Reform group began burial in a Jewish section of Roselawn, with its first burial the mother of Sam Bowman in 1894. When Henry Goldsmith's[12] second wife, Eva, died, the remains of her husband and son-in-law were first moved from the Masonic cemetery to the new Jewish burial ground.

Indifference to Judaism and a meager Jewish communal life paved the way for a disproportionate amount of intermarriage, not only among the early German Jews, but also among the East European Jews of Orthodox background. The latter group came after the Russian pogroms, first in the 80's and then increased after 1905, with a large influx after the creation of the Galveston Plan. The local newspaper remarked on the difference between the older settlers and the new and commented that Pueblo was not getting as desirable a class of immigrants as before.[13] It was from that group that Pueblo's impetus for a sounder Jewish community came.

When the B'nai Jacob acquired their first rabbi in 1905 and even before a synagogue was built, the congregation built a *mikveh*, which was used until the 1921 flood. The new synagogue (an attractive building in an unsuitable section) was built in 1907 for $6,000. Its mortgage was burned three years later. In that period the influx of immigrants increased so that there were attempts to start other Orthodox congregations,[14] but B'nai Jacob continued.

The national organizations opened lodges in Pueblo. Several of the East European lodges and Zionist groups were started as well as a Jewish Relief Society which was in existence in 1911. The devastating flood of 1921 left many of the Jewish business houses in ruins, and the Pueblo Jewish community never forgave the Denver community for what they regarded as its miserly aid.

In 1947 the Orthodox congregation of Colorado's second largest city began to grow as the location of its synagogue deteriorated. With the necessity of a new synagogue, an attempt was made to unite the Reform and Orthodox congregations, but this was abandoned. Instead the Orthodox and Conservatives combined to build the United Hebrew Center in 1950.[15] With the new synagogue the B'nai Jacob ceased to exist. Pueblo's Jews are united on Zionism. The Temple Sisterhood cancels its meetings in favor of the Hadassah fund-raising affairs.[16] There is no American Council for Judaism in the city which numbers about 170 Jewish families.

6

Pikes Peak had been the beacon for the gold-seekers of the nation, yet the beautiful community at its foot was not the outgrowth of a mining camp. The first town there was Colorado City (where the state government held its seat briefly), which was absorbed by the premier resort of Colorado Springs, and Manitou Springs, almost solely a tourist town. The excellent climate and scenery, as well as the abundant mineral springs in the area, attracted vacationers from all over the world. The outlook of Colorado Springs was English, giving the carefully planned city the name of "Little Lunnon."

Jewish life did not begin in this area as early as it did in the more exciting areas, although an Isaac Cohen arrived from France in 1865. The Oppenheimers and Peltas arrived in the early 80's.[17] Another early resident, Louis Ehrich, arrived about 1882. According to Myron I. Myers, the historian of the Jewish community,[18] Ehrich was a well-to-do man, for he lived in the finest section of the city and presented the large tract of land to the Typographical Union on which the Union Printers Home was built.

An unofficial census by Myers' father, Mandel K. Myers, when he arrived in 1892, totaled two families, three widows, ten children, and five bachelors. Out of this small group one man was among the drafters of the first city charter. One of the widows managed to feed and clothe her children by peddling in the mining districts, later founding one of the leading clothing stores in the city.

The flight from tuberculosis was a flight to the Rockies when Myers arrived in the Springs. He had been sent by his doctors to

Colorado with the knowledge that he might not live long enough to arrive. He lived more than a half-century more. Many such stories were told of the sick who came West to regain their health and remained. David May had come to Manitou Springs in 1877 to recover from a cough and stayed to found his vast merchandising firm. The abundance of such stories increased the population around the Peak.

When the Panic of 1893 caused the value of silver to plummet, the gold of the Cripple Creek area nearby saved the state and created an "excitement" in the Springs. With the increase of population, there were enough Jews to hold the first religious services in 1895. Since these services were a *yahrzeit* (a memorial service for a departed relative) a *minyan* was mandatory. "Accordingly," Myers relates, "the leader solemnly locked the door, put the key in his pocket, assigned a watcher to guard the windows, and the prayers went on to their completion."

That fall and thereafter the holidays were observed in an unbroken sequence. In 1900 when a collection was taken for the purchase of a *Sefer Torah,* there were twenty-one donors, representing a much larger community indifferent to its religion. Two years later the group of Jews met to form a religious organization, the Sons of Israel Association.[19] The twenty-five members assessed themselves dues of ten cents a month, which was soon raised to fifty cents. The most urgent task of frontier Jewish communities—providing for burial—was undertaken immediately. Burial grounds were put to immediate use early in 1903 by the Orthodox and Reform alike, saving them the expensive and unpleasant task of burying their dead in Denver or in the east.

In 1908 the *Jewish Outlook* reported that the Colorado Springs hero, General William J. Palmer, then in England, was donating a site for a synagogue.[20] Later the newspaper edited by the Reform rabbi of Pueblo expressed its admiration for the congregation, even though it was organized "to worship according to the obsolete and incomprehensible tenets of the now effete Jewish Orthodoxy of the Middle Ages." The *Outlook* urged that the Reform Jews form their own congregation, for the Orthodox and Reform could no more mix than oil and water.[21]

The admiration was premature. Internal dissension within the group prevented the building of a synagogue, and the Sons of Israel lost a considerable amount of money. The weakened group purchased a church, spending as much on repair and remodeling as it had on the structure, in order to convert it into a synagogue, which they first used in 1911.

In 1901 the Colorado Springs *Telegram* reported that a B'nai B'rith Lodge and Council for Jewish Women were to be organized and a Jewish Temple was to be formed.[22] The two organizations were formed and remained, but no Temple resulted. In 1910 the *Outlook* reported that the first services of Reform Temple Bethel were held on a Friday night in the summer of 1910.[23]

During this period there were about 150 Jews in the area, until the pogroms sent another immigration wave to the United States from 1906 to 1915. The Jewish population increased to about 225. From the latest group of immigrants, which lived close together, came a strictly Orthodox congregation, the Sons of Abraham, formed in 1908. Before either of the existing groups could do so, the new congregation built the first synagogue in El Paso County in 1909. It was a tiny synagogue, but it boasted the only *mikveh* in the area.

Jacob Schiff, on a visit to Colorado Springs in 1915, reproached the small community with three congregations and no rabbi. Because it was the great American Jewish leader who proposed it, an attempt at unity was made with the formation of a committee representing the Sons of Israel, the B'nai B'rith and the Sons of Abraham.[24] Nothing came of the hope for unity.

The Reform congregations of Pueblo and Colorado Springs solved their problem in 1925 by sharing the services of a rabbi, who lived in Pueblo but came to the northern town weekly. For a time the Jewish community had a *schochet*-cantor, and almost always a Hebrew teacher. "Sunday schools were started and stopped, innumerable times, but few students ever penetrated beyond the Red Sea," Myers records. In 1935 the two Orthodox congregations merged as the Sons of Israel. Three years later all three congregations were partially united under one rabbi. For a time the prospects were encouraging, but the goals of religious unity were not realized. The Reform group, made up of eleven families, withdrew in 1942 to organize a temple under the previous name of Beth El. In 1949 the Temple Beth El was built and the Sons of Israel dedicated a new synagogue in 1951.

As was true elsewhere, *tsdokoh* took precedence over all other Jewish activities. In Colorado Springs it was also the victims of tuberculosis, most of them on their way to Denver, who needed the greatest help. The Hebrew Benevolent Society was organized at the end of the nineteenth century.²⁵ This became a permanent organization. It was followed by a Free Loan Society and a Hebrew Ladies' Aid Society, to which were added the Jewish Welfare Board, the United Service for New Americans, and the Federated Charities.

The B'nai B'rith lodge formed in 1901, followed by a month the one formed in Cripple Creek, and the following week one was opened in Pueblo. This created a new link among the Jewish communities in Colorado. Joint picnics were held for several years in Palmer Lake, so that Denver could join in the festivities. Both Colorado Springs and Pueblo share more of their social life with Denver than they do with each other.

Among the communal leaders of America who have visited the Springs or lived there are many lustrous names. One of them, Henry Sachs, made the city his home. Sachs, whose philanthropies were on a national scale and who was a national figure in the business life of the United States, left, in Colorado Springs, the Sachs Foundation which Mrs. Marx Lorig, the historian of the Temple Beth El, terms a godsend to the Negroes of the area.

Between three and four hundred Jews live in the area, some of them serving in the military installations. In the twentieth century, Pikes Peak overlooks a new kind of "boom town," this time resulting from the recreation-seekers and from the location of the United States Air Force Academy.

FOOTNOTES

[1]*Trail*, Vol. XIII, No. 11, p. 31; *RMN*, Dec. 24, 1871.
[2]*RMN*, April 24, 1873.
[3]WmSF Scrapbook, Oct. 27, 1892.
[4]*IJN*, Feb. 8, 1932.
[5]*DJN*, July 6, 1921.
[6]*ICA, op. cit.*
[7]*AJY*, 1919-20; *DJN*, 1919.
[8]Interview, Mrs. Fred Meyers; *JO*, Mar. 2, 1906.
[9]Goldsmith-Bowman interview, *op. cit.*
[10]Denver *Times*, Sept. 4, 1899.
[11]BB minutes, Apr. 28, 1895.
[12]Goldsmith-Bowman interview, *op. cit.*
[13]*JO*, Jan. 3, 1908.
[14]Milton Braun found an old rubber stamped paper with the imprint "Tiphereth Israel, Pueblo, Colorado." *ICA*, B'ney Abraham Congregation. According to Braun this was only temporary. *ICA* gives a date of July 14, 1919.
[15]Abe and Adelyn Raich, "A History of the Congregation," *Dedication Program*, United Hebrew Center, Sept. 10, 1950.

[16]"The Pueblo Shofar," March, 1957, p. 2.
[17]*JO*, Nov. 24, 1905.
[18]Myron I. Myers, "The Early History," *Dedication Program*, B'nai Israel Synagogue, Sept. 23, 1951.
[19]Art. Inc., Feb. 26, 1910.
[20]*JO*, Aug. 14, 1908.
[21]*JO*, Oct. 23, 1908.
[22]WmSF Scrapbook, Mar. 18, 1901.
[23]*JO*, June 10, 1910.
[24]*DJN*, Apr. 30, 1915; June 18, 1915.
[25]*AJY*, 1919-1920. Gives date 1898. Myers gives date 1902.

The Sublime Ones

1

Among those who came to Colorado to "chase the cure" were musicians, poets, and artists. Colorado, the pristine West, was also an international destination, to be enjoyed by the leaders of government and the royalty of Europe. The state not only attracted talent, but also to some extent those who appreciated it.

Among the early musicians[1] in addition to the pioneer orchestra leader, Henry Kline, was "Professor" Sam Koenigsberg, who provided band music and accompanied visiting soloists in Denver. It was he who furnished the music for the balls of the early social clubs and paraded the downtown streets advertising the new May Company in Denver. Among those whom he accompanied was the community's child artist, "Master" Benny Jarecki. The boy pianist appeared locally as early as the age of seven. Although the family were poor, they denied themselves for twenty years in order to send him east and abroad for his musical education. At the age of nine he gave a concert in New York's Chickering Hall, and went on to study in Berlin. Coming home for a short visit, a "grand" concert was arranged for him at the Tabor Grand.[2]

The music-lovers of the community were heart-broken when the young pianist, whom the newspapers had acclaimed as "second to none," died in 1894.[3] The young man's aim had been to become a symphonic conductor, but the dream died with him.

Early day musical activity is described by Dr. Frank Damrosch, who arrived in Denver on July 1, 1879. As a pioneer in the city's musical life, he formed a string quartet in which he played the cello. That same year he served as organist and choir director of two churches and also the "Synagogue"—which was the Temple Emanuel—where he took part in the Jewish communal life with the young people. Damrosch remained in Denver until 1885, when his father died in New York. During his years in the west, he formed the Denver Chorus Club, first assuming the expenses of the hall rent and the music, until the group insisted that they, as a society, assume the "financial burdens." As the first director of music of the Denver Public School, he gained experience which he regarded as helpful when he took charge of the music in New York's schools, where he had 11,000 teachers and 600,000 children to guide.[4]

Another early day description is supplied by Dolce Grossmayer, whose family arrived in Denver in 1882:

> At that time we had a neighbor with whose daughter and son I played daily. "Papa" was a Count von Jochmus, who landed in Pueblo where he married a lovely girl. They moved to Denver, and shortly afterward "Papa" received, in one lump sum, the amount of $250,000. He was devoted to music and a highly educated man. He immediately bought a home, Steinway piano, etc.
>
> Feeling the need of fine music and seeing the lack of it in Denver in those early days, he agreed with several others to bring an orchestra for several concerts. He also agreed to foot most of the expenses, which he really did.
>
> And so, the New York Symphony Orchestra, directed by Dr. Leopold Damrosch, journeyed to Denver in 1883. These concerts were the first symphony concerts ever given in Denver.
>
> I happen to know this story because I rode to one concert on Dr. Damrosch's knee being then about seven years old, and already feeling myself an authority on Mozart's Sonata, which I performed, without embarrassment for the benefit of Dr. Leopold Damrosch. At any rate it was a Jew who directed those first symphony concerts in Denver, and that is noteworthy.

Miss Grossmayer also remembers that Frank Damrosch opened a small music store in Denver, for which the Count also supplied much of the money. Since much of Denver's cultural life was centered in the Grossmayer home, and since her father, Nathan, was on intimate terms with the great of Europe and America, the Grossmayer story is important beyond the boundaries of Colorado. His correspondence, which has been preserved, included a letter from Louis Kossuth, the liberator of Hungary, written from Turin, Italy. The letter was in reply to an inquiry as to the origin of an adopted baby, which was left with Grossmayer's father-in-law. The baby's parents had claimed that the child was of the Hungarian nobility. The letter is an important document, because in it Kossuth names each one of his cabinet, and gives the name of the traitor who betrayed him into exile. Other letters in the collection include letters from U. S. Grant, C. A. Dana, John Hay, and Edwin Stanton, and an article from the Baltimore *Sun* of April 27, 1863, in which it is reported:

> Senator Wilson presented a bill to Congress in which Mr. Nathan Grossmayer forwarded $1,000 to President Johnson as a portion of a fund to be raised in memory of A. Lincoln— to erect a military and naval hospital for all men disabled in the service of their country.[5]

The Grossmayers did not confine their interests to the cultural life of the city, but took part in Jewish activities. George Grossmayer was a conscientious worker on the employment committee of the B'nai B'rith for many years, when employment for the ex-patients and the immigrants was a major communal problem. Miss Grossmayer and her sisters, Clara and Rachel, not only taught music and performed, but they also taught at the Temple Emanuel Sunday school and were active in the Council for Jewish Women. Dolce Grossmayer organized the Amateur Musical Club for musically-inclined Jewish young women about 1910, to which nearly fifty Jewish vocalists, violinists, and pianists, from both sides of Cherry Creek, belonged. From her teaching came a full generation of competent and talented musicians. She was honored as one of the "Representative Women of Colorado,"[6] when she won the bronze medal as a pianist and composer at the World's Columbian Exposition. The family left Denver in 1918 for California, where she was elected and re-elected director of the State Board of Musicians.[7]

Dolce Grossmayer left a void in the cultural and educational life of the Jewish community, which her well-trained pupils tried to fill with the help of the talented health-seekers who had made Denver their home. One of the latter was Morris Bezman, an internationally-known violinist, who organized the Mansfield quartet. His early death in 1910, a year after Mischa Elman had taken him to Europe to study,[8] left the quartet temporarily without a leader, but that year another violinist took his place in the community. David Abramovitz at seventeen was the youngest member of the Cincinnati Symphony. In Denver he was one of the leading teachers in the city, and considered a "polished gentleman, a conscientious teacher, loyal friend, and generous and important member of the musical fraternity for twenty years."[9] He was a director of the Denver Grand Opera Company, under the management of Victor Neuhaus and Julian Wilensky, its operatic director. In 1920 he was the dean of the Wolcott Conservatory of Music.

Alexander Saslavsky, who had been the concertmaster of the New York Symphony, founded the Saslavsky Chamber Music group, composed of Saslavsky, Finkelstein, Weisman, and Renard, which gave concerts from 1913 to 1924 in the Brown Palace ballroom. In the summer he was concertmaster of the Cavallo Symphony Orchestra at Lakeside Park. These concerts were "very elite and well attended."[10] One of his pupils in Denver was Dr. Gerald Frumess, president of the Denver Chamber Society in 1956.

Jacob Perlmutter played with the Mansfield String Quartet. Another Perlmutter, Maurice, who was considered one of the best violinists in the city, played with the Denver String Quartet. Later violinists Dr. Lewis Chernoff, Gregor Cherniavsky, David Eisenberg and Edward Millstone furnished music for concerts and played in the symphonies. Theodore Reiss was considered by Dolce Grossmayer to be "one of the first-class violinists" in the city while she lived there. Walter Eisenberg, the former concertmaster of the Denver Symphony, became the director of the Colorado Springs Symphony. From Colorado Springs came the talented Victor Polant, who was later the concertmaster of the Detroit Symphony.

Among the vocalists were the Shwayder children (as has been related) Matilde Prezant, Bertha Weiner Kobey, and later Hilda Eisenberg Ohlin. From the native-born Jewish vocalists in Denver came two internationally-known figures, Frances Rose and Mascha Kavelin.

Frances Rose, the daughter of Leopold Rosenzweig, grew up in a German Orthodox Jewish home and attended the public schools of Denver, graduating from East High. She then studied in Cleveland and Vienna, where she received the offer of *prima donna* of the Breslau Opera. In America she had refused a handsome offer from the Metropolitan Opera because she wished to be with her husband in Europe. She remained there as first soprano of the Royal Opera, in Berlin, but traveled with Richard Strauss throughout Europe, singing before the King and Queen of England, Prince Henry of Prussia, and other crowned heads. One of the world's outstanding Wagnerian sopranos, she was in the

United States at the outbreak of World War I and could not return to Germany. Her husband, Theodore Konrad, a tenor with the Swedish Royal Opera Company, died in London in 1921. The singer returned to the family home around 1936, after her retirement,[11] where she remained until her death in 1956. Her fame had not spread to her home town, and she was buried quietly in Mount Nebo Cemetery.

Mascha Kavelin was born Minna Weinberg, the daughter of a *mohel* in West Colfax. Her talent was recognized by the Allied Arts Society of the city which gave help to many young musicians. She, too, went east and to Europe to study. As a brilliant colortura, she was eagerly taken into the La Scala in Italy, where she remained.

Although outstanding musicians have made various cities in Colorado their home from time to time, and have performed during the summer at Aspen or served on the faculties of the various colleges, only one who lived in Colorado Springs did much of the work there which brought him international recognition. This was Rubin Goldmark, lecturer, composer, and critic, who founded a music conservatory on the campus of Colorado College in the 80's. He later directed the Colorado College School of Music from 1895 to 1901. In his impressive list of compositions appear his "Ode to Colorado" for mixed voices and his four "Prairie Idylls" for piano and strings, which won the Paderewski Prize in 1909.[12]

From the time the Jews had participated in the Denver Maennerchor, the Denver Grand Opera Company, and the various musical clubs; supported with enthusiasm the concerts of the celebrated cantors Zavel Kwartin and Josef Rosenblatt; remained active through the later days of the first century of Jewish life in Colorado, they were always identified with the musical life of the city. Rounding out this century was the revitalized Denver Symphony Orchestra, which in 1945 had a new conductor, Saul Caston, formerly the associate conductor of both Leopold Stokowski and Eugene Ormandy. In Denver Caston arranged to bring good music not only to the city's social leaders, who annually sponsor a lavish Symphony Ball, but also to the humbler music-lovers of the region. In order to do this he organized family concerts to which entire families were admitted for $1.20 each; periodic concerts for school children in the public and parochial schools; and concerts in outlying cities including those in Wyoming and Nebraska, for which buses were chartered to transport the orchestra.[18] Another of the musicians attracted to Colorado as a permanent resident is Heinrich Schalit, the composer of Hebrew liturgical music, who was the organist in the Great Synagogue in Munich and music director of the Great Synagogue in Rome.

Many cantors have served Denver, both residents and celebrities brought for the holidays. Among the names most easily recognizable is that of Gregor Kwartin (the brother of the famed Zavel), who organized choirs and quartets throughout the city as well as conducting the B. M. H. music. Another cantor who served at the B. M. H. is the former Palestinian, Aaron Turner.

An unusual event was held in Denver in 1955, perhaps unique in its history, when the three cantors of the three largest synagogues gave a concert in which they sang solos and trios of Yiddish and Hebrew themes. The three were Jacob Lefkowitz, who had served the Alliance for sixteen years before leaving in 1956; Irving Gross of the B. M. H., and Abraham Mendelsberg, of the Beth Joseph, Denver's only native-born cantor to serve in his home city.

2

Music fared well in Denver. Not so art. Only the name of David Spivak seems to have attained more than local note. However, there are several young men who are being watched for the promise they have shown. They include Roland Detre, Bill Sanderson and Akiba Emanuel, recent-comers, and a young man who grew up in West Colfax, Mel Silverman, whose shows have already been a source of pride to his community.

That the plastic arts were neglected was deplored by Boris Schatz of the Belzalel Art School of Palestine, while on tour in Denver in 1931.[14] A few months later Schatz died at the Beth Israel Hospital after an operation.[15] How true he was in estimating the interest in art can be gathered from the fact that after he died no local person or group cared enough to pay for the transportation of his body back to Palestine. His remains were left in a Jewish mortuary until his son, with the help of the Zionist organizations of America, was able to send for it many months later.[16]

3

Because some of the giants of Hebrew and Yiddish literature made Colorado their home at various periods in their lives, the native talent, by comparison, was meager and uninspired. As a writer, Rabbi Judah Ginsburg attained the heights in religious literature with his commentaries. Another of the Hebraists, although not of the religious group, was Naphtali Herz Imber, best-known as the writer of *Hatikvah*. Imber spent time in Denver, not for his health, but on one of his adventures, and managed to write, with a sober pen and tongue-in-cheek, an article for the *Rocky Mountain News*, which must have had an interesting effect on the community.

On Christmas day, 1899, there appeared in the newspaper a lengthy article, "Christmas Celebrations of Peculiar People. How the Arabs and Jews Join Joyfully on Jesus Birthnight, By Prof. Naphtali Herz Imber." He wrote, in part:

> I recalled the Happy Christmas days [in Galicia] so joyfully spent by the Hebrews, especially by the children. In half Asia, Christmas is, as its name implies, a Christian feast. Nevertheless, it is a Jewish holiday; in Russia and Poland where orthodox Armenian Judaism reigns supreme, where the dial indicates the noon hour, all the Hebrew schools are closed and the children go home to enjoy their holiday. From noon until the next morning, the Hebrews are not allowed to open any Hebrew book, not even the Bible, to read or study. Christ was a great Hebrew scholar, and they will not study that language on Christmas day . . . . The pious Jews gather in groups to listen to the reader who reads to them from the "Gospel of Jesus." This book glorifies Christ even more than the Gospels do, despite the fact that its tenor is that of an opponent.

One of the poets, recognized as one of the greatest, left only a tragic mark on the Jewish history of Colorado. David Edelstadt, whose poignant writings stirred the hearts of the oppressed Jews everywhere, lived in Denver before the twentieth century. In Russia he had written about the misery of his people, and in America, where he worked as a garment worker in the sweatshops of the East, he continued his writing and hoping for "social justice." Tuberculosis struck him, and he came to Denver, where he is said to have started a paper on which he worked at night while he worked as a garment worker by day. The struggle was too much for him, and he died before he reached the age of thirty. It is said that there were only about ten or twelve present at his funeral, and that he was buried by the county of Denver in a pauper's grave in 1892.

As his writings became more and more admired, the Workmen's Circle raised enough funds to erect a suitable monument to him. It took several years to find his grave. When it was found, the remains of the handsome, sensitive, young poet were transferred to the Golden Hill Cemetery. In fitting ceremonies the group unveiled the stone, in 1915, into which was carved his celebrated poem, "My Will."[17]

Another of the Yiddish poets, Solomon Bloomgarden—Yehoash (although his name appears as "Jehoash" on at least one book) —was considered by many the greatest, and was locally dearly loved. The young man came to Colorado for his health and lived in what was then South Denver, where he engaged in clerking and bookkeeping. He was at all times on intimate terms with the East European Jews, and took a very active part in the B'nai B'rith lodge as well as devoting much time to Industrial Removal Work.

On one occasion, he and his friend, Bernard Hurwitz, who doted on a certain brand of Russian tea, found it difficult to obtain the tea in Denver. Instead of bewailing their misfortune, they decided that to send for small packages of the tea was not a feasible way of insuring a permanent supply. They pooled their assets and announced to their wives that they were going into the tea business; therefore, as distributors, they needed a large supply. They ordered cases and cases of tea. When it arrived, to the consternation of their wives, they made no search for customers but used it themselves, rejoicing in the ample reserve they had slyly acquired.[18]

During the first five years of the poet's life in Denver, he wrote 214 poems, which his friend, Dr. Spivak, said, "represent a native product of Colorado." Spivak adored his friend and tried with articles in the *Jewish Outlook* to keep the poet's name before the Denver Jews. When his volume *Collections of Poems by Jehoash* was published, Spivak wrote two articles about the poet. He described Yehoash as a comparatively young man, his own teacher and guide, who had acquired a knowledge of Latin, Greek, Russian, German, French, and Italian. Until he was seventeen his family had hoped he would become a rabbi, and sent him to the Woloczin Yeshiva where his one term was his only school experience. According to Spivak, most of his writing was "moved primarily by the past and secondarily by love. Questions of the day concern him but little." This was unlike the subjects of the other Yiddish poets who were moved by the lot of the immigrants in the sweatshops.

> It took Kishineff, Gomel and Zhitomer massacres to arouse him to produce a dozen poems d'occasion.... I believe that every resident of Denver and Colorado will feel happier and prouder because he walks the street whereon Jehoash treads. Here in our midst Solomon Bloomgarden toiled, suffered, sorrowed, loved and sang.[19]

Spivak brought Bloomgarden into activity on the board of the J.C.R.S. when it was organized, and the poet worked on the staff of the sanitarium until it became a successful institution He remained a member of the board and worked for it until his death in New York in 1927.

The frail, boyish-looking poet, who died a few days after Ahad Ha'am, was deeply mourned in Denver, especially because of the poverty in which he had been forced to live while he struggled against tuberculosis. It was remembered that in Denver he and Dr. Spivak had written their Hebrew-Yiddish dictionary, and here he had begun his monumental task of translating the Bible into Yiddish, because he wanted the common people to have the book in the vernacular. He worked on this book for twenty years, but died the year of its completion, leaving it to his wife, Flora, and daughter and son-in-law to publish.

The Workmen's Circle now kept a watchful eye on the patients at the J.C.R.S. They took it upon themselves to see that obscurity and poverty would not go hand in hand with talent. In the early 20's the group became patrons of another young poet, M. Lunansky, who took the penname of Mates L. Lune. In 1922 a concert was given for his *Offene Toiren* (Open Portals) by the group and its affiliated societies. The Literary Group of the Workmen's Circle published the book which included poems about Colorado, the mountains, and Denver. Lune was never nationally recognized, and he died as a young man in 1929.[20]

A one-time paperhanger, the genius with words, H. Leivick (Leivick Halper), was also a patient of the J.C.R.S. in the 30's. The master dramatist and poet wrote his *Leider fun Gan Eden* (Songs of Paradise) while he was recovering his health. In this volume of poems are his "Again Dies a Neighbor," on the death of a patient, "A Eulogy on the Death of a Guinea Pig with Red Eyes," and what is regarded in Denver as his best and most beautiful work, "The Ballad of Denver Sanitarium,"[21] to a fellow patient and friend who succumbed to the White Plague.

FOOTNOTES

[1] Another early musician who may have been a Jew, was Jacob Kauffman, whose violent death was described October 24, 1885 in *RMN*, p. 3, col. 1.
[2] *RMN*, July 19, Sept. 13, Sept. 14, 1885.
[3] WmSF, clipping, Nov. 24, 1894.
[4] Dr. Frank Damrosch, "Years in Denver," *The Lookout from the Denver Public Library*, Vol. I, No. 1, "Music in Denver."
[5] Correspondence, Dolce Grossmayer.
[6] J. Semple, *Representative Women of Colorado*, p. 137.
[7] *DJN*, Feb. 26, 1925.
[8] *JO*, April 30, 1909.
[9] *Lookout from DPL, op. cit.*, p. 29. Also *DJN*, Aug. 31, 1921.
[10] *Ibid.*
[11] *JO*, Apr. 27, 1906, Mar. 18, 1910; interview, Bertha Weiner Kobey.
[12] *Lookout from DPL, op. cit.*
[13] *Time* magazine, Oct. 29, 1951.
[14] BB minutes, Nov. 24, 1931.
[15] *DJN*, Mar. 25, 1932.
[16] *DJN*, Sept. 16, 1932.
[17] *DJN*, Nov. 26, Dec. 3, 1915; *IJN*, Nov. 10, 1927. Mrs. J. S. Shatz says the date of 1892 on his tombstone is incorrect. According to her, he died several years later.
[18] Ida Hurwitz papers.
[19] *JO*, Sept. 7, 1906.
[20] *DJN*, Oct. 25, 1922; Aug. 7, Aug. 23, Oct. 11, 1923; *AJY*, Vol. 30, p. 154.
[21] Interview, Ben and Bessie Glass.

Jews in the Armed Forces

Prior to World War II no official records were kept giving the number of Jews from Colorado who served in the nation's wars. An unofficial Honor List of Colorado's Jewish Boys, compiled by the Jewish Welfare Board for the Denver *Jewish News*, and broken up in the issues of April 30, May 7, and May 14, 1919, contains 717 names. Apparently this list was not complete, for at the same time a service flag with 734 stars was presented at a meeting of the League of Jewish Youth at Progress Club. During these weeks coupons were printed in the newspaper asking for additional names and data.

Figures compiled for Denver only at the end of World War II showed that, as in the rest of the country (and as had been the case in World War I), the proportion of Jews in service was higher than that of the rest of the population. From Denver the total population was represented by 8.5 per cent, while the Jews in service constituted 11.8 per cent. With the organization of a branch of the Jewish War Veterans in Denver in 1947, a list of service men killed in World War II and thereafter is annually published in the *Intermountain Jewish News*. The names in the following list, in addition to those in the *Jewish News*, were obtained from news items and from one tombstone.

IN MEMORIAM

Spanish-American War

Isidor Amter

World War I

Morris Fishel
Asher Levis Joel
Julius Teitelbaum

World War II to Present

Badion, Joseph L.
Berger, Ben
Blanc, George
Bloom, Ben (La Junta)
Brill, Ivan
Brizman, Morris
Caplan, Alexander
Caplan, Morris
Coleman, Melvin
Copp, Max
Devine, Samuel
Dranoff, Isadore
Fabricant, Irving
Fenchel, Gerd
Foreman, Jerome
Forman, Mitchell
Friedman, David
Glass, Edwin
Grimes, Charles
Gross, Morton
Hirsch, Gene
Hoffman, Ben
Holtzman, Harry
Karon, Sam
Kershner, David
Kiefer, Yale
Kline, Vincent
Krohn, Joseph

Kurzinger, Frank
Mariam, Robert
Marx, J. Simpson
Obendorf, Lee H.
Quicksilver, Nathan
Rike, Bernard
Roberts, Albert Sid
Rose, Maurice
Rosenbaum, Alvin
Rosenbaum, Robert
Roth, Charles
Safron, Howard
Shapiro, Lester
Shapiro, Robert
Sherman, Albert
Shradsky, Bernard
Silver, William
Singer, Gerald
Spiegelman, Edwin
Suson, Gerald
Teronsky, Samuel
Tepper, Edward I.
Victor, Leonard
Weiner, Marvin
Wilmore, Stanley
Zeidenfeld, Alvin X.
Ziskin, Morris
Zudik, Alfred

Chronology

The future is changeable but not known; the past is known but not changeable.
　　　　　—PAUL WATZLAWICK, *How Real is Real*

All is foreseen, and free will is given.
　　　　　—PIRKE AVOT

1598　Secret Jews, escaping the Inquisition, accompany Juan de Oñate into southern Colorado.
1803　Most of eastern Colorado acquired by Louisiana Purchase.
1854　Solomon Carvalho photographer for Fremont Expedition.
1858　Gold discoveries precipitate Pikes Peak gold rush.
1859　Jewish Fifty-niners arrive.
　　　Rosh Hashanah falls on September 29. Fifteen "Israelites" organize as Beth Elohim Ha-Midbar (the Holy Congregation of the Lord in the Wilderness). A. Jacobs chairs the meeting held on December 28. Officers elected are A. Goldsmith, president; Jacobs, vice-president; and Joel Gottlieb, treasurer. S. Rothschild, L. Bohm, J. Strassberger, F. Poznansky, and Jacobs are appointed to committees.
1860　Jacobs writes to the *Israelite*, describing how the group is organizing a congregation for their brethren and their families who intend to come out.
　　　Denver and Auraria merge into Denver City.
　　　The Denver Town Company donates "10 good city lots of considerable value for the purpose of building a House of Worship." The same January report from Jacobs tells that the congregation also has acquired ten acres of "good land about two miles from the city limits" for a "Burying Ground

which we will hold in trust and for the Benefit of those who may come."

Hebrew Cemetery Association formed when Mrs. Henry Goldsmith dies in giving birth to Clara, the first Jew born in Colorado.

Isaac Cahn family arrives in Colorado Springs from France.

R. E. Whitsett, not "Whitesett" (page 69).

1861 Colorado becomes a territory.

Pioneer Denver Lodge No. 5 AF and AM formed, meets in Abraham Jacobs's building.

Henry Kline marries Rose Lowenstein (not Rosa Lobinstein) in first recorded Jewish wedding in Denver.

1863 Fire almost destroys Denver.
1864 Cherry Creek floods Denver.
1865 Lincoln assassinated.
1866 Colorado Pioneers Association formed.
1867 Denver chosen capital.
1870 Dr. Elsner establishes municipal hospital.

A.Z. Salomon marries H.Z.'s sister-in-law, not niece (p.41).

1871 Hebrew Benevolent Association formed.

B'nai Brith Lodge No. 171 formed.

1873 Otto Mears negotiates treaty with Utes.

Although the Jewish community is credited with opening the first tuberculosis sanitarium, P.T. Barnum and his son-in-law, Dr. William Buchtel, open Prospect Villa on Capitol Hill for "respiratory disease and dyspesia" (euphemism for tuberculosis).

1874 Articles of incorporation, Temple Emanuel.
1875 First Temple completed at Nineteenth and Curtis Streets.

Baron E. de Rothschild visits.

1876 Colorado admitted to Union.

Standard Club formed.

Benjamin Wisebart elected mayor of Central City.

Otto Mears, state elector, casts decisive vote for Rutherford B. Hayes; earns nickname of "President-maker."

1877 Emanuel joins Union of Hebrew Congregations.

First Orthodox minyan meets.

Colorado Jewish population estimated at 422 [see Leadville 1879].

1878 First Jewish services in San Juan country.

	B'nai Brith Lodge in Trinidad.
1879	Leadville: Congregation Israel, Hebrew Benevolent Association, B'nai Brith lodge. Claims to have more than 400 Jewish residents.
1880	Ohava Emuno orthodox congregation incorporated.
	City social clubs closed to Jews.
1881	First Jewish charity ball, Denver.
	Russian pogroms.
1882	Cotopaxi colonists arrive under auspices of HEAS (not HIAS, p. 174); *Israelite* reports that they are "flourishing beyond all expectations," despite verified reports of suffering.
	Otto Mears of Saguache helps install new B'nai Brith lodge in Pueblo.
	Evergreen cemetery, Leadville.
	Rosh Hashanah service, Gunnison.
	Twin Cities Lodge, B'nai Brith, Pueblo.
	Jews acquitted of arson in Leadville; bigotry injected into trial.
	P.T.Barnum orders the "shysters" and "moneyless Jew brokers" to "float away and take their stink with them."
	In Berlin, scientist Robert Koch identifies tubercle bacillus.
1883	Congregation Aaron, Trinidad; cemetery purchased.
	Orthodox Ohava Emuno buys Temple Emanuel building.
1884	Barnum closes out Denver estate named for him, adjacent to West Colfax, to daughter Helen and husband, Dr. Buchtel, good friend of neighborhood Jews.
	Temple Israel dedicated in Leadville on land deeded by H.A.W. Tabor, cost $4,000.
	Hebrew Cemetery Association, Denver, wins civil suit.
	Hattye Dreyer (Reibscheid) born in Buena Vista.
1885	Congregation Mogen David next to Platte River.
	Progress Club.
1886	Congregation Rodef Zedek.
	B'nai Brith Lodge, Pueblo.
1887	Type locality and type specimen of *Triceratops Alticornis*, the Three-Horned Dinosaur, found in north bank of Dry Creek, between Federal Boulevard and Hazel Court near West Tenth.
	Gross Medical College opens, admits Jews and women.
	Charity Organization Society, first federation of charities and

forerunner of United Way, formed. Founders include Frances Jacobs and Father William O'Ryan (not O'Brien, p.120).

Chebra Kadisha O. Bickur Cholim, burial society.

Congregation Shomro Amunah on banks of Cherry Creek.

Congregation Zere Abraham.

1889 Mass meeting at Temple Emanuel to decide on hospital.

Temple Aaron dedicates building in Trinidad.

Capitalist Louis Ehrich, Yale '69, donates eighty acres for printers' union home.

1890 Rabbi Elya Hillkowitz in Denver.

Queen City Lodge, Order B'nai Abraham.

Jewish Hospital Association incorporated.

Audience at Coliseum mass meeting for earlier store-closing hours is moved by Frances Jacobs's eloquent plea for equal pay for equal work and for women's suffrage.

Fifty-niner "Poznansky the Polander" commits suicide because of extreme poverty.

1891 Agudath Achim congregation.

Town of Colfax incorporated.

Town of Brooklyn incorporated within Town of Colfax.

Chevra Mishno, advanced Talmud study group.

Anshe Emuna congregation.

Denver population estimated at 1,000 Jewish families and nine religious groups.

Cheltenham School opens.

1892 Kneseth Israel (Orthodox), Leadville.

Rodef Shalom (first synagogue by that name).

Jewish Ladies' Aid Society.

Death of Frances Wisebart Jacobs, age forty-nine.

Death of David Edelstadt (not 1896 p. 125).

United Hebrew Cemetery Association incorporated.

Jewish population of Gunnison: seven families and twenty-five singles.

1893 Silver Purchase Act repealed. Panic.

Council of Jewish Women.

Hospital named for Frances W. Jacobs.

1894 Congregation B'nai Israel, Cripple Creek.

Rose Lawn Cemetery, Fort Collins.

	Atwood Colony.
1895	Jewish Protective Association.
	Ladies' Hebrew Relief Society, West Colfax.
1896	Shearith Israel at Fourteenth and Lawrence.
	Jewish burials begin at Riverside Cemetery.
	Dr. Charles D. Spivak moves to Denver.
1897	Town of Colfax annexed.
	Beth Hamedrosh Hagadol (BMH) organized.
	Temple Emanuel fire.
1898	Shomro Emuno merges with Shearith Israel.
	"Snobocracy" decried by *RMN*. "Jews should be glad to be excluded from social clubs."
	Hebrew Ladies Aid Society and Hebrew Benevolent Society, Colorado Springs.
	Ladies Temple Association formed, Pueblo.
1899	National Jewish Hospital for Consumptives dedicated. First free sanitarium for the indigent.
	Congregation Emanuel, Pueblo.
	Temple Aaron built, Trinidad.
1900	National Workmen's Circle founded.
	Israel Kortz synagogue.
	Frances Wisebart Jacobs and Otto Mears selected for stained glass windows in new state capitol.
	Council of Jewish Women formed in Pueblo.
1901	B'nai Brith lodges in Colorado Springs, Cripple Creek, and Pueblo.
	Colorado Springs Ladies Aid Society buys twenty lots in Evergreen Cemetery. First burial for Benjamin Kahn.
	Hebrew Free Loan Society and Jewish Welfare Board.
	Hebrew Ladies' Benevolent Society and Hebrew Benevolent Society Denver, merge into Jewish Relief Society.
	Tiphereth Israel congregation incorporated, lasts until 1943.
1902	B'nai Jacob, Pueblo, *mikveh* and Jewish cemetery.
	Rabbi Charles Kauvar at BMH.
	1903 Kishinev pogroms.
	Jewish Outlook begins publication.
	First meeting leading to Jewish Consumptives Relief Society.
	Congregation Shearith Israel buys Episcopalian Emmanuel chapel.

Dorshe Zion Institute, Zionist congregation.
Yad Achaas Rumanian congregation.
Agudas Achim congregation buys building.
Free Loan Society, Denver.
Sons of Israel congregation incorporated in Colorado Springs.

1904 Sons of Israel acquires three acres in Evergreen Cemetery.
Reform Temple Beth El organizes in Colorado Springs.
Kheleth Jacob congregation, Denver.
Mount Nebo Cemetery.
Central Committee of the Rocky Mountain Region for Russian Jews formed.
Jewish Consumptives Relief Society dedicated.

1906 Kesher Ohava congregation.
Need for a sheltering home for Jewish children discussed at home of Fannie Lorber.

1907 U.S. Senator Simon Guggenheim elected by state legislature.
Ostrover Beth Jacob congregation.
Knesseth Israel, the Hooker Street shul.

1908 Golden Hill Cemetery.

1909 Alpha Yiddish theatre, Ella Sobol, proprietor.
B'nai Abraham erects first synagogue in Colorado Springs.
Temple Beth El, Colorado Springs,

1910 Shwayder Trunk Manufacturing Company.
Colorado Jewish population estimated at 8,000. Yeshiva Etz Chaim, West Denver Hebrew School and Synagogue.

1911 Emanuel section at Fairmount cemetery.
Jewish community begins removal of bodies from city cemetery; removal continues until 1923, but is never completed.
Rabbi Kauvar says he single-handedly saved kosher slaughtering from attempt by Denver Humane Society to forbid it.

1913 Yeshivas Toras Chaim, the Ostrover shul.
Beth Israel Anshei Matzover Chevra Volin congregation.
Goldie Mabowitz, (Golda Meir) runs away from home to her sister in Denver. The fourteen-year old attends North High School for two years, where she earns all As.

1915 *Denver Jewish News.*

1916 Emily Griffith Opportunity School opens.
Hospital building originally named for Frances W. Jacobs is

	renamed for William S. Friedman.
	Isaac Solomon, BMH member, murdered in his store.
1917	West Colfax viaduct completed, called the "Passover bridge, the longest bridge in the world, from Denver to Jerusalem."
1919	Hebraic Studies at University of Denver, I. Rude benefactor.
	Beth Israel Hospital and Home Society founded by Bella Mintz.
1920	Congregation Oheb Zedek formed when insulted members leave BMH when the Hungarian cantor (*hazzen*) is referred to as a Hungarian *hazzer* (pig).
1921	Pueblo flood.
	Cheltenham Annex, the "fresh-air" school, opened by Denver Public Schools.
	Zere Israel, Lithuanian congregation, results from row at combined services with the Ostrover.
1922	Official date for founding of Beth Joseph congregation.
1923	Theatre idol Louis Josephson at Palm Theatre, second theatre on West Colfax after Alpha (Sobol's Barn).
	New Yad Achaas synagogue.
1923	Beth Israel Hospital and Home opens.
1924	Immigration Act slams door on East European Jews.
1925	*Intermountain Jewish News* new name for paper.
	KKK takes over state government.
	Beth Israel congregation, Greeley.
	Name change to "National Jewish Hospital at Denver."
1926	Labor Lyceum on Julian and Conejos.
	Death of Dr. Spivak, age sixty-five.
1928	Green Gables succeeds Progress Club.
	Hold of KKK broken.
1932	Hebrew Educational Alliance built on Meade Street. First Rabbi Manuel Laderman remains its only rabbi until his retirement.
	"Thousands" at funeral of Rabbi Isaac Braude.
1933	Nazi book burning.
1934	Eighteenth Amendment repealed.
1937	B'nai Israel congregation formed by merger of B'nai Abraham and Sons of Israel, Colorado Springs.
1938	Kristallnacht.
	Zere Abraham buys Labor Lyceum for synagogue.

1939	Hitler and Stalin sign nonaggression pact.
	Hitler and Stalin invade Poland.
1940	Nazi activity in Fort Collins.
1941	Babi Yar massacre.
	Pearl Harbor.
	Denver rabbis will not perform weddings in public places.
	Yeshiva Toras Chaim completed, but is used as a synagogue rather than a yeshiva.
1943	Robert Gamzey and Max Goldberg take over *IJN*.
1944	Denver Jewish population: 18,400.
	Congregation Beth El, Colorado Springs, reorganized.
1945	Rabbi Shloime Twerski at Zere Abraham.
	Saul Caston conductor of Denver Symphony Orchestra.
1946	Allie Feldman named Denver Fire Department Chief.
1947	Town Club.
	"Lavender Hill Mob" risk their lives to save the unborn state of Israel by smuggling arms.
1948	BMH hires and fires Conservative Rabbi Lewis Sacks.
1949	BMH hires and fires Conservative Rabbi Morris Margolies, who rescued Torah from burning BMH.
	Beth El building dedicated, Colorado Springs.
1950	United Hebrew Center of Pueblo.
	When African-American entertainers have few places to stay in Denver, Lily and Bernie Halpern open their home to them.
1951	B'nai Israel, Conservative congregation, Colorado Springs.
	B'nai Brith Hillel Foundation at University of Colorado.
	New Beth Joseph congregation, formed partly by members of existing congregaton and young couples in new neighborhood, hires Rabbi Daniel Goldberger.
1953	BMH hires and fires Conservative Rabbi Ephraim Bennett.
	Rabbi C.E.H. Kauvar retires from BMH, now rabbi emeritus.
	Hillel Academy opens.
	Joint Passover-Easter program.
	CARIH (Children's Asthma Research Institute and Hospital).
	Rabbi Abraham Joshua Heschel at first BB Mountain States Institute of Judaism in Estes Park.
1955	BMH hires and fires Conservative Rabbi Gershon Winer, whom they accuse of approving non-kosher cookies for

annual sale. Winer sues Bowman Biscuit Company. (Actually controversy is over sacrifice. Conservatives refer to sacrifice in the past, Orthodox in the future. The prayer books are rubber-stamped for future sacrifice.) Winer supporters leave BMH and form Conservative Rodef Shalom, the second split from BMH [see 1920].

Congregation Beth Joseph holds services in new building.

Temple Emanuel ground-breaking at Hilltop location.

1956 Author Joanne Greenberg and husband Alfred make Colorado home.

Congregation Rodef Shalom formed.

New rabbi at Temple Emanuel, Earl Stone, and ADL urge Rabbi Winer to drop cookie lawsuit, and Rabbinical Assembly sends out investigator. BMH denies controversy is between two rabbis (Kauvar and Winer).

Rabbi Shloime Twerski asks for end to interdating.

Mierle Laderman, rabbi's daughter, symphony ball debutante.

Jewish Educators Council organized.

1957 BMH no longer member of Conservative movement. New Rabbi Samuel Adelman is Yeshiva graduate.

Conservative Jewish Theological Seminary gets belated annual allocation after Allied receives assurances that "efforts will be made to attain withdrawal of cookie lawsuit."

1958 Zere Israel Synagogue on Federal Boulevard to be razed for Colfax interchange.

1959 Bowman Biscuit Company publicly apologizes to Rabbi Winer and settles cookie suit.

Julia Braun named "Woman of the Year" in Pueblo.

Thirteen-year-olds banned from dating at Beth Joseph events.

Madeline Korbel, future Secretary of State, who does not know that her parents were Jews, leaves Catholic Church to marry Episcopalian Joseph Albright.

1960 Temple Emanuel three-day dedication of Grape Street Building.

Theodore Maiman, West Colfax native, discovers LASER at Hughes Laboratories.

1961 Beth Shalom congregation, Littleton.

Temple Micah moves into futuristic-styled building.

Jewish section in Air Force Academy chapel.

Edward Pringle named to state Supreme Court.

1962 Jewish Community Center opens on Hilltop.

	East Denver Orthodox Synagogue.
	Hilltop Jewish population increases with opening of George Washington High School.
1963	Shearith Israel becomes artist's studio.
	Colorado Hebrew Chorale.
	Congregation Beth Shalom, Littleton.
	Colorado Jewish Reconstructionist Federation. B'nai Havurah, Reconstructionist congregation, Denver.
	Denver Institute for Jewish Studies.
	Conservative Rabbi Robert (Reuven) Hammer of Rodef Shalom offered pulpit at BMH.
1964	Rabbi Raymond Zwerin at Temple Emanuel.
	Temple Emanuel expanded building dedicated.
	Mikvah of Denver opens next door to Yeshiva.
1965	Platte River flood.
	Land for Babi Yar Park is acquired by Lil Hoffman and Rabbi Raymond Zwerin from mayor of Denver, Bill McNichols.
1966	Hillel Academy new building.
	American Medical Center and Ex-Patients merge.
1967	Yeshivas Toras Chaim begins original learning function.
	Har Hashem Congregation, Boulder.
	Rabbi Zwerin, first rabbi of new congregation Temple Sinai.
	Denver's Jewish population: 23,000.
	Golda Meir prime minister of Israel.
1968	Beth Jacob High School for Girls, one of two Jewish girls' boarding schools in U.S., opens in former synagogue building donated by Ben Samett.
	About 600 Jews in Pueblo.
1969	Colorado Society for Humanistic Judaism.
	Dr. Stanley Biber performs first sex-transfer operation at Trinidad's Mt. San Rafael Hospital and makes the unlikely town "the Sex-Change Capital of the World," a magnet for thousands of transsexuals.
1970	Bais Medrash Kehillas Yaakov congregation (Talmudic Research Institute) started by Rabbi Twerski.
	Edward E. Pringle, West Colfax native, named Chief Justice of the Supreme Court of the state of Colorado.
1971	President Richard Nixon nominates Sherman G. Finesilver, West Colfax native, to the U.S. District Court in Colorado.
	Temple Shalom in Colorado Springs formed from merger of

	B'nai Israel (Conservative) and Temple Beth El (Reform). It is affiliated with both the United Synagogue of America and the Union of American Hebrew Congregations.
	Rabbi Stephen Foster at Temple Emanuel.
1972	Rabbi Stanley Wagner at BMH.
	Allied Jewish Apartments open on Steele Street.
	First Israel Study Tour.
	Miriam Goldberg assumes the position of her late husband, Max Goldberg, on the *Intermountain Jewish News*.
1973	Yom Kippur War.
	CAJE (Central Agency for Jewish Education of Colorado).
	ARE, Alternatives in Jewish Education Publishing formed.
1974	Congregation Beth Evergreen.
	Community High School of Jewish Studies established.
1975	Rabbi Wagner establishes Center for Judaic Studies, encompasses five areas of study at University of Denver.
	Herzl Jewish Day School.
	Aspen Jewish Center.
1977	Denver starts unique joint conversion program, later known as "The Denver Plan."
	Hospital name changed to "Rose Medical Center."
	Congregation B'nai Vail.
	Informal group praying and studying under name of "Kohelet."
1978	Chabad-Lubavitch of Colorado.
	Congregation Har Shalom organized, Fort Collins.
	B'nai Butte, Crested Butte.
	National Jewish Hospital and National Asthma Center merge.
	Julian Street home of Golda Meir discovered shortly before her death. Mel and Esther Cohen (Strauss) take lead in saving it despite community disapproval.
1979	Rocky Mountain Hebrew Academy (RMHA).
	Temple Micah moves to Park Hill.
	City of Karmiel Park named for sister city, Karmiel, Israel.
	Zita Weinshienk first woman appointed judge of the U.S. District Court of Colorado.
	Helen Ginsburg appointed adviser to Commission on Holocaust by President Carter, resulting in the Holocaust Museum in Washington, D.C.
	"The Scroll K" created as emblem of Vaad Hakashrus (kosher

	supervision).
1980	Boulder Conservative Synagogue, predecessor of Bonai Shalom.
	Rabbi Stephen Foster succeeds Rabbi Stone.
	Rabbi Mordecai Twerski, twenty-sixth rabbi in line of Twerski dynasty and descendant of Baal Shem Tov, succeeds his father, Shloime Twerski. Only native-born rabbi to hold his father's pulpit.
1981	Holocaust Memorial in Mineral Palace Park, Pueblo.
	Congregation Ohr Shalom, Grand Junction.
	Gardenswartz. Memorial Bridge, Durango.
	Rabbi Wagner, chaplain of state senate.
	Denver-Boulder Jewish population 38,600 according to study.
1982	Mizel Museum housed in BMH synagogue.
	Judge Sherman Finesilver named Chief Judge of the United States District Court.
1983	Babi Yar Park unveiled years after President Carter's approval. Founders Jim Buchanan, Alan Gass, Helen Ginsburg, Ted Ruskin, and Rabbi Zwerin remain involved.
	Joint conversion program ends.
	TRI changes their kosher approval emblem to a reclining lion.
1984	Stepping Stones to a Jewish Me.
	Alan Berg, talk show host, assassinated.
	Community Talmud Torah established by Rodef Shalom, BMH, BJ.
1985	West Side reunion, Jerry Lande, prime mover.
	New building for Beth Jacob High School.
	Chabad of Colorado Springs.
1986	Jewish chapel at Air Force Academy, paintings by Shlomo Katz, Torah mantles by Phillis Kantor and Arielle Miller-Timen.
	Smithsonian recognizes Babi Yar Park as noteworthy site.
	Beth Israel sold to St. Anthony Hospital.
	United Way finally recognizes Frances Jacobs as a founder.
1987	B'nai Torah congregation, Westminster.
	Temple Sinai new home on Hampden.
1988	Golda Meir home moved to Auraria campus.
	Phil Winn confirmed as ambassador to Switzerland.

Congregation Bonai Shalom, Boulder.

Time reports American Jewish Committee puts national rate of intermarriage at 30 percent and Denver's at 60 percent.

1989 Larimer County Chevra Kadisha burial society using part of Rose Lawn Cemetery, Fort Collins.

1990 Rocky Mountain United Chavurot, Colorado Springs.

Western Center for Russian Jewry, Denver.

Colorado Jews for Jewish Identity, anti-missionary response to pseudo-synagogues.

JFCS renamed "Jewish Family Service."

1991 Chabad House in Boulder.

Colorado Congregation for Humanistic Judaism.

1992 Temple Beit Torah started by small group of Jews, military and Air Force Academy people in Colorado Springs.

Congregation B'nai Chaim, Littleton.

Beth Israel at Shalom Park opens.

Estimated Jewish population of Greater Denver: 42,000.

Or Chadash Synagogue.

Har Mishpachat, Steamboat Springs.

1993 Joyce Foster, first Jewish woman on Denver City Council.

DAT (Denver Academy of Torah) dedicated.

Dedication of Frances Wisebart Jacobs Park in Denver.

Second Colorado Hebrew Chorale.

1994 Estimated Denver Jewish population: 45,000.

Jewish Renewal Community of Boulder, affiliated with ALEPH the Alliance for Jewish Renewal.

Irv Moskowitz, superindent of Denver Public Schools.

Boulder Jewish Day School.

1995 (General) Rose Hospital sold to Columbia Rose Medical Center, $175 million goes to establish Rose Community Foundation.

COJAC, Colorado Jewish AID Coalition.

With election of Susan Barnes-Gelt, two Jewish women serve on Denver city council.

Southeast Center for Judaism.

Rabbi Abe Raich returns to Pueblo to serve both Conservative and Reform congregations.

1996 Colorado Committee for Soviet Jewry disbands shortly after death of Lil Hoffman.

About 5,000 ex-Soviet Jews in Denver.

JCC dedicated as the Robert E. Loup Jewish Community Center.

BMH and Beth Joseph merge into BMH-BJ congregation.

Hebrew Educational Alliance moves and joins Conservative movement.

Joseph B. Singer Art Gallery.

Chevra Kadisha burial society founded in Boulder.

1997 "The Max Frankel Hillel House" at the University of Denver is named for popular educator and humanitarian.

CHAI (Community Help and Abuse Information) organized as a result of local Lubavitcher rabbi excommunicating doctor and her husband. Denver Jewish community outraged. Extremes in community move further apart, reflecting worldwide Jewish polarization.

Yeshivas Toras Chaim moves into old HEA on Stuart.

Mikvah of East Denver.

Babi Yar memorial completed with dedication of fountain.

Chief Justice Pringle honored with one of two stained glass windows in the State Supreme Court.

Crypto-Jews in San Luis Valley said to have urged non-Jewish ranchers to form Ranchers Choice Coop for kosher slaughtering under Baltimore rabbinic supervision. Primary market Los Angeles.

1998 Allied Jewish Apartments open at Lowry.

Herzl Jewish Day School and RMHA merge.

Denver-Boulder Jewish population: 63,000, a 64 percent increase since 1981 study.

Steven Farber, West Colfax native, named most powerful Denverite in list of twenty-five; law partner and childhood chum Norm Brownstein is fourth; Rabbi Stephen Foster, twenty-fourth; and Dick and Eddie Robinson, also natives, twenty-fifth place.

Vision 2020 organized to chart future of Denver-Boulder area, Micky Miller, chairman.

Temple Beit Torah congregation in Colorado Springs joins UAHC.

Colorado Small Synagogue Consortium formed.

John Temple new editor of the *Rocky Mountain News*.

Local newspaper recognizes international writer Joanne Greenberg in the "Best of Denver."

	Unity in Diversity attempts to connect and support all branches of Judaism.
	Outreach Roundtable funded to bring unaffiliated Jews into the Denver-Boulder Jewish community.
1999	Boulder forms its own Jewish community center.
	Yiddish language and literature now on University of Denver curriculum.
	Vision 2000 results in Action 2000 and Synagogue 2000.
	Colorado State Historical Society honors Golden Hill Cemetery with historical designation and award for care of paupers' section by volunteers.
2000	Orthodox Rabbi Chaim Chaitovsky, Reform Rabbi Steven Foster, and Hasidic Rabbi Mordecai Twerski make history when they share a Friday night pulpit.
	Federal jury awards $10.5 million to couple accused of anti-Semitism. The losers, the Anti-Defamation League and Director Saul Rosenthal, are accused of defamation and of using a police scanner to obtain evidence.

Acknowledgments

The research for a book of this nature is dependent on scores of informed persons, but without the authorities as guides, not only facts would be difficult to find, but also the whole work useless. I am most deeply indebted to Dr. Jacob Marcus, pre-eminent in the field of American Jewish history, who suggested the outline for this book, who furnished me with valuable material from the American Jewish Archives of Hebrew Union College, and whose own writings suggested pertinent questions. Rabbi Isidore Meyer of the American Jewish Historical Society also gave me his kind advice on the content of this book, as did Dr. Solomon Grayzel of the Jewish Publication Society.

In Denver, the Western History Department of the Denver Public Library and the Colorado State Historical Society are the sources of most of the historical material in this book. To Ina T. Aulls, Opal Harbor, and Elizabeth Hawkins of the library, who kept this project in mind for eight years, I am grateful for the hours spent in ferreting out information. To their counterparts at the historical society, Frances Shea and Dolores Renze, I express the same gratitude.

To Ida Hurwitz, my good friend, whose interest in Colorado Jewish history is at least equal to mine, I owe thanks for making available her family papers, for the hours she spent from Chicago to San Francisco finding the persons who participated in many of the events recorded in this book, and for assuming any task I gave up because it was too difficult. To Robert S. Gamzey, editor of the *Intermountain Jews News,* who did not merely give me permission to examine the newspaper file, but also brought the weighty volumes to my home so that I could use them at my convenience, and who gave me encouragement and support when I needed it most, I am forever grateful.

To William Wolf, my teacher and friend, who was available at odd hours for translations and corrections, I express thanks and regrets that I cannot be as useful in his literary work. I am grateful to Fred Rosenstock, collector of Western Americana, who trusted me with documents which helped me establish the authenticity of this book.

For the use of precious documents, I am grateful to Hyman Goodstein, who permitted me to read the B'nai B'rith minute books and other material; to Sam Rose, who let me use his office while I read the minute books of Congregation Emanuel; to Morris Maimon, who supplied a typewriter while I abstracted the J.C.R.S. minute books; to Saralee Pollock, who permitted me to take home those minute books of the Council of Jewish Women in her possession; and to George B. Clark, of the history committee of the Masonic Grand Lodge of Colorado, who spent time in checking names for me in the Colorado Masonic Archives.

For permission to quote from their books, which I used constantly, I am pleased to thank David Lavender, author of *The Big Divide*, and Muriel Sibell Wolle, author of *Stampede to Timberline*. Josie Moore Crum gave me the same generous permission to quote from her original research in *The Otto Mears Passes*, and Rabbi Martin Weitz, in addition to other material, gave me permission to quote from his *Year Without Fear*.

I would like to extend my thanks to my personal friends and even casual acquaintances who sustained their interest in this research over the long period, but so many names would be meaningless. However, I cannot omit Cecil Zeitlin, who kept me from making mistakes, and Hermina Goldfarb, who helped with the proofreading, and Maureen Nidess, who drew the end papers and the art work for the dust jacket.

Thanks are due to Deborah and Vicki Uchill, who were babies when I began my research and were old enough to help with the proofreading and the preparation of the index.

To Sam Uchill, my beloved husband, I am grateful for the unselfish sacrifices he made—those I know about, and those he succeeded in keeping from me.

Bibliography

(Not included in this bibliography are single newspaper references or material in the various collections and scrapbooks. This material will be found in the pertinent chapter notes.)

PRIMARY SOURCES

ORIGINAL DOCUMENTS

B'nai Brith Lodge No. 171, Minutes, 1872-1943; *Ledgers,* 1872-1913; *Cash Receipt Books,* 1911-1921. Denver Lodge Office.

Congregation Emanuel Minutes, 1874-1885; *Burial Register; Indices to Burial Register; Account Book of the Hebrew Cemetery Association,* 1890-1900. Temple Emanuel, Denver.

Congregation Emanuel Interment Register, Oct. 1, 1912–; Fairmount Cemetery, Denver.

Council of Jewish Women, Minutes, 1898; 1903-1907; *Minutes of Junior Council.* Mrs. Saralee Pollock, Denver.

John Elsner, M. D., *Record of Circumcisions,* 1866-1905. Fred Rosenstock, Denver.

Jewish Consumptives' Relief Society Minutes, 1903-1905. American Medical Center, Spivak, Colorado.

United Hebrew Cemetery Association Burial List. Rose Hill Cemetery, Denver.

PUBLIC RECORDS

Articles of Incorporation, Amendments, Dissolution, etc., Secretary of State, Denver.

Articles of Incorporation, Amendments, Dissolution, etc., Marriage Certificates, County Clerk and Recorder, Denver.

Wills, Naturalization Records, County Court, Denver.

United States Census, State of Colorado, 1880. Original at State Historical Society. Microfilm at Denver Public Library.

SCRAPBOOKS, CLIPPING COLLECTIONS, MISCELLANEOUS

Milton Braun Scrapbooks, United Hebrew Center, Pueblo, Colorado.

Adolph and Delphine Cohen Family Photograph Collection, Miss Anna Johnson, Denver.

Denver Medical Society Physicians' Files of Reprints. Society Library, Denver.

Denver Public Library, *Clipping Files,* Denver.

Simon Fishman Scrapbook, Mrs. Simon Fishman, Denver.

William S. Friedman Scrapbook, Denver Public Library.

Samuel Schaeffer Scrapbooks, Mrs. Samuel Schaeffer, Denver.

Temple Emanuel Sisterhood Scrapbooks, Aimee Greenbaum, Denver..

Tombstone Inscriptions, Emanuel Cemetery, Rose Hill Cemetery, Mount Nebo Cemetery, West Side Benevolent Cemetery, Denver; Evergreen Cemetery, Leadville.

Hurwitz Papers and Photographs, Miss Ida Hurwitz and Mrs. Sophie Pelton, Denver.

Dr. J. M. Morris Papers, Dr. Morris, Denver.

Dr. Charles Spivak-Milton Anfenger Correspondence, Robert Gamzey, Denver.

UNPUBLISHED WORKS

Bromwell, Henrietta, "Colorado Argonauts of 1858-1859, A Fifty-Niners Directory," 2 vols., Denver, 1926.
—"Colorado Portrait and Biography," 4 vols. with 2 vol. supplement, Denver, 1934.
Denver City Town Company, "Charter."
Denver Museum, 'Officials of Denver and Colorado, 1858-1933."
—"Index to Officials of Denver and Colorado." Denver, 1934.
"Inventory of the Church Archives of Colorado, Jewish Bodies" (Works Projects Administration), Denver, 1942.
Mayor's Minority Report, Anti-Defamation League, Denver.
McGrath, Maria Davies, "The Real Pioneers of Colorado," 3 vols., Denver, 1934.
Morris, Ernest, "Gathering Much, An Historical Narrative," Denver, 1937. Mrs. Ernest Morris, Denver.
"Proceedings of the Auraria Town Company and St. Charles Town Company, Denver, 1859." Colorado State Historical Society, Denver.
Reese, Rena, "History of the Denver Public Library," Denver, 1928.
Satt, Flora Jane, "The Cotopaxi Colony," University of Colorado, Master's Thesis, Boulder, Colo., 1950.

PERIODICALS

In addition to those listed here, Dr. Jacob Marcus made available many publications (referred to in the chapter notes) through the American Jewish Archives.

American Jewish Archives, Cincinnati.
American Jewish Historical Society, Publications of the, New York.
Colorado Magazine, State Historical Society, Denver.
Denver, *Jewish News,* 1919-1925.
Denver *Post.*
Denver *Times.*
Intermountain Jewish News.
Jewish Outlook, 1903-1913.
Rocky Mountain News.
Solid Muldoon, Ouray, Colorado.
West End Press, Denver.

DEDICATION, ANNIVERSARY, AND MEMORIAL PROGRAMS AND ISSUES OF PERIODICALS

"Temple Aaron Biblette," Temple Aaron, Trinidad, Nov. 11, 1949.
Beth Hamedrosh Hagodol Synagogue, Golden Anniversary Edition, *Intermountain Jewish News,* Mar. 25, 1948.
Denver Lodge No. 5, A. F. and A. M., Fiftieth Anniversary, 1909.
Seventy-fifth Anniversary, Brochure, Temple Emanuel, Denver, 1949.
Dedication Manual, Denver Lodge No. 171, B'nai B'rith, Denver, 1929.

Dedication Program, B'nai Israel Synagogue, Colorado Springs, 1951.
Dedication Program, Congregation Hebrew Educational Alliance, 1953.
Dedication Program, United Hebrew Center, Pueblo, 1950.
Thirty Years of Saving Lives, The Sanatorium of the Jewish Consumptives' Relief Society, Spivak, Colo., 1904-1934.
Parkhill, Forbes, 'The May Story," Denver *Post,* Sept. 23, 1952. Seventy-fifth Anniversary, The May Company.
Reform Advocate, "The Story of the Jews of Denver, October, 1908."
Memoir, Mrs. Frances Jacobs, Denver, 1892.
In Memoriam, Belle Gertrude Kauvar, Denver, 1936.
Spivak Memorial Issue, the *Sanatorium,* Oct.-Nov.-Dec. 1927.
Guest Register, Vendome Hotel.

DIRECTORIES, ROSTERS, AND INDICES

Denver, 1859, 1866, 1876–.
Colorado State Business Directory, 1876–
Denver Club Yearbooks, 1888-1899.
Council of Jewish Women.
Blue Book, Allied Jewish Community Council.
Golden Rule, Chapter O. E. S.
Columbine Lodge, A. F. & A. M., Denver, 1949.
Master File of the Grand Lodge of Colorado, alphabetical listing of all members of the Masonic Lodges of Colorado.
Index to the *Rocky Mountain News,* Denver Public Library, Western History Department, 1865-1885.
Edgar A. Burton Index, Denver Public Library.

SECONDARY SOURCES

American Jewish Yearbook, The, Philadelphia, 1899–.
Anfenger, Milton L., *The Birth of a Hospital,* Denver, about 1942.
Baker, James H. (ed.) and Hafen, Leroy R., *History of Colorado,* 4 vols., Denver, 1927.
Bancroft, Caroline, *Famous Aspen,* Aspen, 1951.
—Silver Queen, the Fabulous Story of Baby Doe Tabor, Denver, 1950.
Beebe, Lucius, *Highball,* New York, 1945.
—*Mixed Train Daily,* New York, 1947.
Bell, John C., *Pilgrim and the Pioneers,* Lincoln, Nebr., 1906.
Block, Benjamin, *Colorado, Its Resources and Its Men,* Denver, n.d.
Bloomgarden, Solomon (Yehoash), *Gezamelte Leider fun Yehoash* (Collection of Poems by Jehoash), New York, 1910.
—*The Feet of the Messenger.*
Boyd, David, *A History: Greeley and the Union Colony of Colorado,* Greeley, 1890.
Brady, Cyrus Townsend, *Indian Fights and Fighters,* New York, 1913.
Brigham, Lillian Rice, *Historical Guide to Colorado,* Denver, 1931.
Byers, William N., *Encyclopedia of Biography,* Chicago, 1901.

Carvalho, Solomon, *Incidents of Travel and Adventure in the Far West*, New York, 1857; Reissued, Philadelphia, 1954.
del Castillo, B. Diaz, *The True History of the Conquest of Mexico*, London, 1928.
Central City Opera House Association, *The Glory that was Gold*, Denver, 1932.
Clark, George B., *Our Masonic Heritage*, Denver, 1936.
Colorado Springs *Evening Telegraph, The Fortunes of a Decade*, Colorado Springs, 1900.
Colorado State Bureau of Mines, *Biennial Report*, 1909-1911.
Colorado State Medical Society, *A Jubliee Volume*, Denver, 1921.
Conklin, Emma Burke, *A Brief History of Logan County, Colorado*, Denver, 1928.
Crippen, Helen and Hafen, Ann W., *Index to the Colorado Magazine*, 1923-1948, Denver, 1948.
Crum, Josie Moore, *The Otto Mears Passes*, Durango, 1948.
Darrow, Clarence, *The Story of My Life*, New York, 1932.
Davidson, Gabriel, *Our Jewish Farmers*, New York, 1943.
Davis, E. O., *The First Five Years of the Railroad Era in Colorado*, Golden, Colo., 1948.
Denver Social Record and Club Annual, Denver, 1909—.
Dill, R. G., *History of Lake County, History of the Arkansas Valley*, n. p., 1881.
Donnelly, Thomas C., *Rocky Mountain Politics*, Albuquerque, 1940.
Dubois, Rene and Jean, *The White Plague*, Boston, 1952.
Edelstadt, David, *Schriften*, London, 1909.
Ellis, Anne, *Life of an Ordinary Woman*, Boston, 1929.
Evans, Dannette, *Spotlight on Pueblo*, Lakewood, Colo., 1952.
Ferril, Thomas Hornsby, *I Hate Thursday*, New York, 1946.
Fleming, John, *The Community Chest*, Denver 1887-1937.
Fowler, Gene, *Timberline*, New York, 1933.
Friedman, Lee M., *Pilgrims in a New Land*, Philadelphia, 1948.
Fritz, Percy S., *Colorado, the Centennial State*, New York, 1941.
Fuller, Edgar I., *The Visible of the Invisible Empire*, Denver, 1925.
Gamzey, Robert, "Trail Blazers of Philanthropy," Denver *Post Empire*, Mar. 9, 1947, p. 5.
Garth, Thomas R., *Life of Henry Augustus Buchtel*, Denver, 1937.
Grant, W. W., *Such is Life*, Denver, 1952.
Grayzel, Solomon, *A History of the Jews*, Philadelphia, 1950.
Greeley, Horace, *An Overland Journey from New York to San Francisco*, New York, 1860.
Griswold, Don L., and Jean Harvey, *The Carbonate Camp Called Leadville*, Denver, 1951.
Hafen, Leroy R. and Ann, *The Colorado Story*, Denver, 1953.
—*Colorado and Its People*, 4 vols., New York, 1948.
Hale, William H., *Horace Greeley*, New York, 1950.
Hall, Frank, *History of Colorado*, 4 vols, Chicago, 1895.
Hentschel, William R., *The German Element in the Development of Colorado*, Denver, 1930.

Hill, Agnes Leonard, *Colorado Bluebook*, Denver, 1892.
Hill, Alice Polk, *Tales of the Pioneers*, Denver, 1884.
Hirschler, Eric E., *Jews from Germany in the United States*, New York, 1955.
Jewish Encyclopedia, The, 12 vols., New York, 1901-6.
Jocknick, Sidney, *Early Days on the Western Slope of Colorado*, Denver, 1913.
Jordan, Harvey, *Program 1941 Regatta*, Sloan's Lake, Denver.
Karsner, David, *Silver Dollar*, New York, 1932.
Kline, Samuel J., *Recollections and Comments*, Los Angeles, 1924.
Kohut, Rebekah, *My Portion*, New York, 1925.
Korn, Bertram W., *American Jewry and the Civil War*, Philadelphia, 1951.
Lavender, David, *The Big Divide*, New York, 1948.
—*One Man's West*, New York, 1943.
Learsi, Rufus, *The Jews in America*, Cleveland, 1954.
Leivick, H., *Leider fun Gan Eden* (Songs of Paradise), Chicago, 1937.
Levinger, Lee, *A History of the Jews in the United States*, Cincinnati, 1949.
Lindsey, Judge Ben, *The Dangerous Life*, New York, 1931.
Lookout from the Denver Public Library, Music in Denver and Colorado, Denver, 1927.
—*Art in Denver,* 1928.
MacMechen, Ed., *Robert W. Speer: A City Builder*, Denver, 1919.
Marcus, Jacob R., *Memoirs*, 3 vols. Philadelphia, 1955.
Margolis and Marx, *A History of the Jewish People*, Philadelphia, 1945.
Masserman, Paul and Baker, Max, *The Jews Come to America*, New York, 1932.
McMurtrie, Douglas C. and Allen, Albert H., *Early Printing in Colorado*, Denver, 1935.
Mumey, Nolie, *History of the Early Settlements of Denver*, Denver, 1942.
Nankivell, Major John H., *History of the Military Organizations of Colorado, 1860-1935*, Denver, 1935.
Ormes, M. D. and E. R., *Book of Colorado Springs*, Colorado Springs, 1933.
Pathorne, E. B., *Musical History of Colorado*, Denver, 1889.
Pioneers of the San Juan Country, Sarah Platt Decker Chapter, D.A.R., 3 vols. Colorado Springs, 1942, 1946. Vol. 3, Durango, 1952.
Postal, Bernard and Koppman, Lionel, *A Jewish Tourist's Guide to the U. S.*, Philadelphia, 1954.
Proceedings of the M. W. Grand Lodge of A. F. & A. M. of Colorado, Denver, 1890.
Quiett, Glenn Chesney, *Pay Dirt*, New York, 1936.
Representative Men of Colorado in the Nineteenth Century, Denver, 1902.
Representative Men of the West in Caricature, Denver, 1904.
Schoberlin, Melvin, *From Candles to Footlights*, Denver, 1941.
Semple, James, *Representative Women of Colorado*, Denver, 1911.
Smiley, Jerome, *Semi-Centennial History of Colorado*, 2 vols., New York, 1913.
—*History of Denver,* Denver, 1901.
Social Year Book, Denver, 1898-9; 1901-2.
Steinel, Alvin T., *History of Agriculture in Colorado*, Ft. Collins, 1926.
Stone, Wilbur F., *History of Colorado*, 5 vols., Chicago, 1918.

Thompson's Elite Directory and Club List of Denver for 1891-92.
Universal Jewish Encyclopedia, 10 vols., New York, 1939-1943.
University of Colorado, *Colorado, Short Studies of Its Past and Present.* Boulder, 1927.
Vickers, W. B., *History of Clear Creek and Boulder Valleys,* Chicago, 1880.
—*History of the City of Denver,* Chicago, 1880.
Watters, Leon L., *The Pioneer Jews of Utah,* New York, 1952.
Wechter, Dixon, *The Saga of American Society,* New York, 1937.
Weitz, Martin, *Year Without Fear,* New York, 1955.
West, Ray (ed.), *Rocky Mountain Cities,* New York, 1949.
Wharton, Junius E., *History of the City of Denver,* Denver, 1866. including D. O. Wilhelm, *Business Directory.*
White, William L., *Bernard Baruch, Portrait of a Citizen,* New York, 1950.
Whittaker, Milo Lee, *Pathbreakers and Pioneers of the Pueblo Region.* Pueblo, 1917.
Wiernick, Peter, *History of the Jews in America,* New York, 1912 and 1931.
Willard, James F. and Goodykoontz, Colin, *Experiments in Colorado Colonization,* Boulder, 1926.
Willard, James F., *Union Colony at Greeley,* 1869-1871, Denver, 1918.
Willison, G. F., *Here They Dug the Gold,* New York, 1946.
Who's Who in American Jewry, New York, 1926.
Who's Who in World Jewry, New York, 1955.
Wolle, Muriel Sibell, *Cloud Cities of Colorado,* Denver, 1934.
—*Ghost Cities of Colorado,* Denver, 1933.
—*Stampede to Timberline,* Boulder, Colo., 1949.

CORRESPONDENCE AND INTERVIEWS

Only letters containing specific information used in this book are here included. This is true of the interviews, although dozens not included were valuable for corroboration of factual material.

Amter, Isidore
Anfenger, Milton
Appel, Walter
Berry, Hannah Shwayder
Block, Augusta Hauck
Blumberg, Dr. A. M.
Blumberg, Ben
Bowman, Victa Newman
Braun, Milton
Bresler, Anna Hillkowitz
Cohen, Abe B.
Cohen, Faye
Ellsberg, Edna
Enger, Herman

Fishman, Mary Fine
Flaks, Minnie and Tillie
Freedheim, Mr. and Mrs. Alfred
Freedheim, Rose Weil
Gelt, Mr. and Mrs. Louis
Ginsberg, Charles
Glass, Mr. and Mrs. Ben
Goldberg, Max (Mattis)
Goldhammer, Henry
Goldsmith, Lena
Gordon, Mrs. Ben
Green, Dena Raich
Greenbaum, Aimee
Greenblatt, Sarah Goodstein

Gresham, William
Grossmayer, Dolce
Hart, Robert
Hayutin, Max
Heller, Wolf
Hershkowitz, Mr. and Mrs. Emanuel
Hillkowitz, Minnie Pinter
Hornbein, Philip
Janowitz, Sidney
Jarecki, Theresa Wisebart
Johnson, Anna
Karsh, Dave
Kauvar, Rabbi Charles E. Hillel
Kay, Dora Kobey
Kobey, Bertha Weiner
Krohn, Dr. Morris
Levand, Louis
Levy, Tillye
Lieberman, J. J.
Lifton, Amy Salomon
Lorig, Mrs. Marx
Mayer, Mr. and Mrs. Adolph
Mayer, Colonel Frank
Meyer, Carl J.
Meyers, Mrs. Fred
Miller, Joe
Miller, Minette
Moore, Florence
Morgan, Mary
Morris, Mrs. Ernest
Morris, Dr. J. M.
Morris, Percy S.
Myer, Myron I.
Nidess, Mr. and Mrs. Ary
Olcovich, Florence Saft
Orenstein, Rose Milstein
Pelton, Sophie Hurwitz
Pepper, William
Potashnick, Max
Pomeranz, Esther

Pomeranz, Rose
Preiss, Sam (Price)
Queree, Pearl
Quiat, Ira L.
Quicksilver, Mr. and Mrs. Frank
Radinsky, Ethel Milstein
Raich, Mr. and Mrs. Abe
Rhoades, Harry
Ridgway, Arthur
Roller, Elizabeth
Rose, Bernard
Rosen, William
Rosenberg, Nathan
Rosenthal, Phoebe Cohen
Rossman, Lou
Rotenberg, Sam
Rothschild, Nathan
Rothstein, Ed
Salomon, Fred Z. (St. Louis)
Samett, Benjamin
Sanders, Mr. and Mrs. Gilbert
Schaeffer, Mrs. Samuel
Strauss, Deena Spivak
Schwartz, Mrs. Henry, Jr.
Schwartz, Nathan
Seeman, Julius Freyhan
Shapiro, Rabbi Zalman
Shatz, Mrs. J. S.
Smith, Joseph Emerson
Smith, Marian P. (Poppy)
Sobol, Mrs. Eli
Sosny, Joseph
Weil, Dan
Weinberger, Arnold
Weinberger, B. W.
Whatley, Barney
Wikler, Mrs. I. W.
Wittelshofer, Mr. and Mrs. Edwin
Wittow, Samuel
Wolfson, Pearl Hayutin

Index

Abramovitz, David, 299
Abrams, Morris, 70
Adams, Alva, 149, 150
Adams, Charles, 54
Adath Zion Congregation, Boulder, 288
Adler, Moses, 71
Agudas Achim Congregation, 169, 214
Agudas Dovrei Ivris, 231
Agudas Evriah, 230
Ahaves Achein Verein, 227
Aidelman, E., 243
Aleph Zadik Aleph, 140
Allied Jewish Campaign, 133, 271, 275
Allied Jewish Community Council, 275-6, 278
Alpha Theater, 228
Amateur Musical Club, 299
Amercian Committee for Ameliorating the Conditions of the Russian Exiles, 189
American Council for Judaism, 83, 292
American Jewish Committee, 253
American Jewish Congress, 253, 271
Amter, Marks, 139, 204, 205, 208
Anfenger, Louis, 73, 94, 135, 138, 148, 149; Milton, 74, 136, 137, 138, 141, 148, 149, 160, 277-8
Anti-Defamation League, 82, 162, 163, 239
Anshe Amunah Congregation, 212
Anshe Emuno Congregation, Boulder, 288
Appel, A. M., 134; J. S., 116, 123, 179; Walter, 150, 163, 208-9
Arager, Solomon, 176, 204, 205, 212, 225, 226
Arkush, Samuel, 28, 71
Atwood Colony, 140, 177-183, 266

Auraria and Denver Chess Club and Literary Society, 21, 36
Auraria Lodge, U. D. (Masonic), 19, 20

Ballaban, Bro., 136
Bamberger, Leopold, 204, 207
Barnum, P. T., 40, 195
Baruch, Bernard, 105
Beaumont, Commodore Louis, 88, 99, 100, 101
Beebe, Lucius, 60
Beilschowsky, Moritz, 10
Benjamin, Carrie S., 141, 157
Bennett, Ephraim, 210
Berlinsky, Garfield, 272-3
Bernhardt, David, 243
Bernheim, I. W., 88
Berry, Bernard, 28, 134
Beth Am Congregation, 221
Beth David Hebrew School and Center, 218
Beth Ha Medrosh Hagodol, Synagogue, 197, 209, 219, 220, 224, 229, 237, 255
Beth Israel Anshei Matzover Chevra Volin Congregation, 217, 218
Beth Israel Congregation, Greeley, 288
Beth Israel Hospital and Old Folks Home, 83, 94, 170, 263, 264, 274, 275
Beth Jacob Congregation; see Ostrover Beth Jacob
Beth Joseph Congregation, 220
Bezman, Morris, 299
Bickur, Cholim, 260
Block, Emanuel, 148
Block, Joseph, 23, 24, 25 n 26, 75
Block, Simon, 165-6, 207
Bloomfield Park, 227, 228
Bloomgarden, Flora, 256, 305

Bloomgarden, Solomon (Yehoash) 179, 185, 244, 252, 253, 256, 304-5
Blumberg, A. M., 286-7; Ben, 279
B'nai B'rith: Denver Lodge No. 22, 27, 39, 42, 45, 65, 67, 73-4, 76, 83, 84, 86, 105, 115, 125, 132, 133, 134-41, 159, 160, 162, 177, 181, 182, 185, 186, 192, 229, 247, 261, 262, 267-9, 270, 273, 274, 285; Forum Series, 39; Girls, 141; Youth Organization, 141
B'nai B'rith College of Jewish Studies, 82, 139
B'nai Jacob Congregation, Pueblo, 290, 291-2
B'nai Zion, 280
B'nai Zion Congregation, Fort Collins, 287
B'ney Abraham Congregation, Pueblo, 295 n 14
B'noth Zion, 281
Bogen, Boris D., 274
Bornstein, Louis, 243
Bowman, Sam, 291
Boyd, David, 40, 41
Braude, Isaac A., 234-5, 239; William, 239
Britwar, Israel, 213
Bronfin, I. D. 202, 251
Brunot, Felix, 56
Bryan, William Jennings, 148
Buchtel, Dr. William, 195
Buffalo Bill; see Cody, William F.
Butcher, Sam, 200
Byers, William N., 36, 69, 71; Mrs., 35

Cahan, Abraham, 244, 249
Cantor, Eddie, 264
Capitol Hill Cemetery; see Jewish cemetery,
Caplan, Maurice L., 164 n 21, 185
Carson, Kit, 33, 51
Carvalho, Solomon N., 10
Caston, Saul, 301
Central Committee of the Rocky Mountain Region for the Russian Jews, 81, 265, 266, 269

Central Conference of American Rabbis, 82
Central Jewish Council, 138, 237, 252, 267-271, 275, 276, 277
Charity Organization Society, 120-2
Chatz, Israel, 215
Chebra Kadisha O. Bickur Cholim, 212, 224
Cheltenham Annex, 261
Cherniavsky, Gregor, 300
Chernoff, Dr. Lewis, 300
Chesed Shel Emeth, 223
Chevro Mishno, 227
Chisdes, Jacob, 144
Chotsky's Synagogue, 215
Chovevei Zion, 280
Cleveland Orphan Asylum, 78, 103, 114, 134, 137
Cody, William F., 152-4
Cohen, Charles B., 106
Cohen, David, 200
Cohen, Mrs. Delphine, 114; Henry, 125, 242, 252
Cohen, Gustave, 107, 142
Cohen, Isaac, 292
Cohen, Louis (Georgetown), 107, 167
Cohen, Louis (San Luis), 107
Cohen, Montague, N. A., 277
Cohen, Sam (Fairplay), 107
Cohn, Elias, 104
Collins, Moses, 247, 277
Colorado Council of Zionists, 280
Colorado Springs: B'nai B'rith, 295; Council of Jewish Women, 294; Free Loan, 295; Hebrew Benevolent Society, 294; Hebrew Ladies Aid Society, 295
Colorow, Chief, 107
Community Chest, 80
Cooper, Charles I., 272
Cooper, Jacob, 243
Cotopaxi Colony, 140, 173-4
Council of Jewish Women, 42, 125, 137, 141, 189 (New Orleans), 190, 229, 231, 247; Colorado Springs, 294; Junior Council, 142

335

Cripple Creek: B'nai Abraham Congregation, 106; B'nai Israel, 106; B'nai B'rith, 106
Crum, Josie Moore, 62
Cronbach, Abraham, 112
Cummings, A., 53, 72, 73

Damrosch, Frank, 297-8; Leopold, 298
Davidovich, Chaim, 239
de Hirsch, Baron Maurice, 173; Fund, 174, 177, 181-3
Deitsch brothers, 27, 28, 90; Isadore, 27, 35, 70, 134, 156; Jonas, 27, 35, 70, 72; Moritz, 27
Denver Hebrew School, 45, 137, 229, 237
Denver *Jewish News*, 252, 271, 272, 277
de Solla, J. Mendes, 80
Detre, Roland, 302
Diamond, Benjamin, 242
Dickinson Branch Library, 218, 232
Dorshei Zion Society of Denver, 215, 222 n 44, 280
Doyle, J. B., 13-17, 26, 33, 37
Dreyfuss, J. S., 208

Edelstadt, David, 125, 257, 303
Edgerton, Harriet, 252
Ehrich, Louis, 292
Eisenberg, David, 300
Eisenberg, Walter, 300
Eisenhower, Dwight D., 264
Elbroch, Harry, 243
Elchanan, Isaac, 233
Elkin, M., 45
Ellis, Anne, 59
Elman, Mischa, 299
Elsner, Edward, 46, 47; John, 42-48, 49 n 33, 66, 74, 85, 92, 133, 134, 166, 205, 246, 280, 282; Lena, 46, 94, 166; Leopold, 42, Record of Circumcisions, 24, 45-6, 100; Rose, 46-7
Emanuel, Akiba, 302
Emanuel Cemetery, 48, 86
Engel, Israel, 136

Epstein, Isaac, 139
Evergreen Cemetery Association, 102
Ex-Patients Sanatorium, 161, 220, 261-3, 274

Farband, 282
Farber, R., 209
Fareber, Mr., 135
Feirstein, M., 280
Field, Eugene, 28, 146, 147
Fine, Louis, 177, 181
Finkelstein, 300
Fischer, Jacob, 243
Fishberg, Maurice, 203, 241
Fishman, Mary Fine, 177-183
Fishman, Simon, 182
Flacks, Abe, 286
Fleischer, A. H., 77, 134
Forman, Meyer, 179
Frances Jacobs Hospital, 65, 100, 124, 251
Frank family, 285
Frankle, Henry, 117, 205
Free Sons of Israel, 133
Fremont, John C., 10
Fribourg, Amdée L., 148
Freudenthal, Alfred, 110-1; Fund, 110; Leopold, 110; Sam, 110
Friedenthal, A. L., 205
Friedenthal, Sigmund, 204, 205-8
Friedenberg, J., 205
Friedheim, Alfred, 108; family, 107-8
Friedman, David, 230
Friedman, Emanuel, 202
Friedman, Herbert S., 239
Friedman, Meyer, 94, 269, 270
Friedman, William S., 66, 78-83, 97, 100, 117, 122, 124, 125, 133, 138, 159, 179, 189, 212, 213, 229, 236 243-4, 246-7, 265, 270, 277, 280, 285
Fromenson, A. H., 280
Frumess, Gerald, 300
Funk, Rudolf, 211

Gamzey, Robert, 278

Galveston Plan, 138, 291
Garbarsky, Marks, 176, 204, 206-7, 225, 229; Mrs. 225; Tena, 225
Gilpin, William, 32, 52
Ginsberg, Charles, 159, 160, 161
Ginsburg, Eta, 236; Judah Leib, 235-6, 303
Glazerlach, 198, 213
Goldbaum, Flora, 71
Goldberg, Max, 278
Goldberger, Daniel, 238
Goldburg, Grumpert, 23, 24 n 24, 28, 71
Goldhammer family, 100; Hall, 228
Golden Hill Cemetery, 223-4, 257, 303
Goldman, Edward, 141; Frank, 141
Goldmark, Rubin, 301
Goldrick, O. J., 14, 15
Goldsmith, Abraham, 19, 20, 22, 70, 289-90; brothers, 91; Clara, 70; Eva, 291; Henry, 10, 24 n 16, 70, 289, 290, 291; Mrs. Sam, 24 n 16
Goodstein, Abraham, 196, 243; Isaac, 194, 195, 196, 227
Gotthelf, Isaac, 52, 54, 58, 66, 91, 130
Gottlieb, Ellen, 23; Flora, 22, 24 n 24; Joel, 22, 24 n 24, 85, 166; Joseph, 22, 23, 70, 85; Mrs. J., 130
Gottlieb, Leo, 110, 111
Grabfelder, Samuel, 247, 267
Grabosky, Ella, 23
Graetz, Heinrich, 206
Grant, Ulysses S., 38, 56, 57, 119, 145, 168
Greeley, Horace, 26, 39, 40, 57
Green Gables, 130, 132
Grimes, Sam, 203 n 12, 226
Gross, Irving, 302
Grossmayer, Clara, 298; Dolce, 298-9, 300; George, 299; Nathan, 298; Rachel, 299
Guggenheim, Meyer, 97; Simon, 87, 97, 110, 144, 151
Guldman, L. H., 88, 94, 228, 263-4; Community Center, 94

Hachnosas Orchim, 197
Hadassah, 82, 281, 282
Halpern, Ephraim Z., 235
Hanauer, Abraham, 27, 30, 33, 37
Harmony, Social and Literary Society, 132
Harrison, Joseph, 145
Hart, Dean Martin, 121
Hart, E. Samuel, 174; Josiah, 174; Meyer, 175
Hattanbach, Michael, 134
Hayes, Rutherford B., 60
Hebrew Benevolent Society, 73, 85, 114, 120, 133
Hebrew Burial and Prayer Society, 19, 70, 73, 77, 85, 114
Hebrew Cemetery Association, 70, 73, 85
Hebrew Educational Alliance, 218, 230-1, 232, 237
Hebrew Free Loan, 201, 274
Hebrew Immigration Aid Society (HIAS), 172, 173, 174
Hebrew Ladies Benevolent Society, 42, 73, 74, 114, 121, 124, 175, 252
Hebrew Library Association, 232
Hebrew Republican Club, 148
Hebrew Union College, 78, 103, 111
Heilprin, Michael, 173
Heimberger, D. O., 44, 45, 92, 93; Jacob, 93
Heinig, Carl, 95
Hellman, B., 28
Henry, T. C., 177
Hershfield, Louis, 28
Herskowitz, Emanuel, 226
Heublum, H., 243
Hildesheimer, Rabbi, 172
Hill, Alice Polk, 35
Hill, Nathaniel P., 47, 87, 132
Hillel Academy, 231
Hillowitz, Anna, 202, 245; Elias, 233-4, 245; Philip, 191, 202, 244, 245, 251, 268, 280; William, 247
Hirsch, Emil, 247, 290
Holzman family, 28; Solomon L., 28, 108
Hoover, Herbert, 149

Horn, Sol W., 161
Hornbein, Philip, 149, 150, 159, 160, 161, 252, 269, 280, 282
Hughes, Charles J., 104
Hungarian Charity and Pleasure Club, 227
Hurwitz, Bernard, 83, 281, 304
Hyman, Betty, 103; David M., 103, 104
Hyman, M., 243

Idelson, Idel, 234
Imber, Naphtali Herz, 303
Independent Order B'rith Abraham, 227, 244
Industrial Removal Organization (IRO) 138, 185
Ingley, Fred, 65; Mrs., 65
Intermountain Jewish News, 67, 278-9
Irmas, Henry J., 285
Itzkovitz, Mr., 179

Jacobs, Abraham, 19-21, 33-35, 37, 69, 70, 71, 75, 90, 91, 118, 119, 144, 156; Frances Wisebart, 80, 104, 118-124, 129, 247; Evelyn, 119
Jaffa, Arthur G., 109; Joseph, 110, 243-4, 266-7, 268; Sam, 109
Jarecki, Benny, 297
Jehoash; *see* Bloomgarden, Solomon
Jewish Aid Society, 274
Jewish Alliance, 132
Jewish Alliance of America, 250
Jewish Cemetery, 83-87
Jewish Community Centers, 139
Jewish Consumptives Relief Society, 138, 149, 199, 218, 220, 224, 237, 241-7, 251-2, 255, 257, 259, 262, 263, 266, 268-9, 274, 277, 305
Jewish Family and Children's Service, 274
Jewish Free Kitchen, 137
Jewish Hospital Association, 65, 117, 132, 205
Jewish Ladies Aid Society, 197, 274
Jewish National Fund, 280, 282
Jewish National Home for Asthmatic Children, 259-61, 263
Jewish Outlook, 246, 277
Jewish Protective Association, 14, 232
Jewish Social Service Bureau, 274
Jewish Social Service Federation, 138, 272-4
Jewish Theological Seminary, 45, 209, 210, 237, 256
Joel, Cecilia, 41
Johnson, Edwin C., 150
Johnson, Andrew, 72
Joint Distribution Committee, 253

K. S. B., 133
Karsh, Anna, 203 *n* 12
Kastor, I. H., 28
"Katerinchick," 176
Katz, Herman, 243
Kauffman, Jacob, 306 *n* 1
Kaufman, David, 243
Kauvar, Belle G., 281; Charles E. H., 209, 229, 236-7, 269, 280
Kavelin, Mascha, 300
Keheleth Jacob Congregation, 217
Kehillah; see Central Jewish Council
Kesher Ohava Congregation, 215
Kiesler, Adolph, 282
Kiowa Colony, 183
Kirschstein, Arthur J., 278
Klausner, Abraham, 239
Kleiner, M., 202
Kleinstein, 28
Kline, David, 70, 73, 85, 133
Kline, Henry, 28, 71, 73, 91, 297; Joseph, 28, 73, 91-2, 144; Samuel J., 73, 92
Klinkowstein, M., 206, 226
Knesseth Israel Congregation, 217, 218, 227, 235, 239
Kneseth Israel Congregation, Leadville, 102
Kobey, A. S. A., 169, 170; Bertha Weiner, 300; family 168 ff.; Mary, 167-70
Koch, Sam, 239

Koenig, William, 10
Koenigsberg, Sam, 297
Kohn, G. S., 186 n 14
Kolinsky, Mrs. I. J., 281
Kossuth, Louis, 42, 298
Krohn, Morris, J., 170, 202
Ku Klux Klan, 160-3
Kuhn, Abraham, 28; Adam, 28
Kwartin, Gregor, 302; Zavel, 301

Labor Lyceum, 199
Laderman, Manuel, 237-8, 288; Mrs. 238; Paul, 288
Ladies Hebrew Relief Society, 197
Ladies Shroud Society, 225
Lasky, Charles, 206
Lathrop, Mary F., 123
Lavender, David, 51, 64
Law and Order movement, 21
Leach, Samuel, 226
Leadville: B'nai B'rith lodge, 100, 102, 103; Hebrew Benevolent Association, 100, 102; Hebrew Ladies Benevolent, 102
League of Jewish Youth, 228
League of Mercy, 229
Lefkowitz, Jacob, 302
Leiter, Levi Z., 96-7
Lehman, David S., 94
Leivick, H. (Leivick Halper), 305-6
Levin, Louis, 243
Levinger, M., 243
Levy, Isaac, 109
Levy, Gus, M., 205
Levy, Kate, 247
Levy, Robert, 92-3
Lieberman, Jacob, 140, 277
Lifton, Amy Salomon, 40-42
Lillie, Gordon William, 152, 153
Linas Hachesed Society, 227
Linas HaZedek, 227
Lincoln, Abraham, 32, 51, 145
Lind, Jenny, 46
Lindsey, Ben, 42, 162, 163, 190-1
Lobinstein, Rosa, 71
Locke, John Galen, 160
Loeb, 28
Loeb, L., 205

Londoner, Joseph, 31; Julius, 27, 29, 30, 38, 134, 145; Wolfe, 27-30, 46, 63, 65, 87, 130, 144, 146, 147
Long, Mary Elitch, 258
Lorber, Mrs. J. N., 259, 261
Lorig, Mrs. Marx, 295
Lotus Club, 130-1
Lune, Mattes, 305

McCoy, Charles H., 174
McDonald, Jesse F., 150
McKinley, President, 100, 213
McMenamin, Hugh, 162, 163
McMorris, Thomas A., 57
Mandel, Joseph, 220
Marcus, Jacob, 112
Marcus, Mrs. J., 281
Marinoff, Jacob 252
Mauer, A. H., 126 n 4
Maxwell, Lucien, 44
May, David, 86, 88, 98-101, 124, 293
Mayer, Adolph, 19; Leopold, 18, 19, 29, 66, 69, 70, 91, 144
Meadow Hills Club, 133
Mears, Otto, 50-58, 88, 125, 165; Mrs., 55, 66, 66 n 41
Meeker, Nathan C., 39-41, 57
Mendelsberg, Abraham, 302
Menkus, Elias, 204, 224 n 11
Menorah Society, 228
Merchants Protective Association, 38
Meyer, Ferdinand, 107, 113
Micah, Congregation 83-4
Mile High Lodge B'nai B'rith, 141
Miller, Jacob, 202
Miller, Louis, 214
Miller, Minette, 103
Mills, J. Warner, 163
Millstine, J., 243
Milstein, Chana, 196; family, 198, 212-3; Shul Baer, 196
Millstone, Edward, 300
Mitchell, David, 134; Julius, 18, 69, 70, 74, 85, 131
Mizrachi, 281, 282
Mogen David Congregation, 213
Monash, Edward, 100, 124

Montefiore Literary Society, 110; Moses, 140, 207
Mo'os Chittim, 225
Moritz, Arthur, 28
Morley, Charles J., 160
Morris, David, 24 n 24; Esther, 24 n 24; Helena, 23, 24 n 24, 71
Morris, Ernest, 152-5; 266-7
Morris, J. M., 176, 179, 272, 275
Morris, L., 90
Morris, Max, 150
Morris, May, 142
Morris, Mildred, 94
Moses, Albert (Trinidad), 111
Moses, Albert Luria, 285; Penina Septima, 285; Rosa Nunez, 285; William Moultrie, 285
Mountain States Institute of Judaism, 139
Mount Nebo Cemetery, 224, 225
Muller, Alfred, 82, 149, 159, 179, 181, 229, 265-9
Myers, Mandel K., 292-3
Myers, Myron I., 292-3, 294

"Naphtali," 181
Nathan and Meyer, 107
Nathan, Anna Zucker, 23; Edward, 23, 28; Louis, 23, 28; Rebecca, 289; Simon, 23, 27, 95, 96, 288-9
Nathan, Nat, 107
Nathan, Solomon, 27, 283
National Jewish Hospital, 42, 97, 100, 125, 138, 185, 191, 192, 220, 241, 245-7, 259, 261-2, 263, 266-7, 273, 274
Neuhaus, Victor, 279, 300
Newman family, 290
Newton, Quigg, 164

O'Brien, William 120
Oestreicher Kranken Unterstzungs Verein, 227
Ohava Emuno, 205-8, 209
Oheb Zedek, 220, 229
Ohlin, Hilda Eisenberg, 300
Oppenheimer, 292
Ornauer, Henry, 208

O'Ryan, William, 78
Ostrover Kranken Unterstizung Verein, 216, 227
Ostrover Beth Jacob Congregation, 215-7, 238
Ostrover Young Men's Benevolent Association, 227
Ouray, Chief, 53, 55, 57, 58, 108
Owen, Ruth Bryan, 258

Packer, Alfred, 54
Paley, Johann, 244
Palm Theater, 228
Palmer, William J., 293
Patek, Alfred, 93
Patterson, Thomas, 136, 282
Pawnee Bill; see Lillie, William G.
Peabody, James, 149
Peixotto, Benjamin, 134
Pellish's Hall, 228
Pelta, 292
Penrose, Spencer, 254
Perlmutter, Jacob, 300
Perlmutter, Maurice, 300
Pike, Zebulon M., 11
Pioneer Women, 282
Pisko, Edward, 145; Seraphine, 146, 190, 201, 266, 267, 270
Pittsburg Platform, 70
Plonsky, Henry, 204, 205-10, 219, 289
Poale Zion, 282
Polant, Victor, 300
Potashinsky, J., 207
Poznanski, A. J., 90; Felix, 27; Phillip, 27, 70
Poznanski and Cohen, 27, 34, 156
Poznanski, H., 27
Prezant, Matilde, 300
Price, Samuel, 277
Progress Club, 130, 131, 132, 140
Prince, Mr., 135
Pry, Polly, 54
Pueblo: Associated Jewish Charities, 290; B'nai B'rith, 291; Jewish Relief Society, 291

Quiat, Ira L., 16, 161

Rabbinical Seminary of Philadelphia, 206
Rachofsky, Aaron, 277; Abraham, 166-8, 170; family, 166-70
Radinsky, Abraham, 151, 214; David, 214
Reed, Myron, 120
Reiss, Theodore, 300
Renard, 300
Ringolsky, J., 90
Ringolsky, Sol, 202, 225
Ridgway, Arthur, 64
Rittmaster, Alexander, 26, 166-8
Riverside Cemetery, 86
Rivkind, Isaac, 256
Rocky Mountain Lodge B'nai B'rith, Leadville, 100, 101, 102
Rodof Shalom Congregation (1892), 208, 209
Rodof Shalom Congregation (1956), 210
Rodof Zedek Congregation, 208
Roman Nose, 50
Rose, Maurice, 264; Memorial Hospital, 264, 275
Rose Hill Cemetery, 223, 224
Roselawn Cemetery, Pueblo, 291
Rosen, Ephraim, 183-4; Moses, 183-4
Rosen, Joseph, 235
Rosenbaum, Charles, 149, 235
Rosenblatt, Josef, 301
Rosenberg, Ben, 277
Rosenblum, Yehuda Leib, 235
Rosenfeld, Morris, 244
Rosenfeld, William 28
Rosenthal, Philip, 194, 205, 225
Rosenzweig, Leopold, 300
Rossman, Louis, 180
Rothgerber, Ira, 150
Rothschild, Louis, 23
Rothschild, M., 74
Rude, I., 132, 216, 220, 229, 237, 263, 282; B'nai B'rith building, 229; Community Center, 94, 228
Rushnevsky, Melvin, 239

Sachs, Henry, 295

Saft, Bertha, 206; Hyman, 206, 208, 209
Saltiel, Emanuel H., 173-5; John T., 173
Salomon brothers, 13, 18, 71, 77; Adolph Z., 13, 17, 39-42; Fred Z., 13-17, 20, 21, 32-39, 66, 69, 70, 91, 94, 118, 134, 145, 156; Fred (St. Louis), 35, 41, 66; Hyman Z., 13-17, 24 n 2, 33, 37, 39, 41, 50, 70, 72, 85; Matilda, 41
Saly, Susie, 206
Samett Ben, 217-8, 238; Synagogue, 217-8, 238
Sampliner, J. M., 144
Sanders, Gilbert, 109, 110, 111
Sands, A., 27, 90; D., 32; family, 28, 108; J., 27
Sands, Jacob, 105
Sanderson, Bill, 302
Sanatorium, The, 252
Saslavsky, Alexander, 300
Satt, Flora Jane, 174, 176
Schalit, Heinrich, 302
Schatz, Boris, 302
Schayer, Charles, M., 71, 85, 130, 176; H., 27, 92, 123; Herman, 27; Milton, 140; S., 27
Schechter, John, 158; Louis, 100, 158
Schiff, Jacob, 81
Schoenberg, Elias, 99; Joseph E., 99, Louis D., see Beaumont; Moses, 99; Opera House, 128; Rosa, 99
Schott, Max, 88, 103
Schraeter, Jacob, 219
Schreiber, Emanuel, 80
Schulein, Salomon, 27, 28, 32
Schurz, Carl, 42, 57
Schwartz, Nathan, 179-80
Schwartzburg, Samuel, 180
Schweitzer, Albert, 103
Settlement house, 142, 190, 191, 192
Shapiro, Louis, 243
Shapiro, Zalman Shmuel, 238
Shearith Israel, 211, 229, 238
Sheen, Fulton, 23

Shere, Oscar, 202, 251
Schiff, Jacob, 294
Shlesinger, Sigmund, 50-1
Shomro Emuno Congregation, 192 n 3, 297, 210-1, 229
Shwayder, family, 170-1, 300; Florence, 170-1; Hannah, 171; Isaac, 168; Jesse, 170-1; Leibe 171; Rachel, 170-1
Siegle, Max, 243
Silver, Mr., 177
Silver, Herman, 74, 93
Silverman, Mel, 302
Silverman, Benjamin, 196
Slavick, Anne, 285
Smith, Joseph Emerson, 62, 66
Smith, E. L., 135
Sokolow Delegation, 82, 271, 281; Nahum, 254
Solomon, Mrs. Albert, 287
Solomon, Hannah, 247
Solomon, Joseph, 204, 205, 206, 207
Sonneberg, A., 28, 70, 90
Sonneschein, Dr., 87, 209
Sons of Abraham, 294
Sons of Israel Congregation, Colorado Springs, 293, 294
Speer, Robert, 150, 163
Spivak, Charles David, 126, 176, 179, 181, 202, 231, 242-4, 246-7, 249-58, 267-8, 270, 277, 278, 281, 304, 305; David, 302; Institute, 231; Mrs., 247, 250, 256, 258
Standard Social Club, 130, 131, 132, 140
Steadhouse, Abe and David, 70
Stevens, Mr., 96
Strassburger, Isadore, 28
Strauss, Adele, 258; Deena Spivak, 257; Herman, 257-8
Strauss, A., 186 n 14
Strouse, Morris, 108
Strousse, S., 107
Studinski, Mike, 144

Tabor, Baby Doe, 48, 105; H. A. W., 39, 48, 87, 102, 105
Taft, William Howard, 93

Tammen, Harry, 154
Tascher, (Solomon?), 16
Teller, Henry, 104
Temple Aaron, Trinidad, 109, 110, 111, 112, 117; cemetery, 290
Temple Beth El, Colorado Springs, 294, 295
Temple Emanuel, Denver, 39, 45, 65, 73-87, 100, 115, 116, 130, 131, 148, 171, 172, 190, 192, 206, 208, 209, 212, 219, 229, 239, 245, 259; Literary Society, 132; Sisterhood, 141
Temple Emanuel, Pueblo, 289-90
Temple Israel, Leadville, 100, 102
Thomas, Henry, 174
Thomas, Charles S., 54
Tiphereth Israel Congregation, 215, 227, 243
Tiphereth Israel Congregation, Pueblo, 295 n 14
Tobias, Joseph, 195-6
Town Club, 132
Trapp, Louis, 28
Trattner, Ernest, 239
Trinidad: B'nai B'rith, 109; Hebrew Ladies' Aid Society, 110
Trounstine, Phil, 35, 144
Troyansky, Moses, 140; family, 140, 182
Turner, Aaron, 302
Turner, Israel, 239
Twerski, Shloime, 23
Twin City Lodge, B'nai B'rith, Pueblo, 291

Union Colony, 39 ff.
Union of American Hebrew Congregations, 74, 82, 137
United Health Appeal, 275
United Jewish Appeal, 111
United Synagogue of America, 210
Upper West Colfax Hebrew School, 23
Utter, David, 157

Vickers, W. B., 29
von Jochmus, Count, 298

Walsh, Thomas, 225
Washer, Joe, 140, 212, 243
Weil, H., 134
Weil, Leopold B., 27
Weinberg, Charles, 66
Weinberg, Minna; see Mascha Kavelin,
Weinberger, N., 135
Wels, Simon L., 19, 20, 22
Weiner, Adolph, 176
Weisman, 300
Weitz, Martin, 112, 183, 213, 239, 278-9
West Denver Citizens Club, 232
West End Press, 279
West Side Jewish Sheltering Home; see Hachonsas Orchim
Western Council of Zionists, 229
Western Jewish Advocate, 279
Whiteman, Wilberforce, 170
Whittemore, Justice, 23
Whitesitt, R .E., 69
Wilde, Oscar, 46
Wilensky, Julian, 300
Willens, Bessie, 260
Wise, Isaac Mayer, 75
Wise, M., 109
Wisebart, Benjamin, 145, 147; Opera Hall, 128
Witkowsky, L., 186 n 14
Wolcott, Edward O., 63
Wolf, L., 243
Wolf, Simon, 136, 137, 229
Wolfe, Israel, 90
Wolfe, Ruth Spivak, 258
Wolle, Muriel Sibell, 104
Wongrowitz, A., 226
Wood, Harry, 59

Workmen's Circle, 199, 224, 231, 244, 256, 303, 305
Wootton, Richens, 14

Yad Achaas Congregation, 215, 218, 230, 238
"Yankel Koloneist," 178
Yasness, Morris, 243
Yedevitz, Mr., 179
Yehoash; see Bloomgarden, Solomon
Yeshiva Congregation, 231, 239
Yeshiva Etz Chaim, 197, 216, 218, 230
Yeshivas Toras Chaim, 216-7, 218, 230; *also see* Ostrover Beth Jacob
Yiddish School, 230-1
Young Men's Hebrew Alliance, 132
Young Men's Hebrew Association (Y. M. H. A.), 132

Zalinger, B. F., 36, 94; Brunetta, 34, 46; Jennie, 94; Joseph E., 34, 46; Lena; see Elsner, Lena
Zederbaum, Adolph, 243, 244, 251, 265; Alexander, 244
Zere Abraham Congregation, 184, 191, 211, 212-3, 235, 238-9
Zere Israel Congregation, 214, 216, 236, 239
Zigmond, Maurice, 239
Zionist Council of Denver, 282
Zionist Hebrew School, 230, 281
Zionist Organization of America, 253, 282
Zionist Synagogue; see Dorshei Zionist Society
Zolotkoff, Dina, 225; Leon, 244, 251